Stations of the
Divided Subject

Stations of the Divided Subject

Contestation and Ideological Legitimation in
German Bourgeois Literature, 1770–1914

Richard T. Gray

STANFORD UNIVERSITY PRESS

STANFORD, CALIFORNIA   1995

Stanford University Press
Stanford, California
© 1995 by the Board of Trustees of the
Leland Stanford Junior University
Printed in the United States of America

CIP data appear at the end of the book

Stanford University Press publications are
distributed exclusively by Stanford University
Press within the United States, Canada, and
Mexico; they are distributed exclusively by
Cambridge University Press throughout the
rest of the world.

For three women:
Lucretia, Sabine, Cora

Acknowledgments

Numerous individuals and institutions have supported this work in a multitude of ways. Since throughout the book I make a point of the material contingencies on which intellectual production often hinges, it is only proper that I should begin here by expressing my debt to those institutions that have financially underwritten this project over the course of its evolution. An Andrew W. Mellon Faculty Fellowship in the Humanities at Harvard University provided me with the time and the financial support to accomplish the initial research for the book. During the year at Harvard I profited immeasurably both from the resources of Widener Library and from the intellectual exchanges with colleagues and other Mellon Fellows at Harvard, especially with Martha Woodmansee. Mills College provided me with a summer research grant that permitted me to travel to the Deutsches Literaturarchiv in Marbach, Germany, where I researched the Lessing and Schiller chapters. To the Archive and its efficient, friendly, and helpful personnel I wish to express my gratitude. The manuscript was completed while I was in residence at the University of Tübingen, where my work was funded by a generous grant from the Alexander von Humboldt Foundation. I extend special thanks to Prof. Dr. Wilfried Barner of the Deutsches Seminar in Tübingen for sponsoring my research.

Early versions of some of the work presented here were published previously. Segments of the Büchner and Hofmannsthal chapters appeared in volumes 61 (1988) and 62 (1989), respectively, of the *German Quarterly*; parts of the Heine chapter were published in volume 27 (1988) of the *Heinrich Heine-Jahrbuch* and in volume 81 (1989) of *Monatshefte*; a prototype of the Schiller essay appeared in the volume *Fictions of Culture: Essays in Honor of Walter H. Sokel*, edited by Steven Taubeneck (Bern and Frankfurt: Peter Lang, 1991). Thanks are due to these journals and to Peter Lang Publishing for permission to reprint this material in revised form.

I want to express my endless gratitude to that handful of people who have untiringly supported me and my work over the past decade: Jane K. Brown,

Jens Rieckmann, Frank Ryder, and Walter H. Sokel. It is fair to say that without their encouragement and backing I would not be where I am today. Remaining true to convention, I have saved mention of my greatest debt for last; this I owe to my wife and colleague, Sabine Wilke, who has followed and influenced this project from beginning to end. Long before the actual writing began, discussions with Sabine provided the environment in which the then embryonic ideas that have come to make up the chapters of this book could grow and flourish. At later stages she read and constructively criticized the individual interpretations, each of which has benefited from her perceptive commentaries. But Sabine has invested much more in this book than simply her intellectual energy; for without her love, encouragement, emotional support, and patience it would surely never have been completed.

R. T. G.

Contents

A Note on the Citation of Primary Sources

All quotations from and references to primary works are identified in the text itself. Abbreviations used to identify all primary sources can be found in the list of abbreviations that follows. For all primary works and secondary texts originally written in German, numbers in roman type refer to the pages of the German originals, while the page numbers of published translations are given in italics. Whenever a more literal rendering was necessary, translations have been modified; if no italic number is given, the translation is my own. References to plays include citation of the act and scene (in roman numerals) for easier cross-referencing.

Abbreviations

BW	Georg Büchner, *Sämtliche Werke und Briefe*, ed. Werner R. Lehmann, 2 vols. (Munich: Hanser, 1974). *Complete Works and Letters*, trans. Henry J. Schmidt (New York: Continuum, 1986).
CS	Franz Kafka, *The Complete Stories*, ed. Nahum N. Glatzer, trans. Willa and Edwin Muir (New York: Schocken Books, 1971).
Diaries	Franz Kafka, *Tagebücher 1910–1923*, ed. Max Brod (Frankfurt: Fischer, 1949). *The Diaries 1910–1923*, trans. Joseph Kresh and Martin Greenberg (New York: Schocken Books, 1976).
EG	Gotthold Ephraim Lessing, *Emilia Galotti*, in *Gesammelte Werke*, vol. 2, pp. 237–318. *Emilia Galotti: A Tragedy in Five Acts*, trans. Edward Dvoretzky (New York: Ungar, 1962).
Erzählungen	Franz Kafka, *Erzählungen*, ed. Max Brod (Frankfurt: Fischer, 1952).
HB	Heinrich Heine, *Briefe*, ed. Friedrich Hirth, 6 vols. (Mainz: Florian Kupferberg, 1965).
Hochzeit	Franz Kafka, *Hochzeitsvorbereitungen auf dem Lande und andere Prosa aus dem Nachlaß*, ed. Max Brod (Frankfurt: Fischer, 1953). *Dearest Father: Stories and Other Writings*, trans. Ernst Kaiser and Eithne Wilkins (New York: Schocken Books, 1954).
HW	Heinrich Heine, *Sämtliche Schriften*, ed. Klaus Briegleb, 6 vols. (Munich: Hanser, 1969).
History of Religion	Heinrich Heine, *Zur Geschichte der Religion und Philosophie in Deutschland*, in *Sämtliche Schriften*, vol. 3, pp. 506–641. *Concerning the History of Religion and Philosophy in Germany*, in *The Romantic School and Other Es-*

	says, trans. Helen Mustard, ed. Jost Hermand and Robert C. Holub, pp. 128–244 (New York: Continuum, 1985).
Ideas	Heinrich Heine, *Ideen: Das Buch Le Grand*, in *Sämtliche Schriften*, vol. 2, pp. 245–308. *Ideas: Book Le Grand*, trans. Charles Godfrey Leland, Robert C. Holub, and Martha Humphreys, in *Heinrich Heine: Poetry and Prose*, ed. Jost Hermand and Robert C. Holub, pp. 174–228 (New York: Continuum, 1982).
Judgment	Franz Kafka, "Das Urteil," in *Erzählungen*, ed. Max Brod, pp. 53–68 (Frankfurt: Fischer, 1952). *The Judgment*, in *The Complete Stories*, ed. Nahum N. Glatzer, trans. Willa and Edwin Muir, pp. 77–88 (New York: Schocken Books, 1971).
Letter/Father	Franz Kafka, "Brief an den Vater," in *Hochzeitsvorbereitungen auf dem Lande und andere Prosa aus dem Nachlaß*, ed. Max Brod, pp. 162–223 (Frankfurt: Fischer, 1953). *Letter to His Father*, trans. Ernst Kaiser and Eithne Wilkins (New York: Schocken Books, 1966).
Letters	Franz Kafka, *Briefe 1902–1924*, ed. Max Brod (Frankfurt: Fischer, 1958). *Letters to Friends, Family, and Editors*, trans. Richard and Clara Winston (New York: Schocken Books, 1977).
Letters to Felice	Franz Kafka, *Briefe an Felice*, ed. Erich Heller and Jürgen Born (Frankfurt: Fischer, 1967). *Letters to Felice*, trans. James Stern and Elisabeth Duckworth (New York: Schocken Books, 1973).
LW	Gotthold Ephraim Lessing, *Gesammelte Werke*, ed. Paul Rilla, 10 vols. (East Berlin: Aufbau, 1954–1958).
Naive	Friedrich Schiller. *Über naive und sentimentalische Dichtung*, in *Sämtliche Werke*, vol. 5, pp. 694–780. *On the Naive and Sentimental in Literature*, trans. Helen Watanabe-O'Kelly (Manchester, Eng.: Carcanet New Press, 1981).
Nathan	Gotthold Ephraim Lessing, *Nathan der Weise*, in *Gesammelte Werke*, vol. 2, pp. 319–481. *Nathan the Wise*, trans. Bayard Quincy Morgan (New York: Ungar, 1955).
Robbers	Friedrich Schiller, *Die Räuber*, in *Sämtliche Werke*, vol.

1, pp. 491–618. *The Robbers*, trans. F. J. Lamport (Harmondsworth, Eng.: Penguin, 1979).

Romantic School   Heinrich Heine, *Die romantische Schule*, in *Sämtliche Schriften*, vol. 3, pp. 359–504. *The Romantic School*, in *The Romantic School and Other Essays*, trans. Helen Mustard, ed. Jost Hermand and Robert C. Holub, pp. 1–127 (New York: Continuum, 1985).

SB   *Schillers Briefe*, ed. Fritz Jonas, 7 vols. (Stuttgart: Deutsche Verlags-Anstalt, 1893–96).

SW   Johann Christoph Friedrich Schiller, *Sämtliche Werke*, ed. Gerhard Fricke and Herbert G. Göpfert, 2nd ed., 5 vols. (Munich: Hanser, 1960).

Tale   Hugo von Hofmannsthal, *Reitergeschichte*, in *Sämtliche Werke*, ed. Heinz Otto Bürger, vol. 28, pp. 39–48 (Frankfurt: Fischer, 1975). *A Tale of the Cavalry*, in *Hugo von Hofmannsthal: Selected Prose*, trans. Mary Hottinger and Tania and James Stern, pp. 321–31 (New York: Pantheon, 1952).

Woyzeck   Georg Büchner, *Woyzeck*, ed. Egon Krause (Frankfurt: Insel, 1969). *Woyzeck*, in *Complete Works and Letters*, trans. Henry J. Schmidt, pp. 199–241 (New York: Continuum, 1986).

Stations of the
Divided Subject

Toward a Sociosemiotic Literary Practice

We will not oppose the visible to the hidden; we will seek what is more hidden than the hidden: the secret.   —Jean Baudrillard

Every beneficial effect of writing, indeed every effect of writing that in its innermost is not devastating, rests in its (the word's, language's) secret. . . . My idea of an objective and simultaneously highly political style and form of writing is: one that guides us to what the word is prohibited from expressing.
—Walter Benjamin

SINCE ITS emergence at the end of the eighteenth century, German bourgeois literature has performed an anamnesic, memorializing function. Given the increasing dominance of purposive rationality in bourgeois social and economic practice, it fell to literature "to take on the task of memorializing repressed forms of collective socialization and to create images for this memory."[1] This study is conceived as an attempt to sketch a broad historiography of this repressed memorial to collective socialization as it is inscribed within selected works of German bourgeois literature written between 1770 and 1914. In approaching this historiographical task I have not followed the lines of traditional literary history, which commonly privileges the formulation of abstract generalizations over thorough interpretation of individual works. Such "comprehensive" literary histories, guided by the pretense to totality, condemn themselves to superficiality if only because they barely scratch the surface of the literary texts they claim to "comprehend." My inquiry opposes to traditional extensive literary historiography what can be called an intensive historiographical method. I have opted to pursue as my primary strategy the close reading of particular sample texts drawn from specific stages of German literary history and to develop overarching speculative historical inferences out of recognitions derived from these interpretations. In this sense I try to take to heart Paul de Man's admonition that "to become good literary historians, we must remember that what we usually call literary history has little or nothing to do with literature and that what we call literary interpretation—provided only it is good interpretation—is in fact literary history."[2]

The interpretations offered here are joined thematically by their common attempt to interrogate the dialectic of utopian contestation and ideological legitimation that, as I will argue, structures both bourgeois subjectivity and bourgeois literary-aesthetic practice.[3] The interpretive chapters are further linked by the methodological aim of developing a literary-critical procedure that combines detailed textual analysis with broad historico-theoretical theses, as well as by a broadly defined theoretical program. The authors and texts with which my investigation deals are drawn from three seminal periods of German literature: the final decades of the eighteenth century, during which the German bourgeois intelligentsia initially sought to give expression to its emancipatory revolts against oppression from without and from within (Enlightenment and Sturm und Drang); the period of restoration and renewed rebellion from the 1820's to the revolutionary upheavals in 1848 (Young Germany); and the Austrian *fin de siècle*, marked by the dizzying crisis of bourgeois liberalism and its stubborn ideological retrenchment (literary Impressionism and Expressionism). I have chosen these periods because they represent crucial historical junctures in which tremendous sociopolitical tension and instability are accompanied by furious creativity in the sphere of literary aesthetics. For this reason, they provide ideal historical sites at which to probe the dialectic between "symbolic" and "semiotic" components—to use the terminology of Jacques Lacan and Julia Kristeva—in the signifying practices of bourgeois literary texts and simultaneously to explore the imbrications of this textual dialectic with the internal struggle between ideological (self-)repression and utopian-emancipatory critique at work in the bourgeois sociopolitical subject.

One of my principal contentions is that even in the evanescent phase of bourgeois literature at the end of the eighteenth century, middle-class literati in Germany were struggling more against themselves—that is, against the principles of bourgeois sociopolitical and economic practice—than they were against a "class" oppressor from without. Indeed, throughout the three periods under investigation, the internal division of the bourgeois subject expresses itself as a—sometimes more, sometimes less—muffled protest by middle-class writers against the alienating and reifying tendencies of the bourgeois episteme within whose (signifying) parameters they and their texts necessarily operate. By way of example, the figure of the scheming political intrigant who manipulates others by manipulating signs and their significations—a stock character throughout much German bourgeois literature—marks the persistent critique of a perniciously calculative, instrumentalized reason deployed for the purpose of mastery over others. However, this is but one of many symptoms that indicate that these writers had early and important insights into what has come to be called the dialectic of enlightenment, the recognition that, in the words of Max Horkheimer, "at the moment of consummation, reason has become irrational and stultified."[4] Although it has become a literary-historical commonplace to claim that the irrationality of the Sturm und Drang and of German Romanticism was formulated as a critical broadside aimed at the repressively rational culture of the German Enlightenment, the close relationships between this attack and the indictment of certain fundamental principles of bourgeois practice already voiced by some of the major representatives of the literary Enlightenment in Germany—Gotthold Ephraim Lessing, for example—has tended to pass unnoticed. What my investigations will show is that the critique of enlightened reason represents much more than a localized skirmish with the ideology of Enlightenment culture; indeed, it points to a deeper, more unsettling distrust of that form of purposive rationality that founds and underwrites bourgeois economic, sociopolitical, and signifying practices. The motif of internal self-disjunction thus expresses itself throughout the works examined here as a self-contradictory appeal to, and simultaneous denunciation of, specific aspects of bourgeois ideology and practice. The relative proportions and the specific textual concretizations of "semiotic" or "symbolic," of resistant and ideologically affirmative moments, vary widely from work to work and period to period. The analysis of these disparities provides the data that will help situate the individual works in relation to the reigning bourgeois institution of literature, while simultaneously giving clues to the historical transformations that their innovative textual practices effect in this institution.

According to Theodor Adorno, it is precisely art's dual nature as autonomous entity and social fact that makes a linear historiography of art impossible. This leads him to the conclusion that "it is probably more correct to say that art history is a series of nodal points than to view it as being continuous."[5] The historical aim of my study is to take cognizance of the necessary discontinuities of literary history while yet examining certain "nodal points" in the historical genesis of German bourgeois literature. This investigation is thus divided into three historical "stations" that correspond to the periods outlined above. Within each of these periods I examine two distinct works, each by a different author. This organizational principle is intended to permit me to address questions of historical synchronicity within each of

these periods, while at the same time providing some basis for discussing
the overarching theoretical and aesthetic issues the interpretations raise
when viewed diachronically. The juxtaposition of the historically proximate
works from each station, in other words, helps mark off an evolutionary
stage in the bourgeois institution of art. On the other hand, the comparison
of insights derived from the analysis of works from one station with those
drawn from the interpretation of works from the other stations throws into
relief changes, consistencies, and discontinuities in the genesis of the bourgeois institution of literature in Germany over a period of approximately 150
years. Methodologically this organizational structure is further justified by
the wish to achieve in my own critical practice a dialectical equilibrium between detailed textual analysis and generalizing sociohistorical and cultural
commentary.

My study is grounded in the assertion of a structural homology that con-
nects, on the one hand, the relationship between the bourgeois subject and
the ideological, sociopolitical order in which it is inscribed and, on the other
hand, the interaction between the individual literary-aesthetic work and the
bourgeois institution of art. The bourgeois subject and the bourgeois work
of art are both determined by the codifications of what Lacan and Kristeva
call the "symbolic" order; however, their individual signifying practices (Lacan's "imaginary"; Kristeva's "semiotic") are simultaneously determining of
this order. The investigations presented here examine the operation of this
dialectic in the formation of bourgeois subjectivity as well as in the workings of the bourgeois literary work of art. The perception that bourgeois
aesthetic practice is constituted in the tension between systematic domination and its contestation, between an institutionalized ideological framework and its creative, oppositional restructuring, runs like a leitmotif
throughout much recent critical aesthetic theory. As evidence of this, aside
from Kristeva's theory of poetic language, one could cite, for example,
Adorno's claim that the work of art strives for a dissonance that is simultaneously countered by its affirmative collaboration with sociopolitical repression,[6] and Peter Bürger's belief that bourgeois art is defined by the conflict between institutional framework and the potential political substance
of the individual work.[7]

Without anticipating my conclusion too much, I should give notice here
that I believe it is indeed possible to discern a specific phylogenesis—although not a "development" or "evolution" in the traditional sense—in the
dialectic of conformity and resistance that structures the bourgeois subject
and bourgeois literature in Germany. Lucien Goldmann's distinction between the "non-conscious," the "conscious," and the "repressed uncon-

scious" adequately defines the individual stages of this transformation.[8] For Lessing and Schiller, the writers who represent the first historical station, resistance to their own bourgeois ideology can best be termed "non-conscious" insofar as they themselves are not fully cognizant that the principles they are indicting underlie their own thought, action, and literary practices. This expresses itself most prominently in a political-critical equivocation that stems from an ideologically motivated retraction of their own spontaneous critical insights into the guiding sociopolitical, economic, and discursive practices of the bourgeois episteme. This retraction turns the literary work against itself, resulting in internal contradiction and a profound textual ambivalence. These characteristics appear as manifest symptoms of a primary repression of utopian political resistance, a repression that drives it underground into the political unconscious both of the bourgeois authoring subject and of its literary-aesthetic product. By contrast, for Heine and Büchner, the authors who represent the second station, resistance to bourgeois ideology and practice is fully "conscious," no longer restrained by second thoughts arising from the self-indictment implicit in their critical insights. However, because their aim is to exploit the mechanisms of the bourgeois public sphere and disseminate this self-critique throughout their middle-class reading public, they must contend with the resistance to these insights brought by bourgeois readers intent on defending the sociopolitical status quo by which they themselves are empowered. Faced with the incipient hegemony of a bourgeois ideology that protects the existing sociopolitical and economic reality as the bastion of its own (in)vested interests, these writers are forced to develop subtle strategies—conscious manipulations of the dialectic between resistance and affirmation—that will help them smuggle their critical contraband into the mighty fortress of bourgeois (false) consciousness. For Hofmannsthal and Kafka, finally, the writers who represent the third station, sociopolitical resistance has regressed, reverted to the stage of the "repressed unconscious." Here an originary moment of radical political critique is erased, simultaneously effaced by, but kept legible behind highly sophisticated literary-aesthetic strategies. The literary text takes on the character of a palimpsest in which an initial utopian-emancipatory impulse is repressed and overwritten by an intricately structured narrative in whose textual network the repressed nevertheless persistently returns. The historical genesis of aesthetic practices within the bourgeois institution of literature thus appears as a mechanism of sociopolitical self-repression in which the political-emancipatory drive of the bourgeoisie, expressed in the revolutionary fervor of the eighteenth and nineteenth centuries, is driven into a political unconscious by self-subjugation to that socioeconomic and political reality molded by bourgeois practice. This process culminates in a violent return of the political repressed that foreshadows the demise of the bourgeois subject as a dialectically structured, self-divided consciousness.

At a time when the condition of knowledge is shaped, in the words of Jean-François Lyotard, by an "incredulity toward metanarratives,"[9] it has become necessary to justify any wide-ranging historical purview such as the one taken here. Although a certain "narrative" about the German bourgeois subject does indeed emerge from the historical component of this investigation, this narrative makes no claim to the totalizing gesture of "metanarrative." Indeed, what ultimately makes metanarratives suspicious is their proximity to those ideological strategies of legitimation and control that bourgeois culture generated as one of its preferred strategies of cultural-political mastery. But it is important that we not make the fundamental mistake of confusing application with essence: just because grand narratives have been applied to the ends of ideological control does not mean that such narratives are by definition and as such ideologically tainted. Indeed, it is difficult to imagine a grander narrative than the post-structuralist account of the history of "metaphysics" from Plato to Heidegger; and those who condemn this narrative suspect it of ideological collusion, whereas those who praise it cite its critical purpose. It is obvious, moreover, that even Lyotard's "paralogical" project serves an ideology-critical purpose; indeed, its critical strategies are schooled on the theories of the early Frankfurt School, especially on those of Horkheimer and Adorno.[10] Their theory of the dialectic of enlightenment is another prime example of a grand narrative intended to have a decidedly critical function: they tell, after all, the history of Western civilization from Homer to the modern culture industry as a story of reason's infiltration and perversion by myth. Finally, to try to tell history at all—as recent criticism has made us amply aware—is to construct a narrative, and to abandon history simply because it tends toward "grand narrative" would be to relinquish a potentially productive and insightful mode of critical understanding. The crucial question, as Nietzsche pointed out in his essay *On the Utility and Liability of History for Life*, is whether history is employed to distract from or contribute to our critical insight into the conditions of life.

It seems appropriate to offer a few remarks regarding the principles that have influenced the selection of the texts under discussion here, particularly since I have remained solidly within the mainstream canon of German literature. The restriction to canonical texts and writers is inherently bound up with my specific interest in the bourgeois *institution* of literature, an institution that holds primary responsibility for the constitution of the literary canon. Likewise, my exclusive choice of male authors derives from the fact that within this literary institution, authorship was a vocation traditionally reserved for males. Similarly, as we will see, within the bourgeois philosophical discourse on subjectivity, the subject that is theorized is always assumed to be middle-class and male. It was hence the desire to critically interrogate the principles of the bourgeois institution which structures literary-aesthetic production and reception that motivated my decision to examine canonical male authors and their literary creations. At the same time we have to admit, whether we like it or not, that the intellectual academies in which we as literary scholars function are agencies of this same literary institution, and its principles still shape our own receptive practices. Consequently, we are often more dependent on the canon than we would like to admit—especially when we seek to address a broader literary-critical community, as I wish to do in this book, and not merely speak to the specialists of a particular national literature or historical epoch. In this sense my appeal to authors and texts well known and commonly read outside the confines of German Studies derives in part from this mundane practical consideration. The realities of the institutionalized academic marketplace extract concessions even from those who consider themselves to be ideologically resistant scholars; thus, it seems that neither I, as bourgeois critic, nor my book, as critical commodity, can escape the dialectic of ideological affirmation and opposition that I have made the object of my research.

Even the restriction to canonical authors and texts still leaves considerable latitude for the selection of appropriate objects for textual analysis. Given the unavoidable limitation, for reasons of space, to no more than six interpretations, it was clearly necessary to restrict myself to one or two genres to prevent generic questions from interfering with the broader theoretical and historical problems. My analyses concentrate on tragic drama and short fiction in part for practical reasons: the relative brevity of these texts makes them easier to digest and hence facilitates the kind of detailed textual analysis I practice. By the same token, tragic drama and narrative fiction are two genres that especially flourished in the German bourgeois literary institution, and they thus represent literary forms in which considerable creative energy was invested. Moreover, the examination of drama and narrative provides an opportunity to investigate the general trend within German bourgeois literature away from the more immediate, sensual, and communitarian parameters of representation and reception inherent in the dramatic spectacle toward the mediate, internalizing, and privatizing modes of representation and reception characteristic of reading, with its restriction to the textual evocation of fictional worlds. The focus on these two genres thus plays into the question of historical transformations within the bourgeois institution of literature, and it further helps me engage theoretical questions about the privatizing tendencies in bourgeois social practice.

With regard to the specific texts themselves, I have singled out authors and works whose critical reception has been characterized by severe political contestation. In each instance, considerable scholarly debate has revolved around the text's sociopolitical status, and it has been alternately appropriated both for traditionalist interpretations and radical critical analyses. This antagonistic reception is but one signal that these are works in which the dialectic between affirmation and contestation is particularly vital. Adherence to this criterion also explains why explicitly engaged works such as the writings of Bertolt Brecht do not figure in my investigations. Such engaged literature, insofar as it collapses the dialectic of affirmation and resistance into the pole of political contestation, falls outside of (or beyond) the paradigm of a specifically *bourgeois* literature, just as do the products of the culture industry, which collapse this dialectic into the contrary pole of ideological assent. In this context we should recall Adorno's argument that any literature that attempts to realize an immediate critical-political engagement necessarily overlooks the repressive sociopolitical conditions in which it is forced to operate, blithely ignoring the systematic distortions of intercommunicative exchange to which its political message is always already subjected.[11]

Finally, the texts I have selected embody what have universally been considered ground-breaking literary-aesthetic innovations, and this represents a significant criterion given that this study seeks to come to an understanding of the interrelationship between aesthetic revolution and sociopolitical resistance. Indeed, the original working title of my project, "Literary Revolution and Revolutionary Literature in Germany," stressed this aspect in particular. As the ideas developed and matured, however, this issue receded into the background, to be supplanted by the more complex questions of divided subjectivity and the dialectical struggle that distinguishes bourgeois literary-aesthetic practices. The guiding hypothesis of the original project was the supposition—viewed in retrospect, admittedly rather naive—that revolutionary textual practices could somehow be directly linked to conscious revolutionary sociopolitical drives and desires. As my investigations progressed, I became increasingly aware that interpretive analysis did not bear out this one-to-one correspondence. Gradually it became clear that it was precisely the conflict between critique and its simultaneous ideological repression, either conscious or unconscious, that accounted for the literary-aesthetic innovations of these texts. My investigations thus came to focus specifically on what Gilles Deleuze and Felix Guattari term "minor" literature, where "minor no longer designates specific literatures, but the revolutionary conditions for every literature within the heart of what is called great (or established) literature."[12] My conclusion, then, is that in the domain of German bourgeois literature, aesthetic revolution is born of the contradictions and antagonisms that characterize the bourgeois subject and the bourgeois institution of art: the dialectical conflict between ideological repression and its contestation is the primary motor behind literary-aesthetic changes and advances.

No interpretation, as reception theory has taught us, proceeds in a theoretical vacuum; as interpreters we always bring a horizon of understanding to the text, an understanding that—in the best of all possible interpretive worlds—is altered by the provocations of the text itself. In this regard, my study is conceived as a literary-critical project in which literary theory and hermeneutical practice coincide with an insistence on textual detail. However, to interpret means to have a position; and to have a position, as Frank Lentricchia reminds us, means to have a theory.[13] But having a theory does not mean dogmatic adherence to a single theoretical position selected from among the theory-commodities available in today's ever-burgeoning academic marketplace. The investigations collected here draw on a wide variety of critical perspectives in an attempt to exploit the insights of whatever literary-theoretical persuasion seems best able to elucidate the aesthetic practices of an individual text. Readers should hence not be surprised—and I hope they will not be put off—to find that I appeal to extremely diverse theoretical models, from the Critical Theory of the Frankfurt School to hermeneutics and reception theory to Freudian psychoanalytic discourse to post-structuralist conceptions of the subject and of history and, last but not least, to (social) semiotics. To some readers these diverse theories may seem mutually exclusive or even antagonistic, but it is my belief that their interpenetration in the process of interpretation can not only demonstrate how each is particularly suited to illuminate distinct facets of the texts in question, but will also disclose the specific points at which these theories mutually correct and/or supplement one another.

It is avowedly not my purpose, I must immediately add, merely to pursue a broad theoretical eclecticism; rather, my methodological aim is to mark off a theoretical terrain that will help advance the discipline of socio-literary textual analysis. Jürgen Habermas has never tired of reminding us that all knowledge is a function of the interests—acknowledged or unacknowledged—that govern its articulation. The methodological and theoretical interests of the present inquiry can best be described as the desire to evolve a sociosemiotic interpretive practice that fuses a radical political critique with the insights of recent advances in semiotic theory. Consequently, I rely heavily on the sociocultural precepts and terminology of the Frankfurt School, but I lend this critical model a semiological cast by integrating it with the positions of sociohistorical semioticians such as Jean Baudrillard, Michel Foucault, and Jean-Joseph Goux. Semiotic text analysis as commonly practiced has justifiably been accused of idealism or abstract formalism. Obsessed with the infinite openness of signifying chains, it frolics in the *jouissance* of textual play, ignoring the sociopolitical ground rules that always already govern this textual game. Literary sociology, on the other hand, is too often guilty of treating the literary text as a transparent medium that re-presents in fictional worlds specific historico-political contingencies. Sociosemiotic analysis, by contrast, seeks to merge these two critical directions, examining how sociopolitical, economic, and historical conjunctures are inscribed within the signifying practices of a particular, historically determined literary text. Both in their general orientation and their peculiar theoretical procedure, then, my investigations seek to locate themselves in a space between the "rootedness" of dogmatism and the free-floating "detachment" of the liberal bourgeois intelligentsia—in that space between total eclecticism and narrow adherence to a specific theoretical creed, in other words, which Max Horkheimer specifically designated as the site of *critical theory.*[14]

Since an examination of the constitution of bourgeois subjectivity forms the nucleus of this inquiry, the theoretical position that informs my interpretations can best be spelled out by concentrating on this issue. Questions of the human subject and of subjectivity have made a marked resurgence in philosophical and literary studies over the last decade or so. Without doubt, this renewed interest has been kindled by post-structuralist insights into the imbrication of language and subjectivity. This has led, in turn, to reassessments of the nature of subjectivity and consciousness on the basis of the revolutionary redefinitions, introduced by post-Saussurean linguistics, of language as a signifying system. This development culminated in a radical attack on the understanding of subjectivity as it had become institutionalized over the course of what Jacques Derrida calls the history of Western metaphysics. Within this "metaphysical" tradition, the subject is conceived as a free, autonomous, self-determining, (self-)mastering, and inherently rational consciousness whose relationship to itself is characterized by transparency and self-presence. Seen in this way, the subject is, literally, an in-dividual: an indivisible, unitary totality. One of the main thrusts of post-structuralist criticism has been the "deconstruction" of this unitary, autonomous,

and self-present subject, and it has proceeded by tracing the fissures and contradictions that always already divide the subject and rupture its self-presence. This critique culminated in the pronouncement of the subject's
death—assuming that it had ever actually lived. But the very radicality of
the post-structuralist critique of the subject has tended to be post-structuralism's own undoing; for by abandoning the category of the subject, reducing it to the play of signifiers—that is, to the product of an abstract differential system of signification—post-structuralism necessarily commits a
petitio principii, calling into question the very site from which its own critique of subjectivity must be launched. In order to have any descriptive
power, the post-structuralist critique would itself somehow have to escape
the "structurality of structure," thereby establishing itself as a new "subject,"
a new "center" in the long chain of substitutions for the structuring center
that, according to Derrida, constitutes the history of Western metaphysics.[15]

Any theory that attempts such a wholesale abandoning of the creative,
critical subject cannot avoid getting caught up in this same performative contradiction. Moreover, as Andreas Huyssen argues, to jettison the subject as
"author," as initiator and manipulator of signifying systems, is to dismiss the
opportunity of interrogating the ideology of the authorial subject and hence
to cut short questions about how codes, texts, and other cultural artifacts
contribute to the historical constitution of subjectivity.[16] Huyssen's argument is important because it helps dispel the erroneous notion that any defense of the concept of subjectivity is necessarily a form of neoconservative
retrenchment against post-structuralist advances. Although some such
moves are indeed underway,[17] the most substantive challenges to deconstructive theories that write off creative subjectivity as the "sub-jected"—
that is, subjugated—agent of the symbolic order have come from thinkers
who accept certain post-structuralist insights but attempt to appropriate
them for a radical politics. This is true, for example, of theoreticians such as
Louis Althusser, Jean Baudrillard, and Julia Kristeva, who are closely tied to
the post-structuralist camp. But it also applies to critics who approach post-
structuralism from the vantage point of other theoretical discourses. Manfred Frank, for example, who examines post-structuralism from the perspective of German hermeneutical theory, principally objects to post-structuralism's implicit political impotence, and he argues that "individuality,"
understood as the code-forming and code-transgressing potential of the subject, cannot simply be reduced to an epiphenomenon of the signifying system.[18] Frank's insistence on the relevance of hermeneutics as a theory that
can account both for the production and interpretation of texts, on the one
hand, and for the relationship between individuality and the signifying net-

works of language, on the other, underscores how contemporary discourses on the subjectivity of the text and the textuality of the subject dovetail. What is more, by unearthing debates in the German Romantic and idealist philosophical traditions that anticipate some of post-structuralism's seminal insights and point toward potential solutions to its theoretical aporias, Frank also helps us recall that the present controversies about language and its role in the constitution of subjectivity were already prefigured in the eighteenth century by the philosophies of the ascendant bourgeois intelligentsia. This anchoring of debates on subjectivity specifically in the epoch of bourgeois culture represents a significant and necessary move. In much of the current philosophical and literary debate, subjectivity is discussed as though it were a wholly abstract, universal, and generalizable phenomenon. However, this idealistic conception of subjectivity must be subjected to a materialist critique, which simply means that the subject must be radically historicized. The nature of the subject and of subjectivity is always bound up with specific historically determined conditions, and my study attempts to come to terms with the character of subjectivity in the period that can broadly be defined as bourgeois modernism. This historical orientation is, I believe, one of this investigation's distinguishing characteristics.

At their best, deconstructive theories have impressed upon us the textual nature of subjectivity. It is more than a mere metaphor, for example, when Derrida maintains that the noncoincidence of the self with the self parallels the rift that divides the letter into the dimensions of "allegory" and "literality."[19] This metaphor points to an essential homology between divided subjectivity and the counterpoint between exoteric (literal) and esoteric (allegorical) levels in the literary text. What is more, this same opposition corresponds, when projected into the sphere of textual reception, to the distinction between "grammatical" and "psychological" understanding postulated by hermeneutical theory, or, when viewed through the lens of psychoanalytic discourse, to the dichotomy between manifest and latent sense that is integral to Freudian dream analysis. Above all, thinkers such as Derrida and Lacan, by stressing the accession of the subject to the structure of signification, have heightened our awareness of the semiological underpinnings that shape all social practices. However, these insights must also be subjected to a radical historicization. In other words, the symbolic practices described by post-structuralist theory must be identified not as universals, but rather as the epistemic structures that segregate the thought from the unthought, the sayable from the unsayable, and the comprehensible from the incomprehensible in the historically circumscribed epoch of bourgeois modernism.

Important advances in this direction have been made from within the discourse of post-structuralism itself. One thinks here of Althusser's Neo-Marxist transformation of the post-structuralist conception of a subject shaped by language into a theory about the ways in which ideology conditions consciousness.[20] Building on Althusser's position, Paul Smith has recently attempted to retheorize the subject as a dialectic between "the supposedly determining 'individual' and the determined 'subject.' "[21] Smith takes as his starting point Althusser's conception of ideology as a structure that interpellates the subject, but he grafts onto this conception Julia Kristeva's more dialectical model of the subject as both "repressed" and "innovative," thereby working toward a notion of the subject (which he terms the human "agent") that embodies "a form of subjectivity where, by virtue of the contradictions and disturbances among subject-positions, the possibility (indeed, the actuality) of resistance to ideological pressure is allowed for."[22] According to Smith, the differential systems of language and ideological codification create in the texture of their own contradictions a space for an oppositional activity.

In current debates on subjectivity it has largely passed unnoticed that the Critical Theory of the early Frankfurt School, especially the work of Max Horkheimer and Theodor Adorno, staked out a theoretical terrain on which the subject can be conceived as a dialectical construct that succumbs, on the one hand, to ideological pressures while yet retaining, on the other hand, the potential to transcend and overcome ideological dictates. One of the major failings of orthodox Marxism, as the early Frankfurt School theoreticians realized, was its inability to account for revolutionary consciousness. A "vulgar" Marxism that dogmatically defines all consciousness as derivative of material economic, social, and political conditions reduces human subjects so completely to pawns of the system that it eliminates every potential for critical awareness and intervention in that system. In fact, what vulgar Marxism shares with certain versions of post-structuralism is its inability to theorize a creative, system-independent subject. Critical Theory sought to escape this conundrum by developing a philosophy of praxis that stressed the importance of subjectivity, consciousness, and cultural production in the sociopolitical matrix. To be sure, these theoreticians were careful not to hypostatize individuality, subjectivity, and rationality as independent principles, as bourgeois ideology was wont to do, but emphasized instead the dialectical reciprocity between material, sociopolitical, and economic conditions and the conditions of human subjectivity. Thus Horkheimer writes that "the antagonism between individuality and the economic and social conditions of existence . . . is an essential element in individuality itself."[23] The subject, Horkheimer suggests, cannot be conceived apart from its embeddedness in and conditioning by historically determined material conditions within society. But subjective consciousness is simultaneously instrumental in the implementation and maintenance of concrete economic and sociopolitical structures. This can be seen most clearly in the instance of ideology understood as "false consciousness," insofar as it represents a set of mystifications and self-deceptions that permit subjects to affirm those conditions—sociopolitical, economic, psychological—that are the source of their suffering. For Critical Theory, abstract reason becomes just such an ideology; and it recognizes that "the crisis of reason is manifested in the crisis of the individual, as whose agency it has developed."[24]

In their attempts to discover the links that bind the individual to the social fabric, the Frankfurt School theoreticians looked in two directions. On the other hand, they turned to sociopsychological theories as a way to ground the evolution of the individual subject in the socializing practices of society. This theoretical venture, developed particularly in the writings of Erich Fromm and Herbert Marcuse, expanded on Freud's cultural theories, which had proposed that the human psyche is conditioned by a struggle between the need to satisfy base instincts and the demands of the civilizing process. Their basic strategy was to demonstrate that what Freud theorized as universal human nature could in fact be circumscribed as conditions arising from capitalist society. On the other hand, the Frankfurt School theoreticians pursued what can be termed socioepistemic investigations, seeking to discover those rationalizing principles that were specific both to socioeconomic and to cultural practices in modern capitalist societies. This led them away from orthodox Marxism's stress on the conditions of production as the primary determining factor of society and toward a concentration on the concept of exchange as the central principle connecting bourgeois thought and socioeconomic practice. "Above and beyond all specific forms of social differentiation," Adorno writes, "the abstraction implicit in the market system [des Tauschwerts] represents the domination of the general over the particular, of society over its captive membership. . . . Behind the reduction of men to agents and bearers of exchange values [des Warenaustauschs] lies the domination of men over men. This remains the basic fact, in spite of the difficulties with which from time to time many of the categories of political science are confronted."[25] The systematic abstraction that allows one to overlook the concrete and immediate use-value of an object while attributing to it an intangible exchange-value underwrites, according to this view, not only the structures of bourgeois commerce, but the bourgeoisie's strategies for social domination as well. The rational subject who

abstracts from the inherent individuality of objects of nature and fellow human beings to ensure his mastery over them thinks in the same manner as
the person who ignores the particularities of certain commodities to enter
into a negotiation for their exchange.

The socioepistemic and sociopsychological approaches toward coupling
the economic and political processes of material culture (the "base") with
the structures that underlie intellectual culture (the "superstructure") have
remained until today, even in the more overtly politicized versions of post-
structuralism, the principal strategies of radical social theory. The sociopsychological approach is most strikingly evident in the work of Deleuze
and Guattari. The socioepistemic tactic is represented, for example, by the
early Foucault, who in *The Order of Things* develops an archaeology of those
epistemic structures that govern thought and social practice in the Western
world since the Renaissance. Along similar lines, one thinks of Baudrillard's
identification of successive developments in the theory and practice of semiosis with specific stages of Western political economy,[26] or of Goux's hypothesis that economic exchange and signifying exchange are isomorphi-
cally linked by a common semiotics, by a set of identical symbolizing principles.[27] Unfortunately, the Critical Theorists never explicitly developed a
sociosemiotic theory of their own. Such a theory is implicit, however, in
their critique of an instrumentalized reason that operates according to the
principle of abstract exchange and the logic of identity. We get an inkling of
the semiological thinking that underpins the Frankfurt School's critique of
reason in a passage from *Dialectic of Enlightenment* in which Horkheimer and
Adorno attack the doctrine of the arbitrariness of the sign as a mere strategy that allows one to condemn everything that transcends this relationship
as metaphysical. In this semiotic system, they claim, words no longer carry
meaning ("bedeuten"), but instead are reduced to the function of signifying
("bezeichnen").[28]

This position has fundamental similarities with the semiotic theories advanced by Foucault, Baudrillard, and Goux, all of whom, like the Critical
Theorists, draw out the interconnections between economic or monetary
practices and signifying systems. The operative concept that these theories
share is the notion of exchange, and it would not be an exaggeration to assert that these recent theoreticians have helped fill an important gap left by
Critical Theory in that they have elaborated in diverse ways its implicit semiotics. It is this point of imbrication in a shared sociosemiotic theory that
makes the positions of Critical Theory and of these post-structuralist
thinkers mutually supplementary. Merging these theoretical directions will
help me outline the entanglement of the semiotic issues that structure bour-

geois subjectivity both with questions of literary aesthetics and with the problematics of bourgeois economic and sociopolitical practice. In this context it is important to keep in mind that the rise of semiotic thought is cotemporaneous with the emergence of bourgeois modernist culture in the eighteenth century.

Fundamental to my project is the recognition that there is a structural parallel between the semiotic of differentiality heralded by structuralism and post-structuralism and the differential structure that fixes value in bourgeois economic exchange. My interpretations will demonstrate that this problematic was already critically explored in bourgeois literature and aesthetic theory as early as the eighteenth century. Just as in the semiological system individual "elements hold each other in equilibrium in accordance with fixed rules,"[29] in bourgeois economic practice the relative value of any commodity is determined by its submission to the rules governing commodity exchange. In particular, every commodity must submit to having its value established by and expressed in terms of the general equivalent, money. It is certainly no coincidence that Saussure, the "father" of modern structural linguistics, borrowed the concept of "value" from the realm of economics to apply it in the sphere of language.[30] Modern semiotics conceives the process of semiosis, in the words of Charles Morris, as "any situation in which one thing takes account of something else, which is not directly causally efficacious, through the mediation of some third thing; a sign process is thus a process of 'mediated taking account of.' "[31] For Karl Marx, precisely such "mediated taking account of" describes the operation by which money transforms the self-identical object into a non-self-identical commodity. As an abstract "third thing" that mediates between the use-values of two concrete objects, money, the ultimate sign, codifies their abstract exchange-values according to a differential process.[32] To be sure, already in the eighteenth century the French economist Anne Robert Jacques Turgot had recognized certain intrinsic connections between monetary systems and the signifying structure of language.[33] One of the hypotheses that my essays pursue is that the economic conflict between use-value, or intrinsic worth, and exchange-value, or extrinsic worth defined in the differential system of exchange, parallels not only the dialectical struggle constitutive of bourgeois (self-)divided subjectivity, but likewise the structural tensions inherent in the bourgeois work of art.

Throughout this study I employ the phrases "institution of art" or "institution of literature" as a metaphorical shorthand for that partial complex of the symbolic order that holds sway over aesthetic and/or literary discourses. The concept of the "institution," hence, does not necessarily imply a concrete administrative entity or a consciously formulated and externally policed program. At any given historical crossroad, the institution of literature is always greater than given dominant "schools," doctrines, or aesthetic "fashions"; indeed, it encompasses the entire set of rules that make the production and reception of any literary work possible. In *The Order of Things* Foucault defines hermeneutics as "the totality of the learning and skills that enable one to make the signs speak and to discover their meaning" and semiology as "the totality of the learning and skills that enable one . . . to define what constitutes [signs] as signs, and to know how and by what laws they are linked."[34] If we superimpose these definitions onto one another and add to them the modifier "aesthetic," we can define the institution of art as the fusion of those hermeneutic and semiological practices governing aesthetic discourse in any given historical period. The institution of art would thus be constituted as the totality of the learning and skills that enable one to make aesthetic signs speak and to discover their meaning, and the totality of learning and skills that enable one to constitute aesthetic signs as aesthetic signs and to know by what laws they are linked. In Foucault's definitions "hermeneutics" describes the semantics governing the production and reception of signification, while "semiology" names a critical-theoretical syntax that identifies those conditions that make signification possible. Similarly, the concept "institution of art" circumscribes both the production and reception of aesthetic signification and the critical discourse that examines the conditions under which such aesthetic signification becomes possible—in short, aesthetic theory.

As the central precept of the bourgeois institution of art, the doctrine of aesthetic autonomy has figured prominently in debates on the emancipatory potential of literary practice. It holds important implications for an understanding of the irrevocably dichotomous structure of the bourgeois literary work of art as both commodity and protest against the very process of commodification. No interpretation that wishes to pay heed to this fundamental structure of bourgeois literary-aesthetic products can ignore these implications. The first is that the critical potential of institutionalized bourgeois literature cannot be immediately identified with the phenomenon of aesthetic autonomy: the autonomous status of the literary work of art does not alone guarantee that any given text will have a practical sociopolitical effect. On the contrary, the revolutionary quality of any text must be gauged according to its implementation of specific textual practices given the particular historically determined conditions in the bourgeois life-world and in the bourgeois institution of literature that condition its production and reception. Aesthetic form is at once regressive and progressive; it holds, to be more precise, the potential to be exploited for either regressive or progressive political ends, but it does not embody in some essentialist manner either characteristic. This suggests that no abstract theory can come to terms with the revolutionary impetus of literary-aesthetic form; rather, the question of the oppositional aspects of literary products can be decided only on a case-by-case basis through detailed analyses of individual works, analyses that attempt to probe the relative positions of affirmation and opposition, ideology and ideological resistance, manifest in any given text. Such examinations must attempt to contextualize a text within the theoretical-historical sites of its production and reception. This suggests, on the one hand, that we must seek to radically historicize the theoretical development and practical implementation of bourgeois literary-aesthetic practices. On the other hand, it implies a methodology that itself strives for a dialectical balance between detailed interpretation and the cautious formulation of general historical and theoretical hypotheses. Such is the aim of the present study, as it attempts to move toward a sociosemiotic literary practice that combines the microanalysis of specific texts with the macro-context of theoretical and historical abstraction. It is this dialectical quality that sets this study apart both from traditional literary-historiographical investigations, and from theoretical discussions of subjectivity and revolutionary literary aesthetics. I seek to approach general questions about the constitution of subjectivity, the dynamics of the literary work of art, and the historical evolution of the bourgeois institution of literature not by developing my own abstract, generalizing theories, but rather on the basis of interpretive practice, by means of close readings of texts. Insofar as I attempt to work from the particularity of textual analysis to the generality of historical and theoretical hypotheses, my general methodology can be termed inductive.

I concur with the assertion that the most valuable literary criticism contributes as well to social criticism.[35] It is my hope that such a claim can be made for the investigations presented here. I would be satisfied, of course, if this book were read for the individual interpretations it offers or as a kind of social history of bourgeois authorship in Germany. But I would be especially pleased if its conscious fusion of disciplined interpretive practice with critical-theoretical perspectives drawn from literary and social theory could make a contribution, however small, to the development of a sociosemiotic literary-interpretive practice.

CHAPTER ONE

Divided Subjectivity and the Internal Dialectic of Bourgeois Literature

The subject is born divided, because of being born with the signifier.
—Jacques Lacan

Literary works are utopias in one of their roots, but in another they are economic and social products. They not only have responsibilities, but are also facts; and their responsibilities must make accommodations to these facts.
—Robert Musil

IN *Phenomenology of Spirit* (1807), Hegel sketches under the heading of "Unhappy Consciousness" ("das unglückliche Bewußtsein") a conception of the human subject as an entity traversed by self-division and contradiction. This Unhappy Consciousness, although it exhibits the doubling of self-consciousness that Hegel believes is fundamental to Spirit ("Geist"), fails to achieve a unity of consciousness that transcends these internal contradictions. It thus represents for him a historical station of subjectivity that follows upon those stages he terms "Stoicism" and "Scepticism," but yet antedates the culmination of subjectivity in pure *Geist*, which Hegelian idealism posits as a future totality beyond all contradiction.

In Scepticism, consciousness truly experiences itself as internally contradictory. From this experience emerges a *new form* of consciousness. . . . This new form is . . . one which *knows* that it is the dual consciousness of itself, as self-liberating, unchangeable, and self-identical, and as self-bewildering and self-perverting, and it is the awareness of this self-contradictory nature of itself. In Stoicism, self-consciousness is the simple freedom of itself. In Scepticism, this freedom becomes a reality, negates the other side of determinate existence, but really duplicates *itself*, and now knows itself to be a duality. Consequently, the duplication which formerly was divided between two individuals, the lord and the bondsman, is now lodged in one. The duplication of self-consciousness within itself, which is essential in the Notion of Spirit, is thus here before us, but not yet its unity: the *Unhappy Consciousness* is the consciousness of self as a dual-natured, merely contradictory being.[1]

As a specific developmental stage in the evolution of Spirit, Unhappy Consciousness distinguishes itself from Scepticism, the stage of self-division that precedes it, on the basis of its awareness of its own dichotomization; and it differs from what Hegel terms "living Spirit" in that it has not (yet) achieved reconciliation with itself in the form of a dialectical sublation of its opposites into overriding unity.[2]

Essential to the dichotomous condition of Unhappy Consciousness, however, is a perpetual dialectical interplay, a constant recursivity between the two poles of its internal division.

This *unhappy, inwardly disputed* consciousness, since its essentially contradictory nature is for it a *single* consciousness, must for ever have present in the one consciousness the other also; and thus it is driven out of each in turn in the very moment when it imagines it has successfully attained to a peaceful unity with the other. Its true return into itself, or its reconciliation with itself will, however, display the Notion of Spirit that has become a living Spirit, and has achieved an actual existence, because it already possesses as a single undivided consciousness a dual nature.[3]

Unhappy Consciousness, as the penultimate manifestation of Spirit before its absolute, that is, perfected, realization in the unity of Spirit as such is constituted as perpetual dialectical instability. The "unhappiness" of this consciousness stems from this lack of unity; but it is telling that as a solution to this crisis of dis-unity Hegel explicitly precludes the mastery of one of the poles in this reciprocal dialectic over the other. Internal division is constitutive of the subject both as Unhappy Consciousness and as realized *Geist*, with the difference that in the latter a transcendent integrity unifies consciousness into ultimate oneness. Only the self-realization of living Spirit, the projected reconciliation of its particularity ("Einzelheit") with the universal, can provide this incessant dialectical play with a transcendental unity.[4] This unity, however, is one into which this dialectical dynamic is inscribed: in this process of perfect sublation ("Aufhebung"), dialectical play is simultaneously preserved and canceled, retained in its duality while elevated to a higher singularity. In this movement Hegel's *Phenomenology of Spirit* secularizes Christian theodicy by transforming it into a philosophic-historical project. Taking as his point of departure the fundamental recognition that human subjectivity is traversed by a dialectical rift, Hegel posits the "evil" of self-division as the necessary historical condition for the attainment of the stage of pure Spirit in which this self-division is both preserved and transcended.

It is not so much Hegel's totalizing teleology as such that arouses suspicion as it is the ideological self-justification of divided subjectivity that it encompasses; for in this system, non-self-identity is legitimized as the condi-

tion of possibility of human consciousness per se. Within Hegel's philosophical adumbration of human consciousness the ideality of pure Spirit is
counterposed to the reality of Unhappy Consciousness; but in Hegel's teleological system what is real and historically given has significance only insofar as it is the germ of the ideal. The teleological logic of Hegel's investigation allows him to valorize the internal contradictoriness of Unhappy
Consciousness as a necessary way station through which Spirit must pass
on its road to self-identity. This strategy is inherently ideological in that it
essentially allows Hegel to repress his own critical insights into the given historical status of bourgeois subjectivity: he eschews any philosophical inquiry
into the sociopolitical, psychological, or other material causes of divided subjectivity, preferring instead to train his sights on the ideal. Still, what Hegel
offers with his description of Unhappy Consciousness as a self-contradictory
system of "absolute dialectical unrest" is a diagnosis of his own self-divided
consciousness,[5] a condition he shared with his fellow bourgeois intellectuals in Germany. The fact alone that Hegel locates Unhappy Consciousness
as a historical stage that lies beyond certain recognizable past plateaus in the
evolution of consciousness but that has nevertheless not (yet) attained its
utopian aim of perfect self-identity implies that Unhappy Consciousness, as
what lies specifically between that past and this future, marks the historical
site of the consciousness that generates Hegel's own philosophical reflections. Janus-faced, Unhappy Consciousness, like Hegel's own philosophical
system, both looks back on its past and forward to its future in the scheme
of Spirit's coming-to-(self-)consciousness. Thus Hegel specifically characterizes Unhappy Consciousness as an "intermediate position": "It has advanced beyond both of these [Stoicism and Scepticism]; it brings and holds
together pure thinking and particular individuality, but has not yet risen to
that thinking where consciousness as a particular individuality is reconciled
with pure thought itself. It occupies rather this intermediate position."[6]

For Hegel, Unhappy Consciousness names that "intermediate" stage of
subjectivity attained by European enlightened bourgeois man (not woman)
by the beginning of the nineteenth century. Throughout the present study
the term "subject" refers to this historically circumscribed, internally contradictory, and relentlessly (self-)divided male subjectivity constituted over
the course of bourgeois culture—in the period that can broadly be termed
"modernity," that is, from the Enlightenment (ca. 1750) through the era of
so-called High Modernism, ending approximately with the First World War.
Appropriating the terminology employed by Friedrich Schiller to distinguish
"modern" poets from their historical forebears, this historical-cultural epoch
could be called the age of "sentimental" subjectivity, where the concept "sen-

timental" is understood, as Schiller defines it, to denote a "reflected" or "mediated" consciousness. Similar in this respect to Hegel's definition of Unhappy Consciousness, Schiller characterizes the consciousness of the sentimental poet as one perpetually torn by an internal contradiction between the demands of the real and the requirements of the ideal. "The sentimental poet," he writes in *Über naive und sentimentalische Dichtung*, "is constantly dealing with two opposing concepts and emotions, with reality as a boundary and with his idea as the infinite" (*Naive*, 720–21; 42). Schiller's notion that sentimental subjectivity is constituted as a conflict between the limitlessness of ideality and the limitations of given historical conditions has a direct analog in Hegel's description of Unhappy Consciousness as an antagonism between "pure thinking and particular individuality."

Non-self-identity, self-contestation, and absolute dialectical unrest are the conditions of bourgeois subjectivity as Unhappy Consciousness. Although Hegel's exposition of this conflicted subjectivity is unexpectedly brief, he does attempt to specify the oppositions that structure this dialectical tension. On one side of the dialectical field he places "self-liberation," "unchangeability," and "self-identity"; he envisions these being challenged on the other side by "self-bewilderment" and "self-perversion."[7] The positive, stable, self-formative features of bourgeois subjectivity, in other words, are for Hegel always already undermined by a second set of drives that issue from a self-perverting or self-inverting consciousness ("sich verkehrendes Bewußtsein") that contests the ultimate establishment of self-identity. Hegel elucidates this internal antagonism by comparing it with the dialectical interchange between the "lord" and the "bondsman," a relationship he had analyzed in the previous section of *Phenomenology*.[8] What distinguishes Unhappy Consciousness, according to Hegel, is that in it the dialectic of mastery and bondage is not distributed between two individuals, but instead is inscribed into one and the same consciousness. If the lord is characterized as an "independent consciousness whose essential nature is to be for itself," while the bondsman represents a "dependent consciousness whose essential nature is simply to live or to be for another,"[9] Unhappy Consciousness is marked by the dialectical reciprocity of autonomy and bondage in one and the same subject. As the name for bourgeois subjectivity, Unhappy Consciousness thus distinguishes the bourgeois subject as a mode of consciousness torn between independence and dependence, freedom and servitude, autonomy and self-willed subjugation.

This consciousness is therefore the unconscious, thoughtless rambling which passes back and forth from the one extreme of self-identical self-consciousness to the other extreme of the contingent consciousness that is both bewildered and bewildering. . . .

It affirms the nullity of ethical principles, and lets its conduct be governed by these very principles. Its deeds and its words always belie one another and equally it has itself the doubly contradictory consciousness of unchangeableness and sameness, and of utter contingency and non-identity with itself.[10]

The bourgeois subject as perceived by Hegel is thus cleaved by a contradiction that marks it fundamentally as *hypocritical*—to employ the term bourgeois morality would apply to such self-contradiction—a being in which words and actions, thought and deeds fail to coincide. The bourgeois subject, in short, both subscribes to the ethical norms established by the bourgeois social contract and simultaneously rebels against these very norms; it asserts its autonomy while submitting to the heteronomy of externally sanctioned laws of conduct; it maintains its independence and its ec-centricity, thereby resisting the "contingent," while affirming its own dependence on these contingencies. The bourgeois subject as Unhappy Consciousness is, in a word, fundamentally ideological in nature, proclaiming its self-identity, immutability, and autonomy, while simultaneously acceding to the mutable, contingent, heteronomous constraints of its given sociopolitical and economic environment.

The identification of bourgeois subjectivity with Hegel's Unhappy Consciousness does not mean that bourgeois consciousness is simply a monolithic construct—an error that traditional Marxist analysis makes when it attributes to the middle class a fixed and unchanging "class consciousness." On the contrary, precisely because bourgeois subjectivity, as Unhappy Consciousness, is constituted as a dynamic, dialectical system, modifications in the relative balance of the oppositions that structure this consciousness can be discerned. One of the aims of these investigations is to outline some of the distinct historical "stations" through which the self-divided bourgeois subject passes. However, this circumscription of historical stages within the epistemic formation of Unhappy Consciousness is not intended to suggest teleological development or organic growth. The changes that can be detected in the constitution of bourgeois subjectivity, in other words, should not be viewed as purposive, but rather as mutations that take place in the relative nature of this dialectically constituted subjectivity given changing historical, sociopolitical, economic, and psychological conditions. The metaphor "stations" is meant to indicate that these historical stages represent distinct, potentially discontinuous, historical sites which yet stand in a certain nonteleological relation to one another.

The narrative that emerges in the interpretations developed here presents a critical counter-narrative to the ideological self-understanding of the bourgeois subject as autonomous, rational, self-perfectible in-dividual. This ac-

count tells the (hi)story of the subject's often violent political self-disciplining, a self-coercion whose disciplinary methods vary from the extreme of
brutal self-repression to the more moderate mode of cautious political self-
restraint. The history of the bourgeois subject in Germany appears as the
story of a massive repression of certain insights on the part of middle-class
intellectuals into the pernicious political and cultural implications of bourgeois socioeconomic praxis, the insistent and often destructive return of
these repressed self-critical insights, and their renewed repression. Hegel
himself hints at the centrality of this self-repressive moment in the dialectical constitution of bourgeois subjectivity as Unhappy Consciousness when
he explains its internal antagonism as an internalization of the master-slave
dialectic into a single consciousness. Of course, Sigmund Freud also describes the formation of that self-repressive psychic agency, which he calls
the superego and whose function it is to police the subject's unconscious
drives, in terms of just such an introjection of an externally authorized master into the interior of the psyche.[11] In fact, the theory of servitude Hegel
develops in the section of *Phenomenology* devoted to the relationship of master and slave represents a significant intellectual-historical antecedent to
Freud's theory of the psyche. Hegel is intent upon legitimizing servitude as
a position that is superior to mastery, and he hence argues that it is nothing
other than the self-renunciation constitutive of servitude that ultimately
leads to the formation of an independent consciousness. According to this
theory, it is the self-repression demanded by the position of servitude, defined as "consciousness forced back into itself" ("in sich zurückgedrängtes
Bewußtsein"), that creates independent consciousness: the subject must
"withdraw into itself" to be "transformed into a truly independent consciousness."[12] Self-repression is justified by Hegel, with the paradoxical logic
symptomatic of ideological self-deceit, as a prerequisite for the attainment
of autonomy. This paradoxical, ideologically tainted dialectic of self-repression and autonomization—or this confusion of self-repression with the establishment of independent consciousness—proves to be a persistent pattern in literary textualizations of the subject throughout the bourgeois period in Germany. It is this imbrication of bourgeois consciousness with
self-repression that Freud diagnoses with his theory of the superego.

   Hegel's ontology of Unhappy Consciousness dovetails in many ways with
contemporary conceptions of subjectivity as a dialectically structured entity.
The "subject in process / on trial" ("sujet en procès"), as conceived by Julia
Kristeva in her amplification of the theories of Jacques Lacan,[13] shares with
Hegelian Unhappy Consciousness the structure of perpetual dialectical re-
cursivity and unrest. But Kristeva's conception of the subject supplements

Hegel's notion in the significant respect that, pursuing recent insights into the linguistic texture of subjectivity,[14] she conceives it to be structured as a *language*. In *Revolution in Poetic Language*, Kristeva's explicit aim is "to specify the production of this subject as a process, an intersection—an impossible unity"; and her project does, indeed, manifest, as she claims, a "second overturning" of the Hegelian dialectic insofar as it ruptures Hegel's sublation of Unhappy Consciousness's incessant dialectical unrest into the stable closure of *Geist* by insisting on the productivity of this conflict itself.[15] The struggle between "particular individuality" and "pure thinking," which shapes Unhappy Consciousness, reemerges in Kristeva's theory as the conflict between the "semiotic," as the expression of unrestrained "subjective" drives, and the "symbolic," those "objective," systematic codifications of the restraints to immediate expression instituted by concrete historical, sociopolitical, and biological structures. "Because the subject is always *both* semiotic and symbolic," Kristeva writes, "no signifying system he produces can be either 'exclusively' semiotic or 'exclusively' symbolic, and is instead necessarily marked by an indebtedness to both."[16] Her insistence on the cogenesis of subjectivity and what she calls "signifying systems" or "signifying practices" underscores, in contradistinction to Hegel, that subjectivity only makes itself evident in the act of signification, that is, through its expression in language, understood in the widest sense. Thus Kristeva casts Hegel's theory of Unhappy Consciousness into semiotic terms.

Kristeva, to be sure, is not concerned with the semiotics of everyday communication, but specifically with the signifying practices endemic to poetic language. She defends this privileging of literary discourse by pointing to its capacity to transgress systematic codification.

If there exists a "discourse" which is not a mere depository of thin linguistic layers, an archive of structures, or the testimony of a withdrawn body, and is, instead, the essential element of a practice involving the sum of unconscious, subjective, and social relations in gestures of confrontation and appropriation, destruction and construction—productive violence, in short—it is "literature," or, more specifically, the *text*. . . . The text is a practice that could be compared to political revolution: the one brings about in the subject what the other introduces into society.[17]

We can infer from this passage that "literature" names a discourse in which semiotic elements constantly disrupt the institutional codifications of the symbolic order. The site at which the emancipatory, utopian Other repressed by the symbolic confronts and challenges this order marks the signifying practice of poetic language. There are points in Kristeva's argument, in particular where she valorizes the literary avant-garde as the ideal manifestation of what she terms "text" or "poetic language,"[18] where she seems almost to abandon the notion of dialectical balance between the semiotic and symbolic, stressing instead the transgressive force of the semiotic. This tendency is produced by her desire to find in certain literary-aesthetic practices the corollaries of social revolution. In fact, no such equation can be made. On the contrary, as the interpretations of the present study will demonstrate, literary-aesthetic innovation does not derive from mere semiotic transgression of the symbolic, but emerges instead as specific historically determined negotiations of the dialectical conflict between these two positions.

Throughout the philosophical and theoretical literature on subjectivity, this concept is not taken merely to signify human consciousness or self-consciousness in the broadest sense, as the generality of the term would lead one to believe; rather, the notions of the subject and of subjectivity circumscribe a narrowly specifiable manifestation of human consciousness that is distinguishable from this broader philosophical concept in various respects. First of all, the subject treated by philosophical reflection is commonly the philosophically reflective subject. In other words, subjectivity is not something attributed to the "man on the street"—to what Martin Heidegger called *das Man*, the "they" who determine and are determined by everyday societal practice.[19] On the contrary, subjectivity is a form of consciousness generally reserved for artists and philosophers—that is, characteristic only of the intelligentsia—and in this sense it is the pedigree of a certain intellectual nobility. Kristeva implies as much when she identifies the subjectivity concretized in exceptional literature as the paradigm for subjectivity per se: "Literature," she writes, "has always been the most explicit realization of the signifying subject's condition."[20] In the essay "The Artist as Deputy [*Statthalter*]," Adorno justifies the aristocratic status afforded artists in bourgeois society by identifying artistic consciousness as the final refuge of subjectivity in an increasingly reified and administered world. "The artist who is the bearer of the work of art," Adorno asserts, "is not the individual who produces it; rather, through his work, through his passive activity, he becomes the representative [*der Statthalter*] of the total social subject [*des gesellschaftlichen Gesamtsubjekts*]."[21] And in his *Aesthetic Theory* he writes, in a similar vein, that "producers of great art are no demigods but fallible human beings, often with neurotic and damaged personalities."[22] According to Adorno, the individual artist plays the role of a kind of "damaged" vessel into which subjectivity flees in its attempt to escape the reifying effects of bourgeois practice. Artists embody the last outpost of subjectivity, they are neurotic Messiahs, as it were, who represent for all humankind the final hope for salvation from the wholly administered and rationalized world.

This identification of the subject with the exceptional—if damaged—individual is fundamentally grounded in specifically bourgeois conceptions of individuality. The subject is, in effect, an invention of bourgeois philosophy, representing the Enlightenment ideal of the autonomous in-dividual able to make full use of its own reason. This conception is fundamentally ideological in a twofold sense. On the one hand, the theory of autonomous subjectivity is one of the primary weapons deployed by the bourgeoisie in its struggle for emancipation from the political structures and social codes of feudal society. It is to this notion of subjectivity that critical philosophers such as Kristeva and Adorno appeal as a potential for human liberation. On the other hand, the notion of subjectivity also serves the middle-class intellectual as an ideological mask that conceals the reality of the bourgeois subject's internal division and heteronomy behind the dream of autonomy and integrity. But there is yet one more restriction that must be placed on this notion of the subject; for in the bourgeois world, subjectivity is a quality explicitly reserved for *male* members of society. Indeed, one of the patterns that emerges from the texts examined here is that the very constitution of the bourgeois subject is predicated on a repression of the feminine, its often brutal sacrifice for the achievement of some rationally established principle. Hence, in theoretical discourses on subjectivity throughout the bourgeois period, the signifier "subject" almost without exception tacitly refers to the male bourgeois aristocratic-artistic subject—a recognition that has powered considerable feminist scholarship on the definition of the subject.

There is one further quality of the bourgeois subject and bourgeois subjectivity that needs to be noted here: its interwovenness with the Freudian conception of the psyche split into unconscious and conscious drives and governed by the agencies of the id, the ego, and the superego. On the example of Hegel we have already seen that fundamental to the formation of bourgeois subjectivity is a primary act of self-repression, a reflex that suppresses the bourgeois subject's self-critical consciousness and seeks to efface the reality of the subject's status as self-divided, dialectically self-contestational construct by projecting it as the unitary and self-coherent in-dividual. For Kristeva, as well, who closely follows Lacan's extension of Freud's theories, the subject comes into being when the originary semiotic "chora" suffers repression as it enters into the codifying structures of the symbolic order.[23] With this accession of the subject to the order of reason, which takes the form of a primary act of repression, the subject is both constituted as subject and split into the dimensions of the conscious and the unconscious. The bourgeois subject and the Freudian unconscious, as simultaneous products of this primary repression of what is "unreasonable" and "incalculable," are thus genetically interdependent. As Rosalind Coward and John Ellis persuasively argue, "The processes which constitute the language-using subject, i.e. produce the subject in symbolic relations, constitute the unconscious in the same moment."[24] I would modify this statement by substituting for the phrase "language-using subject" the designation "reason-using subject," whereby I would identify "reason" with that symbolic practice of a mediate, calculative, and conventionalized rationality that Michel Foucault identifies with the "Classical" age, a rationality whose sole aim it is "to discover the arbitrary language that will authorize the deployment of nature within its space."[25] The subject produced in symbolic relations is the subject subjected to the reifying practices of the bourgeois enlightened episteme, grounded in the structures of abstraction and exchange. As analyzed by the critical theorists of the Frankfurt School, this arbitrary system deployed for mastery over the life-world comes to shape all interaction in bourgeois existence, until it is ultimately turned against the bourgeois subject itself.

The primary act of repression that gives birth to bourgeois divided subjectivity and causes the bourgeois subject—in Hegel's words—to "withdraw into itself,"[26] repeatedly manifests itself in German intellectual history as a retreat from the sociopolitical realities of the life-world into the internal and private world of the self. It was Max Weber's lasting achievement to have documented the connections that link the ascetic, self-repressive worldview of Protestantism to the "spirit" of the bourgeois era, showing how the Protestant ethical code represents a response to the socioeconomic demands of capitalism.[27] However, in the wake of Weber's persuasive condemnation of the Protestant ethos it has too easily been forgotten that Protestantism, as the name clearly indicates, itself began as a resistance movement against the religious, ethical, and political authority of the Catholic Church, the primary ideological state apparatus of feudal society.[28] Indeed, it is the (perhaps dubious) achievement of the various sectarian movements of the seventeenth and eighteenth centuries that derive from the Lutheran Reformation to have formulated the philosophical and political categories that made it possible even to think the notion of autonomous selfhood so central to the constitution of bourgeois subjectivity.[29] This point was not lost on Heinrich Heine, for example, who in his treatise *Concerning the History of Religion and Philosophy in Germany* extols Martin Luther as "not merely the greatest, but also the most *German*, man in our [the Germans'] history" (*History of Religion*, 538; *151*), and he goes on to identify Luther not only as the initiator in Germany both of freedom of thought and freedom of the press, but also as the necessary intellectual precursor of the French Revolution (see 541, 543, 549; *154–55, 156, 164*). Already with Protestantism, then, the retreat into what Weber calls "innerworldly asceticism" is indefeasibly coupled with rebellion against the ideological bastions of absolutism in the name of bourgeois individual autonomy. Moreover, as the case of Luther so explicitly demonstrates—and as Heine stresses in naming him the progenitor of a new literature in Germany and the instituter of freedom of the press—the inward protest of the bourgeoisie is inherently bound up with the institution of *publication*, with the "free" dissemination of ideas and their "unfettered" reception as they circulated in the form of the printed word both in the bourgeois public sphere and in the bourgeois marketplace.

Among the ways in which the inveterately ideological character of bourgeois subjectivity expresses itself is in the paradoxical constitution of the bourgeois public sphere as a political haven for the private, politically compromising thoughts of bourgeois intellectuals. In this privatized public sphere we discern one manifestation of the bourgeois doctrine of autonomy that ideologically legitimizes the repression of political-emancipatory drives: isolated in the domain of the private, these drives are effectively neutralized where questions of political praxis are concerned. But this privatizing neutralization is disguised behind the ideological vision of the public sphere as the interactive space in which these revolutionary ideas are able to circulate freely. This equivocal association of public-ation with the private domain of the bourgeois citizen finds its correspondence in the increasing shift toward *reading* as the dominant mode of literary reception in the bourgeois epoch. The transmission of literature through the medium of the text extracts it from the immediacy of public spectacle and displaces it into the privatized consciousness of the individual bourgeois subject. The frequent critiques of textuality voiced by eighteenth-century intellectuals reflect an inherent suspicion of this transposition of literary discourse from the public dimension of oral presentation and performance to the private medium of textual representation.

The internal division of bourgeois subjectivity finds concrete expression in the distinction, characteristic of bourgeois thought, between the public and the private person. What Thomas Hobbes describes in terms of the split between the roles of human being and citizen, Jean-Jacques Rousseau and Immanuel Kant view specifically as the cleaving of the bourgeois subject into the functions of the public and the private person. In the essay "What Is Enlightenment?" (1784), Kant attempted to draw a distinction between the public and the private use of human reason. In this treatise, which is universally considered seminal for an understanding of the bourgeois Enlightenment, Kant subjects the terms "public" and "private" to a curious set of semantic permutations, over the course of which they literally exchange their meanings. What comes to light in the semantic shifts these concepts undergo is the struggle of the bourgeois intelligentsia to come to grips with the disjunction between its own utopian political aims and the neutralizing self-containment of these emancipatory drives in the politically impotent space of the internal, private person. "Public" use of reason Kant associates, paradoxically, with the *private* opinions of the citizen as scholar, that is, as free-thinking, autonomous individual; "private" use of reason, on the other hand, corresponds for him to the "legitimate" shackling of any citizen's thought when fulfilling his role as *public* servant. "By the *public use* of one's reason I understand the use which a person makes of it *as a scholar* before the *reading public*. *Private use* I call that which one may make of it in a particular *civil post* or office which is entrusted to him."[30] The obvious inconsistencies in Kant's terminology apparently derive from his correlation of what he calls the public use ("öffentlicher Gebrauch") of reason with the mechanism of publication ("Veröffentlichung"). The "private," "scholarly" thoughts of the autonomous individual must be free to enter into general public circulation through the medium of publication; creative, autonomous thought belongs to the public sphere insofar as it functions to form public opinion through the medium of the written word. This conjuncture of the thought of the individual with the progressive shaping of public opinion points to the utopian design that the bourgeois Enlightenment attached to the public sphere: it circumscribed a privileged island of freedom and political resistance within the greater "public" domain of sociopolitical reality.[31] This explains why Kant stresses that "the public use of one's reason must always be free, and it alone can bring about enlightenment among men."[32] It was from this protected realm of an autonomous public sphere, grounded in the principle of the free, politically unconstrained circulation of ideas, that the middle class sought to gather the strength to assert itself politically against absolutistic oppression.

But what Kant gives with one hand, he takes away with the other: immediately after valorizing the freedom of the public use of one's reason, he admonishes his readers to submit without resistance to restriction of the private use of this faculty. "The private use of reason, on the other hand, may often be very narrowly restricted without particularly hindering the progress of enlightenment."[33] Here, at the very latest, it becomes evident that Kant's semantic manipulations of the terms "public" and "private" serve a strategic, ideological purpose. Only by circumscribing that sphere in which the bourgeois subject performs the duties of the *public* functionary as the merely "private" domain can he in good conscience advise his fellow citizens to submit *without reflection* to the demands of the political order. As civil functionary, that is, as "private" person, the enlightened individual becomes the unreflective agent of the repressive sociopolitical system. By attaching to "public" service the attribute of the "private," Kant implies that the individual as political agent must keep his personal thoughts to himself, especially when they run counter to the system. The employment of reason is free, in other words, only as long as it is effectively reduced to impotence where political critique and oppositional practice are concerned. What Kant designates as the domain of the "private" is thus the site of a principal political repression: the private sphere is defined precisely by submission to established political authority, regardless of whether such self-subjugation goes against the dictates of a genuinely autonomous and critical reason.

The role of the bourgeois subject in furthering the project of enlightenment, according to Kant's arguments, is marked by two antithetical movements: publicization, that is, the making-public or public-ation of private thought in the insular realm of the bourgeois public sphere, where it poses no threat to the political status quo; and the repressive privatization, the making-private and hence keeping-secret of critical reason in the domain of political praxis. The dynamic of enlightenment's philosophic-historical project is thus structured as a contradiction between resistance to the sociopolitical status quo and the simultaneous repression of this resistance in a moment of blind affirmation in which the supposedly reasonable, enlightened subject mindlessly, if voluntarily, becomes the sub-ject, the (self-)subjugated agent of the oppressive State. The utopian political visions of the bourgeois Enlightenment thus seem to be staked entirely on the wager that the public(iz)ation of private reason, the central mechanism of the bourgeois public sphere, will somehow infect and thereby alter the sociopolitical domain in which it is inscribed. Moreover, it assumes that this modification from within will progress at a faster pace than the speed at which this same private reason is further privatized and repressed as it accedes to the demands of quotidian sociopolitical reality. Following Kant's logic, the more the bourgeois subject is taken up into the structures of the State, the more it must repress its own utopian political visions; and political resistance can be cashed in, on the other hand, only at the price of wholesale withdrawal into a public sphere that is entirely isolated from, if yet inscribed within, sociopolitical reality. The public sphere circumscribes an insular political subculture in which reasonable thoughts are permitted to circulate freely only to the extent that they remain pure theory.

The paradoxes of the publicized private and the privatized public crystallize at that moment in which Kant, now a philosophical ventriloquist, mouths the words his ideal enlightened prince would address to his subjects: "Argue as much as you will, and about what you will, but obey!"[34] Split be-

tween freedom of thought and absolute obedience to sociopolitical authority, the enlightened bourgeois subject is constituted as a subject in both
senses: in its publicized private sphere (Kant's "public"), it remains the subject, the author, of its own (purely intellectual) existence, an independent
and autonomous individual; but in its privatized public domain (Kant's "private"), it is the sub-ject of its political master, relentlessly (self-)sub-jugated
and sub-ordinated to the tangible demands of the sociopolitical world. In
this sense the enlightened bourgeois subject propounded by Kant shares
with Hegel's subject as Unhappy Consciousness the fact that it is inherently
ideological in the strict sense: empirically and factually acceding to the requirements of the sociopolitical environment, it conjures up an ideal, internal realm of autonomy that compensates for its outward subjugation. The
philosophic-historical conceptions of a community of autonomous, rational
individuals free of external tutelage, or of a harmonizing *Geist* that sublates
the contradictions of bourgeois consciousness into a superior Oneness, simply mark the projected convergence of the ideal and the real at some nonex-
istent site, at u-topia, in a mysterious and mythic "no-place" that repressively
covers over the reality of the bourgeois subject's self-contradiction and political (self-)repression.

The utopian impulse behind Kant's enlightenment project is thrown into
relief by the self-contradictory concept of a free and unrestrained sphere of
public communication subsisting within the confines of the bourgeois sociopolitical world. The bourgeoisie invests its entire emancipatory political
capital in the belief in the free exchange of information in the bourgeois public sphere. Of course, the workings of this public sphere are patterned after
the *laissez-faire* economic theory of the free exchange of commodities in the
domain of bourgeois commerce. Reinhart Koselleck has identified the secret ("Geheimnis") of this public sphere with bourgeois morality, which, defined in opposition to all that is overtly political, is yet conceived as a covert
political-emancipatory force. According to Koselleck, the secret political
thrust of the bourgeois public sphere gives birth, however, to a state of incessant political crisis, since the very constitution of this secrecy is grounded
on a repression of the political and its sublimation into the purely speculative utopian fancy of bourgeois philosophic-historical projects.

Unable to integrate politics, [bourgeois] moral man stands in a void and must make
a virtue of necessity. A stranger to reality, he views the political domain as a heteronomous definition that can only stand in his way. . . . That politics is fate, that
it is fate not in the sense of blind fatality, this is what the enlighteners fail to understand. Their attempts to allow the philosophy of history to negate historical factuality, to "repress" the political realm, are Utopian in origin and character.[35]

The bourgeois public sphere is thereby constituted as the absolute negation of the political: as the subject withdraws from the influence of the sociopolitical environment, so, too, it strips itself of any sociopolitical effectiveness, of the possibility of having an active and critically shaping influence on this environment. The legacy of this bourgeois utopian dream of a sphere of communication unhampered by sociopolitical constraints, as Jürgen Habermas points out, can be traced through the history of bourgeois hermeneutic theory, which is guilty of overlooking the "systematic distortions" enforced upon communicative interaction by the sociopolitical sphere in which it is inscribed. For Habermas, this tradition reaches its culmination in the philosophical hermeneutics of Hans-Georg Gadamer.[36] What Habermas makes clear—and what Kant and Gadamer, for example, ignore—is that the bourgeois public sphere, while hypostatized as purely autonomous and "free" realm, is itself bisected by the same rift that divides the bourgeois subject. What expresses itself in the bourgeois subject as a dialectic of subjugation and utopian autonomy manifests itself in the ideology of bourgeois literary aesthetics, which Habermas exposes as the moving force behind the bourgeois public sphere,[37] as a dialectic of resigned affirmation and emancipatory contestation of the historically given conditions of the sociopolitical world.

The interweaving of autonomy and subjugation in the fabric of the bourgeois subject is further complicated by the fact that the revolt of the middle class, which is formulated as a rejection of the politics of feudal absolutism, is displaced into an internal rebellion of the bourgeois subject against those principles that structure bourgeois thought and practice themselves. Bourgeois intellectuals harbored the latent suspicion that the creative, utopian potential of "healthy reason" was in danger of being occupied and perverted by the merely calculative, abstractionist, manipulative, and quantifying rationality that structured bourgeois mercantilistic practices. This fear expressed itself in the German Sturm und Drang movement, for example, in the form of a wholesale rebellion against enlightened reason. The semantic dichotomy between "head" and "heart" that structures much of the oppositional discourse of these writers gives voice to more than just a simple antagonism between reason and pure emotion; it prefigures, rather, the juxtaposition of what today we would conceive, following the terminology employed by the Frankfurt School, as the opposition between "instrumental" and "communicative" reason.

The attack against a one-sided, strictly mechanical and formalistic rationality is sounded already in Kant's essay "What Is Enlightenment?" where he discloses the structure responsible for the persistence of human oppression and tutelage as a purely mechanistic employment of the faculties of reason.

> For any single individual to work himself out of the life under tutelage which has become almost his nature is very difficult. He has come to be fond of this state, and he is for the present really incapable of making use of his *reason* [*Verstandes*], for no one has ever let him try it out. Statutes and formulas, those *mechanical tools* of the *rational* [*vernünftigen*] employment or rather misemployment of his natural gifts, are the fetters of an ever-lasting tutelage.[38]

Implicit in Kant's comment is the opposition, partially obscured by the English translation, between *Verstand* as a healthy, free, and creative reason, and *Vernunft* as the subordination of reason to societal statutes and mechanical rules and formulae. *Vernunft* as the *mis*use of reason thus represents a narrow codification of specific rational structures which then become the crutches, so to speak, with which rational tutelage is able to walk.[39] It then mistakes this limping gait for the free stride of autonomous reason (*Verstand*). It is this ideological moment in which mechanical, calculative rationality is misrepresented as autonomous reason that marks what Horkheimer and Adorno would later call the dialectic of enlightenment. Kant's critique of the bourgeois subject's "self-incurred tutelage" presents an early if yet somewhat unfocused indictment of this confusion of purposive rationality with "healthy" reason. This "rational misemployment" of the human subject's "natural gifts," the suppression of autonomous, critical reason by calculative rationality, increases over the course of the bourgeois era, reaching its apogee in scientistic positivism, in what Habermas calls the "absolutism of pure methodology."[40]

This conflict between autonomous reason and the rational formalism of positivism reflects a fundamental epistemic conflict that organizes the internal self-division of bourgeois subjectivity. This antinomy manifests itself in many of the literary-aesthetic documents of the bourgeois period in Germany as the deep-structural antagonism between two competing semiological orders: on the one hand, the formalistic, calculative, and arbitrary semiotic that, founded on the principle of abstract equivalence and exchange, has its correlate in bourgeois socioeconomic practice; on the other hand, a motivated semiotic (in Saussure's sense) in which the relationship between signifiers and signifieds is guaranteed either by the principle of similitude (iconicity), or by a transcendental signifier such as the meaning-producing subject or "God," understood as the rule-governing center that escapes structuration.[41] In the texts under discussion here, this intraepistemic struggle appears in a series of different guises. On the level of literary-aesthetic theory it manifests itself as the tension between contradictory conceptions of the literary work, which is conceived either as the autonomous product of artistic genius, or as the literary commodity subject to evaluation in the process of economic exchange, or as both at once. This conflict expresses one of the fundamental dilemmas of bourgeois authorship. In the textual dimension this intraepistemic equivocation occurs as the opposition between "exoteric" and "esoteric" levels of textual signification. Here we are dealing with the text's constitution as meaningful signifying system and the parameters of its interpretive reception. On the structural level this intraepistemic antagonism is evident in elementary rifts and contradictions that shatter the integrity of the fictional characters and undermine the inherent logic of their fictional worlds. Here the intraepistemic conflict of bourgeois subjectivity expresses itself in the dimension of literary representation per se.

Toward the end of the eighteenth century the covert self-critique of bourgeois epistemic structures began to manifest itself in the conspicuous and persistent denunciation of the abstraction and mediacy of writing and textuality. Viewed from a sociopolitical standpoint, this critique seems paradoxical, since the bourgeois protest against external authority was inseparable from technological advances that established writing, publication, and reading as the primary tools for formulating and disseminating the bourgeoisie's claims to power. This suggests that the indictment of writing initiated by Rousseau and so eagerly assimilated by German bourgeois intellectuals such as Herder and Schiller—to name just two of the most prominent figures—marks a turn on the part of these bourgeois writers against the very institutions and principles on which the bourgeois self-emancipatory project, which they ostensibly aim to further, was founded. As such, it signals a profound if cloaked skepticism about the utopian political designs of bourgeois enlightenment, a skepticism grounded in the sense that its emancipatory purpose had somehow gone astray or been perverted. This self-critical insight is coherent with Kant's admonition that the reduction of reason to instrumental rationality bespeaks its misuse for the ends of ideological (self-) control and sociopolitical (self-)tutelage. Thus this attack on writing is not simply carried out in defense of a metaphysics of voice and (self-)presence, as Jacques Derrida would have us believe; rather, it reflects an essential self-critique of certain principles of bourgeois thought and the economic, sociopolitical, and semiotic practices in which they are concretized. This self-critique takes aim in particular at the arbitrary, rationalist, and calculative semiotic that underwrites bourgeois economic practice, which is symptomatic of a deployment of instrumentalized reason for the purpose of mastery over nature, society, and the self. The Enlightenment's philosophic-historical dream of attaining a wholly transparent system of signs, as manifest in the semiotic theories of such thinkers as Leibniz, Johann Heinrich Lambert, Mendelssohn, Lessing, and others, is the clearest form in which this protest against the bourgeois episteme takes shape.

The interpretations that follow interrogate the theoretical homology between the evolution of bourgeois subjectivity as a dialectical conglomerate of purposive rationality and creative, communicative reason, and the constitution of bourgeois literature as a dialectical imbrication of affirmation (reinforcement of the symbolic order and the codes of the bourgeois institution of art) and contestation (strategic transgression of the symbolic order and the bourgeois literary-aesthetic institution). Just as for Kristeva no signifying practice manifests exclusively semiotic or symbolic characteristics, those literary-aesthetic works born of the dialectical unrest of bourgeois subjectivity are never either totally affirmative textual concretizations of bourgeois ideology—pure literary commodities or products of the culture industry—nor totally autonomous creative artifacts that freely contest the signifying structures of bourgeois discursive practice. The contestational and affirmative moments of bourgeois literature thus can be associated, allowing for some modifications, with Kristeva's distinction between the "genotext" (contestation) and the "phenotext" (affirmation).[42] In a similar vein, Adorno characterizes the "twofold essence" of the work of art in terms of an immanent equivocation between its status as "autonomous entity," on the one hand, and as "social fact," on the other.[43] Adorno's terminology indicates that the structural dichotomy inherent in the bourgeois aesthetic product overlaps with the dichotomous structure of bourgeois subjectivity as autonomous individual and as the sub-ject subjugated to sociopolitical contingencies. This suggests, moreover, that from the perspective of critical analysis, both the bourgeois subject and the bourgeois work of art are principally ideological constructs: they are marked by the self-contradictions inherent in Hegel's Unhappy Consciousness and evince a form of subjectivity that can be described with the Marxian notion of "false consciousness"—if we strip from this term its own ideological and rhetorical veneer. What this means is simply that the bourgeois literary work of art, like the bourgeois subjectivity that it concretizes, is a product of the dialectical tensions between emancipatory critique of the social reality it represents and concession to the repressive facts of this reality.

The fiction of the wholly autonomous literary work, whose transgressive textual practices correspond to the symbolic overthrow of codified societal practices, and the fiction of the autonomous public (but privatized) sphere, in which the free circulation of ideas purportedly guarantees the vitality of emancipatory sociopolitical designs, parallel the ideological fiction of the absolutely autonomous, self-identical, and self-determining bourgeois in-dividual. What these fictions seek to disguise is the fact that literature, the public sphere, and the bourgeois subject alike are inscribed in, and dependent upon, the sociopolitical and economic practices that structure the bourgeois life-world. But to disclose the doctrine of literary autonomy as an ideological guise is by no means tantamount to theorizing bourgeois literature as inherently impotent and thus as inescapably buttressing bourgeois socio-economic and political hegemony. Autonomy, in other words, should neither be strictly identified with the literary work's critical potential nor with silent affirmation of the status quo. Just as Hegel refuses to collapse the contradictions of Unhappy Consciousness into one or the other of its dialectical poles, critical analyses of bourgeois literature must likewise resist the temptation either to flatten the bourgeois literary product into a wholly affirmative ideological construct, on the one hand, or inflate it into pure transgressive-utopian resistance, on the other. The interpretive practice employed in this study attempts to elucidate, while simultaneously doing justice to, this fragile dialectic of the bourgeois literary-aesthetic work.

Debates about the function of aesthetic autonomy in the bourgeois institution of art have centered around two antagonistic assessments of the sociopolitical implications inherent in the isolation of art's signifying practices from those (signifying) practices at work in society at large.[44] Condemnations of the autonomous work are usually predicated on the hypostatization of the bourgeois institution of art as an unadulterated embodiment of bourgeois ideology: the individualism and self-containment of the work of art corroborate and underwrite, according to this view, the pretense of the autonomous bourgeois individual. The "beautiful semblance" of aesthetic form, in other words, is thought to reflect that ideological mask with which the bourgeois subject deceives itself about its own submission to the operative rules of the rationally administered world. On the other hand, those who defend the emancipatory potential of aesthetic autonomy maintain that the insularity of the institution of art from the dominant practices of bourgeois society forms the necessary condition for the critical vitality of the aesthetic work. According to this view, the very otherness of the aesthetic realm rescues the work of art from co-optation by the structures of commodification and reification to which bourgeois epistemic structures otherwise subject the entire life-world, including the human subject itself. As the absolute

Other of the reified bourgeois subject, autonomous art is thought to function as a memorial to an unalienated existence beyond or before abstraction, calculation, purposive rationality, and the order of the symbolic.

This equivocation concerning the implicit politics of the doctrine of aesthetic autonomy can best be examined in the thought of Herbert Marcuse, who over the course of his career alternately defends both positions. In his early and influential essay "On the Affirmative Character of Culture" (1936), Marcuse predominantly takes the negative side in this argument, accusing the "affirmative culture" of the bourgeois era of establishing an illusion of unity, self-identity, and freedom that indirectly endorses and augments bourgeois self-alienation by papering over contradictions in the objective sociopolitical realm. "As the purposeless and beautiful were internalized and, along with the qualities of binding universal validity and sublime beauty, made into the cultural values of the bourgeoisie, a realm of apparent unity and apparent freedom was constructed within culture in which the antagonistic relations of existence were supposed to be stabilized and pacified. Culture affirms and conceals the new conditions of social life."[45] For Marcuse, affirmative culture evolves as a process by which the purposeless and the beautiful—the opposites of the calculative expedience dominant in bourgeois socioeconomic practice—are internalized, withdrawn from the realm of empirical practice into the ideality of the "soul." In this process, the "soul" is hypostatized as that human essence not subject to the otherwise all-pervasive mechanisms of commodification and exchange. This process of internalization, of course, parallels the hypostatization of the (privatized) public sphere as a realm of free and immediate thought-exchange inscribed within the commercial realm of commodity-exchange.

Although indictment of this internalizing process forms the central focus of this early essay, Marcuse simultaneously concedes, in what amounts to a small addendum to his main hypothesis, that the idealism of bourgeois ideology also marks a concealed, secret protest against conditions in the bourgeois life-world and thus bears witness to a profound longing for a revolutionary transformation of the real. "But bourgeois idealism is not merely ideology, for it expresses a correct objective content. It contains not only the justification of the established form of existence, but also the pain of its establishment: not only quiescence about what is, but also remembrance of what could be."[46] Bourgeois idealism, according to Marcuse, is structured around the same duality between ideologically compensatory semblance and implicit critique of really-given historical conditions that Marx termed "false consciousness." However, Marcuse's localization of the hidden emancipatory memory of bourgeois culture within the internal, private sphere of bourgeois consciousness repeats the split between private and public roles that, as we have seen, is constitutive of the bourgeois subject. The aura of "mystery" or "secrecy" ("Geheimnis") with which, according to Reinhart Koselleck, the bourgeoisie masks the rebellious political component of its own thought, signals the withdrawal of political activity out of the public domain into the private sphere of the autonomous—and thus politically detached—individual.[47]

Kant's semantic conflation of the "private" and the "public," as I have indicated, prefigures this retreat of public political critique into the internal realm of the private individual. The convergence of the private with that political rebelliousness that must be kept secret by being internalized and repressed finds expression in the semantic ambivalences of the German word *heimlich*, which signifies both what remains secret or concealed and what is intimate and private. The internal dialectic of this concept and its opposite, *unheimlich* ("uncanny," "un-concealed," "no-longer-secret"), which Freud, in his celebrated 1919 essay "The Uncanny" ("Das Unheimliche"), identifies with the return of the repressed, will form a touchstone for the present investigation. If the dichotomy of bourgeois subjectivity and of the bourgeois institution of art comes about by means of the privatization or occultation of political critique, its internalization into the private-secret (*heimlich*) realm of the bourgeois "soul," then the return of these repressed political drives in the bourgeois subject and in bourgeois literature takes the form of the *unheimlich*, the "uncanny," the mysterious and unforeseeable eruption of this occulted utopian-political desire into the "text" of bourgeois consciousness and bourgeois literature.

Whereas in the early essay "The Affirmative Character of Culture" Marcuse emphasizes the ideological aspect of bourgeois aesthetics while playing down its secret-private (*heimlich*) emancipatory and utopian dimension, forty years later in *The Aesthetic Dimension* (1977) he reverses these proportions. To be sure, this shift in emphasis stems from the fact that this later treatise is largely intended as an attack on institutionalized Marxist aesthetics, specifically on the doctrine of Socialist Realism. Over against the obvious poverty of such a doctrinaire aesthetic theory and practice, the emancipatory utopian potential of bourgeois literature begins to loom much larger for Marcuse. Hence in this treatise he specifically argues against all conceptions of art that subsume aesthetics under the realm of pure ideology, and his own earlier theory of bourgeois affirmative culture is implicated in this critique. "However, this purely ideological conception of art is being questioned with increasing intensity," Marcuse writes. "It seems that art as art expresses a truth, an experience, a necessity which, although not in the do-

main of radical praxis, are nevertheless essential components of revolution."[48] Expanding on Adorno's thesis that aesthetic form is nothing but sed-
imented—that is, censored or distorted—content, Marcuse situates this revolutionary kernel of bourgeois aesthetics in the dimension of form. "Literature can be called revolutionary in a meaningful sense only with reference
to itself, as content having become form. The political potential of art lies
only in its own aesthetic dimension. Its relation to praxis is inexorably indirect, mediated, and frustrating."[49] Marcuse is concerned with the delimita-
tion of literary aesthetics from propagandistic literature, and in this context
immediate political sentiment in literary texts, paradoxically, becomes for
him the symptom of a hopeless didacticism and positivism whose sole purpose is the corroboration of the status quo. In the face of the immediacy of
such an authoritarian aesthetic practice, it is precisely the mediate, indirect
critique of purposive rationality embodied in the autonomous aesthetics of
the bourgeois era that appears as the final critical outpost from which the
real is capable of being questioned and ultimately transformed. That renunciation of radical praxis embodied in the doctrine of aesthetic autonomy,
paradoxically, proves to be the only alternative left to radical praxis given
the hegemony of purposive rationality in the bourgeois world.

Marcuse's valorization of the mediacy of aesthetic form as the revolutionary core of literary textuality only makes sense against the theoretical
backdrop of Adorno's identification of literality and discursivity with the
spirit of positivism. If, as Adorno aphoristically asserts in his *Aesthetic Theory*, "Literalness is barbaric,"[50] then the upshot of this remark would seem
to be that the nonbarbaric only finds expression in the nonexpository or
nondiscursive.[51] In a bourgeois regimen characterized by the mastery of reality through its accession to the discursive, to the symbolic order, all discursivity is implicated in this game of domination and hence becomes politically suspect. The discursive is by definition the conformist, the positivistic, the ideologically co-opted.[52] Given this circumstance, the otherness
of art, expressed in the "aesthetic dimension" of its form, in its presentative,
figural, nondiscursive, or formal-rhetorical properties, becomes the pedigree of utopian resistance to the real.

Marcuse's shift from the negative to the positive assessment of autonomous art's critical potential marks the evanescence of a significant insight into the historical development of bourgeois society. Only once one
recognizes and concedes the absolute hegemony of bourgeois sociopolitical and economic practices, their remarkable ability to deflect and neutralize all forms of opposition and resistance, does the absolute otherness of the
aesthetic dimension cease to be perceived primarily as an ideological mask

and come to be discerned as a refuge of resistance from the all-encompassing threat of political co-optation. Only with the pessimistic insight into the necessary ineffectiveness of radical praxis, in other words, does the revolutionary nonpraxis of aesthetics—revolutionary precisely because it represents nonpraxis in a world in which all praxis has devolved into manipulative control guided by the strategic deployment of instrumental reason—take on supreme importance for theories of resistance. Adorno's and Marcuse's later aesthetic conceptions exist, however, in a kind of historical lag: while they plead the case of a resistant aesthetics, as philosophical documents they mark the historical juncture at which that oppositional potential ascribed to the domain of the aesthetic is transferred to the realm of aestheticized theoretical discourse. Critical Theory thereby becomes the immediate heir to bourgeois aesthetics. However, as amply demonstrated by the debates currently raging on the contemporary critical front about the contestational and/or emancipatory moments of diverse critical theories, theory inherits from this benefactor its fundamental political equivocation as well.

In the final analysis, theory only becomes *critical* theory when it is put into interpretive practice. That is the purpose of the following interpretations.

Repression and the Ideological Constitution of Bourgeois Subjectivity

CHAPTER TWO

Picturing Emilia

Conflict of Representations and the Tragedy of Bourgeois Subjectivity in Lessing's 'Emilia Galotti'

> The individual is an ideological structure, a historical form correlative with the commodity form (exchange value), and the object form (use value). The individual is nothing but the subject thought in economic terms, rethought, simplified, and abstracted by the economy. The entire history of consciousness and ethics (all the categories of occidental psycho-metaphysics) is only the history of the political economy of the subject.   —Jean Baudrillard

IN THE ESSAY "Traditional and Critical Theory," Max Horkheimer comments on the fundamentally ideological constitution of bourgeois individuality:

Bourgeois thought is so constituted that in reflection on the subject which exercises such thought a logical necessity forces it to recognize an ego which imagines itself to be autonomous. Bourgeois thought is essentially abstract, and its principle is an individuality which inflatedly believes itself to be the ground of the world . . . , an individuality separated off from events. . . . Such an illusion about the thinking subject, under which idealism has lived since Descartes, is ideology in the strict sense, for in it the limited freedom of the bourgeois individual puts on the illusory form of perfect freedom and autonomy.[1]

Gotthold Ephraim Lessing's "bourgeois tragedy," *Emilia Galotti* (1772), is one of the earliest literary documents in Germany that testifies to the constitution of the bourgeois individual as a principally ideological entity. Lessing's play thus represents "bourgeois tragedy" in a significant double sense: one of the earliest examples of this dramatic form in Germany, it helps to establish the formal-aesthetic and structural complexion of bourgeois tragedy as genre; however, on the representational level, that is, in its fictional world and its signifying practices, it treats the central tragedy of bourgeois subjectivity, its constitution as false consciousness. *Emilia Galotti* dramatizes, in other words, the deep-structural conflict between the intersubjective ideals promulgated by the bourgeoisie in its struggle for self-definition and the (self-)reifying nature of its actual social practices, which are specifically calculated to maximize control over the life-world. The act of murder in which Odoardo Galotti sacrifices his own daughter to the ideals of an "austere virtue" (*EG* II, v, 260; 24) concretizes this (self-)destructive dialectic of bourgeois ideology. When Odoardo's wife Claudia questions whether such virtue even deserves this appellation, she puts her finger on the ideological nexus of the play. Bourgeois virtue, she correctly suspects, is bought at the price of committing violence against the bourgeois subject itself. In *Emilia Galotti* bourgeois tragedy thus marks the moment at which mastery over the subject (including the self) is legitimized by an appeal to its function as representational proxy for those intangible ideals (virtue, self-identity, autonomy, etc.) which bourgeois ideological reflection projects beyond the facticity of quotidian existence. The subject ceases to be a principal part of the life-world and becomes instead a cultural signifier, a mere material placeholder for abstract values. This signals the moment of the subject's (self-)alienation, its devolution into a heteronomous Being-for-some-other at the very moment of its ideological hypostatization as autonomous Being-for-itself.

The aporetic structure of bourgeois subjectivity as false consciousness is replicated in the bourgeois work of literary art in terms of what we can call, following Adorno, the tension between its "mimetic" and its "constructive" principles.[2] Aesthetic representation in the bourgeois world is structured as a dialectic between mimesis and construction, between imitation as perfectly adequate, transparent representation (the re-creation of nature once more in art) and creativity as artificial or imaginative elaboration on the real (aesthetic supplementation of nature). Adorno translates this dynamic into terminology that reinforces its interconnection with bourgeois sociopolitical and economic practice when he refers to it as a dialectical struggle between nature and mastery over nature.

How can works of art be like windowless monads, representing something which is other than they? There is only one way to explain this, which is to view them as being subject to a dynamic or immanent historicity and a dialectical tension between nature and domination of nature, a dialectic that seems to be of the same kind as the dialectic of society. Or to put it more cautiously, the dialectic of art resembles the social dialectic without consciously imitating it. The productive force of useful labour and that of art are the same.[3]

Adorno's metaphor of the "windowless monad" suits not only the bourgeois work of art but the character of the bourgeois subject as well: both are caught up in the tension between participation in and domination over the realm of sensuous nature. In his *Aesthetics*, Hegel cited the paradox that art moves through the sensual only to transcend it; he views this sublation of the sensual as the condition of possibility of art if it is to fulfill its supreme task, the emancipation of humanity from its enslavement to the natural world.

Art by means of its representations, while remaining within the sensuous sphere, liberates man at the same time from the power of sensuousness. Of course we may often hear favorite phraseology about man's duty to remain in immediate unity with nature; but such unity, in its abstraction, is purely and simply rudeness and ferocity, and by dissolving this unity for man, art lifts him with gentle hands out of and above imprisonment in nature.[4]

The task of aesthetic representation is precisely to rupture the unity between human beings and the realm of the sensuous, to elevate human nature out of the real into the ideal, and thus to cultivate, that is, to master this nature. *Emilia Galotti* depicts the running-amok of this representational function in bourgeois life practice: far from being lifted "with gentle hands out of and above imprisonment in nature," in Lessing's play the human subject is brutally slaughtered by a bourgeois patriarch who elevates the interests of ideological representation over those of material Being. Moreover, Lessing's drama discloses the fundamental dovetailing between those bourgeois signifying practices that repress the materiality of the signifier to valorize the ideality of the signified and the destructive processes of bourgeois (self-)alienation that repress the materiality of the body and its drives by appealing to the ideality of abstract ideological values.

Over the entire course of its receptive history, the equivocalities and ambivalences of *Emilia Galotti* have challenged literary critics; it comes as no surprise, then, that the play has evoked a plethora of often contradictory interpretations, many of which attempt to come to terms with its ambiguous textuality.[5] Frank Ryder has suggested that scholars must turn to questions of literary sociology if they hope to understand this multiplicity of conflicting appraisals. The inherent "illogicality" of Lessing's text, in his view, "proceeds from an ambivalence located elsewhere, an ambivalence which forces the play to respond to contradictory pressures, preventing dramatic unity. This 'elsewhere' consists of the playwright and his time."[6] The problem with Ryder's formulation of this conflict is that he inscribes the critical project of interpretation in an already ideologically predetermined narrative in which the author is the protagonist and the society in which he operates his evil antagonist: "In *Emilia Galotti*," he writes, "society is shown imposing upon its individual members constraints so severe as to distort normal human reac-

tions."[7] This interpretive narrative presupposes the opposition between individual—the autonomous bourgeois subject—and society—the corrupting
impact of the sociopolitical Other on the "norm" of autonomous individuality—which authors such as Lessing, and bourgeois tragedies such as *Emilia
Galotti*, were first attempting to institute. But what makes *Emilia Galotti* especially interesting as historical document—and especially labyrinthine as
aesthetic work—is that although it attempts to establish this ideological narrative, it simultaneously undercuts it by depicting the bourgeois subject as
always already complicitous with those alienating social practices it seeks to
project as the oppressive constraints dictated by a societal Other. Lessing's
play thus displays a complex dialectical structure that both portrays this imbrication of the bourgeois "individual" in the alienating societal praxis it attacks and simultaneously attempts to disguise this fact by appealing to precisely that ideological mask whose dissemblance it has penetrated. This self-
contradictory tension produces the ambivalences of *Emilia Galotti*: its
inconsistencies point to the internal contradictions that mark bourgeois authorship during its ascendant phase in Germany at the end of the eighteenth
century. Lessing's own case is paradigmatic for the situation of the bourgeois
authorial subject at this historical juncture: it is a subjectivity disfigured by
the ideological moment in which insight into its own complicity in the
tyranny of the alienating symbolic codes under which it suffers is repressed
and thereby (re)turned into ideology. This ideological (re)turn leaves the
subject and its aesthetic product hopelessly flawed: the fissures that run
through both the ideological guise of autonomous subjectivity and the aesthetic mask of the well-formed masterpiece can no longer be papered over.

The "enigma" of *Emilia Galotti* as bourgeois tragedy represents in microcosm what Adorno terms the "enigmatic quality" of bourgeois art in general. "Society's discontinuities, its untruths and ideologies," he maintains,
"emerge in the work [of art] as structural discontinuities, as deficiencies."[8]
This ambivalence reflects the prototypical paradox of socially critical bourgeois literature; namely, that it sweeps its (self-)critique under the textual
carpet of its own discursivity while disclosing it in its formal, aesthetically
significant structures.[9] Lessing's play addresses this problematic in its portrayal of the bourgeois artist Conti and the conflicting impulses to which he
and his art submit. The "Conti scenes" of *Emilia Galotti*, which serve as a
prelude to the tragedy, formulate as problems of aesthetic representation
those ideological complexes that shape both the sociopolitical and the ethical dimensions of this tragedy. Lessing's drama reveals that on the level of
epistemic structure, bourgeois aesthetic and ethical, political, and even economic practices are principally interconnected: what occurs in the realm of

aesthetics as the dialectic between mimesis and construction surfaces in the sphere of ethics as the conflict between idealized virtue and its corruption, in the sociopolitical domain as the struggle between bourgeois autonomy and external oppression, and in the economic dimension as the opposition between the glorification of nature qua nature and its reification into marketable commodity. Each of these sets of oppositions is structured in terms of the dialectic of ideology in which the factuality of bourgeois praxis is camouflaged behind a self-exculpating pretext. Their common denominator is the idealization of the world of nature as a strategy for disguising a violent will to master it.

I will pursue this problematic by examining, first of all, the genesis of *Emilia Galotti* as literary work in the context of Lessing's own experience of the dilemmas of bourgeois authorship. Ultimately, it was their own confrontation with the conflicts inherent in the nature of authorship that caused German bourgeois writers of this period to gain critical insights into the aporias of bourgeois sociopolitical and economic practices. Their often tortured awareness that the idealized pedagogical-emancipatory mission they as literary spokespeople were charged to pursue was undermined by the commercial character of the bourgeois public sphere provided them with a perspective from which they could become cognizant of the general ideological reflex of bourgeois society.[10] The publishing industry in Germany was one of the first to introduce the mediation of the bookdealer into the relationship between producer and purchaser;[11] it thereby became one of the first sectors of the economy to introduce full-fledged bourgeois commercial practices. Thus authors such as Lessing, who were forced constantly to deal with the conflict between the ideals of enlightened authorship and the realities of publication in the commercial marketplace, had a privileged vantage point that allowed them to perceive the manner in which bourgeois socioeconomic principles ran interference with the high-minded emancipatory ideals of the bourgeois Enlightenment.

After establishing the crisis of bourgeois authorship as Lessing's window on the conflict between bourgeois ideology and its life praxis and demonstrating that *Emilia Galotti* as literary-aesthetic product evolves out of this conflict, I will examine the Conti scenes of Lessing's play (I, ii–v) as aesthetic concretizations of this problematic. On the example of the artist Conti we witness the cleaving of the bourgeois subject into two rival tendencies, accommodation to given socioeconomic principles, on the one hand, and utopian vision, on the other. Where he makes concessions to the reality of his economic dependence, Conti develops an aesthetic theory that retrospectively legitimates the practices he has no choice but to follow. Where he adheres to his aesthetic intuition, by contrast, aesthetics tends to become pure theory entirely divorced from practice. These two movements prefigure the crisis of bourgeois subjectivity that calls forth the tragic events of the play. Insofar as it moves from an examination of this ideological reflex in the domain of aesthetics to disclosures of its operation in the dimensions of bourgeois subjectivity, morality, and economics, the expository development of Lessing's tragedy replicates the structure by which Lessing as bourgeois author was able to translate his own crises of authorship into critical—if yet repressed—presentiments of the self-destructive dialectic between bourgeois sociopolitical, economic, and signifying praxis, on the one hand, and its self-deceptive adornment and legitimation in bourgeois ideological projections, on the other. From here, finally, we will move to an examination of Emilia Galotti's tragedy as a product of this disjunction between bourgeois self-representation and the reality of its life praxis.

Emilia Galotti and the Crisis of Bourgeois Authorship

The genesis of Lessing's tragedy *Emilia Galotti* covers a long and circuitous route from his initial plan for the drama, formulated in 1757, to its eventual publication and first performance in 1772. Lessing's occupation with the material for this tragedy spans a fifteen-year period that circumscribes a major portion of his creative life: the one-act tragedy *Philotas* (1759) and the comedy *Minna von Barnhelm* (1763–67) are products of this period, as are his major literary-critical projects, *Letters Regarding the Most Recent Literature* (1759–65) and *Hamburgische Dramaturgie* (1767–68), and his important aesthetic treatise, *Laokoön* (1762–66).

The immediate impetus behind the original conception of *Emilia Galotti* as bourgeois tragedy probably stemmed from theoretical reflections on the tragic genre that Lessing formulated in critical response to positions taken by his friends Friedrich Nicolai and Moses Mendelssohn. In the summer of 1756, Nicolai completed his *Treatise on Tragic Drama* and sent excerpts to Lessing. This resulted in a vigorous correspondence among the three friends in which questions about the production and reception of tragic drama were fervently debated.[12] Nicolai's *Treatise* concluded with the promise that he would undertake a second study treating specifically the genre of bourgeois tragedy. In a letter to Nicolai from July of 1756, Lessing remarked that he had ideas to contribute to such a project: "I have jotted down a lot of unordered thoughts about the bourgeois tragedy that perhaps can be of use to you for the proposed treatise, once you have thought them through a little" (*LW* 9: 70).

It is only a few months after the conclusion of this correspondence discussing the aesthetics of tragedy that Lessing reports to Nicolai and Mendelssohn that he is working on a new tragedy that bears the title *Emilia Galotti* (see *LW* 9: 150, 157). The proximity of this play's conception to the reflections on tragedy formulated in the context of this friendly disputation suggests that the motivation behind this drama may have been the desire to exemplify the theoretical issues dealt with there. However, if *Emilia Galotti* was indeed conceived as a prototype of the bourgeois tragedy, then the problems that arise for Lessing in the realization of this work, problems that interfere with its completion, are indicative of dilemmas inherent in the very constitution of this genre.

Lessing concedes even at the earliest stages of work on this play that the process of creation is a very deliberate one, marked by "constant expansions of the plan" and "constant deletion of what has already been completed" (*LW* 9: 157). Although these difficulties cause him finally to set aside this initial draft, the idea of creating a tragic drama that would deal with a "bourgeois Virginia" continues to haunt Lessing. It is no coincidence that he returns to this material once again when he is in Hamburg, that is, at a time when he is composing his *Hamburgische Dramaturgie*, a critical project concerned, among other things, with the nature of tragic drama. This corroborates the hypothesis that Lessing conceived *Emilia Galotti* as a work intended to exemplify his theoretical and critical positions about bourgeois tragedy. But once again compositional difficulties cause Lessing to abandon the plan for this play; and this, in turn, indicates that the problems he faced when attempting to cast the material of this "bourgeois Virginia" into the form of an exemplary bourgeois tragedy appeared to be insurmountable.

The fitful genesis of *Emilia Galotti* sheds some light on questions about the probable causes of the play's contradictory texture. First, the complex and lengthy evolution of the drama, which finally coalesces only on Lessing's third attempt to master the material, is one source of the inconsistencies that characterize the final version of the play. What is more, Lessing remained dissatisfied with the literary execution of *Emilia Galotti* even as he was finishing the final version: "The closer to the end I come, the less satisfied I myself am with it," he wrote to his editor, Christian Voss, in January 1772 (*LW* 9: 489). Thus Lessing remained convinced to the very end that he had not adequately solved the problems presented by this play; and yet he was driven to complete the text despite his awareness of its inherent flaws. The inconsistencies and intellectual antinomies of the final text are thus bound up with irresolvable contradictions endemic to the very conception of *Emilia Galotti* as bourgeois tragedy.

We do not have to look very far to discover the underlying paradox responsible for the intrinsic contradictions of this work: it is nothing other than Lessing's singular desire to depoliticize Livius's account of the tragic fate of Virginia, which served as the model for *Emilia Galotti*, by removing from it "everything that makes it interesting to the State" (see *LW* 9: 157, 502). In Livius's narrative the sacrifice of Virginia stands in a fundamentally political context: because the necessity of her murder reflects on the corruption and tyranny of the ruler Appius Claudius, this act calls forth a popular revolt against his oppressive regime. The desire to depoliticize the story of Virginia's sacrifice runs counter to the substance of this historical narrative, and such a self-contradictory project could scarcely help but produce a self-contradictory work. This depoliticization of the political motivates the very genealogy of bourgeois tragedy as genre.

Given the obvious problems he faced in trying to come to terms with *Emilia Galotti* and his own dissatisfaction with the final product itself, one can hardly help but wonder why Lessing decided to return to the play in 1771–72 and finally complete it. The all too banal answer to this question is that he was driven by purely financial considerations. At this time Lessing was producing a revised edition of his works, which was to include a volume of his collected tragedies. In the context of this project he returned to the manuscript of *Emilia Galotti* with the explicit intention of reworking this "modernized Virginia" (*LW* 9: 504) to add it to this volume. His aim was to supplement the republication of *Miß Sara Sampson* and *Philotas* by printing alongside them this hitherto unpublished tragedy.[13] The addition of this "new" work was intended to enhance the marketability of the collection. In the letter to his publisher in which he promised the manuscript of *Emilia* for this volume, Lessing alluded to his desperate financial situation and expressed the hope that the publication of this new edition would help remedy it.

The new work [*Emilia Galotti*] will definitely be in your hands before the older material has been completely printed. It is progressing quite well; and if I am able to have some peace, so that my debts don't drive me crazy over Christmas, then it will progress even better. For the second volume of my works you should be receiving more manuscript within a week—if you help me, dear friend, to weather this storm, then I don't believe that I will ever burden you again. (*LW* 9: 461)

The publication of this collected edition, and the printing of *Emilia Galotti* as an integral part of this project, stands in direct relation to Lessing's financial woes, which have begun to oppress him especially severely at this point of his life because of his engagement to Eva König and the additional

financial responsibilities that marriage implies. The harried tone of this letter, Lessing's humiliating entreaty to Voss, and the haphazard manner in
which the material for the new publication is collected all point to the ur-
gency of his economic circumstances and the danger that his desperation
will have deleterious effects on his own writing. In the specific instance of
Emilia Galotti, Lessing went so far as to send the first part of the manuscript
to Voss to be typeset before he had even written the conclusion of the play
(see *LW* 9: 489), and nothing could document more emphatically than this
makeshift method of composition that Lessing's economic situation as author was dire enough to menace the very integrity of this work.

It is not surprising that this compositional procedure produced a work
rife with inconsistencies. But the concessions that this situation extracted
from Lessing as author go far beyond the danger of mere shoddiness; indeed, it seduced him into compromising all those aesthetic values he had invested in his theoretical pronouncements on drama itself. This is signaled
by the evolution of *Emilia Galotti* out of a dramatic script intended for stage
production into a text intended merely for publication. In a letter Lessing
wrote to his brother Karl on February 10, 1772—composed just when he was
finishing this play—he recapitulates the milestones on the journey toward
its completion, stressing the differences between the final version and the
original plan. The subject of this play, he writes, "was one of my oldest,
which I then once began to work out in Hamburg. But neither the old version nor the Hamburg reworking were of use for me [in the work on the final version], because the former was divided up into just three acts, and the
latter was planned merely to be performed, and was never intended to appear in print" (*LW* 9: 499–500). This evolution of the dramatic work toward
the status as text, to be sure, occurs in part as a response to Lessing's conviction, especially after the demise of the Hamburg project, that the hopes
for a German national theater were doomed to failure.[14] But even as early
as 1756 Lessing maintained in a letter to Mendelssohn that any truly well-
structured tragedy will retain its effectiveness when read, without the benefit of actors and the immediacy of performance (*LW* 9: 102). And when a
year later he refused to strike passages from *Miß Sara Sampson* that Mendelssohn thought would be impossible to declaim, he justified this by citing
the significance of their philosophical substance, suggesting that at a time
when reading is increasingly supplanting performance as the dominant
mode for the reception of drama, intellectual depth can take priority over
issues of eloquence and declamation (*LW* 9: 138–39). Lessing's gravitation toward the textualization of drama hence represents a practical concession to
the realities of the literary marketplace, to reading as the dominant mode

of literary reception and to the text as marketable literary commodity. However, drama conceived as marketable text runs counter to Lessing's own theoretical reflections that establish drama as the highest genre of literature precisely because of its capacity to elevate the arbitrary signs of language to natural signs in the process of living performance (see *LW* 9: 317–20). The drama as text no longer possesses any specific semiotic advantages that would set it apart from, say, the novel, since the text as text, whether dramatic or epic in nature, utilizes "arbitrary" signs.

Over the course of his entire life Lessing was plagued by financial pressures, and they form a fundamental part of his self-understanding as bourgeois author. In his letters he frequently mentions his growing indebtedness and the struggle to find a position, beyond that of free-lance writer, that would permit him to provide for himself adequately. In critical response to the pirating of his *Hamburgische Dramaturgie*, Lessing composed a short treatise with the title "Live and Let Live" (ca. 1768), subtitled "An Outline for Writers and Booksellers." In this essay he attempted to sketch some remedies for the miserable situation of "independent" bourgeois writers. Lessing, of course, was not able to live by his writing alone; but nor was he able to live without his writing, for the meager salary he was paid, for example, as librarian in Wolfenbüttel for the Herzog of Braunschweig, was simply not enough to provide for his needs. As a result, the money earned through publication of his writings formed a significant and necessary supplement to his regular income, and he was only too aware that the commercial exchange-value of the literary product had precious little to do with its intrinsic aesthetic use-value.

Near the end of his engagement at the theater in Hamburg, at a time when he was again shopping around for some form of stable employment, Lessing condemned in a letter to his brother Karl his own need to write for money: "Soon the time will arrive again when I will not be able to call a single penny in the world my own, except the one that I first have to earn. I will be unhappy if this must occur by means of writing. Take my brotherly advice and abandon your plan to live by writing" (*LW* 9: 276–77). The practical dilemmas of bourgeois authorship drive writers into a basically paradoxical situation: on the one hand, there is the impulse to produce more prolifically, sacrificing artistic quality to the demands of quantity to meet their minimal financial needs; on the other hand, they harbor a profound skepticism about the emerging literary commodity, a skepticism that takes the form of scathing critiques of the prolific writer.[15] Lessing himself delineates this dichotomy between quality and quantity in the business of writing in another letter to his brother, valorizing, not surprisingly, the writer of quality. "If you continue to produce play upon play," he admonishes, "if you don't practice with the writing of essays in between, in order to organize your thoughts and provide your mode of expression with clarity and purity, then I utterly dispute that you will ever produce something out of the ordinary in this field; and your hundredth play will not be one iota better than your first" (*LW* 9: 322–23). He repeats this advice a little over a year later, in November 1770, this time explicitly juxtaposing his brother's situation as writer to his own.

Next, however, I advise you emphatically to write less, that is, to have less published, and to study all the more for yourself. I assure you that I for my part would follow this advice myself much more if my circumstances did not pressure me so much to write. Since I can just barely get by with my regular salary, I simply have no other means, aside from writing, to find gradual relief from my debts. God knows, I have never needed to write for money more than at present; and this necessity, of course, even influences the material about which I write. (*LW* 9: 387)

Lessing obviously understands that the financial pressure to produce literary commodities has an adverse impact on the product itself. His advice to his brother seems well intentioned, since he seeks to direct him away from the pitfalls that Lessing believes have undermined his own position as author. His predicament testifies to the fact that the function of bourgeois authorship is strictly divided between the fabricator of the thrown-together, unlearned, and consequently shoddy literary commodity and the artistic craftsman who deliberately creates and carefully constructs each text as an individual literary work of art. Moreover, he implies that the author functions as the intellectual vanguard upon whose self-education the progressive education of the human race depends. This conception of the author as pedagogical mentor of the reading public draws on the idealized vision of the bourgeois public sphere as a font for the development and dissemination of knowledge. Lessing's remarks to his brother indicate his awareness that this mission is undermined by the economic constraints placed upon authorship. Under the influence of such mundane economic considerations, the bourgeois public(ation) sphere, which aims at the free flow of "pure" knowledge, takes on the character of a commercial marketplace determined solely by considerations relevant to the free flow of profitable commodities. Idealizing himself as the establisher and disseminator of cultural values, in other words, Lessing as bourgeois author finds himself confronted with the reality that in his role as author he has been reduced to a laborer who must create marketable surplus value. This conflict ultimately leads him to question his own status as author and decry the dependence on economic contingencies that undercuts his ideal vision of authorship.

Given his own dreary circumstances as author at the time of the final composition of *Emilia Galotti*, it is not surprising that Lessing would depict the problems of bourgeois authorship in his portrayal of the artist Conti. Conti represents a self-portrait of the author insofar as the dilemmas he faces reflect the crises Lessing himself sensed in his own artistic mission. In *Emilia Galotti*, however, these issues are embedded within the dramatic context of bourgeois tragedy as a sociopolitical, economic, moral, and literary-aesthetic phenomenon. What this play discloses is the principal conjunction of the crisis of bourgeois authorship with conflicts that run deep beneath the surface of bourgeois socioeconomic praxis, conflicts such as the struggle between intrinsic worth (use-value) and extrinsic usefulness (exchange-value), between quality and quantity, between "healthy" reason and instrumental rationality, between "head" and "heart." At the end of the eighteenth century, the emerging bourgeois literary institution in Germany evolved an ideological character strikingly similar in structure and substance to the ideology of the bourgeois individual: the real fact of the dependence of the literary work on the mechanisms of the bourgeois marketplace was camouflaged behind an aesthetic ideology that projected the artist as an independent genius and hypostatized the literary work as an autonomous creation. Thus writers such as Lessing, who were caught in the sophistry of this ideological aporia and had to grapple in their daily existence with the practical conflicts it spawned, were touched very closely by the crises that accompanied the emergence of bourgeois commerce. These experiences opened up a window on the alienating backlash of bourgeois epistemic structures and economic practices. Bourgeois authors came to see how these structures threatened to pervert the healthy interaction among subjects—and between subjects and the life-world—into alienating patterns guided by profitable exploitation. In the analysis of *Emilia Galotti* I will attempt to trace the development of these insights, moving from the questions of aesthetic representation and artistic practice developed in the Conti scenes to broader issues about the constitution of bourgeois subjectivity as ideologically structured (false) consciousness.

The Conti Scenes: Structures of Conflict in the Representations of Emilia and Orsina

> The method of painting is often the repository of much deeper, sometimes socially relevant, experiences than are realistic portraits. —Theodor Adorno

Although the function of the Conti scenes in the dramatic development of *Emilia Galotti* can be counted among the central enigmas of this work, few serious attempts have been made to integrate the debate on aesthetics they present with the tragic events the play unfolds. As a rule, these scenes are accounted for in one of two ways. On the one hand, they are seen as motivators of the tragic plot insofar as Conti's portrait of Emilia fans the flames of the Prince's desire;[16] on the other hand, the differing responses of the Prince and Conti to the aesthetics of the two portraits are identified with the distinct roles played by art in aristocratic and bourgeois society, although these aesthetic attitudes are never linked with the play's tragic conflict.[17] Even those critics who deal explicitly with the aesthetic questions addressed in these scenes rarely devote to them the serious attention and detailed analysis that they deserve. George Wells, for example, although correctly asserting that this episode must be read in the context of the aesthetic theories Lessing developed in *Laokoön*, fails to recognize that this connection is pertinent to the tragic conflicts that structure the drama itself. For him these scenes perform nothing other than an extratextual function, intervening in the controversy on aesthetics that Lessing had been carrying on with his contemporary, Johann Joachim Winckelmann. "In sum," Wells concludes, "what Conti says on art is a good natured quip on Lessing's part, gentle mockery of the views of Winckelmann on the subject."[18] Ilse Appelbaum-Graham comes closer to a substantive analysis, interpreting the "tragic disparateness of mind and medium in art," which Conti expresses in terms of the discrepancy between his ideal artistic vision of Emilia Galotti and his inability to realize this perfection in her portrait, as a prefiguration of the tragic conflict that pits Emilia's emotions and physical drives against the ideal vision of feminine virtue held up and defended by her father.[19] Neil Flax has offered an adroit interpretive analysis of these scenes in the context of Lessing's *Laokoön* and the general project of Enlightenment semiotics. Flax claims that the shift in representational modes with which Emilia is presented in the play, the movement from portrait in these early scenes to *"tableau vivant"* as the dramatic re-presentation of the historical Virginia in the final act, manifests the philosophic-historic project of Enlightenment semiotics as a fusion of natural and arbitrary signs. Flax's conclusion, however, lends the tragic denouement of Lessing's play an unwarranted optimism:

As Odoardo and Emilia perform the ultimate sacrifice and at the same time assume the form of a familiar painting [historical renditions of the slaying of Virginia], pictorial art is instilled with the conceptual force of language, and the abstract language of morality is imbued with instantaneous visibility. The climax of the play therefore marks the fulfillment of the semiotic project as it was conceived by German Enlightenment philosophy: the complete integration of the two orders of human sign-use.[20]

Flax's conclusion still leaves us with the paradox that the fulfillment of this Enlightenment ideal is necessarily accompanied—indeed, it seems causally to result from—the brutal death of the heroine. Drawing Flax's interpretation out to this level undercuts his optimistic thesis by revealing it as just one moment of a murderous dialectic of bourgeois Enlightenment in which progress is bought at the price of doing violence to the bourgeois subject itself. Thus while Flax succeeds in demonstrating that the political dimension of the play is embedded in the "ontologically prior ground" of semiotics and aesthetics,[21] he ultimately ignores the essential political questions that his analysis calls forth. He falls victim, in other words, to the ideology of bourgeois Enlightenment by buying into its self-instituted and self-perpetuated semblance of optimism and progress while suppressing the repressive and violent measures that underwrite the accomplishment of these progressive aims. If Lessing's play depicts the fulfillment of the semiotic-utopian project of the German Enlightenment, then it also demonstrates that it is founded on a primordial act of violence against the autonomous subject. The inextricable aporia of the drama's conclusion suggests that Lessing himself, an author who has traditionally been viewed as the paradigmatic champion of a progressive Enlightenment in Germany, was explicitly not able to make the leap of Enlightenment faith; and this refusal of enlightened optimism makes itself manifest in the irresolvable contradictions of the play. The paradox that the political ascendancy of the bourgeoisie results in violence against the virtuous bourgeois (feminine) subject is merely the most poignant of these contradictions.

Although they are the most stimulating interpreters of the paintings in *Emilia Galotti*, Appelbaum and Flax concentrate solely on the portrait of Emilia, wholly ignoring both the painting of the Countess Orsina, the Prince's former lover, and the implicit aesthetic reflections that this altogether different work elicits from the patron who ordered it and the painter who completed it. However, the ultimate significance of the paintings themselves and the ruminations they prompt only evolves out of their juxtaposition as a contrastive pair. More than simply presenting the likenesses of two different (female) subjects, these portraits represent, both in their subject matter and in their representational patterns, two competing versions of the subject and its signifying practices.

Mimetic representation as conceived by artists in the eighteenth century commonly was broken down into two distinct moments, selection of an appropriate object from nature to serve as artistic model, and transformation of this object into a work of art, that is, its appropriate aesthetification through the application of a specific artistic practice.[22] Both of these steps can be discerned in the creative procedure Conti follows to produce the paintings in *Emilia Galotti*, and for each painting both the criteria for selection of the object and the applied aesthetic practice are distinct. The specification of the Countess Orsina as the subject for a portrait, of course, is not at the discrimination of the artist himself; indeed, this choice is determined by the patronage system within whose logic Conti is compelled to operate. Lessing explicitly stresses Conti's dependence on the unpredictable and changing impulses of his patron by introducing into this scene the irony that between the time Orsina's portrait was commissioned and the time it was completed, the Prince's feelings for the portrayed object have dramatically changed. Moreover, the Prince's response to Conti's aesthetic representation is but a function of the emotions he feels toward the portrayed object itself (*EG* I, ii, 240–41; 4–5). For the Orsina portrait, the criterion of selection is heteronomous, conditioned by impulses external to the aesthetic perception of the artist himself. The selection of Emilia Galotti as the subject of a painting, by contrast, derives ostensibly from Conti's wholly subjective and independent evaluation of the natural object's inherent worthiness of aesthetic representation. The criterion of selection in the case of Emilia's representation can thus be described as autonomous.

Conti points explicitly to the distinct motivations that produce these paintings when he explains his reasons for calling on the Prince: "I've brought the portrait [of Orsina] that you ordered, your Highness. And I've brought another [the portrait of Emilia] that you didn't order; but since it deserves to be seen—" (*EG* I, ii, 240; 4). Emilia's portrait "deserves to be seen," we later learn, because of Conti's belief that there is "no subject [for art] more admirable than this" (*EG* I, iv, 243; 7); and in response to the Prince's query whether he reckons Emilia Galotti among the outstanding beauties of the town, Conti spells out the reasons for his choice of Emilia as the subject of this painting. "But, my Prince, as a painter I will have to tell you this: the fact that Emilia Galotti sat for me has been one of the happiest moments of my life. This head, this face, this brow, these eyes, this nose, this mouth, this chin, this throat, this bosom, this figure—this whole build [*Bau*] has been from that time on my only model of womanly beauty" (*EG* I, iv, 245; 8–9). Emilia is the choice subject of this painting because she represents for Conti, both in her individual physical features and in their harmonious "build" or "construction" ("Bau"), the absolute ideal of natural feminine beauty.

There is an ominous side, however, to Conti's enthusiastic confession, which equates the individual beauty of Emilia with the abstract ideal of feminine beauty. Conti's impassioned speech merely reflects the doctrine, which

Lessing acknowledges in *Laokoön* (*LW* 5: 18), that artistic inspiration is fueled by love. Conti explicitly appeals to this principle when he later asserts that painters "paint with eyes of love" (*EG* I, iv, 243; 7). By the same token, for Conti it is not the specific woman Emilia Galotti who is the object of his love—and it is this that distinguishes the love with which he creates this painting from the lust with which the Prince receives it—but rather the *ideal* that she represents for him. However, such an idealization that abstracts from the concrete traits of the natural object to arrive at aesthetic absolutes also has its negative aspects. Indeed, to the extent that he takes Emilia as an absolutized ideal that transcends her particularity, Conti commits an infraction against a fundamental law of portrait painting. "For although portrait painting allows for an ideal," Lessing comments in *Laokoön*, "this ideal must be governed by similarity: it is the ideal of a *specific* human being, not the ideal of the human being in general" (*LW* 5: 20–21; emphasis added). The aesthetic transgression Conti commits in his rendering of Emilia—her depersonalization—is symptomatic of a transgression against the individuality of Emilia Galotti as subject. Conti's ebullient adoration of Emilia thus manifests what we can call the dialectic of Eros, a paradoxical movement in which the admiring elevation of the object of love simultaneously and necessarily entails abstraction from, and hence denigration of, its individuality. In this sense the aesthetic attitude that underwrites Conti's representation of Emilia parallels the destructive dialectic inherent in Odoardo's fatherly love for Emilia: it is her (false) idealization as paragon of bourgeois (female) virtue that will require her destruction as a flesh-and-blood woman who, like all human beings, is subject to irrational passions.

Not coincidentally, it falls to the Prince, who lusts precisely after the flesh depicted in this portrait, to undo in his act of aesthetic reception the abstract idealizations perpetrated by the artist Conti. His desire for the painting's physical subject permits him to strip away these lofty aesthetic ideals and recognize in the artistic representation the specific traits of Emilia Galotti. Upon seeing Emilia's portrait he thus exclaims, "By God! As if stolen from a mirror!" (*EG* I, iv, 244; 7). This ostensibly innocent comment carries with it two significant implications. First, the Prince affirms the mimetic accuracy of Conti's representation of Emilia by comparing it to a mirror image, and he thereby attests to Conti's artistic success, since for the eighteenth century the value of mimetic representation was measured according to the standard of specular reflection. On the other hand, the metaphor of theft that creeps into the Prince's discourse ("As if stolen from a mirror!") anticipates the actual theft of Emilia that the Prince, with the assistance of the diabolical and conniving chamberlain, Marinelli, will later actually commit.

Moreover, in the Prince's statement aesthetic mimesis and theft are linked, suggesting that Conti's act of artistic representation, which purloins aesthetic semblance, so to speak, from the object it represents, is somehow related to that more concrete theft of Emilia that is the very stuff of this bourgeois tragedy. The representation of Emilia and the responses of the Prince and Conti to this mimetic portrayal thus significantly prefigure the tragic events the play will unroll. Already in this scene Emilia becomes the object both of an abstract idealization that denies the body as empirical fact, and of an erotic desire that perceives nothing but the body as such. The deliberations between Conti and the Prince on the aesthetics of Emilia's portrait thus anticipate the battle for Emilia's definition as (female) subject: idealized representative of bourgeois virtue for father Odoardo, to the Prince she is but the carnal object of (male) lust. Emilia's tragedy is the impossibility of autonomous self-determination, and it is written into this battle between the Prince and Odoardo over their own (heteronomous) representations of her.

The dialectic of idealization and mimesis that is concretized in the portrait of Emilia reflects an equivocation inherent in the notion of illusion as conceived by eighteenth-century aesthetics. What all the arts have in common, according to Lessing, is that they "represent absent things to us as present, semblance as reality" (*LW* 5: 9). However, to the extent that it presents "semblance as reality," aesthetic illusion has the power not merely to re-present what is absent, but also to *mis*represent it. The concept of aesthetic illusion, in other words, inherently encompasses both mimesis and construction, the dialectical poles of bourgeois aesthetics identified by Adorno. In the service of mimesis, illusion signifies the illusion *of* reality, the transparent re-presencing of an object as it is perceived to exist in nature; in the service of construction, illusion signifies illusion (or delusion) *about* reality, imaginative amplification on an object as it is perceived to exist in nature. The doctrine of aesthetic illusion hence circumscribes both imitation as accurate and adequate simulation and counterfeit as divergent dissimulation. For the eighteenth century, semiosis as mediative representation by means of signs inherently embraces both of these potentials, and the valorization of transparent (or "natural") semiosis in the aesthetic theories of this period bespeaks the desire to collapse the dialectic of illusion into mimesis.[23] In his reaction to Emilia's portrait the Prince subscribes to illusion as mimesis, and her painting becomes the placeholder for the physical object he desires; Conti's aesthetic practice, on the other hand, seeks to replace the empirical object with its idealized representation. Like father Odoardo, Conti privileges illusion as the (dis)semblance of idealized perfection over the realities of corporeal existence.

The distinct motivations governing Conti's choice of subjects for these two portraits thus have far-reaching implications for the aesthetic theory that underpins, and the artistic execution that creates, each work. However, this distinction should not be understood as the opposition between a system of feudal patronage and autonomous bourgeois creativity. On the contrary, it reflects—seen from the perspective of the artist himself—merely the difference between a work of art whose production is motivated by economic considerations and one created solely in response to inspiration and aesthetic intuition: art for money's sake versus art for art's sake, to put the distinction crassly. In the case of Orsina's painting, the artistic product functions primarily as a sellable commodity; in the instance of Emilia's portrait, Conti's personal motivations are entirely aesthetic in nature, and the painting thus manifests for him the technical challenge of perfectly representing the ideal of natural beauty Emilia embodies for him.[24] As aesthetic product, the Orsina painting is generated out of impulses extrinsic to the realm of aesthetics itself: it represents a heteronomous art, or, to apply the terminology Hegel proposed in his *Aesthetics*, an "ancillary" art, or an art of "service" ("dienende Kunst"). The portrait of Emilia, by contrast, is created solely with aesthetic considerations in mind: it is what Hegel terms "free" or "autonomous" art ("freie Kunst").[25] By placing these two artistic possibilities in the hands of one and the same artist, Lessing suggests that they are not two utterly distinct aesthetic movements, but rather two directions the artist pursues simultaneously. In the painter Conti, in other words, we are introduced to an archetypical bourgeois artist of this period who, like Lessing himself, is fundamentally divided between adherence to the idealized dictates of the bourgeois institution of autonomous art (Emilia's portrait) and the economic demands that force him to treat his artistic products as mere economic commodities (the painting of Orsina).

If we turn now to the reactions registered by the Prince and Conti in their discussions of these two paintings, we can specify the characteristics of service and autonomy as they structure the dialectic of bourgeois aesthetics, paying heed to the dimensions of aesthetic production and reception alike. The Prince's monolog in scene three of the first act, spoken while he anticipates Conti's arrival with the commissioned portrait of Orsina, presents us with telling insights into his perception of the potency of mimetic representation.

Her picture! So be it! Her picture is certainly not herself. And perhaps I will find in the picture what I no longer see in her personally. But I don't want to find it again. . . . If another picture of her, painted with other colors on another canvas, could find a place in my heart again:—really, I believe I would be satisfied. I was always so carefree when I loved her then, so happy, so exuberant. Now I'm the opposite of all that.—But no; no, no! Happier or not, I am better off this way. (*EG* I, iii, 241; 5)

The Prince reacts to the idea that he will see Orsina's portrait by playing up the discrepancy that separates the true object from its artistic representation. However, the very fact that he must assure himself that the image is not the person herself betrays his tacit esteem of art's representational potency, its capacity to make absent things present, and thus to reinvoke for him the person he now wishes to forget. After voicing this concern, however, he then does a kind of sentimental about-face in which he ascribes to aesthetic mimesis the potential to reinvest him with those emotions he no longer feels for the woman herself. He thereby attributes to aesthetic representation the power to intervene in and alter emotions. But the Prince resists this emotional reinvestment by asserting his will to withstand the erotic power of representation. Throughout the monolog he swings back and forth between these negative and affirmative responses to the mimetic magic of aesthetic re-presencing, ultimately resolving to reject its erotic impact. Two things remain constant in the Prince's projected conception of artistic mimesis, however, despite his emotional swings. On the one hand, he dissociates aesthetic semblance from the object it represents, treating appearance and essence as though they were independent functions. On the other hand, he identifies the sensual immediacy and potentially transformative power of a mode of representation that, like painting, employs natural or iconic signs to invoke its signified. The Prince can only oppose the persuasive sensual rhetoric of an aesthetic mimesis grounded in iconicity by mustering his will to resist its charm.

The discussion between Conti and the Prince elicited by the inspection of Orsina's portrait centers on the first of these issues: the two debate the sources of those discrepancies that distinguish the original from her aesthetic representation. Conti himself calls attention to such discrepancies when he introduces the painting in an apologetic manner, excusing its mimetic defects by ascribing them to the necessary technical limitations of his art.

CONTI: I hope, Prince, that you will consider the limitations of our art. A great deal of what is most enticing in beauty lies completely beyond its limits. Look at it from this angle!

PRINCE *(after looking at it a short time)*: Splendid, Conti; very well done! That may be said of your artistry, of your brush. But you flattered her, Conti; quite infinitely flattered her!

CONTI: The original didn't seem to think so. And anyway, she is actually no more flattered than art must flatter. Art must paint in just the same way that plastic nature—if there is one—conceived of the picture: without the imperfections which the resisting material makes unavoidable; without the decay which time uses in its fight against nature. . . .

PRINCE: And what did the original say?

CONTI: I am satisfied, the Countess said, if I don't look uglier.

PRINCE: Not uglier?—Oh, the true original!

CONTI: And she said this with a facial expression of which this picture admittedly shows no trace, no suspicion.

PRINCE: That's just what I meant; that's exactly where I see that infinite flattery. Oh! How well I know it, that proud, mocking expression, which would distort even the face of a goddess! . . . For admit it, Conti: can the person's character really be ascertained from this picture? It certainly should be. You have transformed pride into dignity, mockery into a smile, and her disposition to gloomy fanaticism into gentle melancholy.

CONTI (somewhat annoyed): Ah, my Prince, we artists count on the finished picture finding the lover just as ardent as when he commissioned it. We paint with eyes of love, and eyes of love must also judge us. (EG I, iv, 241–43; 5–7)

I have quoted this scene at length because it develops in detail the principles of an aesthetics of flattery that stands in diametrical opposition to the aesthetic theory Conti outlines when discussing Emilia's portrait. Indeed, the inherent malleability of Conti's self-reflections on aesthetic issues is emphatically brought to light when we witness the fluctuations in his own assessment of the Orsina painting that transpire even over the course of this brief dialog. Initially Conti admonishes the Prince to consider the limitations of the painter's craft when viewing the portrait. He apparently assumes that the "eyes of love," with which he anticipates the Prince will view the work, will attribute any divergences between the original and its representation to the shortcomings of the artist himself. By depersonalizing the cause of any mimetic flaws and projecting them into the given nature of the general aesthetic medium in which he as individual painter must operate, Conti hopes to deflect any personal repercussions the Prince's potential criticism of the portrait might have for him as artist.

Conti sings a quite different tune, however, once he fathoms that the Prince's (pre)disposition to the "original" of this painting has radically changed since the time when the portrait was commissioned. Indeed, he falls into blatant contradiction when he now defends that very divarication from the "original" that he initially feared would be ascribed to his own artistic inadequacies as conformity to an untransgressible aesthetic law: to the requirement that aesthetic representation "flatter" the portrayed object, that it perfect imperfect nature. Indefeasibly tied to the arbitrary attitudes of his patron, Conti's aesthetic theory and practice fluctuate to keep apace with the Prince's emotional swings: (feigned) despondency about the deficiencies of aesthetic representation thus ultimately gives way to exultant approbation of its—literally—supernatural proficiencies.

Locked into the economic dependence of service, Conti's first duty as artist is to please his patron, even if this means being unfaithful to the aesthetic principles that govern artistic representation. Conti himself alludes to this subservience when he notes that the artist relies on a constancy of sentiment for the portrayed subject on the part of the person who commissions a portrait. By highlighting this destabilizing dependence of the artist on the Prince as the representative of political and economic power, Lessing supplies a critique that applies mutatis mutandis to the eviscerating subordination of the artist to the structures of the commercial marketplace. In fact, it is the economic aspect of the relationship between Conti and the Prince, their roles as principals in a process of exchange, that Lessing stresses. As artistic producer who desires to sell the product of his labor, Conti must bend to the will of the Prince as consumer: the customer, Conti has learned, is always right. The patronage system thus stands as an index for precisely that economic subjugation of the artist under which Lessing himself suffered throughout his life.

In his depiction of Conti's accommodation to the attitudes of the Prince, Lessing paints a subtle picture of the psychological tensions that evolve in the master-slave relationship between the artist and his "patron." The volte-face that characterizes Conti's assessments of his own artistry marks his flight, given the fact of his real subjugation, into the relatively safe haven of affirmative ideological self-posturing. His calculated reinterpretation of the mimetic limitations of his artistic practice as the idealizing and transformative capacity of aesthetic flattery represents nothing other than an ideological self-legitimation. It permits him to portray his art, which is in fact held hostage to the demands of service, as a sublime supplement to divine creation whose function it is to elevate the real, natural world to the perfection of the ideal. Conti's maneuverings thus sketch the logic by which the bourgeois subject constitutes itself as dialectically structured ideological consciousness: beginning with recognition of, and resignation to, his own subjugation, Conti strategically moves to a self-aggrandizing projection that makes a virtue of this sociopolitical and economic necessity. The Conti scenes thereby establish a pattern that simulates the psychological texture of the entire drama. The ideological dynamic that structures his own self-understanding as artist prefigures the ideological reflex that permits the (self-) victimization of Emilia Galotti, as bourgeois subject, to be portrayed as martyrdom in the name of abstract ethical ideals. Emilia, however, is trapped in a finer web of dependencies spun not only by the Prince and Marinelli as the representatives of political and economic authority, but also by her father and mother as representatives of bourgeois moral and social designs. Like Conti, she will respond to these conflicting demands by looking for refuge in the beautiful semblance of ideology, seeking protection behind the moral fortress of unimpeachable virtue.

It is significant that Conti does not merely pull his remarks about art's role as the perfecter of nature out of his creative hat; indeed, with this claim he articulates a principle common to eighteenth-century aesthetics. Lessing's friend Moses Mendelssohn, for example, enunciates this axiom in the treatise *On the Primary Principles of the Fine Arts and Letters* (1771) when he argues that "the object of the fine arts . . . must be decorous [*anständig*], new, unusual, fruitful, etc. . . . From this one sees to what extent art is obliged to depart from nature and to represent [*nachzubilden*] objects not wholly as they are to be found in the original." He continues by specifying the purpose of such rectification of the flaws inherent in nature.

The common statements that artists must *beautify nature*, imitate *beautiful nature*, etc., mean nothing other than this. They seek to depict a certain object in the manner God would have created it if sensual beauty had been his highest aim, and if other more important aims had not been able to occasion such departures. This is the most consummate ideal beauty, which can be found in nature nowhere other than in the totality, and which perhaps can never fully be achieved in works of art.[26]

Aesthetics appears as a necessary supplement to nature, which, diverted away from the perfection of sensual beauty by its concern for other principles, requires the skill of the visual artist to artificially retouch its original creations. The fact that nature embraces the uncomely as well as the comely presented a problem for eighteenth-century aesthetics, since it conceived representation, on the one hand, as imitation of nature, but believed, on the other hand, that art should be restricted to portrayal of the beautiful. This dilemma evoked two distinct responses, one being Mendelssohn's break with a strictly defined program of mimesis as manifest in the claim that art must beautify, that is, transform, the natural world, the other being restriction of the selection of objects for representation, which banished all that is ugly from the world of art. In *Laokoön*, of course, Lessing opted for the second of these two responses in the specific instance of the visual arts, defining their singularity in part by this restriction to portrayal of the seemly (see *LW* 5: 173). Lessing's painter Conti has it both ways: in the case of Emilia's portrait he follows Lessing's theoretical course, selecting a beautiful object and attempting to render it with mimetic precision; in the instance of Orsina's painting he forgoes control over the moment of selection and relies on artistic supplementation of the flawed natural object. The fact that in the execution of Emilia's portrait Conti conforms to the principles Lessing laid down in his own theoretical deliberations suggests that it is this aspect of Conti's Janus-faced artistic practice that Lessing wishes to valorize. Where the artist no longer dictates the criterion of selection, but rather has it dictated to him, he must turn to aesthetification, privileging construction over mimesis. The Conti scenes demonstrate that the aesthetifying practice of a constructivist art of flattery derives from the web of economic and sociopolitical dependencies to which the service artist is subjected. Because the value of the artistic product is here established extrinsically in the structure of economic exchange, the artist relies on aesthetification as a strategy to enhance the appeal—and thus the exchange-value—of the work while adhering to the aesthetic requirement that the artistic product (re)present beauty. The two paintings thus concretize the distinction between the artistic commodity, in which aesthetic (dis)semblance is grafted onto the natural object in the course of its representation, and the genuine work of art, in which aesthetic semblance transparently re-flects and re-presences the intrinsic features of the natural object itself.

There is, of course, a common ground that unites the distinct aesthetic aims Conti pursues in these two portraits. In both portrayals the ultimate aesthetic goal can be described as idealization: the representation of idealized nature on the one hand (Emilia), and the idealized representation of flawed nature on the other (Orsina). Consistent with this is the impassioned oration Conti delivers in response to the Prince's praise of his representation of Emilia, a diatribe on aesthetics that culminates in the assertion that art is fundamentally a mode of perception rather than a set of concrete representational techniques or artistic practices.

Nevertheless, this picture [of Emilia] still left me very dissatisfied with myself. And yet, on the other hand, I am very satisfied with my dissatisfaction with myself. Ha! What a pity that we do not paint directly with our eyes! How much is lost on the long path from the eye, through the arm, into the brush! But the moment I say that I know what has been lost here and how it has been lost, and why it had to be lost: I am just as proud of that, in fact prouder, than I am of what I did not allow to get lost. Because from the former I recognize more than from the latter that I am really a great artist, but that my hand isn't always. Or do you think, Prince, that Raphael would not have been the greatest artistic genius had he unfortunately been born without hands? (*EG* I, iv, 244; 7–8)

In this disquisition Conti touches once again on those questions about the necessary limitations of artistic practice that he initially cited in his apolo-

getic introduction of Orsina's portrait. When he returns to this theme in his
discussion of Emilia's painting, however, the necessity of these limitations
is once again made into a virtue: it is precisely the awareness of the inevitable discrepancies that distinguish the idealized "original" from its necessarily faulty aesthetic representation that becomes the hallmark of artistic genius. Conti's claim that Raphael would still have been the greatest artistic genius even if he had been born without hands underwrites a conception
that projects artistic talent as independent of all material skills, free of the
necessity to concretize aesthetic intuition through the implementation of
specific aesthetic practices that would produce the *work* of art. What Conti
defends, in other words, is the wish-fulfillment dream of a wholly etherealized art that has been extricated from all the contingencies of the material
world, an art that takes on the character of pure aesthetic intuition. Conti
performs a kind of phenomenological reduction of artistic practice, brack-
eting off from it all demands of the material life-world by identifying them
as tainted epiphenomenal disturbances of the otherwise flawless creative
gaze of artistic image-ination. Like the ideological self-deception of the autonomous bourgeois subject, this conception of a dematerialized autonomous art is an ideological fantasy that compensates for the socioeconomic shackles that tie artistic genius to the heteronomous structures of
commodity aesthetics. This inflated notion of artistic genius compensates
for the atrophy of the creative individual in a life-world increasingly dominated by purposive rationality.[27] But Conti's notion of autonomous art
thereby becomes wholly subject-centric insofar as it locates the conditions
of possibility of aesthetics in the artistic consciousness of the "genius" rather
than in the inherent constitution of the natural object or in the manner of
its artistic representation. However, this radical idealization, formulated as
ideological protest against the material, socioeconomic conditions that determine the aesthetic work as commodity, opens the door to a conception
of creative imagination, codified in the eighteenth-century notion of aesthetic genius, that eventually will topple the entire edifice of a mimetic aesthetics: the devalorization of the original sows the seeds from which avant-
garde visions of a nonmimetic art—presentative rather than *re*-presenta-
tive—will spring.

While the process of idealization is operative in the production of both
Emilia's and Orsina's portraits, it occurs in each instance at different moments in the artistic procedure, and this is what accounts for the distinct aesthetic attitudes constitutive of these works. We can distinguish between a
primary and a secondary phase of aesthetic idealization. Primary idealization, indicative of Conti's portrayal of Emilia, occurs on the level of aesthetic

perception itself and resides in the imaginative gaze of the artistic genius; secondary idealization, at work in Conti's rendering of Orsina, takes place in the phase of aesthetic concretization whereby the perception of the represented object itself is enhanced by the labor that produces the material representation as *work* (of art). Where Emilia's portrait is autonomous, independent of crass economic or other practical considerations, Orsina's representation is heteronomous, deriving its principles from the embeddedness of the artistic act in the web of constraints that define the socioeconomic sphere. Where the former is mimetic, re-creating in aesthetic intuition the self-identity of natural beauty, the latter is constructive, exploiting technical skill to shape and perfect the imperfect natural world. Taken together as the artistic possibilities that Lessing places in the hands of a single painter, the bourgeois artist Conti, these conflicting aesthetic drives mark the paradoxical dialectic of bourgeois art: driven to subjective mastery over the natural world, its increasing exploitation and technification, art simultaneously counters this reifying tendency by identifying in the world of repressed nature what Adorno calls the "nonidentical," the last vestiges of an authentic being not ravaged—and not ravageable, since it is wholly dematerialized—by the structures of calculative exchange and the logic of identity.[28]

The two modes of representation concretized in the Orsina and Emilia portraits correspond to distinct applications of material signs for the production of a work of art. In the aesthetics of service, or of artistic flattery, the material signs of painting intervene in the process of mimetic representation and impose upon the original a set of constructive, technical alterations. The Prince explicitly points to the transmogrifying powers of this aesthetic procedure when he claims that in the portrait of Orsina, Conti has "*transformed* pride into dignity, mockery into a smile, and her disposition to gloomy fanaticism into gentle melancholy" (*EG* I, iv, 243; 6; emphasis added). In this transformational process the material signs of painting supplement the wanting materiality of the empirical object: they become a signifying mask, so to speak, and thus constitute a dis-simulation of the empirical object that the painting pretends merely to simulate. The painting's material signs move to the foreground, flattering and thereby simultaneously occulting the essence of the object they purport simply to re-present. This is the moment at which the dialectic of illusion reverts from the pole of mimesis—re-presentation of the absent—to that of creative construction—aesthetic supplementation of nature: instead of re-presentation of semblance, representation as dis-semblance; instead of mimetic re-collection of the absent object, its aesthetic reconstitution and reconstruction. The persistence with which eighteenth-century thinkers, among them Lessing and Mendelssohn, cite the transparency of the aesthetic signifier to its signified as the acid test for accomplished artistic representation bespeaks a profound skepticism about the fundamental mediacy of signs. This is accompanied by the suspicion that semiotic mediation, if not somehow policed, opens up the process of representation to dissimulation, dissemblance, and deceit.[29] In the painting of Orsina, such aesthetic deception is associated with a service art in which the work enters into economic circulation as a commodity. In such instances inflated semblance serves to increase the desirability, and thus the marketability, of the artistic product.

In his notes to the fourth draft of *Laokoön*, Lessing attempts to refine his ideas about the relative functions of natural and arbitrary signs in painting and poetry. Elaborating on his demand that the painter is restricted to the use of natural signs, he admits that to adhere to this rule strictly the painter would have to render all objects in their true-to-life dimensions. Arbitrary signs, therefore, do indeed inevitably find their way into painting; but it is the task of the expert painter to limit their employment as much as possible. While developing this problem, Lessing arrives at a definition, grounded in semiotic considerations, of what he calls a "symbolic picture," a visual representation in which signs eclipse their signified.

A smaller scale human figure is still the picture of a human being; but it is also already in a certain respect a symbolic picture: I have first to expand the scaled-down figure in my imagination back to its true size, and this procedure, regardless of how quickly and easily it transpires, nonetheless prevents my intuition of the signified object from occurring simultaneously with the intuition of the sign. (*LW* 5: 294–95)

Lessing's primary concern whenever he subjects works of art to value judgments, of course, is with their "truth" and "effectivity" (*LW* 5: 294), and it is his belief in the greater receptive impact of natural signs that leads him ultimately to elevate them above arbitrary signs for both the visual and the poetic arts. The reasons underlying this valorization of natural signs are expressed quite clearly in this definition of the symbolic picture. By using the extreme example of mere physical dimensions—as absurd as this example might appear at first glance—Lessing makes it clear that even the slightest deviation from total iconicity between the painterly (that is, natural or iconic) sign and its signified already establishes the semiotic relationship as arbitrary and consequently detracts from the immediacy of the painting's effect. As soon as the observer's power of imagination must assist the sign to reconstruct its intended signified in its true form and real-to-life dimensions, the identity of sign and signified, or the perfect transparency of the sign to the signified, is irrevocably lost. This implies that the moment the observer must engage his/her interpretive skills in an attempt to move from sign to signified, both the aesthetic potency and the relative "truth" of the representation are necessarily diminished. Perfect natural signs, we can infer, would require no interpretation whatsoever: they would be immediately and intuitively fathomable—indeed, sign and signified would fall together to such an extent that perception of the sign would be tantamount to perception of its signified. Lessing imagines the refraction of immediate intuition that occurs in the perception of arbitrary signs as a time-lapse between sign-intuition and signified-intuition, whereby in the ideal instance these two acts would occur with perfect synchronicity. Consciousness of the sign *qua sign* thus turns out to be the index of semiotic arbitrariness for Lessing: the more conscious we are of the sign—the greater its opacity—the greater its degree of arbitrariness.[30]

Lessing's definition of a "symbolic picture" adequately describes the semiotic relation between representation and original constitutive of Orsina's portrait; and the receptive response of the Prince, who must translate Conti's painted signs to recognize behind them the "true original," conforms to the receptive effect Lessing attributes to this semiotic practice. Given the principles Lessing defends in *Laokoön*, the Prince's objection would be enough to condemn the Orsina painting as a hopelessly flawed work, one which, as Lessing expresses it in the foreword to this theoretical treatise, falls short of painting's "true calling" because it transforms its signs into "an arbitrary form of writing" ("eine willkürliche Schriftart") (*LW* 5: 11). Just the opposite is true of Emilia's portrait: the moment Conti unveils the painting, the Prince exclaims, "What's this? Your work, Conti? Or the product of my imagination?—Emilia Galotti!" (*EG* I, iv, 243; 7). Although he does not even anticipate being presented with a painting that has Emilia as its subject, he recognizes her instantaneously in Conti's iconic signs. Indeed, the representation is so "transparent" that the Prince confuses Conti's likeness with the image of Emilia produced in his own imagination: intuition of the painted sign "Emilia Galotti" coincides completely with his mental signified "Emilia Galotti," and thus the Prince can praise Conti's representation with the assertion that Emilia's image has been stolen from a mirror (*EG* I, iv, 244; 7). The authenticity of Conti's representation is guaranteed by the fact that no interpretive lag interferes in the process of transference between the iconic signs of the painting and their mental signifieds: sign-intuition and signified-intuition merge. The painting of Emilia thus exemplifies those characteristics that Lessing associated with successful artistic portrayal in the visual arts.

It would be inaccurate to claim, however, that the Orsina portrait employs arbitrary signs while the picture of Emilia exploits natural signs. Indeed, since both are painted renderings of empirical subjects, they must both be operating, on the level of aesthetic representation, with fundamentally iconic—that is, for eighteenth-century semiotics, natural—signs. The difference between the two paintings, measured particularly by the difference in the receptive responses they evoke, hence must be situated elsewhere than in the semiotics of mimetic representation. Indeed, Lessing complicates the semiotic questions raised in the Conti scenes by depicting these issues on the specific example of portrait painting. For the eighteenth century, the human body, especially the face, is itself the bearer of signs that indicate the emotions or character of the inner person. Thus in the instance of portrait painting it is necessary to distinguish between two orders of semiosis: the "expressive" or "symptomatic" dimension, which, as presentational index of thoughts or feelings, governs the relationship between sentiment and sign production in the living subject of the painting; and the "mimetic" dimension, which, as aesthetic *re*presentation, is concerned only with the capacity of signs to capture the expressive features of the subject.[31] The eighteenth century's fascination with physiognomy, or with what Lessing termed "moral semiotics" (*LW* 9: 680), reflects a preoccupation with the expressive dimension of sign use. This concern is likewise evident in Herder's theory that language evolves out of the human animal's inherent expressive drive rather than the need for intersubjective communication.[32] In the case of portrait painting, these two semiotic functions converge: the portraiture must render the purely sensual traits of the original, its visible features, but it must render them *as expressive signs* that refer simultaneously to the supersensual (or subsensual) features of internal character.

Lessing's Prince clearly approaches the painting of Orsina with just such expectations, since he criticizes Conti's depiction for failing to convey the essential character of the original: "For admit it, Conti: can the person's [Orsina's] character really be ascertained from this picture? It certainly should be" (*EG* I, iv, 243; 6). Conti's representation of Orsina misses its mark because, as the painter himself admits, it does not reproduce the expressive signs of Orsina's character, those facial expressions that are symptomatic of her haughty demeanor and her pride. It is, after all, in the facial expression with which the Countess shows her dissatisfaction with Conti's portrait that the Prince recognizes "the true original," a facial expression of which the portrait "admittedly shows no trace, no suspicion" (*EG* I, iv, 242; 6). The fraud that Conti perpetrates in this painting is thus grounded in an especially insidious semiotic ruse: he exploits iconic, natural signs as a representational artifice that *mis*represents the expressive signs of the portrayed subject, thereby creating an illusion about her character. Illusion serves the ends of delusion; iconic signs, which are ostensibly connected to their signified by the principle of similitude, are deployed here in the interests of dissimulation. The nimbus of semiotic transparency inherent in the iconicity of these signs lends this dissimulative representation the conviction of authenticity.

Among Lessing's reflections on the semiotic constitution of the arts there are deliberations that deal with precisely this problematic. In a celebrated letter to Friedrich Nicolai from May 26, 1769, Lessing applies semiotic categories to distinguish high and low genres in both painting and poetry (see *LW* 9: 317–20). The higher genres he associates in both instances with the predominant use of natural signs, while the lower genres are linked with the increasing application of arbitrary signs. In this context, he amplifies on his understanding of what constitutes arbitrary signs in painting.

However, I call in painting not only everything that is a part of the costume an arbitrary sign, but even also a large part of the bodily expression. To be sure, in painting these things are not actually arbitrary: their signs are in painting natural signs. But they are in fact *natural* signs of *arbitrary* things, which cannot possibly have the same general understanding, the same speedy and quick effect, as *natural* signs of *natural* things. (*LW* 9: 319)

It is noteworthy, first of all, that Lessing reiterates here the conception of temporal immediacy as the measure of aesthetic-semiotic effectivity that appeared in the fourth draft of *Laokoön*. Furthermore, he establishes that the signs of painting themselves must always be considered natural signs as long as they function iconically rather than symbolically.[33] In order to draw his distinction between the higher and lower genres of painting he finds it necessary to differentiate between aesthetic representation as a secondary semiosis and symptomatic semiosis as a primary system of self-expression: aesthetic representation becomes subordinate to an originary self-representation of the natural object (or subject) itself. This self-representation Lessing identifies explicitly with costume and bodily expression. Thus it is not the nature of the representational signs alone that determines the effectiveness of the aesthetic representation, but the nature of the expressive semiosis that is produced by the represented subject itself. In the instance of painting, aesthetic representation of a self-identical subject, one whose expressive signs are natural or motivated (that is, necessary and immediate) indices of its true character, would conform to what Lessing terms the natural signification of natural things; artistic representation of a non-self-identical subject, one whose expressive signs are arbitrary or nonmotivated (that is, contingent and false) signals of its true character would accord with what he calls the natural signification of arbitrary things.

This, finally, is the ultimate dichotomy that discriminates between the Orsina and Emilia portraits, and it displaces the conflict of representation from the second-order realm of aesthetic mimesis into that first-order domain of subjectivity conceived as expressive semiosis, as the subject's self-representation in expressive signs. The Emilia painting represents the subject as autonomous, self-identical in-dividual: the mimetic accuracy of the aesthetic representation derives from its capacity transparently to reproduce this essential integrity on the level of character. Emilia's physical traits, in other words, are the natural expressive signs of her virtue and innocence, and Conti's aesthetic challenge in rendering her is to duplicate in his portrayal the transparency of this (self-)expressive semiosis. The portrait of Orsina, by contrast, represents a subject whose expressive self-representation (the expression of her pride) has been erased and supplanted by arbitrarily chosen natural signs. Ironically, the split between sentiment and its expression, which the Prince criticizes in Orsina's portrait, proves to be an adequate representation of a rift in her actual character. Immediately after she is portrayed in the Conti scenes as a subject in which being and semblance diverge, Marinelli represents her to the Prince as a woman whose words (whose arbitrary signs) are at odds with the facial expressions (the natural signs) that accompany them: "With the most humorous demeanor she [Orsina] said the most melancholy things, and then the most ridiculous jests with the saddest of facial expressions" (*EG* I, vi, 247; 11). The verbal codification of Orsina's emotions conflicts with those expressive signs that the eighteenth century took to be more immediate and reliable indicators of internal states, and this divergence is symptomatic of a disruption in the expressive, self-representative dimension of semiosis. Orsina's sentiments manifest themselves in contradictory signs, and these reflect a deep division that runs through her as subject. Thus both Orsina's portrait and her actual character testify to a self-divided, contradictory subjectivity.

In this sense the portrait of Orsina projects the fate that would befall Emilia if she were to give in to the Prince's solicitations: her own self-representation would thereby be breached, and she would be condemned to existing as a subject split between essence and semblance, between being-for-herself and being-for-another. As courtesan Orsina embodies the subject that has accepted its subjugation to the laws of abstract exchange: her own worth is established extrinsically through her union with the Prince—or some other suitor—rather than intrinsically through autonomous self-definition. As subject, then, Orsina symbolizes the menace facing Emilia's subjectivity, the threat that it will be "seduced," led away from its own self-determination and integrity and condemned to the status of a desirable commodity. Each painting hence marks one side of the ideological rift that traverses both bourgeois subjectivity and bourgeois aesthetics. Emilia's death—and thus bourgeois tragedy—arises out of the attempt to uphold the illusion of the autonomous bourgeois subject, which her painting represents, in the historical context of an increasingly reified and alienated bourgeois life-world. Submission to the fate of Orsina, and to the constructive aesthetics that supplants her authentic (self-)representation, reflects the deliverance of the human subject—as but one component of "beautiful nature"— to the reifying gaze of a desire whose aim is nothing other than mastery.[34]

This analysis of the portraits in *Emilia Galotti* has traced the conflict between the representational systems that constitute these pictures, uncovered the semiotic structures that underpin this dichotomy, and shown that this opposition can be followed into the contrasting modes of subjectivity characteristic of the "subjects"—in both senses—of the two paintings. Ultimately I want to demonstrate that Lessing's drama can be comprehended as a tragic depiction of the collapse of bourgeois autonomy at the very moment of its self-institution and ideological glorification. My point is that the tragic demise of Emilia Galotti, the representative in this drama of the idealized autonomous subject projected by bourgeois ideology, is already anticipated in her juxtaposition with the Countess Orsina in the Conti scenes. The counterpositioning of these two paintings/subjects goes far beyond the simple portrayal of the class division between a degenerate aristocracy and a vital and virtuous bourgeoisie, penetrating into fundamental epistemic tensions that structure bourgeois thought itself. The aesthetic distinction between service art and autonomous art, which rends the aesthetic consciousness of Conti, the prototypical bourgeois artist, into two oppositional sets of artistic values and their corresponding practices, marks that set of subliminal conflicts that runs through the very texture of bourgeois thought.

The juxtaposition of the two portraits demarcates these epistemic oppositions on five distinct levels: the dimensions of economics, aesthetics, semiotics, subjectivity, and morality. The genesis of the Orsina painting is motivated by practical economic considerations: the painter produces it on commission, and from his perspective it is nothing but a mere commodity intended to bring financial gain. As a result, Conti paints not with his own eyes and mind, but with the eyes and mind of his customer. That the painting arrives "a month too late" to be greeted with the Prince's ardor (*EG* I, iv,

243; 7) reinforces both the occasionality of its genesis and its submission as commodity to the arbitrary desires of the consumer. Its value, established in the system of abstract exchange, thus fluctuates in accordance with the fluctuations in the consumer's desire. The Emilia portrait, by contrast, is the product of the autonomous artist, created beyond any mundane considerations such as financial exigency or personal ingratiation to a higher authority. The motivations the painter expresses for rendering Emilia are grounded solely in considerations of an aesthetics whose aim is mimetic representation of natural—if yet idealized—self-identical beauty. The fact that the representation of Emilia, which moves the Prince so violently, is twice removed from the original subject—the text explicitly states that it is but the copy of the originally painted "copy" (*EG* I, iv, 245; 9)[35]—underscores the receptive effectiveness of an artistic practice motivated exclusively by the autonomous creativity of the artist, a mode of representation whose authenticity is guaranteed by the application of natural signs to represent natural things. The attitudes of the two men, Conti and the Prince, to the paintings are emblematic of their attitudes to the women they represent, as well. Orsina, like her portrait, is to both men nothing but a commodity: she is an object in the natural world that can be exploited for economic gain or for personal pleasure. She becomes the object of an abstract exchange between buyer and seller, functioning as a means to life for the artist-seller Conti, and as a means to exploitable pleasure for the buyer, the Prince.[36] Emilia, like her *original* portrait, on the other hand, is for Conti an individual who represents the higher values of an absolute, divinely ordained beauty, something that is to be respected and admired; for the Prince, on the other hand, she too, like Orsina, is but one more exploitable object of nature, something to be desired, purchased, and possessed. To be sure, Conti plays into the commodification principle the Prince represents when he copies the original portrait and takes it to him in the first place. With this act of reproduction, the impending commodification of the bourgeois individual Emilia Galotti and her natural beauty is already set in motion. If the very process of reproduction, as Walter Benjamin claims, marks the transition from the auratic to the technological work of art,[37] then Conti's reproduction of Emilia's portrait for the Prince is a symptom of the bourgeois artist's equivocation between "auratic" and "technological" (commodified) modes of artistic production. Whereas the original portrait of Emilia is still produced under conditions of an auratic aesthetic, in other words, the copy made for the Prince represents the submission of the aesthetic work as well as its human subject to the structures of reproduction and commodification. The imminent menace to the individuality of the subject Emilia Galotti is ominously anticipated by this shift in the status of her aesthetic representation.

In the aesthetic dimension, the Orsina portrait derives from an aesthetics of flattery that exploits the rift between factual being and aesthetic semblance to idealize the empirical object, thereby making its representation more desirable—and consequently more sellable. Just such a splitting-off of sensual semblance from the object itself constitutes, according to Wolfgang Haug, the fundamental structure of commodity aesthetics. "The aesthetics of the commodity in its widest meaning—the sensual appearance and the conception of its use-value—become detached from the object itself. Appearance becomes just as important as—and practically more so than—the commodity's being itself."[38] Such an aesthetic practice manipulates the difference between illusion and essence, exploiting the former to make the aesthetic—the aestheticized—product more "attractive." "In a commodity the relation word, image or meaning and referent is broken and restructured so that its force is directed, not to the referent of use value or utility, but to desire."[39] Commodity aesthetics thus possesses the ability to transmogrify the original, transforming "pride into dignity" and "mockery into a smile" (*EG* I, iv, 243; 6). The aesthetic principle underlying the original portrait of Emilia, by contrast, operates by mimetically representing the identity between appearance and essence that constitutes her very subjectivity: not only does the painting portray Emilia's physical features "as if stolen from a mirror," but it simultaneously represents these traits as natural signs of her virtue and integrity.

On the semiotic level, the representation of Orsina operates with natural signs of arbitrary things, that is, it exploits the iconic force of natural signs to lend credence to the arbitrary, flattered representation of the portrayed subject. From this reliance on natural signs it derives its persuasive force, and it places this power in the service of deception. The potentials of aesthetic semblance and mimetic simulation, in short, are exploited to the ends of dis-semblance and dis-simulation. The Emilia portrait, in contradistinction, is constructed through the implementation of natural signs of natural things, and the perfect coincidence of sign and signified—their natural motivation, or "apt relationship" ("bequemes Verhältnis"), as Lessing termed it (*LW* 5: 115)—in both the mimetic and expressive dimensions of sign use establishes the inherent quality and receptive effect of this representation. In the juxtaposition of Emilia's and Orsina's portraits, similitude stands over against a dis-simulative semiotic relation, and this disjunction reflects distinctions between the subjective characters of the two represented individuals.

The Seduction of Reason: Emilia Galotti as
Victim of Bourgeois Purposive Rationality

> Seduction is that which extracts meaning from discourse and detracts it
> from its truth.   —Jean Baudrillard

The juxtaposition of Orsina and Emilia presented in the Conti scenes circumscribes a set of oppositions between self-division and integrity, deceit
and self-identical verity, dis-simulation and similitude. Orsina, whose name
is an anagram of *raison*,[40] conforms to what Leibniz defined as "symbolic
cognition," a form of knowledge grounded in nonmotivated, arbitrary semiosis and "characterized by a foregrounding of the signifier which at the same
time forces the signified to the periphery of awareness."[41] Emilia, by contrast, embodies what Leibniz called "intuitive cognition," a mode of thought
that operates with motivated, natural signs that are perfectly transparent to
their signifieds. In this sense these figures represent respectively the "higher"
and "lower" human faculties commonly distinguished by German Enlightenment philosophers, and their opposition demarcates an intrasubjective
conflict, not a class-based struggle between aristocratic and bourgeois values. Contrary to conventional interpretations, *Emilia Galotti* is not a tragedy
of interclass conflict. This manifests itself most forcefully in the fact that protagonists and antagonists do not fall neatly into two opposed social classes.
If there is a fundamental opposition that separates the characters into two
potentially inimical groups, then this is the distinction between head and
heart, between purposive rationality and intuitive cognition. This contrastive
semantic pair, which was central to German bourgeois thought in the eighteenth century, structures the tragic emplotment of *Emilia Galotti*.[42] Most of
the character configurations develop as modifications of this tension: the interactions between Emilia and Orsina, the Prince and Marinelli, Emilia and
Claudia Galotti, Appiani and Marinelli, and Pirro and Angelo, for example,
all represent variations on the head-heart conflict. In each of these interactions, reason attempts to seduce intuition. But the form of reason that challenges the avatars of heart is not the healthy human reason exalted by Enlightenment thought; rather, it is a narrow, instrumentalized rationality that
operates according to a means-ends logic.

The head-heart distinction crosses class boundaries in Lessing's play. Critics have often noted, for example, that the Prince embodies an emotional-
ity reminiscent of bourgeois "sentimentalism" (*Empfindsamkeit*).[43] On the
other hand, Claudia Galotti exhibits a manipulative rationality obsessed with
the strategic accomplishment of a well-defined aim: the mating of her

daughter with the most respectable social partner. This clouding of class boundaries is most evident in the figure of Count Appiani, who, although given an ennobling title, solidly represents bourgeois values and interests. Indeed, given his landed wealth, the estate in Sabionetta, even Odoardo Galotti—and consequently his family, as well—seems to be situated somewhere on the borderline between the aristocracy and the bourgeoisie. The deep-structural conflict moving the tragic events of the drama hence is not grounded in an objective sociopolitical hierarchy, as the class questions half-heartedly raised by the text and prefigured in the Virginia story would seem to indicate; rather, it stems from an intrapsychic, intrasubjective struggle that lies at the root of bourgeois thought itself. This is the sense in which we should understand Lessing's claim that in *Emilia Galotti* he depoliticized the story of Virginia's abduction. Operating according to what Theodor Adorno calls "the age-old mechanical principle of the bourgeois spirit," a principle that seeks "relief from the weakness of the ego by reifying subjective accomplishments, by putting them outside of the subject, as it were, and mistaking them for iron-clad guarantees of objectivity,"[44] Lessing's play presents a principally intraepistemic crisis cloaked as a tragedy of interclass intrigue. This explains why *Emilia Galotti* is structured throughout its first four acts as a drama of intrigue but in the final act suddenly makes a radical shift, becoming essentially a psychological drama focused on the internal conflict of the heroine.[45] Only when the play makes this transition from external to internal struggle does it arrive at its true locus; and it is this sudden twist in its emplotment—certainly another primary source of the text's ambiguities—that most convincingly discloses the web of intrigue to be an objectification of the intraepistemic, psycho-logical conflict of a bourgeois subject whose intuitive cognition is in danger of being seduced by the lures of instrumental reason. This also helps explain the otherwise intractable problem of Emilia's curiously amorphous personality and the paucity of her appearances on stage throughout the first four acts of the drama that bears her name.[46] To be sure, Lessing rebuffed this objection to his drama when it was first voiced by his brother Karl: just because the tragedy bears her name, Lessing claimed, does not necessarily mean that Emilia is its protagonist (*LW* 9: 497–98). This has led scholars to identify other characters, most notably Odoardo or the Prince, as the play's true protagonists.[47] If we assume, however, that the dramatic figures should neither be viewed as autonomous characters nor as representatives of opposing social classes, but taken instead as indices of conflicting values and epistemological systems that traverse bourgeois thought itself, then the question about the protagonist of the play becomes moot: all of the characters, in short, are aspects of the overriding and abstracted in-dividuality whose tragedy we witness. Only in the final act are these divergent struggles absorbed and focused into one single conflict: the tension between Odoardo and Emilia that ends in her death.

Orsina has a number of key functions in the structural economy of *Emilia Galotti*. As a subject rent by the split between appearance and being, she prefigures the divided subjectivity that threatens to become Emilia's fate. More important, perhaps, is that she forms a structural link between the representational strategies of service art, concretized in her portrait, and that form of manipulative reason exploited by Marinelli, whose tactics she also seeks to utilize. When Orsina craftily attempts to maneuver Odoardo into the role of her avenger, for example (see *EG* IV, vii, 299–302; 64–67), she replicates the treachery Marinelli employs in his scheme to procure Emilia for the Prince. Beyond this, Orsina also plays a central role insofar as she is the sole character who attains a critical perspective on the dramatic events. Only she truly manages to break free of the carefully spun web of ideological illusion, and this lends her the authority of a commentator whose judgments have the ring of objective verity—despite the author's attempts to discredit her by casting her in the role of the jealous woman. She thus becomes the mouthpiece of critical pronouncements with which the audience can readily identify. Who can resist applauding her, for example, when she castigates the bourgeois-patriarchal fraternity of reason whose bylaws explicitly restrict membership to men: "How can a man love something which, in defiance of him, desires to think? A woman who thinks is just as disgusting as a man who uses make-up" (*EG* IV, iii, 293; 57). More significantly, she successfully penetrates Marinelli's veil of mendacity and even threatens to expose it (see *EG* IV, vi, 297–98; 62). To be sure, she cannot be construed as the unambiguous voice of healthy reason, if only because her insights are diluted both by her passion for revenge and her treacherous attempt to transform Odoardo into the instrument of this vengeance. In its portrayal of Orsina, then, Lessing's text once again seems bent on equivocation. Still, without Orsina to enlighten him, it is questionable whether Odoardo would possess the perspicacity to assess Emilia's situation after the abduction.

ORSINA: The bridegroom is dead: and the bride—your daughter—is worse than dead.

ODOARDO: Worse? Worse than dead? But still dead all the same? Because I know of only *one* thing worse—

ORSINA: Not dead all the same. No, good father, no! She's alive, she's alive. She won't really start living until now. A life full of ecstasy! The most beautiful, the gayest life of leisure—so long as it lasts. (*EG* IV, vii, 301; 65)

Orsina exploits the rhetoric of irony to drive home the double-edged nature of that "gayest life of leisure" which Emilia would lead as the object of the Prince's pleasure. She stresses—and she speaks from experience—that this existence can only last for that brief amount of time it takes the Prince's longing for the not (yet) possessed object to be replaced by the indifference of ownership. As the Prince's mistress, Emilia's "value" will no longer be assessed in terms of autonomous self-worth but will be defined instead as a function of some Other's lack: she will become a commodity whose sole purpose is to fulfill the need of this Other.

As Lessing's bourgeois tragedy moves inexorably—if not always logically—to its violent conclusion, it is Emilia herself who takes on the role of primary instigator of her own death. The trump card she plays to convince her father of the necessity of this sacrifice is an impassioned invocation of the ineluctable power of seduction.

ODOARDO: Get hold of yourself. You, too, have only *one* life to lose.
EMILIA: And only *one* innocence!
ODOARDO: Which is above all might.
EMILIA: But not above all seduction. Might! Might! Who can't defy might? What's called might is nothing: seduction is the only real might. I have blood, my father, blood as youthful and warm as anybody's. My senses are senses, too. (*EG* V, vii, 316; *80*)

When she points to her own sensual nature, to the warmth and youthfulness of her blood, Emilia confesses her own seducibility. But to be seducible in the context of this play is not merely to succumb to the power of one's own passions; it is to capitulate to mis-guidance and se-duction (*Ver-führung*), to fall victim to di-varication in any number of forms, not the least of which is that deceptive deployment of signs that empowers Marinelli's treacheries. As the central problem of *Emilia Galotti*, seduction names that persuasive rhetorical force embodied most diabolically in Marinelli's tactic of inflating the face-values of signs to distract from their genuine significance. It is precisely this semiotic tactic that Baudrillard calls "seduction."

Seduction is that which extracts meaning from discourse and detracts it from its truth. It would thus be the opposite of the psychoanalytic distinction between manifest and latent discourse. For latent discourse diverts manifest discourse not *from* its truth but *towards* it and makes it say what it did not wish to say. . . . In seduction, conversely, it is somehow the manifest discourse, the most "superficial" aspect of discourse, which acts upon the underlying prohibition (conscious or unconscious) in order to nullify it and to substitute for it the charms and traps of appearances.[48]

Seduction is a procedure that plays up appearances at the expense of actual states of affairs, that holds onto signs rather than passing through them to what they signify. If interpretation operates by penetrating manifest discourse to discover the latent sense hidden beneath it, seduction constitutes a form of anti-interpretation, an occultation of latent sense that functions by insistently bringing one back to the literality of manifest discourse. Discursive seduction, in short, shuns semiotic transparency by stressing the materiality and mediality of signs, by exploiting the play of the signifier.

The mechanisms of this discursive seduction are prefigured in Conti's aesthetics of flattery, which, like commodity aesthetics, elevates appearance above essence. Claudia Galotti identifies the mechanics of this seduction in "the insignificant language of gallantry" in which "an act of courtesy turns into a sensation, a word of flattery into a true assertion, an idea into a wish, a wish into a design. In this language nothing sounds like everything, and in it everything is as much as nothing" (*EG* II, vi, 264; *28*). Like the aesthetic practice Conti employs in the portrait of Orsina, the "language of gallantry" exploits appearances to manipulate empirical facts; it deploys arbitrary signs to dress up and thereby conceal authentic significance. Such discourse, as Claudia correctly perceives, levels all differences into monotonous uniformity. Hence it is not in fact an *in*significant language, as Claudia supposes, but rather an *a*significant one, a language that liberates signs from their conventional (latent) significations and arbitrarily institutes (manifest) meanings. Discourse exists as an absolutized structural economy that screens out transdiscursive referentiality. What remains is the system of semiotic calculation in which signs merely become the multiple placeholders of the Same, a tale told by an idiot, signifying nothing, because signifying anything. The logic of this discourse of seduction is the same as the logic that structures bourgeois economics: the closed system of mediately established exchange-values supplants the immediacy of use-value to fuel the infinite circulation of commodities, of objects uprooted from use and directed instead toward desire.[49] *Emilia Galotti* presents the tragedy of its heroine's seduction by the discourse of abstract (semiotic) exchange, a language that strips her of everything that is originally hers and reduces her to nothing. Lessing thus depicts the drama of bourgeois self-alienation as the bourgeois subject's capitulation to a form of symbolic cognition in which signs are divorced from significance, in which structurally established values gain independence from intrinsic worth.

Emilia's seduction, her submission to the logic of commodification, is signaled already, as we have seen, when Conti reproduces her portrait and sells it to the Prince. For the latter, the representation of Emilia is but a totem that stands in for the portrayed woman: the possession of her image augurs well for the possession of the desired woman herself. Consequently, after purchasing this fetish, the Prince explicitly transfers the language of commercial transactions to the flesh-and-blood woman.

As much as he wants! (*Speaking to the picture* [of Emilia]) I got you too cheap at any price. Ah! Beautiful work of art, is it true that I possess you?—And lucky he, who possessed you as well, yet more beautiful masterpiece of nature! Whatever you want for her, honest mother! Whatever you want for her, old grouch! Just ask, just ask! What I most desire is to buy you from yourself, you sorceress! (*EG* I, v, 246; 9–10)

The concept of "buying Emilia from herself" becomes a metaphor for the seduction and self-alienation of the bourgeois subject, its subscription to the reifying process of commodification. As this scene suggests, the Prince's power does not so much reside in his political authority as in the commercial might of infinite capital, the potential to buy anything, and thereby reduce it to a masterable object.[50]

Where the Prince represents the passion and power to possess, Marinelli manifests the means that promises fulfillment of these desires. In this sense they concretize a version of the head-heart dialectic that turns out the negative underside of each term, emotion devolving into blind passion, reason into purposive rationality. The Prince's unbridled passion, in fact, makes him a perfect target for corruption by Marinelli's calculative logic that guarantees gratification. When he subordinates his authority to the manipulative will of his devious Chamberlain, the Prince essentially sells his soul to the devil of self-indulgence: "Think for me," he commands Marinelli when he discovers that his desperate need to possess Emilia may remain unfulfilled (*EG* I, vi, 251; 15). Abandoning himself to the calculations of Marinelli, the Prince childishly submits himself to a form of rational mastery simply because it promises the fulfillment of his every wish. He is thus the first character to be seduced by a reason that has been reduced to purposive rationality.

Scene three of the second act (*EG*, 255–57; 19–21), which presents the interaction between Pirro, a servant in the Galotti household, and Angelo, the robber whom Marinelli has hired to murder Appiani and abduct Emilia, at first glance appears to be but a minor interlude that shores up the motivational framework of the plot. In fact, however, it functions as a kind of parabolic reduction of the structure of self-incurred dependence that characterizes the relationship between the Prince and Marinelli. Against his own better judgment, Pirro allowed himself to be persuaded to become Angelo's accomplice in crime: he knowingly led his previous master into the hands of Angelo and his robbers. Although Pirro has come to regret this egregious offense, Angelo exploits it to extort from him a pledge not to interfere with the attack on Emilia's and Appiani's wedding coach. The scene closes with Pirro's ominous commentary on his own predicament: "Let the devil get ahold of you by *one* hair and you're his forever!" (*EG* II, iii, 257; *21*). But this scene not only reflects retrospectively on the relationship between the Prince and Marinelli; it also proscriptively outlines the interaction between Emilia and her mother, which is depicted later in the same act (II, vi). It thus builds a bridge between the Prince's accession to Marinelli, and Emilia's self-subordination to the will of her mother.

Returning from mass, where the Prince surprised her with his persistent overtures, Emilia resolves to inform her fiancé of this unpleasant encounter. Claudia convinces Emilia to suppress this confession, claiming, rather unpersuasively, that knowledge of the Prince's unrestrained affection would only slowly poison Appiani's love for her. Emilia responds by abandoning her own impulse to be forthright and acquiescing to her mother's reasoning: "You know, mother," she remarks, "how I am always glad to yield completely to your better judgment. . . . I have no will against yours. Ha! (*with a deep breath*) I'm feeling better again, too" (*EG* II, vi, 263; *27*). Freely acceding to her mother's advice, Emilia duplicates the Prince's self-subordination to Marinelli and Pirro's subjugation to the robber Angelo. Once Emilia commits herself to this act of deception against Appiani, her tragedy is irrevocable: once the devil has her by a single hair she is his forever. At this point, at the very latest, Emilia has been seduced, deflected from her own immediacy and innocence, from her spontaneous drive for verity. In effect, Emilia, much like the Prince, commits that most egregious of all offenses against bourgeois personal autonomy: she falls into that self-incurred tutelage that Kant condemned in the essay "What Is Enlightenment?" abandoning her own healthy reason and relying instead on the thought of another.[51] This implies that the initial step on Emilia's path to self-alienation occurs when she is led away (se-duced) from the vigilant eyes of her father and brought by her mother to the city. Indeed, Odoardo's suspicion that it was more than just the possibility of "a decent education" that incited Claudia to bring Emilia to town seems wholly justified (see *EG* II, iv, 258; *22*). Claudia, like the clever merchant, is determined to sell her daughter to the bidder with the most symbolic capital, and consequently she herself is "flattered," as Marinelli correctly surmises (*EG* IV, i, 286; *50*), to think that her daughter should be wooed by a prince. Claudia's social climbing thus presents a variation on the theme of calculative mastery over human subjects, their exploitation as commodities to be exchanged for one's own self-gratification and profit. She is the one bourgeois character in the play—aside from Conti in his role as service artist—who is clearly caught up in that "language of gallantry" which she, in a moment of ideological self-exculpation, projects onto the discourse of the court. Moreover, she seduces Emilia into practicing such deceit, enlisting her as an ally in the campaign of strategic misinformation directed against Odoardo and Appiani. These subterfuges ultimately prove to be essential cogs in the mechanism of coincidence that will lead to Emilia's death.

Chamberlain Marinelli is, of course, the principal figure in *Emilia Galotti* who heralds an incipient dialectic of enlightenment, the reduction of healthy reason to an instrument of cold, rational calculation employed for the purpose of mastery. Like Orsina, Marinelli is a key figure insofar as he lends a certain thematic coherence to the problematics Lessing's play addresses. An examination of some of the specific tactics that make up his treachery discloses the consanguinity of his calculative rationality with the problems of representation and semiosis raised in the Conti scenes. Indeed, Marinelli can be taken as the perfect avatar of what Foucault describes as the epistemic structure of the "Classical" or Enlightenment age, a discursive formation in which "to make use of signs . . . is an attempt to discover the arbitrary language that will authorize the deployment of nature within its space . . . , to fabricate a language, and to fabricate it well—so that, as an instrument of analysis and combination, it will really be the language of calculation."[52] Moreover, in Marinelli this analytical dismemberment and strategic reconstitution of signs and their significations is aligned with the reifying process of universal commodification.

Like the Prince, who subjects Emilia to the discourse of commerce, Marinelli speaks of the procurement of Emilia in terms drawn from the sphere of commodities and their exchange.

MARINELLI: Goods which one cannot have firsthand can be bought secondhand; and usually such goods are all the cheaper for being purchased secondhand.
THE PRINCE: Be serious, Marinelli, be serious, or—
MARINELLI: Although admittedly, for that they are also all the worse for wear—
THE PRINCE: You are getting impudent! (*EG* I, vi, 251; *15*)

This is one of those brilliant scenes that so forcefully brings home Lessing's skill as a dramatist, his ability to throw into relief in a compact dialog the intricate psychological motivations of his dramatic figures and the complexity of their interactions. This interchange derives its rhetorical impact from its ironic juxtaposition with the previous scene, in which the Prince himself referred to Emilia as a purchasable good. Marinelli thus merely makes explicit what was implicit in the Prince's own words. It is highly ironic, of course, that the Prince recognizes in Marinelli's analogy the impudence he fails to perceive in his own language. To be sure, Marinelli is aware that the metaphor of the purchasable commodity demeans the subject to which it is applied; he exploits it, in effect, to mock the Prince's sentimentalist desires. But in so doing he also exposes the Prince's passion as nothing but the passion for possession. In addition, the matter-of-factness with which Marinelli develops his metaphorical conceit betrays his own fundamental callousness: for him human subjects are indeed reducible to the alienated, depersonalized status of movable goods.

Marinelli's primary skill is shrewdness in the use and abuse of language. He is an extraordinarily modern character, given eighteenth-century standards, in that he essentially treats language as a game whose ground rules can continually be revised and redefined. For him, signs by definition have no natural signification: the relationship between signs and signifieds is motivated not by some internal relationship that establishes the adequacy of the sign to its signified; rather, it is controlled simply by willful institutions of meaning, arbitrary attributions of significance. Thus, when the Prince leads Emilia off into a room of his summer palace and commands Marinelli to follow them, the latter stays behind, assigning a contrary meaning to this straightforward imperative: "Follow us—that might mean: don't follow us!" (*EG* III, v, 281; 45). Marinelli's capriciousness is directly connected to the arbitrary use and understanding of signs. He sets himself up as the transcendental signifier, so to speak, that governs all meaningful semiosis: he randomly reinscribes the significance of signs according to his personal whims and desires.

As a play, *Emilia Galotti* is structured around a set of coincidental events that uncannily interlink to construct a logic of tragic inevitability. This overriding structure of fortuitous necessity, to express it in all its paradoxicality, in fact reflects little more than Marinelli's machinations. If from a position outside his own discourse these coincidences seem to be but chance occurrences, from within his discourse they evince the iron rule of means-ends logic. Orsina hence correctly discerns that the fatal coincidences leading up to Emilia's death are guided by some inscrutable design, although she erroneously attributes this to the workings of divine providence. "Believe me, Marinelli, the word 'coincidence' is blasphemy. Nothing under the sun is coincidence—least of all that whose purpose stares so clearly right in your face.—Almighty and gracious Providence, forgive me for having joined this foolish sinner in giving the name 'coincidence' to that which is so obviously your own doing, indeed your direct doing!" (*EG* IV, iii, 294; *58*). Due to the revelatory power of dramatic irony, we as audience are aware that what Orsina palms off on divine providence in fact derives from Marinelli's cunning. It is no *deus* who gives sense to these contingencies, but rather the *deus ex machina* of Marinelli's calculating reason. It is both fitting and ironic, then, that it falls to the deviser of these logical coincidences to equate human design and accident: "Intention and chance: it's all the same" (*EG* IV, i, 287; *51*). Indeed, given the logic of identity and exchange with which Marinelli operates, everything is in fact "all the same": the entire physical and intellectual world appears to him as malleable stuff which his mechanistic reasoning can alchemically convert at will into arbitrary meanings or desirable commodities.

What is most pernicious about Marinelli is his capacity to adulterate the objective world by tampering with signs and their significations: the exploitation of signs becomes the instrument for pitiless exploitation of the life-world. The extreme sophistication of his semiotic tactics is brought out especially well by a specific set of reinterpretations he perpetrates: his various attributions of meaning to the tone of voice in which, according to Claudia Galotti's account, the dying Count Appiani uttered the name Marinelli in his last breath. After being brought to the Prince's country mansion, Claudia recounts to Marinelli the details of the attack on the wedding carriage. Remembering the argument between the Chamberlain and the Count that transpired before her house that morning (*EG* II, x, 268–71; *32–35*), Claudia begins to sense the truth that behind the ostensible robbery lies a conspiracy against the Count authored by Marinelli. "But listen, Marquis. Marinelli was—the name Marinelli was—accompanied by a curse—no, I won't slander the noble man! Not accompanied by a curse—I'm merely imagining the curse—the name Marinelli was the dying Count's last word" (*EG* III, viii, 283; *47*).

First asserting and subsequently retracting her impression that Appiani's remark implied a curse of the Chamberlain, Claudia calls attention to the tone of voice in which this pronouncement was made, suggesting it is a sign of Marinelli's culpability. Indeed, thanks again to the window of dramatic irony, we know that this in fact is the case. Claudia's equivocation—her fear that she might simply be imputing this meaning to Appiani's statement and thus slandering a dead man—underscores the fundamental mutability of signs. Despite this doubt, however, she eventually returns to her original assertion and cites precisely the tone in which the Count expressed Marinelli's name as proof of the latter's guilt.

CLAUDIA (*bitterly and slowly*): The name Marinelli was the dying Count's last word! Now do you understand? I didn't understand it either at first, even though it was spoken in such a tone—in such a tone! I still hear it! Where was my mind that I didn't understand this tone immediately?

MARINELLI: Well, madame? I was always the Count's friend, his most intimate friend. Hence, if he named me while he was dying—

CLAUDIA: In that tone? I can't imitate it; I can't describe it: but it contained everything! Everything!—What? You think they were robbers who attacked us? They were murderers; bribed murderers!—And Marinelli, Marinelli was the dying Count's last word! In such a tone!

MARINELLI: In such a tone? Is it proper to base the accusation of an honest man on a tone heard in a moment of fright?

CLAUDIA: Ha, if I could only produce it in court, this tone! (*EG* III, viii, 283–84; 47–48)

Claudia's insistence on the tone of Appiani's voice as the index of an essential and immediate significance brings us back to the reflections on semiosis occasioned by our analysis of the Conti scenes. To understand the far-reaching significance of this exchange between Claudia and Marinelli, we must appeal to arguments made by Lessing in *Laokoön*. In this theoretical treatise he maintains that the tone of verbal expression is one of the techniques applied by the poet to lend the arbitrary signs of language the force of natural signs. "The signs of poetry [are] not purely arbitrary. Its words, viewed as tones [*Töne*], can imitate hearable objects naturally" (*LW* 5: 265). And in a letter to Nicolai in which he elaborates on the semiotic theory presented in *Laokoön*, Lessing includes tone in the list of techniques that distinguish poetry from prose. "Poetry must definitely seek to elevate its arbitrary signs to natural signs; and only on this basis does it distinguish itself from prose. The means by which it accomplishes this are tone, the [choice of] words, the order of words, meter, figures and tropes, similes, etc. All of these things bring arbitrary signs closer to natural signs" (*LW* 9: 319). Now, the last word of the dying Count, the name "Marinelli," is, taken on its own, the arbitrary sign par excellence: without the tone in which it is pronounced—without being elevated to, or lent the force of, a natural sign—this name has no meaning whatsoever, except to designate the person who is the Prince's chamberlain. Tone, as a natural sign, can supplement and underwrite the meaning of arbitrary signs. The problem, as both Claudia and Marinelli clearly perceive, is that although this tone is the bearer of all meaning, it can neither be imitated nor reproduced, and thus the original significance of Appiani's statement must irrevocably be lost to all except Claudia herself. The tone of Appiani's final pronouncement can be circumscribed in words, that is, it can be recapitulated through the employment of other *ar-*

bitrary signs, but it can never be identically reproduced *as tone,* that is, *as natural sign,* with all of its illocutionary import. To be sure, Claudia, who perceived its original expression, ultimately has no doubt whatsoever as to the significance of this natural supplement with which the arbitrary sign "Marinelli" is expressed: on the basis of this one word Claudia is able to piece together the facts about the attack on the wedding coach and the murder of Appiani.

Viewed from the perspective of bourgeois justice, of course, Marinelli is justifiably miffed that Claudia would defame his character on the basis of something as intangible as a tone of voice. The very intangibility of the evidence she holds up against him, even if for her its verity is undeniable, makes it easy for him to parry her incriminations. He begins by attempting to turn to his advantage the fact that the Count names him in his dying breath, interpreting it as a sign of their intimate friendship. Once again the audience knows from prior statements that this is a baldfaced lie (see *EG* I, vi, 248; 12); and Claudia has reason enough to suspect this as well, given the churlish exchange of words between Appiani and Marinelli she overheard earlier that same day. Ultimately, however, Marinelli exploits the very unreproducibility of Appiani's tone of voice to undercut the validity of Claudia's interpretation. His tactic, simply put, is to confront the intuitive knowledge that Claudia has culled from the natural supplement to Appiani's arbitrary verbal sign with the cognitive knowledge of reason. In a world given over to the despotism of rational proof, the immediate intuition capable of divining absolute truth from natural signs appears to produce nothing but circumstantial evidence. Thus Marinelli legitimately disputes the evidentiary value of Claudia's testimony before the court of bourgeois reason itself, especially since she herself has already admitted that she may have only "imagined" the curse in Appiani's tone of voice.

That Lessing attributed special importance to this scene and the implicit semiotic problems it sketches is demonstrated by its recapitulation, with the addition of an ironic twist, near the conclusion of the drama (V, v). Recounting for Odoardo and the Prince his interpretation of the day's events, Marinelli once again tries to misrepresent himself as Appiani's friend. In response to Odoardo's skepticism about such an assertion, Marinelli appeals both to the fact that Appiani named him in his dying breath and to the tone of the Count's pronouncement; and he cites these two facts as evidence that Appiani intended to charge him with the task of avenging his murder.

MARINELLI: Appointed by him [the Count] personally as his avenger—
ODOARDO: You?

MARINELLI: Just ask your wife. Marinelli—the name Marinelli was the dying
  Count's last word, and in such a tone! In such a tone! May it hound me forever,
  this horrible tone, if I don't use every means to discover and punish his murderers! (*EG* V, v, 310; 74)

Marinelli's seduction of authentic significations, his breaching of the immediate link between sign and significance, reaches its zenith here. Not only
does he reiterate verbatim the words of incrimination Claudia directs against
him, representing them in such a way that they come to mean the opposite
of what she intended with them, he even defends his mendacious interpretation by citing in his own defense precisely that piece of evidence—the tone
of Appiani's voice—that unmistakably proves his own guilt. Because he
knows that Claudia cannot reproduce this evidence, he feels free to deduce
from it whatever he pleases. This tactic has the added benefit that it allows
Marinelli to launch a preemptive strike against Claudia, in anticipation that
she will recount for Odoardo her own interpretation of this natural sign.
Thus Marinelli is portrayed as a shrewd spin-doctor, carefully preparing the
ground on which the seeds—the *semes*—of his corrupt misrepresentations
will grow and flourish.

   When he places tone, as natural sign, in the service of an arbitrary mis-
representation, Marinelli duplicates that strategy of dis-simulation modeled
in Conti's aesthetics of flattery: both strategically deploy natural signs to
designate arbitrary things. This is the most profound sense in which the
commodity aesthetics that Conti develops in response to the economic strictures of the service artist forestructures the calculating semiotic seduction
to which immediate intuition, embodied in Emilia Galotti, will fall victim.
Marinelli's audacious defraction of intuitive truth, his ability to cloud even
the supposed transparency of natural signification, attests to the inherent
frailty of such semiotic immediacy given the (mis)representational potency
of manipulative mediation. Marinelli thus represents the seductive logic of
heartless calculation that threatens the integrity of Emilia Galotti as embodiment of the (yet) unalienated bourgeois subject. However, this menace
does not confront the subject from without; it threatens it, rather, from
within, as a set of signifying practices inherent in the bourgeois epistemic
order. It is to this intraepistemic danger that Emilia refers when she asserts
that "seduction is the only real might" (*EG* V, vii, 316; 80). In face of the veritable omnipotence of that semiotic seduction typified by Marinelli's trans-
valuations of meaning, the immediacy and virtue to which bourgeois subjectivity pretends are factually reduced to utter impotence. Death appears
as the only avenue by which the integrity and self-identity of the subject can
be protected against its (self-)seduction by bourgeois purposive rationality.

Bourgeois Tragedy and the Genesis
of False Consciousness

My investigation of *Emilia Galotti* has pursued two principal arguments: on the one hand, I have attempted to establish the dilemma of bourgeois authorship that Lessing faced and relate it to the conflict of representational strategies pursued by the artist Conti in this bourgeois tragedy; on the other hand, I have sought to trace in the machinations of Chamberlain Marinelli, and thus in the logic of coincidence that structures the tragic development of the drama, reverberations of the semiotic and epistemic problematics raised by the Conti scenes. I now propose to interweave these interpretive strands more tightly by following up on two motifs already examined: the issue of tone as natural sign, a problem that plays a central role at certain nodal points in the text; and a pair of intratextual references that link Odoardo Galotti's attitudes toward Emilia and her tragedy to Conti's aesthetic deliberations.

The interchange between Marinelli and Claudia that turns on the tone of Appiani's dying word lays out the deficiencies of natural signification, the limitations of its immediacy and irreproducibility, especially given the potency of that semiotic mediacy practiced so skillfully by Marinelli. At the end of the fourth act, the play presents a scene with striking parallels to the exchange between Claudia and Marinelli. Again Claudia reports on an interaction she witnessed, appealing to tone of voice as the key to understanding its significance. This time, however, she is relating events to Odoardo, and the incident she is recapitulating is the interchange she has observed between the Prince and Emilia after the abduction.

ODOARDO: Does Emilia know that Appiani is dead?
CLAUDIA: She can't know it. But I'm afraid she suspects it, because he hasn't come.
ODOARDO: And she's moaning and whimpering—
CLAUDIA: Not any more. She's gotten over that now—this is her way, which you're
   acquainted with. She's the most timorous and most resolute person of our kind.
   Never master of her first impressions but, after the slightest deliberation, reconciled to everything, prepared for anything. She is keeping the Prince at a distance; she is speaking to him *in such a tone*—just see to it, Odoardo, that we get out of here. (*EG* IV, viii, 303–4; *68*; emphasis added)

In a drama literally teeming with ambiguities, this passage, which is so central to our understanding of the heroine's psychological condition, is probably one of the most ambiguous. What Lessing continually leaves open in this play is Emilia's precise reaction to the advances of the Prince. They have interacted three times: at the soirée in the house of Chancellor

Grimaldi (*EG* II, iv, 259; *23*); in the church on the morning of her wedding, where the Prince declares his love (*EG* II, vi, 262–63; *26*); and at the Prince's country mansion in Dosalo in the scene Claudia describes here. It is symptomatic of *Emilia Galotti* and its equivocalities that none of these encounters is presented directly on stage; all are simply communicated indirectly through the refracting medium of dramatic report. The only time the audience actually sees Emilia and the Prince together is in the brief encounter immediately following her arrival at Dosalo, where she appears frightened and indecisive, falling to her knees before him (*EG* III, v, 280–81; *44–45*). And yet it is precisely these scenes, hidden from our immediate perception, that hold the answer to one of the principal questions the play poses: does Emilia in fact resist the advances of the Prince, or is she perhaps touched by his seductive charm and/or flattered that she has attracted his attention?[53] In the cited scene, Claudia ostensibly asserts the former. On the other hand, reporting the meeting with the Prince at the church, Emilia herself suggests that she experienced a desire to sin—although she then retracts this admission on the insistence of her mother (*EG* II, vi, 261; *25*). Moreover, the speed with which Emilia recovers her composure after experiencing the robbery and the death of her fiancé throws open the question of whether she has not discovered in the Prince a pleasant diversion from her sorrow. And even Claudia's depiction of Emilia in the cited scene is equivocal, as indicated most clearly by the apparent contradiction between the two qualities she ascribes to Emilia, "timorousness" and "resolution." Given this apparent contradiction, we might be tempted to suspect that Claudia is actually hedging when she alleges the steadfastness of her daughter, afraid, perhaps, to voice her true fears directly to Odoardo—whose "austere virtue," after all, Claudia has already severely criticized (*EG* II, v, 260; *24*).

This hypothesis is confirmed by the curious manner in which Claudia's attitude shifts over the course of her remarks, moving from the confident assertion that Emilia can hold her own against the Prince, to an urgent and emotional appeal for Emilia's immediate rescue. It is no coincidence that this transition in Claudia's attitude turns on her recollection of the tone in which she overheard Emilia speaking with the Prince. We as audience, like Odoardo, are unfortunately not privy to Emilia's tone of voice, since we do not actually witness her dialog with the Prince. If Lessing had presented this scene on stage, instead of relegating it to mediated report, we could presumably read for ourselves the natural sign of Emilia's tone of voice, inferring from this a reliable conclusion about her psychological state. Instead, we find ourselves in a position analogous to that of Odoardo in this scene, or of Marinelli in the exchange with Claudia that turns on the interpretation of Appiani's dying word: since the natural signs that would resolve any uncertainty cannot be mediately reproduced, we can only speculate more or less arbitrarily about their possible significance. Thus, this scene not only underscores the inherent limitations of natural signification, it maneuvers us as interpreters into a position in which we must experience these limitations in our own interpretive practice. In our attempts to reconstruct those natural signs that the drama only presents to us mediately through their reconstitution in dialog, we come to realize that this immediate verity simply cannot be *re*-presented, *re*-produced, *re*-iterated: the immediacy that is its virtue also constitutes its practical inadequacy. If truth can ultimately only be found in immediately perceived natural signs, then its site, Lessing implies, is somewhere *beyond* linguistic discourse, outside of symbolic cognition.

This conclusion is inconsistent neither with Lessing's theoretical reflections on semiotics, nor with his conception that drama is the highest form of literature precisely because it supplements the arbitrary signs of symbolic discourse with the immediacy of dramatic presentation. In his letter to Nicolai from May 26, 1769, Lessing remarked: "The highest genre of poetry is that which transforms its arbitrary signs wholly into natural signs. This is, however, the dramatic genre, for in it words cease to be arbitrary signs and become *natural* signs of arbitrary things" (*LW* 9: 319–20). Now, in *Emilia Galotti* Lessing not only valorizes such natural signification as the only adequate index of intuitive verity, he also indicts it for its practical insufficiencies. The symptom of this indictment is the fact that in this play those crucial interchanges between Emilia and the Prince are banished from immediate dramatic portrayal. Thus while Lessing, in his theoretical remarks, recognizes that the potency of the dramatic genre depends on its capacity to signify immediately and naturally, to recreate on stage the immediacy of human experience, in his bourgeois tragedy *Emilia Galotti* he undermines this potency, refusing to exploit it when it is most crucially needed. It is this deficiency, which amounts to a practical violation of Lessing's own theoretical insights into the efficacy of the dramatic genre, that ultimately accounts for the intrinsic equivocality of this bourgeois tragedy. This is the point, finally, at which we come to fathom how the semiotic undercurrents that run through so much of this play are connected with the inadequacies of its own aesthetic execution. If *Emilia Galotti* circles in its dramatic plot around coincidence as that intuitive verity whose site in the play's developmental logic is marked solely by an apparent logical gap, then as dramatic work this text is also structured around certain key incidents that Lessing refuses to fill out with the plenitude of dramatic portrayal, relegating them instead to the mediacy of narrative account.

The tragedy of Emilia Galotti evolves as a conflict of representational systems, each underpinned by its own semiology. On the level of plot this manifests itself concretely in the fact that Emilia is caught in a tug-of-war between two groups who attempt to enforce heteronomous definitions upon her. The major axis of this struggle runs between the Prince and Odoardo Galotti, of course, with Marinelli functioning as the Prince's second, while Appiani serves as Odoardo's ally. We have considered the attempted alienating commodification of Emilia perpetrated by Marinelli and the Prince in considerable detail. We must now turn to an investigation of Odoardo's vested interests in Emilia and their role in the play's tragic conclusion. We can approach this issue by examining two utterances Odoardo makes near the conclusion of the drama, remarks that allude to pronouncements made by Conti in his aesthetic reflections. These intratextual references support the thesis that the conflict of representations sketched in the Conti scenes has its parallel in the conflicting representations of Emilia held by the parties who struggle to define and master her.

We have seen that in his comment on Raphael's artistic genius Conti dissociates aesthetic intuition from artistic practice, asserting that Raphael would have been a great artist even if he had been born without hands. Odoardo echoes this remark when he finds himself unarmed in the presence of his daughter's abductor. "Here I am now standing in front of the robber's den. (*Opening his coat on both sides and seeing he is unarmed*) It's a wonder that in my haste I didn't leave my hands behind, too!" (*EG* IV, vii, 301–2; 66). If Conti's image of a Raphael without hands is intended to distinguish aesthetic intuition from artistic practice, then Odoardo's unwitting allusion to Conti's remarks suggests that this same distinction holds for him as well, transported, of course, from the aesthetic realm into the sociopolitical domain. The image of an assassin without a weapon invokes the idea of a revolutionary who rejects all concrete political praxis while harboring revolutionary designs in theory. But Odoardo's comment evinces more than just the self-willed political impotence of the German bourgeoisie; it marks a fundamentally broader, specifically ideological reflex in which appeal to intangible ideas, values, and moral scruples excuses passive acquiescence to given sociopolitical conditions. On this level, Conti's and Odoardo's statements mirror the principal refusal of the bourgeoisie to bring its actual social, political, economic, and aesthetic practices into line with the ideals it propagates. Disjunction between critical insight (intuition) and accommodation to the real (practice) thus forms the ideological web in which the constitution of the bourgeois subject takes place. Emilia, as placeholder for what the bourgeois subject suppresses in its everyday practice, is hence caught between capitulation to the real—adaptation to the expediencies of mediation, instrumental reason, abstract (semiotic and economic) exchange, and commodification—and assertion of the ideal—the upholding of virtue, self-identity, and individual autonomy.

Only by ideologically suppressing the (self-)alienation and violence inherent in its own sociopolitical, economic, and signifying practices, and by projecting its own will to mastery onto objectified others such as the Prince and Marinelli, can the bourgeois subject valorize itself as a virtuous and autonomous individual existing in intersubjective harmony both with the natural world and with other monadic subjects. When Odoardo fails to use the dagger on the Prince, the seducer and commodifier of (female) subjects for whom it is intended, turning it instead against his own daughter, the object of the Prince's seduction and commodification, he implicitly throws his support behind the forces of alienation and mastery. Odoardo refuses to strike a blow against the principles that the Prince and Marinelli represent; indeed, he himself becomes their accomplice insofar as he commits the ultimate act of violence against Emilia's subjectivity. The Prince's lust and Odoardo's murder, as it were, both reduce Emilia to a soulless mass of flesh. By demonstrating that he ultimately holds control over Emilia's very life and death, Odoardo merely asserts the priority of his claim on her, thereby coming away with a victory in his personal duel with the Prince. When he "breaks the rose before the storm can rob it of its petals" (*EG* V, vii–viii, 317; 81), he merely supplants the tyranny of passion (the Prince) and calculative rationality (Marinelli) with the despotism of the bourgeois patriarch's ideology of virtue. However, this preemptive strike, intended to rescue bourgeois virtue and integrity, can accomplish its purpose only at the price of destroying the concrete subject who is supposed to be the bearer of these values. The murder of Emilia Galotti thus marks the ideological dialectic of bourgeois subjectivity, its valorization of self-identity and autonomy as theoretical principles or intuitive truths, and the simultaneous denial of these principles in the brutality that characterizes, in practice, its interaction with the autonomous subject.

For Odoardo, as for the Prince and Marinelli, Emilia is but a pawn to be strategically deployed in the *bellum omnium contra omnes* that characterizes human relations in the socioeconomic and political life-world depicted in Lessing's drama. Odoardo never truly considers Emilia to be an autonomous subject; indeed, he defines her solely in relation to others: to himself, to her fiancé, and to her potential seducer—all men, of course. In this sense, Emilia is never anything but a (female) satellite forced into orbit around different (male) suns. That Emilia's fate concerns Odoardo primarily for selfishly ego-

centric reasons is brought out well in the scene in which Claudia recounts
for him the Prince's fascination with Emilia.

CLAUDIA: Haven't I told you yet that the Prince has seen our daughter?
ODOARDO: The Prince? And where did that happen?
CLAUDIA: At the last soirée at the Chancellor Grimaldi's, which the Prince honored
    with his presence. He acted so graciously toward her—
ODOARDO: So graciously?
CLAUDIA: He conversed with her so long—
ODOARDO: Conversed with her?
CLAUDIA: Seemed so enchanted by her liveliness and her imagination—
ODOARDO: So enchanted?
CLAUDIA: Spoke of her beauty with such high praise—
ODOARDO: High praise? And you're telling me all this *in a tone of delight*? Oh, Clau-
    dia! Claudia! You vain, foolish mother!
CLAUDIA: What do you mean?
ODOARDO: All right, all right! That, too, is over with now. Ha! Even the idea—that
    would be precisely the place where I can be most mortally wounded! (*EG* II, iv,
    259; 23; emphasis added)

Odoardo is justly vexed by the tone of delight with which Claudia relates
the Prince's infatuation with Emilia: he clearly understands that this tone,
as natural sign, expresses all too adequately Claudia's "vain" and "foolish"
ambition to see Emilia enter into a union with the Prince. The fact that, on
the very day when Emilia will be wed to another, Claudia finds delight in
this vision underscores that she, too, merely sees Emilia as a tool for her
own self-gratification: the favor her daughter receives from the Prince reflects favorably on Claudia as her mother. Odoardo accuses Claudia of precisely this when, earlier in the same scene, he admonishes her not to "con-
fuse [her] own delight in [Emilia] with [Emilia's] happiness" (*EG* II, iv, 258;
22). However, even for Odoardo himself the fear of Emilia's seduction is not
his first thought when he learns of the Prince's admiration; instead he expresses concern for *his own* vulnerability: he views Emilia merely as a vehicle through which he himself "can be most mortally wounded" by his com-
petitor. Emilia is thereby reduced to the status of an adjunct to her father's
subjectivity; she is that unprotected appendage of his self that he feels is
most vulnerable to attack. Odoardo's anxiety over Emilia's virtue thus is unmasked as pure self-absorption. In essence, then, his interest in Emilia is
every bit as self-serving as is the Prince's or Claudia's: all three are united by
their attempt to define Emilia as a trump card to be played out at a strategic moment in their competing games of self-gratification.

The inimicality between the Prince and Odoardo Galotti is not grounded in political strife, but rather, as indicated early in the play (*EG* I, iv, 243–44; 7), in their rival claims to ownership of the estate in Sabionetta. Their struggle over Emilia evolves as an extension of this proprietary conflict. As her father, Odoardo defends, as it were, his squatter's rights to Emilia. When his daughter comes of age and he must forgo his monopoly on her, he agrees to Appiani's friendly takeover. However, once this merger has been prevented and Odoardo is faced with the Prince's hostile takeover attempt, he destroys the object of their dispute rather than let it fall into the hands of his rival. On this level, his interests in Emilia are no different than those of the Prince: his aim is simply control of, and mastery over, what he considers to fall within his dominion, even if this means its extinction. When he applies overblown rhetoric to defend Emilia's virtue, Odoardo is merely inflating the currency in which he measures the value of his own assets. His murder of Emilia turns out the vicious underside disguised behind patriarchal love, exposing the destructive drive implicit in his—as well as the Prince's and Marinelli's—will to manipulate and exploit the natural world. A bourgeois King Midas, Odoardo—in this respect quite similar to Marinelli—kills whatever he touches by translating it into the discourse of abstract values.

The parallelism between the Prince's and Odoardo's perspectives on Emilia is brought out clearly in the second intratextual allusion that links Odoardo's attitudes to the problematics sketched in the Conti scenes. We recall that in the soliloquy he delivers after purchasing from Conti Emilia's portrait, that "beautiful work of art," the Prince confesses his desire to "own" Emilia herself, this "more beautiful masterpiece of nature" (*EG* I, v, 246; 9–10). In the penultimate scene of the play—the same scene in which Emilia is killed—Odoardo echoes these words of the Prince, himself identifying Emilia—and woman in general—as the "masterpiece of nature." "I've always said it: nature wanted to make woman its masterpiece. But it erred in the tone, it made her too delicate. Otherwise everything about you is better" (*EG* V, vii, 315; 79). This passage forms a nexus that intertwines some of the principal motivic threads of Lessing's text. First of all, the idealization of Emilia in particular, and of woman in general, that Odoardo articulates here replicates that process of idealization described by Conti in the context of his portrait of Emilia. Moreover, where Conti bemoaned the inability of any aesthetic practice to adequately reproduce Emilia's beauty, Odoardo now transfers this insufficiency to nature itself: nature, like the artist, inevitably "errs," falls short of its ideal, even when it is creating its most perfect "masterpiece." Odoardo thereby conjures up once more the disjunction between intuition and practice that marks the ideological moment of bourgeois thought. What is more, he legitimizes this false consciousness, which rec-

ognizes perfectibility but resigns itself to the flawed condition of the given
(sociopolitical, economic) life-world by hypostatizing it as a law of creation
itself: human imperfection is excused as an error in nature, a fatal flaw to
which human beings can only respond with passive acceptance. Emilia's seduction—which, after all, is the product of human design—is once again
made to appear the result of providence or a coincidence of nature. The
bourgeois subject thereby exculpates itself from any responsibility in her—
and by extension, in its own—oppression.

Significantly, nature's defect resides specifically in the *tone* in which it creates its masterpiece. Throughout Lessing's tragedy, the word "tone" marks
that complex of semiotic questions concerned with the relative authenticity and governability of signification. As the natural supplement to arbitrary
(visual or aural) signs, inimitable tone represents the intuitive guarantee that
validates the adequacy of signs to their significations. Throughout *Emilia
Galotti* the valorization of such semiotic immediacy as the essence of truth
is coupled with the negative insight into its practical deficiencies. Odoardo
now provides an explanatory commentary on this inadequacy: nature itself
is imperfect in its representations, in its concretizations of the ideal. There
is, then, no absolute immediacy in the natural world; rather, immediate perception, like perfect aesthetic intuition, is an unattainable ideal. Consequently, one must resign oneself to mediacy; indeed, one can even affirm it
as the way of (fallible) nature. In the final analysis, then, the tragedy depicted
in *Emilia Galotti* is the tragic necessity of mediation: that Raphael was born
with hands; that Emilia is a sensual being with warm blood; that the soul
requires the vehicle of the body to exist in nature; that significance must be
codified in signs; that aesthetic intuition must be concretized as artistic work,
and hence as (potential) commodity; that the immediate presentation of
drama must pass through the ciphers of textual signs; that the bourgeois
subject is not simply an autonomous monad but is inscribed within a concrete life-world; that theory can never free itself of the demand for praxis.

Odoardo's statement accomplishes one further important thing: it draws
the line of conflict that runs through this tragedy as one of gender. His idealization of women has the tacit function of segregating them, as the "you,"
from men, as the "we." Moreover, Odoardo's statement implicitly aligns him
with Marinelli and the Prince, both of whom are well acquainted with the
inner sanctum of power. This hierarchization establishes women, in the words
of Julia Kristeva, as "an *Other* entity, which has no value except as an *object
of exchange* among members of the *Same*."[54] To be sure, this marginalization
is accompanied by the idealization of women as the "masterpiece of nature,"

unfortunately still flawed; and Odoardo maintains that this sets them above men. But to be included in the club of the Same, as Orsina correctly recognizes, is to employ reason—that is, to calculate, to manipulate, to mediate, and thus to corrupt and seduce. It is those principles perfected in Marinelli, in other words, that define Odoardo, the Prince, and the Chamberlain as members of the Same. The marginalization of women thus comes to represent the marginalization of the bourgeois subject's own ideals: they are left only with the options of capitulation and adaptation to the structures of calculative rationality—as in the cases of Orsina and Claudia—or acquiring the status of pure ideals that have no place in, and are therefore banished from, the practical life-world—the fate that befalls Emilia.

As tragedy, *Emilia Galotti* concludes structurally in its penultimate scene, which depicts the physical violence against Emilia that has been inscribed in the logic of the play from the very beginning. But this bourgeois tragedy is drawn out specifically into the tragedy of bourgeois subjectivity by the addition of a final scene in which, while Emilia melodramatically expires, the three male principals who have fought over her possession throughout stand gathered around their collective victim. The addition of this appendix, which plays no integral role in the structural economy of the play, seems to have the function of creating a space within which these three men could infer some lessons from Emilia's tragic end and reflect on their own culpability. However, anyone who expects Emilia's murderers to arrive at self-critical enlightenment is sorely disappointed. Far from owning up to their individual and/or collective roles in this calamity, each points the finger at the other, so that Lessing's drama ends as a kind of merry-go-round of self-exculpation.

ODOARDO: Well now, Prince! Do you still like her [Emilia]? Does she still excite your desires? Still, in this blood, which cries for revenge against you? *(After a pause)* But you're waiting to see how all this will end? Perhaps you expect that I will turn the blade against myself and crown my deed like an empty tragedy? You're mistaken. Here! *(Throwing the dagger at his feet)* Here it is, the bloody witness to my crime! . . .

PRINCE *(after a period of silence while observing the body with horror and despair, to Marinelli)*: Here! Pick it [the dagger] up.—Well? You're hesitating? You good for nothing! *(Ripping the dagger from his hands)* No, your blood is not to be mixed with this blood. Get out, and disappear forever! [*Geh, dich auf ewig zu verbergen!*] (EG V, viii, 317–18; 82)

Odoardo, the actual perpetrator of Emilia's murder, assigns the responsibility for this deed to the Prince. Although Odoardo admits the obvious, namely that he indeed has killed Emilia, he exonerates himself by claiming that the intrigue of the Prince and Marinelli has forced his hand. Odoardo refuses to turn the knife against himself—that is, to accept his guilt—because that would reduce his action to "empty tragedy." But significantly, he also fails once more to use the knife against the Prince. The Prince, in turn, responds to Odoardo's incriminations by passing them along to Marinelli. However, after first encouraging the Chamberlain to use the knife on himself, the Prince then takes it away from him. The Prince, Odoardo, and Marinelli all survive the dagger that at different junctures seems poised to destroy them. What is more, Marinelli, the treacherous mediator, the scheming manipulator of signs, the spinner of a web of rational calculations, the arbiter of abstract exchange—the concentrated embodiment, in short, of all those principles that have resulted in Emilia's death—is admonished merely to "disappear," to "conceal himself" ("sich verbergen") forever. No direct attack is launched, in other words, against these principles themselves; they are spared, as are the men who exploit them, from feeling the thrust of the dagger. In the end, then, neither Marinelli nor the seductive might he represents are truly cast off; they are simply covered over, driven from the overt into the covert. This occultation marks the inception of the dialectic of bourgeois enlightenment, the reversion of bourgeois self-consciousness into ideological false consciousness.

While *Emilia Galotti* unfolds many of the hazards inherent in bourgeois epistemic structures and their concretization in sociopolitical, economic, and semiotic practices, thus potentially preparing the way for a purging bourgeois self-critique, it succumbs to a moment of ideological self-legitimation that undercuts this critical thrust. The calculations deployed by the bourgeois subject's own purposive rationality and the alienation that results from its total commodification of the life-world are either hypostatized as the divinely ordained if flawed order of the natural world—theodicy—or projected outside of bourgeois consciousness itself onto straw men like Marinelli and the Prince, where these principles can be safely attacked as corruptions whose sources lie beyond bourgeois subjectivity itself. In Lessing's play the death of Emilia Galotti signals this ideological constitution of bourgeois subjectivity. What makes Lessing's tragedy ultimately into bourgeois tragedy, a depiction of the tragedy that constitutes bourgeois subjectivity, is that it demonstrates the inability of the bourgeoisie to salvage its own ideals as anything other than pure, intangible theories. As the idealization of the feminine turns dialectically on the concrete extermination of women, the ideal of the self-identical, self-determined, and autonomous bourgeois individual survives merely as an etherealized ideal, an ideal that disguises, moreover, the fact of the bourgeois subject's capitulation to self-division, heteronomy, and self-commodification, its accession to a form of reason that has been reduced to calculative, purposive rationality.

In the examination of Friedrich Schiller's *The Robbers*, which forms the focus of the next chapter, I will attempt to outline the epistemic and semiotic sources of the conflict of representational systems that, according to Lessing's play, marks the inception of bourgeois tragedy.

CHAPTER THREE

Righting Writing

Semiotic Conflict, Hermeneutical Disjunction, and the
Subl(im)ation of Revolt in Schiller's 'The Robbers'

Your holy signs, oh Truth, have been usurped by deceit.
—Friedrich Schiller

Revolution as Conflict of Semiologies

In his "archaeology of the human sciences," *The Order of Things*, Foucault
plots three epochs in the history of Western culture, distinguishing them on
the basis of their characteristic epistemological paradigms (epistemes) and
their essential semiologies.[1] Deliberating on the evolution of the institution
of literature in the eighteenth and nineteenth centuries, he suggests that literature's autonomous status in the bourgeois age derives from its preservation of a superannuated semiology discordant with that which dominates
bourgeois thought in general. Modern literature "achieved autonomous existence, and separated itself from all other language with a deep scission,
only by forming a sort of 'counter-discourse,' and by finding its way back
from the representative or signifying function of language [characteristic of
Western thought since the Classical age] to this raw being that had been forgotten since the sixteenth century."[2] Three aspects of this theory hold out
promise for investigations into the evolution of the institution of autonomous bourgeois literature in Germany in the final decades of the eighteenth century: Foucault's insistence on the semiological dimension as that
realm in which autonomous literature attains its self-constitution; the implied historicizing thesis which suggests that autonomization occurs when
literature "finds its way back," that is, historically re-turns, to a semiotic
mode antecedent to the paradigm shift to Classical (Enlightenment)
thought; and Foucault's assertion that in the counterdiscourse of modern

literature, language escapes the merely representational function to which it is reduced in Classical thought.

As Manfred Frank has recently maintained, the inherent weakness of Foucault's historical archaeology rests in its veritable antihistorical obsession with genealogical formations of history to the total exclusion of the processes or mutations that might account for the transformation from one paradigm to the other.[3] The methodological paradox inherent in Foucault's archaeology, although he insists on "ruptures" and "discontinuities," is that he focuses primarily on the stable epistemological formations that take shape before and after such ruptures. This problem looms all the larger given Foucault's desire to theorize history as a set of structural transformations conceived as the architectural ground plan according to which the subject and its practices are constructed. What Foucault's analyses ignore, as his metaphor of archaeological "strata" indicates, are the breach-points, the ruptures that mark the transformation from one episteme to another. Foucault's historical archaeology thus needs to be supplemented by a theory that, departing from the telos of the Hegelian-Marxian model of revolution, attempts to define the space of discontinuity between epistemic paradigms as the locus of revolution.

This critique applies to Foucault's implicit archaeology of literary history as well. Although one might quibble with his identification of Hölderlin's poetry as the first manifestation of a truly autonomous and semiologically other literature, one can scarcely deny that a major paradigm shift takes place in German literature between about 1770 and the first decades of the nineteenth century. The literary and philosophical texts of the Sturm und Drang mark the transition between two relatively stable epistemic formations: the representational literature of the German Enlightenment, on the one hand, and the absolute literature of early German modernism, on the other. What interests me here is not the indisputable fact of such a transformation, but the nature of the historical struggle within the institution of literature that accompanies this modulation from the Enlightenment paradigm of representation to the pure autonomy of literary modernism. On the example of Lessing's *Emilia Galotti* we have seen how the awareness of intellectual upheaval manifests itself as a conflict between two competing representational systems, and how the literary text itself evolves as a product of this antagonism. This drama, it should be noted, exerted considerable influence on the young writers of the Sturm und Drang generation, largely because the dilemmas that produced this bourgeois tragedy reflected their own intellectual predicament.[4] Literary historians have tended to take the writers of the Sturm und Drang to task, condemning them for their political ambivalence and viewing them either as failed revolutionaries or adolescent rebels without a cause.[5] However, this critique is grounded in a teleological and subject-centric conception of revolution, modeled either on conditions in revolutionary France or borrowed from Marxism and retrospectively projected onto the German bourgeois revolution. This perspective has skewed our interpretation of this generation and the historical epoch in which they lived and wrote. By contrast, I suggest approaching this era with a different notion of revolution, considering it, and the literature it produced, in terms of a fundamental epistemic conflict, a struggle between two competing epistemological paradigms of which the human subject is primarily an agent, not an initiating, creative, revolutionary subject in the traditional sense.

In his contribution to the *Yale French Studies* volume, *Literature and Revolution*, Jacques Ehrmann theorizes a structural conception of revolution that locates it at the fault-line between two antagonistic conceptual systems. "Revolution is subjectless. The true subject of revolution is history. . . . Revolution is situated at the juncture of two histories, appearing as the moment when the relationships between politics and history become disjointed for lack of a suitable language to articulate these relationships, and also for lack of a language (that is, a symbolic conceptual system) fit to articulate reality."[6] Ehrmann's reflections are basically consistent with Foucault's conception of historical "strata," but they point to a more dynamic configuration that is better rendered with the metaphor of the fault between two continental plates, a metaphor that stresses the factors of tension, resistance, and conflict at work at the juncture of two "histories." Such a conception of revolution, it seems to me, can fruitfully be applied to the incipient bourgeois era in Germany and especially to the writers of the Sturm und Drang. Employing Ehrmann's conception of revolution as a subjectless structure of epistemic conflict makes it possible to comprehend the contradictions so prevalent in the literature of the Sturm und Drang as the effects of an epistemological struggle to which these bourgeois intellectuals as subjects are subjected, and to which they attempt to formulate critical responses. It is historically anachronistic, at best, and historically naive, at worst, to expect these writers to possess an autonomous subjectivity that stands over against and can freely shape their given sociohistorical conditions. In fact, as subjects they exemplify that dialectical self-division to which Hegel gave the name of Unhappy Consciousness. In this sense the waffling for which they have so often been condemned should be understood as the irrevocable expression of their own intrasubjective strife. Modifying Heinrich Heine's famous dictum, one could maintain that since the subjectivity of these poets stood in the middle of the intellectual-historical world, it could hardly help but be torn in two by the rupture that ran through this world.[7] This does not mean, however, that as subjects these bourgeois literati were mere passive marionettes whose actions were dictated by structural configurations. On the contrary, their literature must be read in terms of their response to the experience of epistemic rupture, a response that pursues an identifiable course of reaction against the sociohistorical circumstances endemic to the emerging bourgeois world.

A further aspect of Ehrmann's reflections seems especially relevant to a reinterpretation of the revolutionary features of the Sturm und Drang: this is his notion of the revolutionary period as one characterized fundamentally by a struggle for articulation that evolves out of the conflict of competing and inimical discourses. Viewed from such a standpoint, the near-obsessive reflections on language proffered by this generation, including their concern with issues of semiotics and the process of signification, as well as the characteristic verbal flailing about of their dramatic characters, take on added significance. The literature of the Sturm und Drang can be productively understood, as I hope to show on the example of Schiller's inaugural drama *The Robbers* (1781), as the product of a discursive conflict that manifests itself as the struggle between two competing semiologies.[8]

In his late drama *Nathan the Wise* (1779), Lessing depicts his protagonist facing the recognition that in the modern world two systems of understanding and expression, each of which articulates its own "truth," contest one another. In his audience with the Sultan, Nathan is taken unawares when, expecting to be petitioned for a loan of money, he is asked instead to make a statement of absolute truth. Before responding with the famous parable of the three rings, Nathan deliberates on this request in a trenchant monolog:

> I thought of money;
> And he wants—truth. Yes, truth! And wants it so—
> So bare and blank—as if the truth were coin!—
> And were it coin, which anciently was weighed!—
> That might be done! But coin from modern mints,
> Which but the stamp creates, which you but count
> Upon the counter—truth is not like that!
> As one puts money in his purse, just so
> One puts truth in his head? (*Nathan*, 402; 74)

Challenged to a statement of truth in a situation with potentially menacing personal and political ramifications, Nathan recognizes that he must choose between two distinct forms of truth, the "ancient" and the "modern." His

reaction when confronted with this choice is typical of bourgeois intellectuals of the eighteenth century in Germany: he dodges an unequivocal commitment to either of these modes of truth by taking refuge in literature, nar-
rating the parable of the three rings. The struggle of opposing systems of
understanding, especially in a context rife with sociopolitical implications,
is sublated and sublimated in a literary discourse that attempts to walk a narrow line between these mutually exclusive systems.

The comparison of language and coin, which Lessing employs to enun-
ciate this clash of rival discourses, occurs frequently in texts of this period,[9]
and it resounds almost a century later in Nietzsche's analogy of language's
well-worn metaphors to coins whose symbolic inscriptions have been
rubbed away with use.[10] This metaphor implies that Nathan's conflict of
truths is essentially an antithesis between diverse systems of value. In ancient times the currency used to measure worth had its own inherent value,
established intrinsically by the preciousness of the material—gold, silver—
that represented value; in the modern age, by contrast, value becomes extrinsic and systemic. It no longer resides in the material through which it is
expressed but has become instead purely symbolic—the paper currency that
feeds the economic expansion of the bourgeois age. Lessing's contemporary,
the French economist Turgot, formulated this distinction in his *Reflections
on the Formation and Distribution of Wealth* (1766), asserting that "gold and silver [are] constituted money, and universal money, and that without any arbitrary agreement among men, without the intervention of any law, but
only by the nature of things. They are not, as people imagine, signs of value;
they have a value in themselves."[11] Turgot's valorization of specie over paper currency is formulated in terms reminiscent of those in which eighteenth-century intellectuals, including Lessing in his *Laokoön*, championed
natural signs over arbitrary signs. Turgot insists, first of all, that it is in the
nature of specie to possess a certain value, and that this value hence is independent of any arbitrary human conventions. Moreover, he denies that
specie represents value as a sign represents a signified, maintaining instead
that it is what it signifies. This is analogous to the idealization of natural signs
as a transparent, nonsymbolic mode of signification in which, as we saw in
our examination of Lessing's deliberations on the ideal form of semiosis,
sign-intuition and signified-intuition are perfectly synchronous. Both conceptions attack symbolic mediation and appeal for a return to a relationship
of immediacy. The exaltation of specie and the glorification of natural signs
both manifest a protest against representation, against a symbolic order like
that of Foucault's Classical age, in which signs come to stand in for what is
nonpresent.[12]

Herder's *Treatise on the Origin of Language* (published 1772) is a central intellectual-historical document from this period precisely because it specifically focuses this denunciation of modernity as a critique of language. Following Rousseau, Herder imagines a historically prior, utopian state of existence characterized by immediacy, authenticity, and an intimate bond both among human subjects and between these subjects and their life-world. Contrasted with this ideal, the modern age appears as a state of degeneracy in which immediacy has been lost.

The most heroic deeds of the human spirit, which it could only produce and express in engagement with the living world, have become school exercises in the dust of our pedagogical dungeons; the masterpieces of human literature and oratory have become childish trifles through which senile children and young children learn phrases and cull rules. We seize upon their formalities and have lost their spirit; we learn their language but do not feel the living world of their thoughts.[13]

The common denominator of these laments is the diagnosis of a process of human (self-)alienation: substance is displaced by rules and formalities, spirit by letter, thought by language, immediate interaction with the life-world by second-hand experience derived from books. For Herder this state of affairs crystallizes around a basic modern misunderstanding of human language. This conflict between mediate understanding and immediate perception manifests itself for him, as for many of his contemporaries in France and Germany alike, in the dichotomy between dead letter and living word, textual mediation and immediate verbal expression. Indeed, the condemnation of writing so prevalent at this time is but a vehicle for a more general critique of symbolic mediation, which is perceived as the root of human alienation.

One of Herder's primary aims in the *Treatise* is to deny that human language exists primarily and originarily as a communicative, intersubjective medium that binds human beings together. Indeed, interhuman communication already represents for him an estrangement from language's authentic expressiveness. "Least of all is it [language] agreement, *an arbitrary convention of society*. The savage, the hermit living alone in the forest, would have had to invent language for himself, even if he had never spoken it. It was an *agreement of his soul with itself*, and just as necessary an agreement as it is necessary that man is man."[14] This campaign against any merely sociopragmatic conception of language's development links Herder's thought with more general tendencies throughout Europe at the time. His assault on arbitrary conventions, for example, is formulated in words reminiscent of Turgot's critique of paper money. Just as Turgot valorizes specie as a currency in which value is guaranteed intrinsically, Herder seeks a definition of language as a "currency" in which truth is vouchsafed by some intrinsic relation between expression (sign-use) and the human "soul." Thus Herder discovers language's originary purpose neither in its representational function, its ability to depict things by becoming their symbolic proxies, nor in its appellative function, its role as an intersubjective link, but rather specifically in its expressive function.[15] As expressive system, language testifies solely to the integrity of the human spirit (soul) and its emotive expression in signs. Herder's theory of the origin of language hence can be read as a symptom of what Foucault describes as the attempt by (literary) discourse to find its way back from language's representational function to its forgotten "raw being."[16] Herder designates the aim of such a return as the (re)discovery of a discourse in which "soul" and "expression" are intrinsically one. Language in this form—and for Herder this is its primordial form—operates as an external signature of the speaker's internal sentiments: it bears testimony to the integrity and autonomy of the speaking subject. Herder condemns the breach of this symptomatic function, the estrangement of expression from the immediate and essential experiences and emotions of the speaker, as the cause of modern humanity's sense of alienation.

Herder's disavowal of language as a system of arbitrary conventions expresses precisely that skepticism about symbolic cognition and mediative signs that underwrote Lessing's insistence on natural semiosis as the ultimate aim of all the arts. In our examination of the semiotic questions raised in *Emilia Galotti* we saw that for him, as for Herder, the expressive function of the sign circumscribes a realm of primordial signification in which human sign-use is integrally bound up with internal character. Both of them defend what we might call a physiognomics of language, and it is no coincidence that Johann Kaspar Lavater's physiognomical theories, which are structured around the same semiotic principles, were tremendously popular throughout Europe at this time. Lessing gives this expressive form of semiosis the name "moral semiotics." The telos of Lessing's semiotic theory—the reinstitution of a natural system of signs as one of the fundamental goals of German Enlightenment culture[17]—appears in Herder's theory as the demand for a return from the degenerate language of convention to one of genuine expression. There is, then, a principal similarity between the Enlightenment view of language, especially when viewed semiologically, and the conceptions of the Sturm und Drang. This continuity easily passes unnoticed if one belabors, as traditional literary history has tended to do, those aspects of the Sturm und Drang that evolve as a protest against enlightened reason in its most schematic forms. Below the surface these movements are unified by the utopian, philosophic-historical dream of infusing the cultural world with the immediacy of the natural world, of (re)attaining a state of being in which signs are immediately comprehensible and in which hermeneutics, as a science of interpretation, consequently becomes superfluous.

The common thread of Schiller's aesthetic projects is precisely this impulse toward the nostalgic return to, and recovery of, a lost state of immediacy. For Schiller, as for Lessing, the sphere of aesthetics appears as that redemptive medium through which culture must pass if it is ever to recover lost nature. There is a fundamental semiotic undercurrent that runs through Schiller's deliberations on the redemptive function of aesthetics, one that links his theories with Lessing's aesthetic reflections. The aim of this chapter is to establish Schiller's awareness of what I have described as a conflict of semiologies and to position his aesthetic program within this fault-ridden intellectual-historical terrain. This will serve as the backdrop for my examination of *The Robbers*.

Schiller's Sentimental Redemption of the Naive as Semiotic Re-Turn

If, as John Frow claims, the "sentimental redemption of the naive" represents the prototypical strategy of modernist literature, then Schiller, like the Stürmer und Dränger in general, is the modernist par excellence—and not merely because he authored the terminology that makes this definition possible.[18] Indeed, Schiller's entire literary-aesthetic project, from the rebellious early plays to *On the Aesthetic Education of Man in a Series of Letters* (1795) and *On the Naive and Sentimental in Literature* (1795) and beyond, can be characterized as a critical rejection of the devolving contemporary world in favor of a nostalgic return to the lost origin of an authentic, unalienated, and immediate existence. Schiller defines the "sentimental" poet, in fact, as a seeker after lost nature (*Naive*, 712; 35). But even as late as 1803, in the essay "On the Use of the Chorus in Tragedy," Schiller still formulated the task of the modern tragic poet as the retrotransformation of the "modern common world into the ancient poetic [world]," and his attack on the contemporary age continues in these characteristic and telling terms: "The palace of the kings is now closed, the courts have retreated from the gates of the cities into the interior of houses, writing has displaced the living word, the people [*Volk*] itself . . . , where it does not simply effect cruel violence, has become a State, that is, a concept" (*SW* 2: 819–20). The poet's mandate is to reverse these circumstances, to restore the immediacy that has disappeared from the practical interaction between individuals and the life-world, to undo the

processes of abstraction, internalization, and privatization that have transformed the interactive community of the *Volk* into the monadic, modular
subjects of the modern State. It is significant that Schiller reduces this juxtaposition of the ancient and the modern to the dichotomy between "living
word" and "writing," the conceptual dyad that became a shorthand for the
critique of alienation with this generation of writers.

Schiller's aesthetic redemption of the naive is marked by the dilemma
that, in order to attain the promised land of originary immediacy, transparency, and authenticity, the artist must accept and make accommodations
with the givenness of humanity's alienated condition. This project can thus
be termed revolutionary only if, following Baudrillard, we define revolution
as "planned reversal."[19] Schiller conceived his aesthetic theories as guidelines
for a return to genuine human dignity. This aesthetic redemption of humanity turns on the paradox that the ultimate renunciation of dissimulation
can only be accomplished by exploiting dissimulation in the form of aesthetic semblance. "Humanity has lost its dignity," Schiller writes in a celebrated passage from the ninth letter of *Aesthetic Education*, "but Art has rescued and preserved it *in significant stone* [*bedeutenden Steinen*]; Truth lives on
in the midst of deception, and from the copy the original will once again be
restored" (*Naive*, 594; 52; emphasis added). The crisis of modernity, if we take
Schiller at his word, is the crisis of the human counterfeit: humanity has lost
its original value, has become a counterfeit of itself. But art preserves the
last genuine copy of human dignity, from which the original can and will be
restored. Implied in Schiller's metaphor of "significant stone" is a conception of aesthetic discourse as a hieroglyphic tablet, that is, as a durable if yet
illegible text that preserves an enigmatic mode of signification in which truth
hibernates, so to speak, waiting to be decoded and to announce with the
reappearance of its authentic meaning the return of an unalienated, im-me-
diate humanity. The "significant stone" of art preserves an alternate semiotic order whose code has been lost to the modern world. This semiotic undercurrent runs throughout much of Schiller's thought on an almost subliminal level; turning out the semiological lining in some of his theoretical
statements on aesthetics exposes precisely the degree to which Schiller, like
many of his contemporaries, conceived the *querelle des anciens et des modernes*
as a fundamental conflict of semiologies.

Reflections from "Theosophy of Julius," part of the "Philosophical Letters" Schiller composed in conjunction with his friend and mentor Christian Gottfried Körner—a work whose conception, like that of *The Robbers*,
goes back to Schiller's final years at the academy in Stuttgart—suggest that
even at this early date Schiller discerned two different epistemological sys-

tems whose distinctness was attributable to their reliance on divergent semiotic relations. Early in his theosophical deliberations, Schiller's Julius formulates a conception of the symmetry between the physical, objective world
and the internal realm of the human soul, a conception that reads like an extension of Lavater's physiognomical semiotic, allowing it to encompass all
of nature as the signifying material that gives expression to the human soul.

Every condition of the human soul has some parable in physical creation by which
it is signified; and not only artists and poets, but even the most abstract thinkers
have drawn from this storehouse. Lively activity we call fire; time is a stream that
rapidly flows on; eternity is a circle; a secret is cloaked in darkness; and truth is like
the sun. Yes, I am beginning to believe that even the future fate of the human spirit
is announced beforehand in the obscure oracle of physical creation. (*SW* 5: 345)

The external, organic world takes on the role of a secondary phenomenon:
it exists as the perceptible metaphorical vehicle that lays bare the impercep-
tible tenor of the human soul; it is the external signature of the internal
world of the human spirit, and what binds these two spheres together is a
tertium comparationis revealed by the power of analogy. For Foucault it is precisely this principle of similitude, the analogical understanding of the visible as a sign for the invisible, that defines the semiotic of the Renaissance
episteme.

The face of the world is covered with blazons, with characters, with ciphers and
obscure words—with 'hieroglyphics'. . . . And the space inhabited by immediate
resemblances becomes like a vast open book; it bristles with written signs; every
page is seen to be filled with strange figures that intervene and in some places re-
peat themselves. All that remains is to decipher them. . . . The sign of affinity, and
what renders it visible, is quite simply analogy.[20]

Foucault goes on to make two points about this iconic semiotic that are relevant to the arguments pursued here. He stresses, first of all, the relative un-
productivity of this mode of cognition: "By positing resemblance as the link
between signs and what they indicate," he writes, "sixteenth-century knowledge condemned itself to never knowing anything but the same thing."[21]
This epistemic structure represents a closed system of pre-given identities,
and the task of knowledge is limited to uncovering these hidden affinities by
applying the principle of similitude. This semiotic, then, is not concerned
with the discovery of the new, but only with the affirmation of the given. It
is not linear and utilitarian, like Classical thought, but circular and confor-
mative. Second, this iconic semiotic does not discriminate between natural
and cultural orders (of signs), between world and word. "There is no difference between marks and words in the sense that there is between observa-

tion and accepted authority, or between verifiable fact and tradition. The process is everywhere the same: that of the sign and its likeness, and this is why nature and the word can intertwine with one another in infinity, forming, for those who can read it, one vast single text."[22] Schiller's Julius valorizes this interweaving of world and sign as the originary oneness of divine creation. He thus invokes a state of human existence that antedates the breach between "living word" and "writing," between natural and cultural signs, between reality and text. The quasi-oracular semiotic vision articulated by Julius in his theosophical meditations projects one version of that idealized norm against whose standard of truth the semiological order of the modern world falls infinitely short.

While he apparently subscribes to just such a quasi-oracular relationship between the visible world as sign and the human spirit as its signified, Schiller's Julius is simultaneously able to formulate a thoroughly modern semiotic theory, one which, structured around arbitrary signs, stands in stark contrast to this iconic-parabolic theory.

Our entire knowledge is ultimately based, as all the wise ones of the world concur, on a conventional illusion through which, nonetheless, the most rigorous truth can be sustained. Our purest concepts are by no means *pictures* of things, but rather merely their necessarily determined and coexistent *signs*. Neither God, nor the human soul, nor the world are really what we take them to be. . . . But the power of the soul is singular, necessary, and eternally self-identical: the arbitrariness of the materials through which it expresses itself does not change anything about the eternal laws according to which it expresses itself, as long as this arbitrariness is not in contradiction with itself, as long as the sign remains completely true to its signified. In the same way as the power of thought develops the relations among idioms, so must these relations really be present in the things themselves. Hence truth is not a characteristic of idioms, but rather of deductions; it does not subsist in the similarity of the sign with its signified, of the concept with its referent, but rather in the agreement of this concept with the laws of thought. (*SW* 5: 355–56)

In this passage Schiller's Julius displaces significance from the adequation of sign and referent into the logical structures that establish congruency between sign-relations and states of affairs; he explicitly subscribes to a theory of conventionality and arbitrariness as a way of explaining the linkage between expressive signs and their referents. However, he admits that this conventionality is a deception, although one which, nonetheless, is capable of sustaining the most rigorous truths. Abstract signs, according to this view, are incommensurable with the intellectual or physical objects to which they refer; signs are not re-presentations, similitudes of the objects they signify, but symbolic proxies whose representational function is vouchsafed by "eternal laws" that are themselves extrinsic to the relation of signification. "God," "soul," and "world"—indeed, all referents—acquire the virtual unattainability of the Kantian thing-in-itself. The principle of adequation, as the condition of possibility of veritable signification, is replaced by a structure of relationality, the coincidence of "concept" with the "laws of thought" or with the "necessary" self-identity of the power of the "soul." Schiller, in this regard a precursor of the logical positivists and the early Wittgenstein, thus articulates a paradigmatically modern—if yet rudimentary—conception of a formal or structural model of truth in which verity is guaranteed by the conformity of expression with certain eternal (logical or rational) laws. Nothing could deviate more from the substantivist, iconic semiotic grounded in similitude propagated earlier in the same essay, and the rather confounding side-by-side of these two semiologies in one and the same text is symptomatic of Schiller's intellectual-historical position on the fault-line between two antagonistic epistemic orders.

The proximity of Schiller's conventional semiotic grounded in formal-structural relations to modern semiological thought is brought out further by the examples he provides to elucidate his conception. He cites, interestingly enough, the ability of mathematics to calculate, on the basis simply of signs on paper, the future appearance of a comet, as well as the daring of the explorer Columbus, who traverses uncharted seas in the conviction that the laws of logic guarantee that reality will conform to his conceptual map of the world. Both of these examples highlight the purposive and instrumental function of this type of thought: this structural, logical, and conventional semiotic permits productive, projective calculation on the basis of unchanging and infallible rules. What Schiller outlines, in fact, accords well with the symbolically mediated semiotic of the Classical age as described by Foucault.

In the Classical age, to make use of signs is not . . . to attempt to rediscover beneath them the primitive text of a discourse sustained, and retained, forever; it is an attempt to discover the arbitrary language that will authorize the deployment of nature within its space, the final terms of its analysis and the laws of its composition. It is no longer the task of knowledge to dig out the ancient Word from the unknown places where it may be hidden; its job now is to fabricate a language, and to fabricate it well—so that, as an instrument of analysis and combination, it will really be the language of calculation.[23]

The coexistence in Schiller's early thought of the modern symbolic semiotic of arbitrariness and calculation with the superseded iconic, reiterative semiotic points to the fundamental equivocation he shares with many of his contemporary bourgeois intellectuals. The nostalgia for an iconic semiotic in which the adequacy of signifier to signified is immediately guaranteed by resemblance is the persistent symptom of a skepticism and deep-seated uneasiness on the part of these thinkers about the modern bourgeois episteme. If they were among the first bourgeois intellectuals to gain insight into what has come to be called the dialectic of enlightenment,[24] then this critical awareness was grounded in fundamental perceptions about the semiotics of bourgeois exchange and the potential repercussions of this structural-conventional system of value when transported to the realms of human interaction and moral conduct.

In *On the Naive and Sentimental in Literature* Schiller again addresses this semiological problematic; in this instance, however, he does so to valorize the iconic semiotic, which he identifies with the genius endemic to the naive mode of cognition. Contrasting naive thought and expression with the logic and grammar of "the academic mind" ("Schulverstand"), Schiller's reflections culminate in a juxtaposition of the semiotic relations that govern these conceptual systems.

If there [in the case of the academic mind] the sign will always seem of a different kind from its signified, then here [in the naive mode of thought] language springs from the idea as through inner necessity and is so much at one with it, that even underneath the corporeal covering the spirit stands revealed. This kind of expression, where the sign completely vanishes in the signified and where speech leaves the thought which it expresses as it were naked, *while the other type can never represent it without at the same time concealing it,* this is what in style one calls above all inspired and the work of a genius. (*Naive*, 706; *30*; emphasis added)

Naive cognition is characterized by a remainderless conjunction between signifier and signified: the signifier (language) is produced by the signified (thought), not vice versa. Moreover, the process by which the signifier is produced derives from internal necessity. Semiosis, in other words, consists in a relation of self-determination, self-identity, and immediacy whereby the signified naturally and organically, as it were, gives birth to its expressive signifier. Schiller's language in this passage makes amply clear that the noncommittal juxtaposition in "Theosophy of Julius" of a substantive iconic semiotic and a formal-structural semiotic of manipulative control has given way to a firm hierarchization. Iconicity finds its rightful place in the counterdiscourse of "naive" art, while instrumentality is condemned as a symptom of "academic" thought or bookish erudition ("Schulverstand"). The rules of logic, held up by Schiller's Julius in the earlier work as the basis of correspondence between thought and world, are condemned in the later treatise as the cross on which words and concepts are crucified: "The academic mind, always afraid of a mistake," Schiller remarks, "nails its words, like its concepts, to the cross of grammar and logic" (*Naive*, 706; 30). But more stinging than this rhetorically charged incrimination is Schiller's critical assessment that "academic" thought functions in terms of a dialectic between transparency and concealment. Thus Schiller ultimately reduces the distinction between naive semiosis and "the cross of grammar and logic" to the dichotomy between transparency and opacity, the same oppositional pair that informs the semiotic theories of German Enlightenment thinkers. Naive cognition is auto-nomous: the signifier "vanishes" into the signified, leaving it "naked" and thus im-mediately perceptible. By contrast, "academic" cognition, which Schiller explicitly associates with "representation," is hetero-nomous: it only attains expression at the price of concealing, that is, of displacing, what it signifies. Representation by means of hetero-nomous, arbitrary, or conventional signs is thus inextricably caught up in a dialectic of disclosure and enshroudment in which expression necessarily entails occultation. This moment of concealment not only clouds the desired transparency of truth, but also opens up an ungovernable, unpoliceable blind spot in the logic of representation. There is no manifest guarantee that signs, as arbitrary proxies, truly represent what they are supposed to signify. This blind spot is identified as the site of deception and potential manipulation, of illusion, no longer conceived in the positive sense of aesthetic semblance, but rather understood in the negative sense of treacherous delusion.

Schiller's early drama *The Robbers* raises questions about the compatibility of the iconic and the modern, structural semiotic. In the confrontation between the two brothers Franz and Karl Moor, Schiller plays out the struggle between these two epistemic paradigms, between the deceptive mediacy of "academic" thought (Franz) and the immediacy of naive cognition (Karl). In this drama Schiller exposes the practical insufficiency of the naive semiotic in a life-world increasingly dominated by calculation, arbitrariness, abstract exchange, and economically legitimated deceit. Although he concedes the practical inferiority of an iconic semiotic in an open contest with instrumental reason, however, Schiller attempts simultaneously to remedy this condition. He seeks a resolution to the conflict of semiologies, in other words, that will protect naive semiosis against the dissimulations of calculative rationality. His ultimate pedagogical aim is to initiate a process of "planned reversal" by which human thought will be returned from the mediacy of the "academic mind" to the immediacy and transparency of naive genius. The solution he proposes is the institution of a divided subjectivity that preserves naive semiosis in an autonomous inner sphere, while surrendering its external, societal self to the mediative semiotic of bourgeois purposive rationality. His own aesthetic practice in this "dramatic novel," as he termed *The Robbers*, which fuses dramatic immediacy and the mediative reflection of the written / read text, is fashioned as a corrective to the arbitrariness of abstract, manipulable, and manipulating signs.

Semiotic Conflict and Hermeneutical Disjunction in *The Robbers*

> The written word and things no longer resemble one another. And between them, Don Quixote wanders off on his own.   —Michel Foucault

In the preface to the first edition of *The Robbers*, Schiller characterizes Karl Moor as a "strange Don Quixote" whose ideals and "enthusiastic dreams of greatness and effectiveness" are smashed by prevalent conditions in the "unideal world" of the time (*SW* 1: 486). I propose to take this assertion literally and construe Schiller's protagonist as a direct descendant of the naive, idealizing fool, Don Quixote, who, taking the superseded books of chivalrous romance at their word, sets out on an absurd campaign in which the banal reality of the life-world is confronted with the ideality of the written word. Schiller's allusion clearly suggests that the problematics of reading and the adjudication of written text with existing social, cultural, and political conditions—the "conditions of bourgeois society" ("bürgerliche Verhältnisse"), as he refers to them in his preface (*SW* 1: 486)—are central to this drama.

In his ground-breaking essay on the function of letters in Schiller's early plays, Oskar Seidlin situated the conflict between the brothers Franz and Karl in *The Robbers* in the linguistic realm, describing it as the struggle between two distinct conceptions and uses of language. Written texts, specifically letters, are associated throughout the drama with Franz, who, as Seidlin points out, exploits the distance between the writer of such messages and their readers, setting himself (and others) up as "intermediaries and middlemen" who manipulate and falsify the original messages.[25] Franz capitalizes, in other words, on the moment of concealment Schiller diagnosed in the representational dialectic of modern semiosis. As self-established mediator between Old Moor and Karl, father and son, Franz, the veritable incarnation of the abstract, heteronomous sign, controls and distorts their relationship. By strategically deploying written signs, Franz, the paradigmatic corruptor, manages to disrupt even the blood relationship between father and favorite son.[26]

Schiller made no secret of the fact that Franz was intended to represent the negative potentials inherent in the enlightened and modern tendencies of the age. In his "Self-Review" of the play, Schiller identifies the reasoning underpinning Franz's "system of vice" as "the result of enlightened thought and liberal study" (*SW* 2: 627). Franz thus embodies the qualities of the "academic mind" that Schiller would later castigate in *On the Naive and Sentimental in Literature*. Schiller underscores the modernity of the material treated in *The Robbers* when he objects to the plan of Wolfgang von Dalberg, the director of the Mannheim theater who first staged the play in 1782, to transpose the dramatic action into the Middle Ages. Schiller notes that Franz and certain other characters in his play are, in his own words, "too enlightened, too modern" (*SB* 1: 45–46), and that they hence would appear anachronistic in this historical displacement. He realizes, in short, that to dramatize his play in any other time but the historical present would be as absurd as retrocontextualizing Cervantes's *Don Quixote* in the era of chivalry: the entire structure of the dramatic conflict, which is predicated precisely on the opposition between modern reality and the naive ideals of the past, would thereby collapse. In *On the Naive and Sentimental in Literature* Schiller describes the collision between the innocence of naive thought and the depravity of the contemporary world in terms of just such a quixotic disjunction.

A naive way of thinking can, therefore, never be a characteristic of corrupt people but only of children and of people of childlike disposition. These last often act and think in a naive way in the midst of the artificial relationships of the great wide world; because of their own noble humanity they forget that they are dealing with a depraved world and even at the courts of kings behave with an ingenuousness and innocence such as is only to be found in a pastoral world. (*Naive*, 702; 26)

Karl's "childlike disposition" and "noble humanity" appear as dysfunctions given the "artificial relationships" characteristic of human interaction in the "depraved world."

Because commentators on *The Robbers* have tended to interpret Karl as a tragic hero rather than a comic figure in the tradition of *Don Quixote*, they have generally failed to fathom the direction and thrust of the critique of modernity he voices. Even Seidlin prevents his own insights from bearing real fruit by attempting to force Karl into the mold of the tragic hero, viewing Karl's "decision [!] . . . to fuse sign and meaning into immediate and self-evident communication" as an act of tragic hubris.[27] Such a critique sides with the corruptions of Franz and fails to perceive the marginalization of Karl's naive semiotic as a threat. If Schiller criticizes his protagonist, it is certainly not because he relies on a naive semiotic, the same semiotic Schiller himself later defended and explicitly associated with poetic genius; rather, it is the insufficiency of this semiotic principle in the context of a world given over to the manipulative power of semiotic mediacy and arbitrariness to which Schiller calls our attention. As a result of this crucial misreading, Seidlin goes on to interpret Karl's ultimate reconciliation with the law of the land, whose hypocrisy he has otherwise attacked, as a renunciation of "his heroically sinful insistence on directness" and as the symptom of his "acceptance of the communicative sign."[28] Karl's resignation thus becomes resignation in a more specific sense: he is "re-signed," that is, re-oriented and re-integrated into the bourgeois order of mediative signs. But such a re-signing interpretation has the effect of completely stripping the revolutionary impetus away from this work, making out of a utopian project of "planned reversal" a drama of conciliation with, and capitulation to, the principles represented by Franz and the rest of the semiotic counterfeiters in this "depraved world." Karl's submission, in other words, would signify the surrender of the ideal of naiveté, the enemy of dissimulation, to the paramount power of dissimulation. Such a conclusion is not only out of keeping with the parameters of this play, but also inconsistent with the aesthetic-pedagogical project Schiller pursued in different ways over the course of his entire life.

Karl Moor's position with regard to written texts is from the outset a paradoxical one. His famous first words, "I'm disgusted by this ink-smearing century when I read in Plutarch of great men" (*Robbers* I, ii, 502; *35*), establish a number of fundamental points about his character and his assessment of the contemporary life-world. His position vis-à-vis the present historical conditions is one of outspoken inimicality, grounded in his assertion of the degeneracy of this age in contrast to a past ideal. Most important, perhaps, is that the measure Karl employs to gauge this discrepancy between past ideal and present reality is the contrast between their modes of textuality. He does not play off writing against speech, as do, for example, Rousseau and Herder,[29] and even Schiller himself in other instances; rather, he juxtaposes one kind of writing, Plutarch's *Lives*, to the type of texts proliferating during his own time.[30] This nuance is of crucial importance, especially since Schiller defends his own reliance on the textual medium for the composition of this very drama. The valorization of Plutarch's *Lives* as an authentic form of textuality over against the degenerate writing that proliferates in the modern era probably derives from Rousseau's remark in *Confessions* that Plutarch cured him of his dependence on popular novels,[31] and it thus points to the incipient bifurcation within the bourgeois literary institution of two distinct endeavors, serious literature, on the one hand, and the popularized literary commodity, on the other. This phenomenon, as Christa Bürger has argued, is a side effect that accompanies the subjection of literature to the bourgeois marketplace.[32] The distinction Karl draws between the "ink smears" of modern textuality and the genuine writing of Plutarch's *Lives* is thus essentially one between disingenuous textual commodities, whose authors are incapable of immediate identification with the conjunctures they relate—Schiller's example is a "consumptive professor" who holds "lectures on *vitality [Kraft]*" (*Robbers* I, ii, 502–3; *35*)—and genuine textualizations whose authority is guaranteed by the authors' immediacy to, and identity with, their subject matter. This intimate connection must be grounded either in direct personal experience or, in historical investigations such as Plutarch's, in a projective hermeneutical empathy that conjoins authorial character with the subject that is related. Literary quality thus comes to be defined in terms of a coherence and integrity between authorial character and its textual manifestation, an idea that implicitly appeals to bourgeois moral conceptions. In his review essay of a volume of poems by Gottfried August Bürger, Schiller explicitly elucidates this self-identity of authorial spirit and its artistic expression by comparing it to the coincidence of character and action in the domain of ethics. "The same is true for aesthetics as is true for morality: just as for the latter it is solely the morally excellent character of a human being that gives his individual actions the stamp of moral goodness, so also for the former it is only the mature, the consummate spirit from which the mature, the consummate flows" (*SW* 5: 972). What Schiller formulates here can be termed a physiognomy of aesthetic creation, for he imputes an immediate and necessary connection between the "character" of artistic expression and the essential "character" of the authorial personality: literary-aesthetic value arises when texts emerge as immediate and unfalsifiable signatures of their author. This theory points once more to Schiller's proximity to the thought of Lessing and Herder, who define the expressive or symptomatic dimension of language as the locus of truth and authenticity.

All would be well with Karl Moor if he were to act and interpret in accordance with his own theoretical insights into the disingenuousness of modern life and its textual products. Unfortunately, this is not the case, and the fundamental paradox of Karl's character is grounded in the disjunction between this theoretical insight and his practical inability to recognize inauthentic texts and interpret them appropriately. Karl shares this interpretive gullibility, as we shall see, with Old Moor and Amalia. But to condemn the interpretive incompetence of these figures as improbable and artificial, as critics have tended to do,[33] is to pass over the very conflict that Schiller seeks to examine. It is precisely the inadequacy of a naive, iconic semiotic when confronted with the manipulative and deceitful practices made possible by the intermediative semiotic of modernity, mastered by such beguilers as Franz and Spiegelberg, that Schiller's drama throws into relief. Franz's dissimulations catapult the play's naive protagonists into a pervasive state of hermeneutical confusion precisely because their idealizing mode of cognition does not permit them to interpret messages other than as perfect similitudes of authorial essence. Karl, Amalia, Old Moor, and even Kosinsky are successfully marginalized in the "ink-smearing century" because their semiotic expectations, and, as a consequence, their hermeneutical practices, are out of touch with dominant tendencies. However, Schiller's drama not only presents a protest against such marginalization; it also initiates a kind of problem-solving search for a means to remedy this situation. *The Robbers* seeks a solution, in other words, that will permit figures like Karl to preserve and protect the counterdiscourse of iconic semiosis from the encroachments of semiotic inter-mediacy and its all too effective corruptions of meaning.

Franz, as representative of this inauthentic inter-mediacy, functions primarily as an alienator of meanings: he exploits the distance between authorial expression and its codification in written signs, on the one hand—interference in the symptomatic functioning of language—and distorts the connection between scriptive symbols and their interpretations, on the other—disruption of the appellative linguistic function. He interferes, in other words, both in the productive and receptive dimensions of semiotic-communicative transfer, and in this sense he embodies those socially grounded mechanisms of "systematic distortion" that, according to Jürgen Habermas, disrupt and displace any naive and immediate hermeneutical interchange.[34] Despite his awareness that such systematic distortion is typical of communicative exchanges in the modern world, Karl proves to be a hermeneutically naive reader, and it is this interpretive maladroitness, not simply Franz's willful corruptions, that calls forth the misunderstandings underpinning the dramatic plot. Karl's reading of the letter from home in the second scene of the play reveals his interpretive naiveté with regard to written expression, his own inability to recognize in this letter a paradigmatic example of the hypocritical and mendacious textuality he has just vehemently attacked. Karl's initial words of response upon seeing the letter, "My brother's hand!" (*Robbers* I, ii, 508; 42), encapsulate the irony of his interpretive gullibility: while correctly recognizing Franz's "hand" as the author of the written symbols, he fails to perceive Franz's "hand," his devious authorship, in the substance of the message itself.[35] What Franz communicates as his father's "very words" (*Robbers* I, ii, 509; 42) are in fact Franz's own, as we as readers know based on the discrepancy between this message and the actual statements made by the father in the previous scene (see I, i, 449; 31–32). Dramatic irony thus places us in a position superior to that of Karl and discloses to us his fateful misinterpretation. Karl falsely concludes on the basis of this letter "in his brother's hand" that his father has rejected his repentant plea for forgiveness, and he goes on to accuse his elder of love-lessness and hypocrisy. Karl's inability to understand Franz's misrepresen-tation of the father's attitude is predicated on a fundamental principle of the naive hermeneutic with which he operates: the supposed transparency of the mediative sign. Because Karl assumes that Franz is playing the role of a simple, transparent, noncorrupting communicative intermediary between him and his father, he fails to apprehend that this mediation brings with it intentional obfuscations and distortions. For Karl, true to Schiller's concep-tion of a naive semiotic, mediative signs should be purely transparent trans-mitters of authorial expression; hence it is Karl's gullible reliance on this ide-alized semiotic of immediacy, his failure to penetrate the moment of occul-tation in the dialectic of representation, that allows Franz's distortions to pass unnoticed.

Karl's misreading, although understandable given the parameters of his thinking, elicits a series of ironic effects. For one, it prevents him from fol-lowing up on his resolution to abandon his misguided intrigues in Leipzig and return home to an authentic existence. His diagnosis of this deviant be-havior as the product of a disjunction between speech and genuine senti-ment is consistent with his indictment of the modern age in general, whose representative he obviously understands himself to have become: "My heart knew not the vain things my tongue spoke" (*Robbers* I, ii, 506; 39), Karl as-serts in self-condemnation when Spiegelberg reminds him of their roguish exploits. But his resolve to unify the sentiments of his heart with the ex-pressions of his tongue is dissolved after reading Franz's letter. Only at this point of total disillusionment does Karl succumb to Spiegelberg's sugges-tion that they form a band of robbers. The most bitter irony, perhaps, is that with this move Karl fulfills Franz's earlier prophecy that his brother will be-come the leader of a band of highwaymen (see *Robbers* I, i, 496; 28). Indeed, what makes Franz's deceitful mediations so pernicious is that they ultimately proliferate those principles of self-alienation around which his conceptual system is structured. Not only does he succeed in changing the image the father has of Karl, as well as the image Karl has of his father, making each believe that the other has succumbed to the hypocrisy so rampant at this time; he actually maneuvers Karl into a position, through the treacherous manipulation of mediated signs, of carrying on an existence that is out of keeping with his own desires and his essential character. In his monolog of protest against his father, Karl unwittingly evokes the transmogrifying power of Franz's calculating semiotic: "When blood kinship [*Blutliebe*] turns traitor, when a father's love becomes a raging fury," he exclaims, "oh, then catch fire, manly resignation, become a furious tiger, gentle lamb" (*Robbers* I, ii, 514; 48). Convinced that his father's love has somehow been perverted, he takes this conviction as legitimation for his own conversion from "gentle lamb" to "furious tiger." Thus ultimately one must ascribe to Franz's calculating, enlightened semiotic veritable alchemical powers: reality conforms to the manipulative might of his words, his arbitrary signs take control over and master their signifieds.

Amalia, too, suffers calamitous defeats when confronted with Franz's (textual) deceptions. In a scene that closely parallels in its substance and images the depiction of Karl's misinterpretation of the letter from home, Amalia likewise falls victim to one of Franz's textual hoaxes (see *Robbers* II, ii, 529–33; 64–68). Franz sends Hermann, disguised as one of Karl's military comrades, to Amalia and Old Moor to report the fiction that the beloved son, hounded by his father's curse, has died in battle. Franz's aim is twofold: on the one hand, he hopes to torture his father by foisting upon him the responsibility for Karl's death, thereby accelerating the old man's end; on the other hand, he hopes to win Amalia by convincing her that Karl's dying wish was to unite her with his surviving brother. Amalia at first sees through this subterfuge, correctly identifying Hermann as a "vile deceiver" who has been "bribed" to lie (*Robbers* II, ii, 531; 66). She is finally persuaded of Karl's death only when Hermann produces two pieces of concrete evidence supplied by Franz: the bloody sword, which, according to convention, proves that a soldier has fallen in battle, and a portrait of Amalia that Karl is supposed to have given Hermann before his death. To the convention of the bloody sword Franz adds a characteristic twist: he forges a text, written putatively by Karl with his own blood, in which the dying hero bequeaths Amalia to his brother. Amalia is duped by this rather obvious ruse into believing that Karl's "hand" has authored the bloody text: "God in Heaven!" she exclaims, "it is his hand,—He [Karl] never loved me!" (*Robbers* II, ii, 532; 67). Convinced that this counterfeit text was written by Karl, Amalia draws a false conclusion about his sentiments toward her. She thus replicates Karl's spurious condemnation of his father in the parallel scene that portrays his misreading. Like Karl, Amalia has faith in the transparency of signs, and she thus fails to detect the distortions effected by Franz's mediation. Amalia's error, however, is more severe than Karl's; for while he at least correctly recognized

Franz's signature in the written symbols, she fails even to recognize Franz's rather blatant forgery. Her mistake is excused, of course, by the fact that Franz has miraculously produced some overwhelmingly convincing evidence, not least of which is the portrait of Amalia that Karl carried with him.

Although it is easy to cite the improbability of this scene as testimony to Schiller's literary immaturity or to attribute it to carelessness, it seems more instructive from an interpretive standpoint to analyze the possible text-strategic impulses that might have motivated such improbability. We must assume either that Schiller's reasons for implementing such farfetched devices outweigh the logical deficiencies they entail, or that improbability itself is a strategic device that calls attention to specific motivic complexes addressed in the play. The latter hypothesis, indeed, seems to apply in this instance. It is no coincidence, first of all, that Franz supplies a portrait to support his assertions, since throughout the play portraits function as symbols representing the guarantee of resemblance, the voucher that underwrites the iconic semiotic employed by the drama's naive protagonists. Second, the portrait is associated throughout the play with Karl as an emblem of his insistence on immediate communication, whereas the epistle and its manipulable mediacy is connected with Franz. The portrait, which "is what it represents" and thus "appears as the seal and voucher of genuineness,"[36] is skillfully exploited by Franz in this scene: it vouches, so to speak, for the genuineness of the counterfeited Karl that Franz seeks to bring into circulation. If throughout *The Robbers* hand and portrait are the vouchers of intrinsic genuineness, in the scene in which Amalia is deceived by Franz this deception is predicated on his ability to counterfeit both. His success, improbable as it may seem, thereby underscores two complexes we have already examined: on the one hand, it testifies once more to the overwhelming, near-alchemical powers of Franz's cunning, his ability to produce practically at will convincing if yet counterfeit signs; on the other hand, it stresses Amalia's reliance on the semiotic of similitude and underscores the insufficiency of this conceptual pattern, given the distortive capacity of Franz's semiotic counterfeits, as a hermeneutical strategy.

The problematic of naive misreading is augmented by a further dimension as this scene develops. Finally convinced that Karl has died, Old Moor asks Amalia to read him the biblical story of Jacob and Joseph. At the point in her narration where the jealous sons produce Joseph's bloody garment as evidence of his death, Franz suddenly leaves the room, only too aware that the deceit perpetrated in the biblical tale is the perfect similitude of his own deception (see *Robbers* II, ii, 534; 70). But the guileless interpreters fail to draw the analogy between the biblical parable and the reality of their own circumstance: Old Moor and Amalia take the parable merely as confirmation of Karl's death, instead of understanding it as a key that will unlock the prison of Franz's hoax. Shortfall of interpretation, predicated on an innocence that prevents penetration of the simple face-values of textualizations, is the common denominator of all these examples of misreading.[37] This single failing leads to divergent results, however, depending upon whether the interpretive object is an example of genuine textuality such as the Bible, or a disingenuous, inter-mediary textual commodity such as Franz's forgeries. In the latter case their misprision causes the naive interpreters to take fiction for fact; in the former case they fail to recognize the analogical factuality of fiction, that is, to comprehend the profound relevance of the authentic, noncommodified (biblical) text as a similitude of their actual situation. This suggests that in an age dominated by "counterfeiters of truth" (*Robbers* II, iii, 553; 90), it has become impossible adequately to distinguish genuine from counterfeit texts. Schiller does not repeatedly expose the interpretive incompetence of these naive readers merely to condemn their gullibility; he is concerned, rather, with the hermeneutical confusion into which good-willed and guileless individuals are thrown in a world marked by the conflict of competing semiologies and their respective textualities. The incipient bourgeois age—to keep within the economic and numismatic metaphors Schiller exploits throughout the drama—is characterized by the dissemination of counterfeit textual currencies, worthless symbolic inscriptions that make pretense to authoritative value. The naive readers in Schiller's play take these counterfeits, on the one hand, to be empirical verities, and, on the other hand, they are no longer capable of recognizing in genuine textual currency the index of their actual circumstances. Schiller's own play, the dramatic novel *The Robbers*, is addressed as a caveat to just such naive readers; it offers them a lesson in the segregation of the authentic, genuine literary text, of which Schiller intends his own to be an example,[38] from the cheap dissimulating counterfeits, the literary commodities, that he sets out to expose. Thus Schiller does not simply lodge a protest against the marginalization of naive cognition in the modern world; on the contrary, he composes *The Robbers* with a specific pedagogical aim in mind: he seeks to teach a strategy that will allow his readers to preserve naive semiosis from the encroachments of bourgeois instrumental reason, a tactic that will allow them to exist in the "depraved world" as representatives of naive cognition without, however, being condemned to playing the role of quixotic fools.

Semiotics, Economics, and the "Inverted World"

> Since money, as the existing and active concept of value, confounds and ex-
> changes everything, it is the universal *confusion* and *exchange* of all things, an
> inverted world, the confusion and exchange of all natural and human
> qualities.   —Karl Marx

According to Jean Baudrillard, throughout the history of Western society
fundamental mutations in the law of value are paralleled by mutations in
the order of representation. For the "classical" period from the Renaissance
to the industrial revolution, which is founded on the natural law of value,
counterfeit is the dominant representational scheme.[39] An obsession with
the counterfeit, of course, is by its very nature nostalgic since its aim is the
rediscovery of the lost original, of what is unique and individual. *The Robbers* tells the story of the victory of the counterfeit over the original as the
ascendancy of exchange semiotics over the naive principles of iconic similitude, on the one hand, and as the triumph of abstract moneyed economies
over the trust and immediacy of precapitalist good-faith economies, on the
other. Although he registers the fact of this triumph, however, Schiller continues to envision a nostalgic return to naiveté, understood, in the definition offered by Kant, as "the eruption of the sincerity that originally was natural to humanity and which is opposed to the art of dissimulation which has
become our second nature."[40] To this end, Schiller's play argues for a fundamental change of strategies in the struggle against the modern episteme.
We have witnessed how Schiller lays bare the relative incompetence and in-
efficacy of the iconic semiotic when confronted with a world of disseminating counterfeits; the only alternative left to the guilelessly beguiled, it
would seem, is to play the part of counterfeits themselves: only by coun-
terfeiting counterfeits, as it were, can they survive in the world of exchange
and simultaneously struggle against its determining principles. Just as the
naive can only be restored through the medium of the sentimental, and original truth recreated from the counterfeit semblance of art, the iconic semiotic, paradoxically, can only be reconstituted if one is able to operate within
the semiotic of the dissimulative counterfeit to ensure the survival of similitude. In this project of strategic adaptation, aesthetics—high art—makes a
double move: first, it sets out to establish itself as a semiotic Other in the
world of bourgeois exchange, serving as a reminder of the longed-for guarantee of iconic similitude; second, it seeks to function simultaneously as a
pedagogical instrument that models and thereby discloses hermeneutical
strategies appropriate to an unmasking of the counterfeit. Insofar as it
teaches how to reveal the intrinsic essence concealed behind the extrinsic

guise, art becomes a tool of ideological critique. Conceived in terms of literature's semiological otherness vis-à-vis the bourgeois semiotic of conventionality and exchange, aesthetic autonomy is by no means incompatible with pedagogical function; on the contrary, semiotic autonomy is the condition of possibility for literature's revolutionary effectiveness.[41]

In the view of Horkheimer and Adorno, the "constitutive principle" ("Urprinzip") of the bourgeois world is the law of abstract (mediative) exchange. When confronted with this principle, they maintain, the human subject is presented with only two alternatives: "the choice between deceit or going under [*unterzugehen*]."[42] The paths taken by the brothers Franz and Karl Moor represent divergent responses when faced with this choice: Franz opts for deceit and its financial rewards; Karl resolves to "go under," understood not in the sense of "to succumb," however, but in the more specific and subtle sense of "to go underground." *The Robbers* relates Karl's journey from "the sincerity that originally was natural to humanity" to the "dissimulation that has become our second nature" in terms of the ever increasing and more effective repression of resistance to bourgeois epistemic structures and socioeconomic practices. In the first stage of this rebellion, Karl goes underground by establishing himself as the leader of a countersociety of robbers, whose lawless acts he conceives as a form of overt protest against the economically and socially legitimated deceit perpetrated by such people as Franz. Karl derives the justification for this violent campaign against society, as we have seen, from his mistaken conclusion that even his father has joined ranks with the treacherous beasts. Upon later discovering that his destructive rebellion was triggered by an error in interpretation and judgment, however, he realizes that as an outlaw he has merely fostered the very brutality he sought to oppose. At this point Karl seems to accept his own complicity with the principles of the "inverted world," and he turns himself in to the societal authorities. Any assessment of the moral-political thrust of Schiller's drama turns on the interpretation of this action. Typically, critics have viewed it as a sign of Karl's reform, of his ultimate acquiescence to the laws of bourgeois society. By contrast, I will argue that this act merely marks the shift of Karl's opposition from the overt to the covert, its repression from the conscious into a political unconscious. Karl's final strategy of resistance is the attempt to rescue the kernel of his naive sincerity by driving it inward into a submerged, insular, and private realm that is totally divorced from the sphere of societal, intersubjective practice. Viewed in this way, Karl's apparent knuckling under at the play's conclusion represents a radical act of dissimulation, feigned submission for the purpose of preserving naive semi-

osis as the last glimmer of opposition to the mediacy of the modern episteme. But to arrive at this interpretation we must first establish the ways in
which the conflict of epistemes shapes the economic subtext of this play.

In his *Economic and Philosophical Manuscripts of 1844*, Marx denounces
money as an *"inverting* power" (*"verkehrende* Macht"). Money, he writes,
"changes loyalty into treason, love into hate, hate into love, virtue into vice,
vice into virtue, servant into master, master into servant, nonsense into reason and reason into nonsense."[43] Later in the same treatise, Marx derogatorily describes logic as the "money of the mind," the abstract system that
makes speculative, exploitative thought possible, and his critique is reminiscent of Schiller's attack on the sterile logic of the "academic mind." "*Logic*
is the *money* of the mind, the speculative *thought-value* of man and of nature,
their essence which has become completely indifferent to all real determi-
nateness and hence unreal, *alienated* thought, and therefore thought which
abstracts from nature and from real man; *abstract* thought."[44] He thereby
suggests by association that logic, like money, is also an "inverting power"
that manipulates and alienates reality by abstracting from its concrete and
immediate givenness. In this early treatise money and abstract logic come
to symbolize for Marx the transformative, value-perverting, reifying powers of bourgeois thought and economic practice.

One year after the composition of Marx's *Economic and Philosophical Manuscripts*, the socialist philosopher Moses Hess drew a similar conclusion
about the devaluation of human worth that is brought on by the inversion of
being and appearance inherent in the principle of bourgeois exchange. In
the essay "On the Nature of Money" (1845) he asserts: "Whatever cannot be
exchanged, whatever cannot be *sold*, has no value. Insofar as human beings
can no longer be sold, they are no longer worth *a single penny*—they are only
of value insofar as they *sell* or 'hire' themselves out."[45] Hess ultimately
equates writing and money, condemning them both as "destructive means of
exchange" ("tödtende *Verkehr*smittel") that constitute the *"inverted* world"
(*"verkehrte* Welt").[46] The puns on the word *Verkehr*, denoting at once "commerce," "intercourse," "inversion," and "perversion," run like a leitmotif
throughout Hess's writings on the problematics of money, and his attack on
mediacy as the root of all evil in the bourgeois episteme crystallizes around
the semantics of this word. His vision of a utopian future involves a world
without "dead letters" that choke off human spirit and without "dead
money" that strangles life. In this world "no foreign entity, no third *middle
thing* will intervene between us, in order outwardly and ostensibly to 'mediate' between us, while in fact it separates us and divides us inwardly."[47]

Similar in this respect to Hess's utopian dream, Schiller's aesthetic theories are formulated as a means for realizing a world without mediation, a world in which all signs are perfectly transparent and hence expose authentic significance in its naked verity. According to modern semiotic theory, of course, such a dream is "utopian" in the sense of being purely imaginary. Charles Sanders Peirce, for example, defines the tripartite structure of mediation as the very essence of a "sign": "By semiotics," Peirce writes in a now famous formulation, "I mean . . . an action, or influence, which is, or involves, a cooperation of *three* subjects, such as a sign, its object, and its interpretant. . . . My definition confers on anything that so acts the title of a 'sign.' "[48] The remarkable parallels between the definitions Marx and Hess give of money—and in the instance of Marx, of logic as well—and Peirce's concept of the "sign" underscore the isomorphic relationship between modern theories of semiotic mediacy, the structures of symbolic exchange that underwrite bourgeois communication and commerce, and the abstracting, reifying logic of purposive rationality.[49]

As a semiotic magician who transforms reality by manipulating mediative signs, Franz Moor is the avatar of that alchemical power Marx ascribed to money and logic, this calculating semiotic that functions on the basis of exchange and deceptive mediacy. The scene in which Franz transmutes his father's "sleep" into "death" paradigmatically evinces the abstract principle of semiotic-semantic exchange that underwrites his will to mastery. *"Dead!* they cry, *dead! Now* I am your *master.* A hue and cry in all the castle: *dead!*— But what, perhaps he is only *asleep?* to be sure! a sleep from which one never awakens to a good-morning again—Sleep and death are but twins. Let us just exchange the names! Welcome, brave sleep! We will call you death! (*Closing his father's eyes.*)" (*Robbers* II, ii, 535; 70). Franz's initial words divulge that behind his linguistic manipulations lies a will to exchange: the long-awaited death of the father will finally allow him to transfer the sign "master" from the referent "father" to the referent "Franz." Upon discovering that the father is merely unconscious, however, he exploits the metaphorical proximity of the signifieds "sleep" and "death" to exchange their signifiers and thereby alter reference, allowing him to pass off his father's "sleep" as "death." Franz employs the manipulative exchange of equi-valent signs, in other words, to produce equi-vocations that permit him to intervene in and alter the reality these signs signify. He thus is the paradigmatic representative of the "inverted world," of the inversion of the semiotic relation between signifier and signified. Instead of the signifier evolving necessarily and immediately out of its signified, as Schiller envisioned for the ideal(ized) semiotic of naive thought, in Franz's world the signifier controls and masters its signified, enforcing upon reality the manipulations it has effected in the abstract, mediative realm of pure signs.

In keeping with Franz's embodiment of a transformative "money of the mind" is his consistent application of metaphors of money, credit, and exchange when deliberating on his own aims and strategies.[50] In the extended monolog that concludes the first scene of the play, Franz carries on a diatribe against nature and its "holy" bonds, an excursus that serves as the philosophical legitimation for his devious plot to gain mastery in his father's house, even if it means transgressing all natural laws of blood and kinship. This speech of self-justification turns on a rhetoric that blatantly exploits economic metaphors.

Might is right, and the limits of our strength our only law. It is true, there are certain common pacts men have made to drive the pulses that turn the world. Honest name! A valuable coin indeed, one to drive a fine bargain with for the man who knows how to spend it wisely. Conscience—yes, indeed! an excellent scarecrow, to keep the sparrows from the cherry trees!—that too is a well-written check [*Wechselbrief*] with which even the bankrupt can get by in a pinch. Yes indeed, most admirable devices to keep fools respectful and to hold down the mob, so that clever people can live in better comfort. (*Robbers* I, i, 500–1; *33*)

Franz's identification of the limits of law with the limits of self-empowerment succinctly characterizes his conscienceless drive for mastery. He overwrites the laws of nature in the name of cultivated laws of abstraction and exchange. The central image in his monolog is that of the "well-written check"—the "Wechselbrief," whereby "Wechsel" denotes both "exchange" and "change" or "alteration"—and this image joins into a single symbol the issues of corrupt writing and of deceptive economic practices, both of which are grounded in the use of false signs that make promises inconsistent with the reality they signify. Franz makes a mockery of the conventions that vouch for trust and obligation in intercommunicative and economic exchange, making intersubjective values such as "good name" and "conscience" into symbolic tools to be manipulated for personal profit. He intends to capitalize his meager personal assets by investing the collateral of his family name and then taking advantage of others' faith in his promises. He will exploit, in other words, society's reliance on the institutions of moral and economic trust just as he exploits Amalia's, Karl's, and Old Moor's faith in semiotic transparency. Franz transforms these societal bonds into mere symbols without substance; thus his would-be "honest name," the calling card of a just and fair tradesman, becomes a coin whose inflated value—a prescient image of the modern-day credit card—allows him to spend beyond his economic and moral means. He transforms credibility into credit and conscience into a junk bond not backed by any real collateral.

In what Pierre Bourdieu refers to as the precapitalist "good-faith economy," the trader "practises no exchanges involving money and all his relations are based on total confidence; unlike the shady dealer, he has recourse to none of the guarantees (witnesses, written documents, etc.) with which commercial transactions are surrounded."[51] Franz represents the "shady dealer" interested solely in "commercial transactions"; he is the confidence man who mercilessly exploits the confidence of those "naive" figures who do not operate as he does. The result of his practices, as he himself foresees, is the demise of those "common pacts men have made to drive the pulses that turn the world." The principles of abstract, symbolic exchange, in short, destroy the immediate "confidences" and obligations that vouchsafe economic interaction in the good-faith economy, just as the principles of semiotic exchange, which Franz so masterfully deploys, disrupt communicative interaction and hermeneutical understanding. Suspension of interpersonal obligation in the economic sphere thus parallels the suspension of the guarantee of similitude in the semiotic realm.

Baudrillard stresses this coincidence of the institution of the modern, arbitrary sign with the demise of interpersonal obligation.

The arbitrary sign begins when, instead of linking two persons in an unbreakable reciprocity, the signifier starts referring back to the disenchanted universe of the signified, common denominator of the real world toward which no one has any obligation. End of the *obliged* sign, reign of the emancipated sign. . . . The modern sign dreams of the signs of the past and would well appreciate finding again, in its reference to the real, an *obligation*: but what it finds again is only a *reason*: this referential reason, this real, this "natural" off which it is going to live.[52]

Baudrillard describes not only the shift to a semiotic of arbitrariness, but also its repercussions in the dimension of human interaction. Accompanying the emergence of the arbitrary sign comes a shift in emphasis from the symptomatic function of language and economics, a focus on their roles as immediate and transparent bonds that link individuals in a relationship of mutuality and trust, to concentration on their representational function as symbolic mediators between abstract thought and objects in the world. The paradigm shift from the "Renaissance" to the Enlightenment semiotic, in other words, bespeaks a displacement of the semiotic relation from the sphere of intersubjective interaction in the life-world—from communicative action, to employ Habermas's terminology[53]—to instrumental reason, that is, to concerns about the deployment of objects in the (life-)world. It is this transformation that forms the historical backdrop for *The Robbers*, and the brothers Franz and Karl Moor come down on opposite sides of this epistemic divide.

Only in the context of a society caught up in the process of instituting breach of promise as its modus vivendi, a society bent on reifying living things and commodifying natural objects, does Karl's perverse, even pathological obsession with the oath of brotherhood that binds him to the band of outlaws make any sense whatsoever. The price of release from this oath is the death of his beloved Amalia, and the necessity of this payment ultimately signals for Karl the failure of this counterproject, its insufficiency over against the principles of abstract exchange. The scene in which the robbers, surrounded and heavily outnumbered, reject the temptation to buy their own freedom by turning their leader Karl over to the authorities (*Robbers* II, iii, 536–55; 71–92) elucidates how Karl attempts to reestablish in this brotherhood the blood-bond he has lost with his real brother and his father, instituting a countersociety structured around the principles of reciprocity and interpersonal obligation. Two arguments that tie in closely to the thematics and motifs examined thus far figure centrally in the robbers' decision to fight for their lives and that of their ringleader. They are offered the choice between the *verbal* oath that unites them as a group, and the *written* contract offered them by the Priest as an assurance of amnesty. Given the pattern established throughout the play that written texts are the index of deceit and that signatures, easily forged and not necessarily given in good faith, have lost all power of obligation, the robbers have every reason to be skeptical of the piece of paper the Priest offers them containing their "general pardon, signed and sealed" (*Robbers* II, iii, 554; 91). Karl, at any rate, responds by admonishing his comrades that they would have to break their oath to him and each other in order to accept this written offer, and he points out that by thus making themselves into traitors, they would give just cause to legitimate a breach of the written promise made to them.

KARL: Look, look! What more can you ask?—Signed with his own hand—it is mercy beyond bounds—or are you afraid they will break their word, because you have heard that one does not keep one's word to traitors?—Oh, have no fear! Politics could make them keep their word, even if they had given it to Satan himself. Who would ever believe them again? Would they ever be able to play the trick again?—I would swear that they mean it! . . . Is it not so, Father [*Pater*]?

PRIEST [*Pater*]: What is the name of the devil that speaks out of him?—Yes, yes, it is so—the fellow has me spinning. . . .

MOOR: What, still undecided? Or do you think I will resist if you attempt to bind me? Look! see me lash my right hand to this oak branch, I am defenseless, a child can conquer me—Who will be the first to abandon his captain in his hour of need? (*Robbers* II, iii, 554–55; 91–92)

Here, as in his speeches throughout this scene, we witness how Karl, no longer a naive Don Quixote who is duped by signatures and texts, has himself become a master of arbitrary signs, exploiting them to perpetrate a classical instance of ironic double-speak. The Priest, unable to decipher the ironic undertones in Karl's words as he ostensibly encourages his comrades to accept the pardon, responds with understandable shock and disbelief. When Karl's challenge culminates in the provocative rhetorical question, "Who will be the first to abandon his captain in his hour of need?" the robbers jump to his support and send the Priest away with the message that "not a single traitor" can be found in Moor's entourage. For Karl this is the decisive point in the entire action of the play, and he responds to the faithfulness of his comrades with the emphatic statement, "Now we are free— Comrades!" (*Robbers* II, iii, 555; 92), implying that only once their oath of brotherhood has been put to and survived this crucial test are they truly "comrades" and free men—free, we suppose, from the institutionalized structures of deceit rampant in the dominant world of bourgeois exchange. The challenge presented to the outlaws' *verbal* oath by the *written* pardon offered by the "Father" ("Pater")—the designation itself suggests the association of this false "father" with the ostensibly false father, Old Moor, against whom Karl's rebellion is directed—becomes for Karl the fundamental test case of their fidelity and the genuineness of their interpersonal obligation.

The improbability of their victory over vastly superior military forces represents another case in point where logical deficiencies in the motivational structure of the drama can be attributed to Schiller's desire to underwrite specific thematic complexes. For just as the robbers are distinguished from the institutionalized powers by the dichotomy between verbal oath and written promise, they are also differentiated on the basis of their personal motivations. Although they are outnumbered twenty to one, Schweizer remains unperturbed, reminding his "brothers" that the enemy soldiers have none but monetary interests: "Brothers! brothers! there's nothing to worry about. They [the mercenaries] gamble their lives for a few coins, aren't we fighting for our necks and for freedom?" (*Robbers* II, ii, 548; 85). It is the outlaws, in other words, who, as true "brothers," are fighting for genuine and immediate values, for life and liberty, as well as for the bonds of interpersonal obligation, while the mercenary soldiers fight only for symbols of value, for abstract (monetary) signs of worth. Interpersonal obligation is demonstrated to be superior to the symbolic dependencies that structure human relationships in society at large. In the brotherhood that binds the highwaymen, Karl seeks to reconstitute the immediate blood-bond of nature, the bond between brother and brother and father and son that Franz's mediacy has successfully undermined.[54] That such relationships of reciprocity and mutual obligation are wholly marginalized, choked off into a countersocietal underworld, renders a devastating commentary on the perverse structures that govern human inter(ex)change in this society. The robbers' victory over the mercenaries in fact provides the only glimmer of hope in the otherwise wholly pessimistic vision projected in *The Robbers*, which ultimately concedes, however begrudgingly, the ascendancy of the Enlightenment episteme.

The solidarity of the outlaws only represents one aspect of this subcommunity. Indeed, the robber band itself is split between adherence to intersubjective bonds and the pursuit of corrupt self-interest. This internal antagonism is reflected in the conflict between Karl and Spiegelberg and the contrary pursuits they hope to realize when they form the band of highwaymen. Karl, of course, sees himself as a modern Robin Hood and the outlaws as unwitting accessories to his brand of justice. In this role he transfers the demand for transparent mediation to the economic domain, establishing himself as a direct conduit, a noncorrupting mediator oblivious to self-interest and personal gain, who redistributes wealth from the rich to the poor. Spiegelberg, by contrast, represents the infiltration of the brotherhood of obligation by the principles of corruption and deception: he is a second incarnation of the false brother, a replication of the characteristics associated with Franz, but one that highlights more the economic than the semiotic aspects of the enlightened episteme. When Spiegelberg asserts, for example, that "bringing idle money into circulation" is the essence of honesty (*Robbers* I, ii, 511–12; 45), his words echo those of Franz in the speech in which he defines "honest name" as a "valuable coin." Indeed, even the pacts Spiegelberg seals with the robbers stand in stark contrast to the oath of interpersonal obligation that Karl demands of them. The robber Grimm, for example, joins ranks with Spiegelberg by claiming, "I can be had by the highest bidder" (*Robbers* I, ii, 513; 46), suggesting that he understands this union as a kind of slave trade. Similarly, Roller concludes his contract with Spiegelberg by asserting, "I hereby mortgage [*verpfände*] my soul to the devil" (*Robbers* I, ii, 513; 46), and Schwarz accurately designates this hiring-out of human beings as a form of "prostitution" (I, ii, 512; 46). This Mephis-

tophelean pact, sealed in the promise of monetary wealth, is the obverse of
the oath of brotherhood Karl establishes and tests in the temptation scene
examined above. The struggle between Karl and Spiegelberg for leadership
of the highwaymen thus reflects in microcosm the struggle between two
sets of conflicting semiotic-economic principles.

Like Franz, Spiegelberg is a devilish mediator who exploits the alchemical powers of deceit to corrupt honest but downtrodden individuals. Raz-
mann aptly calls him—and this appellation suits Franz as well—"another
sort of Orpheus" ("ein anderer Orpheus") (*Robbers* I, ii, 513; 46). If Orpheus
possessed the power to mollify wild beasts with the beauty of his song, then
Franz and Spiegelberg, as another sort of Orpheus, reverse this process, turning men into civilized beasts by singing their consciences to sleep. Much as
Franz transmutes Karl from "gentle lamb" to "furious tiger" (*Robbers* I, ii,
514; 48), Spiegelberg, more a Circe than an Orpheus, changes men into swine
who pursue actions that spell their moral demise. If Orpheus represents the
civilizing power of art, its capacity to tame the beast in humankind, these
other Orpheuses, and the economic and semiotic principles they exploit,
represent a kind of anti-art, and as such they embody an insidious threat to
any utopian, philosophic-historical project of aesthetic education.

Karl's and Spiegelberg's competing conceptions of the outlaw band and
its societal function represent a displacement of the conflict of semiologies
manifest in the antagonism between Karl and Franz. In a drama that consistently presents the triumph of the mediative semiotic of exchange over
the naive semiotic of iconic similitude and interpersonal obligation, it comes
as no surprise that, despite Karl's ability to waylay the threat to the oath of
solidarity presented by the written pardon, Spiegelberg's principles ultimately reign supreme. Upon turning himself in for the monetary price
placed on his head—irrespective of the extenuating circumstances that motivate this move—Karl implicitly abandons the axiom of intrinsic, autonomous value that he has otherwise upheld throughout the play and embraces the convention of extrinsically determined, hetero-nomous worth.
When Karl submits to the juridical authority of the state and to the laws of
a prostituting economic exchange, he signals his own apparent co-optation
by the ruling logic of abstract value. We recall here Moses Hess's assertion
that in the bourgeois world whatever cannot be exchanged or sold has no
value, and that even human beings only attain worth "insofar as they *sell* or
'hire' themselves out." Abandoning the integrity he has struggled to uphold,
Karl subjects himself to the reifying mediation of symbolic equivalences. If
his own being is already rent by the breach between essential character and
societal (inter)action at the moment he becomes the robbers' ringleader, it
is not until this point of literal sellout that he accepts and accedes to this self-

division. Thus Franz and Spiegelberg, as the objectifications of deceit and abstract exchange, disappear the moment Karl absorbs these principles into his own subjectivity: the objectified confrontation between inimical brothers becomes an intrasubjective tension introjected into Karl's psyche, a tension that constitutes his subjectivity as Unhappy Consciousness.

Karl's ultimate capitulation to the structures of mediated exchange is corroborated by the rhetoric that informs his language in the closing scene of the play, which is dominated by allusions to commodities and their exchange—the discourse identified throughout the text with Franz and Spiegelberg. The oath of brotherhood, as the murder of Amalia makes clear, has metamorphosed into an economic contract: with her sacrifice Karl repays the debt he incurred when the robbers saved him from capture at the hands of the mercenaries; her life is given in exchange for the rescue of Karl's.

KARL: You [the robbers] sacrificed to me a life that you could no longer call your own, a life of horror and disgrace—I have slaughtered an angel for you. Look, look, I say! Are you satisfied now?

GRIMM: You have paid your debt with interest. You have done more than any man would do for his honor. And now come with us!

KARL: You say that? Indeed, the life of a saint for the lives of rogues, it is an unequal exchange, is it not? . . . The scars, the Bohemian woods! Yes, yes! of course, that had to be repaid. (*Robbers* V, ii, 616; *158–59*)

Karl's words are charged with bitterness and irony as he transfers the principle of abstraction that underwrites bourgeois economic exchange to the realm of human interchange, trading one life for another. But Karl's capitulation does not necessarily imply surrender to, and acceptance of, the principles of abstract exchange, as most critics have tended to read the play's conclusion[55]—an interpretation almost certainly grafted onto Schiller's original text by analogy to the later, revised version.[56] Instead, it merely indicates that his *overt* rebellion against these principles has miscarried. There is evidence to suggest that with this capitulation Karl accedes to the real ascendancy of the principle of mediative exchange, without however embracing this principle as his own. Read as an *ironic* appropriation, Karl's ostensible compliance would indicate that his revolt has now gone deeper underground. He recognizes, in other words, the futility of overt insurrection and turns instead to the subtler forms of *covert* revolt: his exploitation of the metaphors of economic-semiotic exchange hence betoken an exploitation of the game-rules of bourgeois society that turns these rules against the principal players themselves. Earlier in the drama, Amalia opted for a similar stratagem when confronted with Franz's open hostility: only by appropriating the technique of dissimulation was she able to avoid being overpowered by Franz (see *Robbers* III, i, 558; 95–96). Karl likewise buys into the principles of exchange only as a last-ditch effort to rescue his resistant rebellion. From this moment on, when the ascendancy of the bourgeois status quo is recognized and accepted, overt rebellion is appropriate only to fools like Don Quixote, and the revolutionary project of planned reversal to the epistemic status of the naive semiotic of similitude becomes a sentimental redemption of the naive, a covert, underground resistance operation that outwardly accepts mediative exchange to carry on its struggle under the dissimulative disguise of resigned—"re-signed"—collusion.

"Quae medicamenta non sanant, ferrum sanat, quae ferrum non sanat, ignis sanat" ("What medicines will not cure, iron will cure; what iron will not cure, fire will cure"), Schiller reminds us in his epigraph from Hippocrates (*SW* 1: 491). It is important to note, however, that Schiller deletes the concluding line of the original Hippocratean aphorism when he appropriates it for *The Robbers*. This line reads: "Quae vero ignis non sanat, insanabilia reputari oportet" ("But what fire cannot cure, must be considered incurable."). This deletion suggests, if the epigraph can be taken as a similitude for Karl Moor's and Schiller's originary sociocritical operation, that such resigned conclusions have no place in this project and must consequently be effaced. When confronted with the failure of specific cures, one must regroup and turn to the implementation of new methods and strategies. This implies that when Karl Moor faces the principles of bourgeois society and must either "deceive" or "go under," as Horkheimer and Adorno express it, he ultimately chooses *both*. If in the underground of his outlaw existence Karl's rebellion proved unsuccessful, then this is simply because he sought to adhere to naive principles of similitude, of identity between character and action, which were doomed to failure given the existing socioeconomic conditions. Only when he consciously appropriates deceit as a weapon against deceit can Karl's potential for rebellion be salvaged. This means that insurrection must go yet further underground, that it must be absorbed into the very being of the rebellious subject itself. Unable to preserve the iconic principle of resemblance between the internal self and the external expressive signs of the self, the bourgeois rebel must sublate / sublimate his rebellion as a fracture that runs through his very subjectivity. Indeed, in the final analysis, even Karl's position as ringleader of the highwaymen is possible only by means of implementing such a strategic disjunction: outwardly a robber and murderer, he never ceases inwardly and in his private actions to be a benefactor to the oppressed and downtrodden. Karl ultimately gives in to this *oppression* only insofar as he transforms it into *repression*, internalizing his revolt, turning what for robber Moor had been a public campaign into a private and secret (*heimlich*) crusade that lies outside the confines of bourgeois self-expression. Karl's development thus exemplifies the birth of the divided subject out of the repression of socio-economic resistance.

This interpretation is borne out by the Hamletesque monolog he delivers in the final scene of the fourth act. In this speech Karl deliberates on, only to reject, the possibility of suicide, and he formulates his reasoning in the following words: "No! No! A man must not stumble—Be what thou wilt, nameless *Beyond*—If I but remain true to myself—Be what thou wilt, let me only take my *self* with me.—Externals are but the varnish upon the man— I am my heaven and my hell" (*Robbers* IV, v, 591; *131*). The generalizing, ob-jectified statement that Karl distills from his self-reflections, "Externals are but the varnish upon the man," is clearly inconsistent with the principle of iconicity as the guarantor of human truth and integrity, the principle he de-fended and represented at the beginning of the play. This insight must be viewed as the culmination of a painful process of education: throughout the course of the drama Karl is effectively weaned of his dependence on naive principles of immediacy. He does not abandon, however, an insistence on the integrity of the self; indeed, his monolog is marked by an insistence on selfhood that is independent of the external varnish on the individual. To be sure, the bourgeois in-dividual proves to be a dividual, an entity divided be-tween external expression and a now wholly internalized (self-)being. Self-identity has become something that is wholly private and insular, existing solely in the internal realm of the soul and independent of the external signs expressed, and the actions carried out, by the empirical self. In other words, self-identity is no longer configured as the similitude between the external and the internal, but becomes a property inhering in the internal itself.

In Karl's ultimate turn to, and acceptance of, the principle of self-division, we witness the birth of the classically divided bourgeois rebel, split between public personality and private sentiment, action and concealed desire, open-ness and secrecy, self-assertion and self-repression. Fidelity to the private, in-ternal self, irrespective of the external actions and expressions of the public person, becomes the measure of human self-worth. Outmaneuvered by the semiotics of arbitrariness, the principle of iconicity and wholeness, which had vouched for the moral integrity of the naive individual, retreats into the sphere of internal self-identity. Hypocrisy is institutionalized and legitimized as the necessary behavioral paradigm in a world governed by the axioms of symbolic abstraction and exchange. Nevertheless—and this is the crucial point—the reversion of the potential revolutionary to the innerworldly as-ceticism of the bourgeois subject remains marked by the dialectic between rebellion and its concealment: revolutionary public ambitions are repressed and relegated to the realm of the private, that is, they become *heimlich* in both senses of that word as analyzed by Freud. Paradoxically, only by being drawn within is Karl's revolutionary potential able to survive, and with this interiorization, Karl, as rebellious bourgeois subject, subjects *himself* to the dialectic of representation as constituted in the bourgeois episteme, to self-(re)presentation and self-occultation. It is this paradox of revolution and its repression that marks the constitution of the German bourgeois intelligentsia in this period and relegates future bourgeois revolutionary projects to the strategy of the sentimental redemption of the naive, the covert recapturing of a moral high ground that has proven itself practically indefensible in the context of the modern episteme. Reinhart Koselleck has demonstrated the degree to which "secrecy" ("das Geheimnis") evolves as a necessary consequence out of the conflict between enlightened burgher and the absolutistic state in eighteenth-century Germany. The burgher develops a "private" and "secret" sphere in which bourgeois morality both takes refuge from the corrupting influence of the politico-economic realm and defines the locus from which it will launch its own revolt against this corruption: "Secrecy [*Das Geheimnis*] was the dividing line between morality and politics. It safeguarded and delimited the social sphere in which morality was to be realised."[57]

Karl Moor paradigmatically embodies this circumscription of a private, internal realm in which integrity is insulated and protected from the corruption of the sociopolitical, economic world beyond the self; but as his case demonstrates, this interiorization is a by-product of the bourgeois intelligentsia's encounter not so much with the constraints of the feudal-absolutistic state as with its own alter ego, its own Franz/Spiegelberg as the embodiment of extrinsic value, corrupt intermediacy, and abstract exchange. Sentimental redemption of the naive defines the recovery project by which the socioeconomic life-world will eventually be salvaged and re-turned to the semiotic-economic integrity of similitude. But prerequisite for this long-range re-volution is the retreat of iconicity into the privatized and secret core of the bourgeois subject, as well as into the privatized and secret revolutionary kernel of bourgeois literature. Karl Moor—in this sense exemplary of the German bourgeois artist of the period—implements a strategy defined by outward collusion with the enemy in an attempt to circumscribe and thus preserve a realm of private and secret revolt. Covert rebellion is not simply the path of least resistance, as one might be tempted to surmise; it is the only available viable path of resistance. Only by himself embracing deceit, exchange, and the symbolic mediacy of money can Karl preserve within his own subjectivity a potentially explosive kernel of resistance. This subli-

mation of rebellion marks the bourgeois intellectual as an aesthetic construct, divided between semblance and essence, bourgeois formality and repressed rebellious drives. Given this, it is not surprising that aesthetics would
appear to Schiller and his contemporary bourgeois intellectuals as the paradigmatic battleground from which the campaign for the sentimental redemption of the naive, the rescue mission intent on delivering the bourgeois
subject from the condition of self-alienation, would have to be launched. It
is in the field of aesthetics, by means of aesthetic education, that the rift dividing the (self-)rebellious bourgeois subject, a rift that signals an internalization of the revolutionary conflict of semiologies, must eventually be
mended.

In a central passage from *On the Naive and Sentimental in Literature*, Schiller claims that the conflict between the world as liminal, limiting phenomenon and the infinity of the ideal is the constitutive experience of the "sentimental" poet. "The sentimental poet therefore is constantly dealing with
two opposing concepts and emotions, with reality as boundary and with his
idea as the infinite, and the mixed feeling which he excites will always bear
witness to this double source" (*Naive*, 720–21; 42). In *The Robbers* we witness
Karl's transmogrification from an integral, unified, naive character who has
difficulty comprehending that he is out of step with reality, into a sentimental, (self-)divided character who, after butting his head against the limits of socioeconomic, epistemic reality, interiorizes this discord as an internal struggle between public concession to the real and secret-private (*heimlich*) assertion of the ideal. The play hence asserts the practical impossibility
of the "naive" in a world dominated by the principles of the "academic
mind." It legitimates "sentimentality"—divided subjectivity—as the only viable return path to the ideal of naive cognition. *The Robbers* presents a blue-
print for this sentimental redemption of the naive, the recovery project by
which the utopian kernel buried within the bourgeois world will be salvaged
and the bourgeois subject re-turned to semiotic transparency and the intersubjective trust of the good-faith economy.

Righting Writing—Righting Reading: *The Robbers* and the Formulation of a Literary Practice for Divided Subjects

The paradox that Karl Moor denounces the mediacy of writing by appealing to a written text (Plutarch) mirrors a similar paradox that characterizes
the constitution of *The Robbers* itself as literary work. In his expository pref-
aces to this work, which must be considered among his very first theoretical deliberations on literary aesthetics, Schiller stresses that this play is ex-

plicitly conceived as a text to be read rather than as a drama to be performed.[58] Critics of this work are thus confronted with the question of how to reconcile Schiller's defense of textual mediacy for the aesthetic constitution of a work that denounces the mediacy of the textual medium as a symptom of the "ink-smearing century." The answer to this question is contained in the thematic development of the drama, in its demonstration that naive obliviousness to the omnipresence of mediation is not an effective means of opposition against it. Karl's realization that the only way to resist the principles of bourgeois enlightenment is ultimately to appropriate them informs the aesthetic constitution of *The Robbers* as re-volutionary work: in the dimension of literary reception, this text attempts to model and initiate in its readers a redemption of the naive that passes through the medium of the sentimental. Hence the conflicts Karl Moor experiences and the lessons he learns reflect those of the bourgeois writers of this period. Schiller himself came to understand the crisis of bourgeois authorship in the process of composing *The Robbers*, and this text develops as an answer to this crisis.

In a letter to Wilhelm Petersen written in spring of 1781, Schiller attempts to enlist his friend as a middleman whose charge it would be to arrange for publication of *The Robbers*. In the course of encouraging Petersen to accept this role, Schiller cites three inducements that especially spark his interest in publishing this work, and these motivations provide an insightful commentary on the problems of literary authorship at the end of the eighteenth century. As the "first and most important reason" Schiller names "that all-powerful mammon, who has never found lodging under my roof suited to his taste: money" (*SB* 1: 35). At this point Schiller tries to encourage Petersen to become a literary agent who could profit from the publication of this work: he promises Petersen the balance of any sum above fifty gulden that he can negotiate for the manuscript. Only after stressing this financial consideration does Schiller express his final two reasons for wishing to publish *The Robbers*.

The second reason, as you will certainly understand, is the judgment of the world, to give what I and a few friends have viewed with perhaps exaggeratedly favorable eyes over to the unpredisposed judge, the public. . . . Of course I would like to know what kind of a fate I can expect to have as a dramatist, as an author.

And then finally a *third* reason, which is totally genuine, is this: I have no other prospect in this world than to *work* in an area, . . . at a post where I can develop and use my physiological and philosophical studies. . . . Writings in the realm of literature, tragedies, etc. would stand in the way of my plan to become a professor of physiology and medicine. Therefore I'm trying to get them out of my system here as soon as possible. (*SB* 1: 35–36)

Although even the order in which Schiller arranges his list of motivations is in itself telling, the substance of each individual deliberation sheds considerable light on the problems inherent in his concrete situation as (would-be) bourgeois writer. Publication—going public—with his literary products implies both concession to the laws of the market—to the principles of commodification—and acceptance of the tastes and expectations of the public, the bourgeois public sphere, as ultimate "unpredisposed judge" of his work. The common denominator of the first two justifications is Schiller's desire to have his work enter into circulation, on the one hand as an object whose monetary value is established in a process of commercial exchange, and on the other hand as an object whose aesthetic value is determined by public taste. In both instances the work and its author submit themselves—as does Karl Moor at the conclusion of the play—to external, extrinsic tribunals of evaluation. Such mundane, practical considerations contrast starkly with the philosophy of poetic genius propagated by the Sturm und Drang generation, a poetics that shunned all notions of conventionality, resisted the norms of public taste, and argued that the intrinsic worth of literary products was anchored in the immediacy of artistic expression. The conflict between this expressive ideal, which Schiller, in fact, defends in *The Robbers*, and the quotidian realities mentioned in this letter provides evidence that this conception of artistic genius was an ideology formulated in reaction to these glaring social and economic dependencies. The hypostatization of artistic autonomy simultaneously lodges a protest against, and ideologically masks, the reality of this practical subjection. The poetics of genius evolves, in other words, as an attempt to rescue individual literary productivity from the dangers of a standardized bourgeois production.

Whereas the first two reasons Schiller gives for desiring publication of *The Robbers* concern questions about the (economic and aesthetic) evaluation of the literary work, his third reason addresses questions about society's assessment of the institution of literary authorship. Schiller believes that his literary pursuits are inconsistent with the goal of establishing himself in a stable bourgeois profession. Literary activity, he suggests, represents a private indulgence incompatible with a solid bourgeois lifestyle, and he argues that publication will help him overcome this youthful aberration. Curiously enough, this assertion goes contrary to what Schiller maintains in his second point, namely that publication will give him the opportunity to confirm or deny his own literary talent. This contradiction points to equivocations and uncertainties he entertained about his own future at this formative stage of his development. Although he has a sense of his own literary calling and wishes to test the viability of authorship as a future course in life, he simultaneously realizes that he must be prepared to make concessions to the practical demands of bourgeois society, even if that means abandoning his literary ambitions altogether. Schiller's own existence in the period of creation and publication of *The Robbers* is thus marked by a conflict similar to the one that structures the fate of his robber-protagonist, Karl Moor. The literary practices that constitute *The Robbers* as work spring from the tension created by these contradictory demands: concession to the requirements of the marketplace and public taste, on the one hand, and the formulation of a utopian vision that expresses opposition to the need of such acquiescence, on the other. When Schiller admits that *The Robbers* is marred by fundamental "errors . . . that are rooted in the basic design of the play" (*SB* 1: 42), he hints at the aporias around which this work is structured. This division in the constitution of the text reflects the self-division of the would-be oppositional bourgeois author, a tension manifest in Schiller's letter to Petersen.

In the essay "On the Affirmative Character of Culture," Herbert Marcuse expounds a theory linking the institution of bourgeois art to the repressive self-disciplining of the bourgeois subject. "In affirmative culture," he asserts, "renunciation is linked to the external vitiation of the individual, to his compliance [*Sich-Fügen*] with a bad order."[59] Schiller's *Robbers* represents a significant literary-historical document insofar as it portrays on the thematic level this process of (self-)renunciation and repression that is the condition of possibility of bourgeois re-volutionary authorship. This text demonstrates that the emergence of the (self-)divided bourgeois subject and the inception of that process by which literature seeks to "find its way back" from representation to a language of pure being are contemporaneous phenomena. Both divided subjectivity as Unhappy Consciousness and the modernist literary project that attempts to redeem the naive by passing through the sentimental are characterized by the dialectical interplay between collusion with, and rebellion against, the epistemic principles of the bourgeois age. As the bourgeois subject evolves within the waxing structures of abstract exchange and reification by hypostatizing the "soul" as that human kernel of self-identity not subject to the extrinsic laws of exchange,[60] bourgeois literature responds to the threat of literary commodification by postulating the autonomy of the literary work. The reality that extrinsic market forces increasingly determine literary value is accompanied by the danger of the de-auratification of literary aesthetics; the doctrine of aesthetic autonomy represents the attempt to re-auratify literature. What arises in the bourgeois subject and is expressed in the institution of bourgeois authorship as a dialectic between collusion and rebellion thus develops in the bourgeois institution of literature as a dialectic between commodification and autonomization. Literary texts that seek to pursue oppositional politico-cultural strategies must accept the moment of politico-cultural affirmation as the necessary concessional phase of their utopian project: they must accept, as Schiller attempts to demonstrate in *The Robbers*, that one can reattain the naive only by exploiting the mediacy and reflection of sentimental literature. The challenge presented to the oppositional-utopian bourgeois writer thus becomes the strategic negotiation of this dialectical rift in the creation of the literary-aesthetic work.

In *The Robbers* the negotiations of this dialectic appear in two manifestations: as the contradiction, on the one hand, between the indictment of writing contained in the thematics of the play and Schiller's insistence on the necessary constitution of this work itself as written text; and, on the other hand, in Schiller's literary-aesthetic tactic of fusing dramatic and epic genres. In the suppressed foreword to the first edition of the play, Schiller explicitly denies that *The Robbers* is a "theatrical drama," calling it instead a "dramatic novel" (*SW* 1: 482). To be sure, it is only as text that *The Robbers* becomes a marketable commodity that promises to bring the author financial rewards. We could speculate that one of the unexpressed reasons for this play's explicitly textual format is submission to the economics of the literary marketplace. In the suppressed foreword, of course, Schiller defends the textual form on a completely different basis, citing the generic fusion of drama and epic as his primary objective. It is worthwhile examining the arguments Schiller brings in defense of this strategy, since they focus once again the dichotomy between mediacy and immediacy that forms the thematic core of the text. In these theoretical reflections, however, this conflict is displaced into the realm of aesthetic reception.

In the preface published with the first edition of *The Robbers*, Schiller describes this work as "a dramatic narrative [*eine dramatische Geschichte*] that exploits the advantages of the dramatic method, namely its ability to expose the most secret [*geheimsten*] Operations of the soul" (*SW* 1: 484). My interpretation of the play has indicated the significance of this technique of disclosure, which manifests itself primarily in the structure of dramatic irony. Lacking the double vision this tactic provides, Schiller's readers would be unable either to see through Franz's hoaxes or to gain insight into the interpretive incompetence of naive cognition in a world of dissimulation and human counterfeits. Application of dramatic irony thus permits Schiller to situate his readers in a position that is hermeneutically superior to that of his naive protagonists. The modeling of this hermeneutical double vision in the dimension of literary reception represents one of Schiller's fundamental literary-aesthetic aims in this play. It is only consistent, after all, that a text that seeks to further utopian opposition to the enlightened world while simultaneously demonstrating that such opposition must take the form of a private-secret (*heimlich*) protest would have to encourage its readers to apply a complicated interpretive-receptive strategy; otherwise they would never penetrate the camouflage of the text's own dissimulations and discover its secret, its hidden center of resistance.

Clearly, the receptive attitude such a strategy requires of its audience is a highly reflective one, and Schiller's legitimation of this dramatic narrative precisely because of the reflection it demands stands in diametrical opposition to the immediacy that Lessing, for example, viewed as the (semiotic) virtue of the dramatic genre. As we have seen, however, in *Emilia Galotti* Lessing also demonstrates his awareness of the practical limitations inherent in the immediacy of natural signs. In Schiller's forewords to *The Robbers* the seeds of these doubts blossom into a full-fledged skepticism. To be sure, in the suppressed foreword Schiller pays lip service to the "living perception" of drama, contrasting it favorably with the "historical knowledge" of narrative literature. Indeed, he praises drama for its "sensual portrayal," its ability to present the world and human emotions as if they were immediately "present." But he insists that this virtue remains in evidence regardless of whether the play is experienced as a performance on stage or received indirectly through the process of reading, and he ultimately champions the mediate reception of reading (*SW* 1: 481–82). In fact, it is precisely the immediacy of dramatic performance, when viewed from the perspective of reception, that arouses Schiller's most profound skepticism. In a central passage found near the conclusion of the suppressed foreword, he juxtaposes dramatic viewing and reading as different receptive strategies, focusing this contrast in metaphors of sight and blindness. "The viewer, blinded by the intense light of sensuality, often overlooks both the most delicate, beautiful passages [of a drama] as well as its unwitting flaws, which are only disclosed to the eye of the contemplative reader" (*SW* 1: 484). The practical-theoretical considerations that motivated Schiller to play down the significance of theatrical performance for *The Robbers* ultimately comes down to these questions of mediacy and immediacy. The immediate sensuality of performance blinds the viewer to the significant details of the work, which can only be perceived through the reflective process of reading.

Schiller's discrimination between the literary public as immediate viewer and as reflective reader points to the beginnings of a historical upheaval in the constitution of literary reception in the bourgeois public sphere. If the Enlightenment demand for a literature in the service of the philosophic-historical aim of *Bildung* manifested itself in Germany primarily in the drive to found a national theater, Schiller's skepticism about the ability of the literary public to penetrate the immediate veil of performance signals the end of this critical-pedagogical project. *The Robbers* as "dramatic novel" marks the beginnings of a significant transition in the bourgeois literary institution from the immediate perception of viewing to deliberate reading as the preeminent mode of literary reception. Thus *The Robbers* can be considered a "tragic drama" in Walter Benjamin's sense, a "drama for the reader" ("Lesedrama"), whose audience must "brood" over the dramatic "text," approaching it with "the same thought and attentiveness as the reader."[61] To the "eye of the contemplative reader" Schiller relegates the task of liberating, in the process of privatized reading, the revolutionary potential forced underground by its confrontation with the treacherous dissimulations of the bourgeois episteme. Preserved in the subliminal sphere of the literary text and of the bourgeois subject is the ideal(ized) potential for a redemption of the naive that only reflective application of a sophisticated hermeneutical procedure can emancipate.

Schiller recognizes that a world addicted to mediacy cannot simply break this addiction cold turkey. The sentimental redemption of the naive, as an aesthetic project of planned reversal, takes the state of human (self-)alienation as a given and attempts to move backward through this state to a condition of originary immediacy and authenticity. The principal tool it employs is contemplative reflection, a double vision that yet depends on the textual medium and the process of mediate reading, but which is structured to produce critical insights. In this sense what Schiller undertakes in *The Robbers* can be viewed as a literary-aesthetic attempt to right writing, that is, to stand what has been "inverted" back on its feet, to create a form of textuality that exploits an involuted textual dissemblance as a tactic for countering the dissembling "ink smears" of modern textuality. In the dimension of literary reception, the task of righting writing corresponds to the aim of righting reading, of training modern readers to employ a sophisticated hermeneutical strategy that will allow them to penetrate the veil of textual dissemblance and thus to distinguish between genuine (re-volutionary) literature and the mere textual counterfeits of the bourgeois age. It will remain for Heinrich Heine, in his literary travelogues, to perfect this oppositional literary strategy, bringing it to bear specifically on the creation of narrative texts.

Literature as Therapy for Divided Subjects

CHAPTER FOUR

Free-Lancing

Heine's 'Ideas: The Book Le Grand' and
Literature Between Service and Servitude

Fortunately books are for most people merely *literature*.
—Friedrich Nietzsche

THE NAME of Heinrich Heine evokes quite contrary images among literary
scholars. Whereas for some he is the ultimate spokesperson of late German
Romanticism, for others he is a radically revolutionary writer, Germany's
foremost political satirist and an outspoken advocate of the ideals of the
French Revolution. The convergence in Heine of these ostensibly antagonistic literary personae has destined him, in the words of Theodor Adorno,
to be a "wound" for German cultural history and for generations of literary
critics.[1] These two Heines are, to the dismay of almost all, inseparably intertwined: as a result, those who would befriend him as a sympathetic love
poet find themselves confronted with the political rebel; and those who seek
to enlist him as a comrade in their political cause are forced to deal with the
melancholy sentimentalist. Heine was aware of this schizophrenia: he commonly referred to it as his "tornness" between two opposing tendencies. Yet
Heine insisted that this trait was characteristic of the contemporary historical situation in Germany and that it thus marked him as the true child of
his time. In *The Baths of Lucca* (1830) Heine wrote, in a famous formulation:

Oh, dear reader, if you want to bemoan this tornness, then bemoan rather that the
world itself is torn down the middle. For since the heart of the poet is the center of
the world, it simply had to be miserably torn in the present time. Whoever boasts
that his heart has remained whole only admits that he has a prosaic, secluded, back-
water heart. The great world-rift, however, runs through mine; and it is precisely
for that reason that I know that the gods have blessed me above many others and
have held me worthy of the poet's martyrdom. (*HW* 2: 405–6)[2]

Characteristic of this statement is the ironic pathos in which Heine cloaks his self-assessment. But underlying this pathetic guise are certain fundamental principles of Heine's poetics, relevant especially for the period of *Travelogues*, composed between 1826 and 1831. Central among these principles is the alignment of the poet's sentiments with the deep-structural "spirit of the age"; Heine takes his own proclivities and attitudes to be a measure for the spiritual ills of the historical present, and he interprets his "martyrdom," that is, his sensitivity to these fundamental historical crises, as the ultimate testimony to his poetic genius. No doubt, Germany in the Restoration period was a society torn, like Heine, between Romanticism and revolution, between glorification of a mythic past and struggle for a transformed future. As the principal philosopher of this epoch, Hegel gave this tornness the designation Unhappy Consciousness, and Heine's literature both concretizes and consciously thematizes the dialectical instability of this divided subjectivity. Heine shares with Hegel the belief that this unsatisfactory state of human consciousness represents but a way station along the teleological course to a self-realized human spirit. For Heine, however, this telos is not immanent to or inscribed in the course of History itself, as it was for Hegel, but rather must be instituted by human subjects operating from within their (self-)divided state. Although he displays the Janus-face peculiar to the divided subject, Heine ultimately looks ahead to a revolutionary future rather than backward into an idealized past, as did Schiller, for example. The same cannot be said, however, for the majority of his German contemporaries who constituted the literary public. Heine's poetic "martyrdom" hence was complicated by the fact that the progressive visions he sought to disseminate by means of his critical literature were not necessarily welcomed by those to whom he addressed his texts.

Heine's revolutionary political persona does not simply supplant the Romantic persona he established in his early love poetry. However, it is not the case, as has often been claimed, that his Romantic and political tendencies exist in a relationship of mutual ironic repudiation. On the contrary, Heine's transformation from a Romantic love poet to an engaged political writer occurs as a critical (self-)appropriation in which the discourse of his Romantic persona is reassimilated and refunctionalized to be placed in the service of his political (ad)venture. This appropriative mechanism makes itself paradigmatically evident in the travelogue *Ideas: The Book Le Grand* (1826), the text which by Heine's own admission signals his shift from Romantic complacency to revolutionary political engagement. In this work Heine's Romantic past is consciously sublated, canceled out as a viable attitude given the conditions of his sociopolitical life-world, but preserved as a literary-aesthetic strategy that ensures the appeal of his texts to a reading public that has not yet been weaned of its dependence on literary—and political—Romanticism. In *Ideas* Heine exploits the conventions of literary Romanticism as a strategy for depicting his own overcoming of Romantic attitudes. His revolutionizing of Romantic poetic conventions thus bespeaks his desire to revolutionize a German (reading) public that in his opinion remained mercilessly enslaved to a Romantic worldview that masochistically valorized individual suffering in the face of ignoble sociopolitical maltreatment.

Although it has generally been recognized that Heine's *Travelogues* constitute a significant literary innovation, one whose impetus stems from the desire to revolutionize literature in order to place it in the service of revolutionary politics,[3] few significant attempts have been made to document by means of the close reading and detailed analysis of individual texts precisely how Heine approaches this task. Observations on the revolutionary textual practices he pursued in these narratives tend to emphasize two general points: his adaptation of the travelogue, a genre of popular literature; and the symbolic transgression of linguistic and literary conventions. Although both of these critical positions accurately describe the general directions in which Heine moves in his attempt to establish a literature with politically revolutionary effect, they do not illuminate in sufficient detail the specific relationship between revolutionary literary practice and revolutionary political praxis. How, in other words, are the textual strategies implemented in the *Travelogues* supposed to have a specific bearing on political praxis given the sociohistorical conditions of Restoration Germany? This question, which addresses the concrete political efficacy of a revolutionary literature, was central to Heine at the time he was composing these narratives. To understand how he answered this question we must investigate his conception of the interaction between the revolutionizing text and its audience, between the oppositional political message manifest in the text and the receptive awareness of the reader as hermeneutical partner. Heine's project presupposes an interactive hermeneutical dialectic in which the political horizon of the reading public will undergo a transformation in the encounter with his text.[4] *Ideas: The Book Le Grand*, a pivotal work in Heine's *Travelogues*, is particularly well-suited for such an examination because the reader, apostrophized as an enigmatic "madame," is taken up into the narrative structure of the text. In the interaction between narrator and its textually represented reader, this narrative presents Heine's conception of the hermeneutical exchange between the politically provocative text and its reader. An analysis of this embedded textual exchange hence can elucidate how Heine foresees and forestructures the hermeneutical relationship between his oppositional text and its audience.

This interpretive analysis must be accomplished against the backdrop of the sociopolitical and intellectual-historical contexts in which this projected hermeneutical transfer is inscribed. Heine was well aware that these factors have a determining influence on the character of literary-interpretive reception. His realization that hermeneutical relations are inevitably filtered through the constraints of the sociopolitical environment complicates the rudimentary hermeneutical conceptions of Romantic theoreticians such as Friedrich Schleiermacher, much in the manner Jürgen Habermas complicates Hans-Georg Gadamer's theory of hermeneutics by pointing to the sociopolitical determinants that unconsciously shape interpretation.[5] Faced with the reactionary political oppression of the so-called "Pre-March" (Vormärz) period in Germany, the years leading up to the revolutions in March of 1848, Heine came to understand that sociopolitical strictures intervene in the hermeneutical equation between author, text, and reader. Heine was clearly aware that communicative interactions, in Habermas's terminology, are subject to "systematic distortions" that somehow must be anticipated and preemptively counteracted if the literary text is to achieve an oppositional political effect. Heine perceived the impediments that stood in the way of his program for what I will call, borrowing a term from Hegel, a politically engaged "service" literature. The textual strategies implemented in *The Book Le Grand* must be viewed in the context of a literary practice that jettisons the insular autonomy of literature in the German Classicist tradition and exploits the sociopolitical embeddedness of the literary text, its author, and its public.

Literary Service and Literary Servitude in Restoration Germany

As a political writer Heine faced the problem of developing a literature of service that could free itself from the constraints imposed by the sociopolitical circumstances of Restoration Germany. We should imagine Heine asking himself the question: "Can literature do *service* without being servile?" Formulated in this way, with the emphasis on the problem of service, the question addresses practical issues about the tactics that a politically emancipatory literature might employ. Yet the same question could be put with slightly different emphasis; it could, for example, highlight the question of whether literature *as such* is capable of fulfilling the function of political service: "Can *literature*," the question now reads, "do service without being servile?" With this emphasis the question becomes a theoretical one inquiring into the very possibility of a literature that functions as a medium of sociopolitical change. During the period of the *Travelogues*, Heine entertained no doubts in theory about the potentially emancipatory character of literature and thus answered the second of these questions with an emphatic affirmation. Only later, with the turn to journalism in the 1830's, did he shift the emphasis of this question from the practical to its theoretical aspect, a shift that indicates his growing skepticism about the adequacy of literary aesthetics for the mission of political service. In these two differing enunciations of one and the same question, the two primary attitudes on the interrelation of (literary) aesthetics and politics in the Vormärz period converge. To clarify Heine's standpoint during the creation of the *Travelogues*, a period in which he adamantly adhered to the position that literary aesthetics has a role to play in the drama of political emancipation, it is instructive to juxtapose his stance to a contemporaneous position that denies the possibility that (literary) aesthetics can fulfill any such service function.

This posture is defended most lucidly and uncompromisingly by Hegel in his *Lectures on Aesthetics*, in which he advances the by now (in)famous claim that art in his time has lost, and will never regain, its supreme calling. "In all these respects art," Hegel writes, "considered in its highest vocation, is and remains for us a thing of the past."[6] The motivations underlying this assertion, and its ramifications for the literature of the German Vormärz, supply a necessary conceptual horizon for an understanding of engaged literature in this period.[7] Hegel understands art's supreme vocation as the disclosure of a higher, more veracious Being ("Dasein"), one that transcends the empirical and historical givens of the phenomenal world. This conception, of course, is consistent with the self-understanding of aesthetics in the German Enlightenment, as well as with Schiller's notion that art preserves an originary human dignity that aesthetic education will restore. According to Hegel, however, art is no longer capable of fulfilling this task. This does not mean, of course, that the philosophical-historical project hitherto associated, especially by German thinkers of the late eighteenth century, with the domain of aesthetics must itself be abandoned; on the contrary, that function which, for Hegel, art itself can no longer fulfill is assumed by the philosophy of art, that is, by aesthetic theory, as a reflective science ("Wissenschaft") of art. "The *philosophy* [*Wissenschaft*] of art is therefore a greater need in our day than it was in days when art by itself as art yielded full satisfaction. Art invites us to intellectual consideration, and that not for the purpose of creating art again, but for knowing philosophically [*wis-*

senschaftlich] what art is."[8] Considering Hegel's claim purely in the context of literary aesthetics, it is clearly coherent with a change in course that I have traced in my examination of *The Robbers*: in Schiller's theoretical observations on this play I documented a turn away from immediate perception to contemplative reflection as the programmatic mode of literary reception. This transformation finds its theoretical concretization and historical justification in Schiller's distinction between naive and sentimental literature. This tendency away from the naive toward the reflective, which has its beginnings in Germany in the literature of the Sturm und Drang, culminates over a century later in the dramatic theories and practice of Bertolt Brecht. Hegel, however, essentially denies the viability of such projects: (literary) aesthetics does not provide a medium in which critical reflection can be furthered. In his view, sentimental or reflective literature would be a contradiction in terms.

Hegel's sense that reflective philosophical investigation into the function of art would replace the production of art itself also finds empirical confirmation in the prominence attained by aesthetic theory in the seventy years after the publication of Alexander Gottlieb Baumgarten's *Aesthetica*, the founding treatise on aesthetics, in 1750. Lessing's *Laokoön*, Schiller's diverse theoretical undertakings, and Kant's *Critique of Judgment* represent but some of the major milestones traversed by this new, swiftly evolving philosophical discipline. The German Romantics' pursuit of philological studies and the upsurge in popular literary and art criticism among the authors of the movement called "Young Germany" (Junges Deutschland) is a further index of this burgeoning interest in critical reflection on art in the bourgeois age. What distinguishes Hegel's attitudes from those of Schiller, for example, is that he wants no part of the nostalgia inherent in the reverse telos of aesthetic education. Thus, if for Schiller the reflective stance of the sentimental poet is a necessary evil through which one must pass before returning to the immediacy of the naive, for Hegel reflection becomes the critical motor driving all human progress. This belief is basically shared by Heine and the writers of Young Germany. Indeed, for Heine it is precisely the backward gaze of the German Restoration, its erection of barriers against that sociopolitical progress represented for him in the ideals of the French Revolution, that makes it the object of his satirical attacks. The project of return valorized by eighteenth-century aesthetics as the seminal function of art is thus identified as a principally conservative, antiprogressive endeavor. Given this assessment, one can certainly understand why Hegel pronounces art dead and goes on to perform a thorough autopsy on it in his voluminous lectures on aesthetics.

The contemporary age, in Hegel's view, is dominated by reflection, and it is this irreversible historical fact that necessarily spells the demise of art: "Thought and reflection," he maintains, "have spread their wings above fine art."[9] Although he himself sees this outpacing of art by reflection as a progressive development, he realizes that his contemporaries, to the extent that they are willing to accept at all his certification of art's death, will likely mourn its loss as but one more symptom of the degeneracy of the contemporary age.

Those who delight in lamenting and blaming may regard this phenomenon as a corruption and ascribe it to the predominance of passions and selfish interests which scare away the seriousness of art as well as its cheerfulness; or they may accuse the distress of the present time, the complicated state of civil and political life which does not permit a heart entangled in petty interests to free itself to the higher ends of art. This is because intelligence itself subserves this distress, and its interests, in sciences which are useful for such ends alone, and it allows itself to be seduced into confining itself to this desert.[10]

Hegel makes clear that while this critique of the modern world is justified, lamentations and nostalgia are inappropriate responses. Instead, one must give oneself over to reflection—here Hegel replicates Schiller's affirmation of reflection as a historical necessity, while yet deflecting it from the nostalgic project of sentimental redemption of the naive—and thereby further the reflective coming-to-consciousness of Spirit that Hegel views as the purpose of human history.[11] But the most interesting aspect of Hegel's remarks is undoubtedly his diagnosis of those ills he deems responsible for the "corrupt" state of modern existence: on the one hand, he blames this condition on the selfish indulgence of human passions; on the other hand, he cites the subjugation of human intelligence to the narrow-minded interests of scientific utility, which he derogatorily compares to a barren desert. This double-barreled critique, which takes aim at the abuse of humanity's sensual and intellectual faculties alike, locates Hegel's deliberations in an intellectual-historical trajectory that delineates, in diverse thematic variations, one of the primary lines of modern German thought. One of the earliest manifestations of this problematic can be found in the fourth letter of Schiller's *Aesthetic Education*, where savagery and barbarism are identified as the Scylla and Charybdis of human existence. "But Man can be at odds with himself in a double fashion," Schiller maintains, "either as savage if his feelings rule his principles, or as barbarian if his principles destroy his feelings."[12] Of course, for Schiller only art is capable of mediating between human passions and human reason, and the aesthetic sphere thus becomes that domain in which the "cultured human being" ("der gebildete Mensch") is constituted, a human being in whom these drives exist in perfect balance and harmony. Between the publication of Schiller's *Letters on the Aesthetic Education of Man* in 1795 and Hegel's lectures on aesthetics, which were first presented in the 1820's, a radical shift in the historical evaluation of aesthetics has occurred. Hegel demotes art, once the means for rescuing humanity from itself, to a mere object of reflective study. To be sure, he believes that the formative role of aesthetics has been assumed by philosophy, which hence inherits art's supreme calling. But it is precisely his jettisoning of art that gives rise to the suspicion that the reflective therapy he proposes is but a symptom of the illness he means to cure: the supplanting of art by philosophy would seem to signal the victory of reason over sensuality and thus bespeak the migration of humanity further into that "desert" of narrow, particularistic knowledge.

This suspicion is justified by the arguments Hegel makes against art and in favor of reflection. Whereas he hypostatizes art as the expression of a "higher reality," as a "truer existence" ("das wahrhaftigere Dasein") over against the empirical world, he simultaneously denies that art is the "highest and absolute mode of bringing to our minds the true interests of the spirit" because it is restricted to the portrayal of what expresses itself in the sensual world.[13] The banishment of art thus seems to imply a suppression of those sensual, individual truths that lie within its domain. This supposition is confirmed by the language with which Hegel outlines the domineering function of reflection in the life of modern human beings. "The development of reflection in our life today has made it a need of ours, in relation both to our will and judgement, to cling to general considerations and to regulate the particular by them, with the result that universal forms, laws, duties, rights, maxims, prevail as determining reasons and are the chief regulator. . . . Consequently the conditions of our present time are not favourable to art."[14] Hegel's arguments move precariously in the direction of what Adorno would later criticize as the repression of the nonidentical by the universalizing strategies of the logic of identity, or as a secularization of what Max Weber called Christian asceticism, which he defined as a "systematic method of rational conduct with the purpose of overcoming the *status naturae*, to free man from the power of irrational impulses and his dependence on the world and on nature."[15] In other words, Hegel's proposition about the end of art reflects the very repression of the sensual and immediate that forms one of the principal reflexes of the dialectic of enlightenment: the exploitation of reason to "regulate the particular" by means of "universal forms and laws," submitting the human being and the world of nature to the principles of (self-)mastery.

The conception of aesthetics on which Hegel forms his judgment about the historical inadequacy of art is restrictively narrow. Indeed, for the instance of literature, at least, his theory falls historically behind developments already initiated in the literary practice of Schiller and other writers of the German Sturm und Drang. If we examine the logic Hegel follows to arrive at his assertion of art's "pastness," we discover that he is guilty of a petitio principii, since this conclusion is already preordained by the narrow circumscription of aesthetics that he takes as his point of departure. Hegel's radical historicizing conclusion is reached by passing through a series of conceptual dichotomies and exclusions, the most significant of which is the distinction between "service" or "ancillary" art ("dienende Kunst") and "free art" ("freie Kunst"). This preemptive differentiation, which allows him to expel "service" art from the sphere of aesthetics, is based on a questionable judgment about the relative "worthiness" ("Würdigkeit") of two types of artistic practice.

As regards the *worthiness* of art to be treated scientifically [*wissenschaftlich*], it is of course the case that art can be used as a fleeting play, affording recreation and entertainment, decorating our surroundings, giving pleasantness to the externals of our life, and making other objects stand out by artistic adornment. Thus regarded, art is indeed not independent, not free, but an ancillary art of service. But what *we* want to consider is art which is *free* alike in its ends and its means.[16]

This passage divulges the extent to which Hegel represents the aesthetic position held by bourgeois ideology; for what he glorifies as "free" art is nothing other than the autonomous art hypostatized by the bourgeois institution of art. With this distinction between "service" and "free" art Hegel underwrites the division between high and low aesthetics through which the bourgeois institution of art attains its self-constitution. Just as he banishes "service" art from the inner sanctum of aesthetics—that is, from the realm of *fine* art—the bourgeois institution of art instituted the dichotomy between "serious," autonomous art and the "ornament" or "entertainment" associated today with the products of the culture industry. However, this idealizing gentrification of art fails to take into account the realities of its production in the bourgeois age, the necessary subordination of art and artist to the practical demands of the socioeconomic sphere. Indeed, it consciously attempts to cordon off the idealized realm of aesthetics from the real socioeconomic dependencies which cause art to "degenerate" into mere ornament and entertainment.

Like Hegel, Heine and the other writers of Young Germany recognized the dangers inherent in the subjugation of (literary) aesthetics to the economic principles of the bourgeois marketplace; but unlike Hegel, they also recognized that the popular appeal of "service" art, as an aesthetic of entertainment and ornamentation, provided a potentially fruitful medium, if properly exploited, for the dissemination of critical perspectives. They thus sought to harness the popularity of "service" art—of artistic commodities— by appropriating it as a medium for sociopolitical education. In this sense Heine and the authors of Young Germany carry on Schiller's project of aesthetic education, with the significant revision that it is service art, not autonomous art, that becomes the medium of this pedagogical mission.

The paradox of Hegel's arguments on aesthetics is that it is only his valorization of "free" art that ultimately permits him to declare art passé. What he pronounces dead, in short, is nothing other than the aesthetics of autonomy that he seeks to defend. However, because it is preemptively banished from the sanctum of "genuine" aesthetics, service art, ironically, is spared the executioner's blade. This is the point at which Heine latches onto and simultaneously abandons Hegel's arguments; for while he welcomes the passing of autonomous art, he nevertheless refuses to accept that its end can be equated with the demise of (literary) aesthetics in toto. For Heine the question instead becomes one of how to reshape literary-aesthetic practice given, on the one hand, the death of autonomous (literary) art and, on the other, the sociopolitical and economic realities of Restoration Germany. Consequently, in the programmatic statement in defense of the literature of Junges Deutschland that Heine articulated in *The Romantic School* (1833–35), he stresses that he and his fellow writers merge politics with art, science, and religion, and he celebrates this merger as a "wholeness" that he contrasts favorably with the partiality of autonomous literature. "This characteristic, this wholeness, we also find in the writers of present-day Young Germany, who likewise wish to make no distinction between life and writing, who never separate politics from science, art, and religion, and who are simultaneously artists, tribunes, and apostles" (*Romantic School*, 468; *100*). The "wholeness" Heine attributes to the writers of this movement—and, by extension, to himself—is not defined in terms of the closure and autonomy of Classical aesthetics, but rather, in explicit opposition to this, by the linkage of art and life, literature and politics: the aesthetic sphere and empirical lifeworld explicitly dovetail and interact.

Whereas Hegel acknowledged and underwrote the bourgeois institution of autonomous art—even if only ultimately to bury it—Heine openly attacks the aesthetic autonomy of what he derogatorily dubs the Goethean Kunstperiode, the age of German classicist art, denouncing Goethe and his epigones for treating art "as an independent second world" detached from "all activities of human beings." By asserting the supremacy of art, Heine argued, these writers turned their backs on "that original real world," that is, on the sociopolitical world (*Romantic School*, 393; 34). Heine and Hegel thus agree that autonomous art is dead; but Hegel, who cannot conceive of a nonautonomous art, infers from this art's historical end, whereas Heine merely draws the conclusion that art must be reborn in an altogether new form, one that is adapted to historical conditions.

Heine believed that modern literature could play a fundamental role in the coming-to-consciousness that Hegel projected as the purpose of human history. In *Concerning the History of Religion and Philosophy in Germany* (1834), Heine praised modern literature for its individuality and skepticism, maintaining that it was not "objective, epic, and naive," like classical literature, but rather "subjective, lyric, and reflective" (*History of Religion*, 552; 164). With this definition Heine invokes Schiller's discrimination between naive and sentimental literature, identifying the former with classicist writing and the latter with modern reflective literary texts. This association is consistent with the thrust of Schiller's distinction, and the recourse to Schiller provides Heine with a theoretical position that permits him to uphold the distinction between the naive, "objective," that is, autonomous literature of the Kunst-periode and the reflectivity of the modern age—without, however, coming to Hegel's conclusion that the age of art per se lies in the historical past. For Heine the historical conditions of the modern world do not demand the forsaking of literary aesthetics in favor of the science of art, but rather a refunctionalization of literature itself. Like Schiller, Heine inscribes the distinction between the naive and the reflective *within* the sphere of (literary) aesthetics, whereas Hegel employs this distinction to juxtapose art and philosophy and thus to establish philosophical reflection as art's historical heir.

Hegel brands service art with qualities that indicate its secondariness to something else; it is a mere externality wanting of any self-contained essence. "Service," in other words, is synonymous with servitude, and this negative implication is brought out clearly by the juxtaposition of service with "free" art. Heine overthrows this evaluation, interpreting the supposed vices of externality, secondariness, and linkage to the transitory events of the sociopolitical world as the ultimate virtues of a literature of service. Yet Heine also realizes that in the move from a theory of the service potential of literary aesthetics to the praxis of a service literature the problem of servitude remains a very real consideration. Once he makes the decision to dedicate his literature to service in the cause of oppositional politics, Heine is still left with the problem of devising literary techniques that will allow him successfully to infiltrate the sphere of public communication and the consciousness of the reading public to plant his revolutionary opinions. This was no simple task, especially in view of the repressive sociopolitical conditions in the Germany of Metternich, with its watchdog control over the sphere of public communication.

Some of Heine's reflections on the interaction between word and deed leave one with the impression that he possessed an idealized, optimistic, and even naive conception of the power of language as the mediator between thought and human practice. In *History of Religion and Philosophy in Germany* he writes, for example: "Thought strives to become action, the word to become flesh. And marvellous to relate, man, like God in the Bible, needs only to express his thought, and the world takes shape" (*History of Religion*, 593; 201). The immanent telos of all thought, Heine proposes, is to be concretized as action, and linguistic expression is the transparent medium of this metamorphosis. Heine thus conceives language as a tool, ascribing to it the power to transform the life-world through a process of human labor. Viewed from this perspective, the autonomous literature of the Kunstperiode employs language in a manner that violates its originary purpose by extricating it from this interaction with the world. Hence Heine views his task as the recapturing and reassertion of this language of practical efficacy, which has been overshadowed by the useless language of Goethean classicism. "A deed is the child of the word," he remarks in *The Romantic School*, "and Goethe's beautiful words are childless. This is the curse on everything that has originated in art alone" (*Romantic School*, 395; 36). Only by abandoning the pursuit of absolute beauty, by becoming more than "free art" and reasserting its rhetoricity, can literature have a hand in shaping the life-world. In this sense what Heine seeks to accomplish can be described as a revival of the rhetorical capacity of literature.

Martin Luther represents for Heine the historical example of an individual who productively exploited the potentials of such a rhetorically functional language in the service of a critical project. Luther, according to Heine, gave the Germans "not merely freedom of movement, but also the means to move, that is, he gave the spirit a body. He put the thought into words. He created the German language" (*History of Religion*, 554; 157). What he most admires in Luther is the ability of a single individual to stand up victoriously against the corruption of an institution like the Catholic Church. Luther thus becomes the model for a form of critique that employs language as a weapon against the dominant ideological institution:[17] what Luther succeeds in accomplishing vis-à-vis the church is exemplary for the critique that Heine seeks to unleash against the ideological bastions of Restoration Germany. Furthermore, Luther consciously developed his language with an eye—and an ear—for its universal comprehensibility among a diverse German populace that spoke variant dialects. Heine perceives his own literary challenge as one that parallels Luther's creation of the German (literary) language: defining his function as that of a popularizer, a disseminator of critical thought, he too must create a literary language coherent with this mission. "To this efficacy," Heine admitted in the preface to *Conditions in France* (1832), "my life remains devoted: it is my office [*Amt*]" (*HW* 3: 91).

Despite his seemingly naive optimism about the immediate translatability of language into political actions, Heine was painfully aware that the formulation of such a critical literary practice presents a delicate and difficult task. In the "Preface" to *Lutetia* (1840–43), he reflects on the kinds of concessions the oppositional writer must make to find a satisfactory compromise between his own critical discourse and the capacity of ideological mechanisms to parry its offensive.

A writer who is political in every respect has to make many compromises with brute necessity for the sake of his cause. There are enough obscure local papers in which we could pour out our heart . . . but these have only a meager and uninfluential readership. . . . We are much wiser when we temper our ardor, and, with sober phrases—perhaps even in a guise—avail ourselves of a newspaper which is justifiably considered to be of international repute and which informs several hundred thousand readers all over the world. Even with these pitiful distortions the word can thrive here; the most paltry hint sometimes brings forth a bountiful harvest in unfamiliar soil. (*HW* 5: 229)

The final metaphor of this passage betrays Heine's stubborn faith in the revolutionary potency of the word. By the same token, he was by no means unaware of the extenuating circumstances of the sociopolitical environment in which his words were expected to sprout, and he concedes that they are subject to (self-)mutilation by the concessions these circumstances extract. Nevertheless, he insists that words and their rhetorical effectiveness can survive this process of systematic distortion.

Scholars dealing with the literature of the Vormärz have justifiably emphasized the external agencies—governmental censorship—responsible for this systematic distortion of communication.[18] The effects of this official censorship, however, were not always debilitating; on the contrary, institutionalized censorship often proved beneficial for the literature of the period insofar as it provided writers with incentives for developing creative forms of literary subterfuge. In addition, the banning of a book by the censors, paradoxically, was commonly taken by the public as a sign of its intrinsic worth, so that the act of suppression unwittingly became a productive marketing technique.[19] Institutional censorship hence was ultimately something that talented writers such as Heine could not only get around, but could even turn to their own advantage.[20] However, if the government censors ultimately were, to allude to Heine's poignant satirical attack in the twelfth chapter of *Ideas*, merely "blockheads" (*Ideas*, 283; *205–6*), the more covert effects of censorship, and the repression to which it testifies, had profound consequences for Heine's literary program. The most efficient filters Heine had to counter were not those deployed by the primary censorship propagated in official channels, but those of the *secondary* censorship unconsciously assimilated into the collective psyche of the German public in reaction to the severe political intimidation characteristic of Restoration society. Since Heine perceived his role as that of a disseminator of critical thought, there could be little sense in preaching to those who already shared his convictions. But if the task of persuasion is difficult enough under ideal circumstances, it is infinitely more arduous when one attempts to reach and influence an audience who—for whatever reasons, but in this specific instance, for reasons of simple political survival—is predisposed to reject the ideas one is propounding. Because Heine's readers did not perceive his political overtures to be in their own best political interests, their internalized censorship mechanisms could be expected to work hard at eradicating his oppositional viewpoints—unless, of course, he were able to devise a discourse that would stealthfully smuggle his intellectual contraband past these psychological censorship mechanisms.[21]

The solution Heine arrives at in the *Travelogues* is to take a double-track approach to his public: one the one hand, he devises a language calculated to appeal to his readers' popularized literary tastes, thereby lowering their psychic defense mechanisms; on the other hand, he attempts to communicate his political message in a form that, although disguised, nevertheless remains recognizable. This is the precarious situation of "service" literature in the sociopolitical circumstances of Restoration Germany: the drive for revolutionary political service is constantly threatened by the demand of servitude to the public it seeks to serve. This servitude expresses itself for Heine, as a free-lance writer financially dependent on the marketability of his literature, in his concrete material dependence on a public that is both the consumer of his literary commodity and the potential revolutionary whom his rhetoric hopes to affect and awaken to political action.

How can the writer present to the same public on whose goodwill and benevolence he economically depends those discomforting, unsettling truths that a critical stance demands? This is the dilemma Heine attempted to solve in *Ideas: The Book Le Grand*. As we have seen, submission to the literary marketplace and the tastes of the purchasing public already constituted a practical dilemma for Lessing and the young Schiller. For Heine, however, this predicament, characteristic of the free-lance bourgeois writer, is further complicated by his overtly rebellious political stance and the oppressive sociopolitical conditions of the Restoration era. Nevertheless, Heine identifies Lessing as a significant precursor who shares with him his woes as economically dependent author. Maintaining that Lessing's chronic poverty is symptomatic of the fate of all critical spirits in Germany, Heine ironically comments that this literary talent, whom he heralds as the "founder of modern German national literature," unfortunately lacked the ability "to turn stones into bread." This "curse," Heine predicts, can be "eliminated only by political liberation" (*Romantic School*, 371–72; 13). The conundrum of Heine's situation, however, is that as a free-lance writer who lives in a time prior to this projected political emancipation, he must find a way both to eat—that is, to write—and to struggle for the very political emancipation that constitutes the condition of possibility of this writing. Given the circularity of this dilemma and his refusal to abandon his political project, Heine must exploit his literary creativity to develop a textual practice that will permit him "to turn stones into bread." As free-lance writer, to state the problem aphoristically, Heine was not free to lance indiscriminately. The complex texture of *Ideas: The Book Le Grand* manifests a specific set of literary strategies calculated to loosen the shackles that tie literary-political service to literary-economic servitude.

Ideas: The Book Le Grand and the "Miserable Economy" of Literature

Heine's *Travelogues* are the product of a period of permutation in his life, a time when he was struggling not only to establish literary authorship as the basis for his material existence, but also attempting to realize sweeping changes in his intellectual attitudes and literary practice. These texts evolve in those transitional years between the Romantic poems and dramas of Heine's early creative phase and the journalistic criticism of the 1830's and beyond. In a letter to Karl Simrock written in 1825, Heine depicts the dilemma of this period as the impossibility of adjudicating his own creative drives with the expectations of the German literary public. "No one senses more than I how difficult it is to offer something literary that has never been done before, and how unsatisfying it must be to every more profound spirit to write merely to please the idle masses" (*HB* 1: 248). This brief comment is significant for two reasons. First, it indicates Heine's awareness that his texts are addressed to a specific bourgeois reading public, one with enough leisure ("idle" time) to pursue literary interests, on the one hand, but which, on the other hand, he simultaneously disparages as "idle *masses*" without individuality and on whom intellectual depth is wasted. Second, he specifically conceives the conflict between the writer and his public as an artistic dilemma: he experiences it as the difficulty of presenting his readers literary works that break with the norms of the popularized literary commodity on which they thrive. This antagonism between the "more profound spirit" of the author and the lowly, institutionalized tastes of the "idle masses" characterizes the conundrum both of Heine's literary and political ambitions: in both domains he senses that his impulses toward the novel and unfamiliar run counter to the attitudes of the Restoration public, which prefers to remain comfortably within the ordinary. Revolutionary politics and innovative literary practice thus converge for Heine in the period during which the *Travelogues* are composed. Given that he anticipated resistance both to the political message of these texts and to their aesthetic novelty, their popular success represents a truly monumental literary-aesthetic achievement. *Ideas: The Book Le Grand*, from the second volume of *Travelogues*, provides the most striking example of a text that advances Heine's revolutionary political position and still manages to win him the popularity he so keenly desires.

According to Heine's own assessment, *Ideas* formed the centerpiece of the second volume of *Travelogues*. In a letter to Moses Moser written immediately after the publication of this volume, Heine described his satisfaction with this collection, stressing the centrality of *The Book Le Grand* in its makeup.

I imagine *Le Grand* has probably pleased you; everything else in the book, with the exception of the poems, is fodder for the masses, who are also consuming it with great appetite. Through this book I have achieved an enormous following and popularity in Germany; if I get well again, I will be able to accomplish a great deal: I now have a voice that resounds for great distances. You shall hear it often, thundering against those who police our thoughts and suppress our holiest rights. (*HB* I: 315–16)

These remarks highlight the centrality of questions of political effectiveness and popular reception for the composition of *Ideas* in particular, as well as for the conception of this collection as a whole. Heine implies that the majority of texts in this volume were primarily buffers, intended both to absorb the shock of the political and aesthetic radicality of *Ideas* and to stimulate the appetite of the public, baiting the reader to swallow the political outspokenness and literary adventurousness of this radical narrative. Heine unabashedly expresses his pride in this achievement, describing the book's success in terms of the liberation of his critical voice.[22]

Throughout the planning and composition of the second volume of *Travelogues*, Heine stressed the uniqueness of these new texts. In December of 1825, for example, he maintained that the second and third volumes would present "a new sort of travelogue" (*HB* 1: 244). Above all else, it was the success and recognition of the first volume that encouraged Heine to continue with this genre in more daring form, since he believed that this positive reception assured him of an audience. "The travelogues are for the present the medium through which I can present to the public whatever I want" (*HB* 1: 290), he wrote almost a year later to Karl Immermann. And in a letter to Wilhelm Müller from June of 1826, he explicitly aligned the shift from poetry to prose with the critical stance he assumed in this new literary endeavor.

Prose is taking me up in its broad arms, and you will be able to read in the next volumes of *Travelogues* much that is prosaically insane, acrid, injurious, and annoying: it will all be remarkably polemical. The times are much too evil, and whoever possesses the strength and the unfettered courage also has the duty to enter into serious combat with this bloating evil and with that mediocrity that makes itself so expansive, so unbearably expansive. (*HB* 1: 270–71; cf. also 1: 303)

Curiously, a comment found in a letter to Varnhagen von Ense written just a few weeks later appears openly to contradict these remarks. "I am presently busy with the second part [of *Travelogues*]," Heine remarks, "and I've tried to make it as attractive [*anziehend*] as possible" (*HB* 1: 276). Far from being contradictory, however, these comments in fact document the mutually supplementary, if ostensibly antagonistic, tactics Heine was attempting to combine in the texts of this collection: bitter critique in the service of political emancipation, on the one hand; ingratiation and concession in the interest of public appeal, on the other. This give and take of courtship and critique, appeal and accusation, constitutes the formative principle underlying *Ideas: The Book Le Grand.*

In November of 1826, when Heine sent Rudolf Christiani an excerpt from a draft of *The Book Le Grand*, which at this early stage was entitled "Ideas on History," he felt it necessary to introduce the text with the following caveat: "Don't damn my harshness; I have been forced to take up the sword. But oh!, I know very well that those who live by the sword will die by the sword. Truly, my position never favored my development into a gentle minnesinger—the call aux armes! armes! was always ringing in my ears—Alea jacta est" (*HB* 1: 297). This declaration indicates that from the very outset Heine viewed *Ideas* as a text that bore witness to the repudiation of his past as Romantic minnesinger. The "harshness" of this work, as he implies by means of semantic opposition, stands in stark contrast to the "gentleness" of his Romantic love poetry. Furthermore, by maintaining that "the die has been cast" ("Alea jacta est"), he underscores the irreversibility of this crucial transformation from Romantic poet to political advocate. It is interesting that Heine cites his "position" as the circumstance responsible for this essential metamorphosis. This suggests that this transmogrification does not evolve organically, as it were, out of his own personality and proclivities, but rather is forced upon him by external factors. Although he does not specify exactly what he means with this reference to his "position," it seems obvious that he is pointing to the plight of the sensitive, free-thinking individual given the unspeakably repressive sociopolitical circumstances of Germany at this time. He is most likely also referring to his "position" as free-lance writer, a posture that lends him a certain degree of autonomy and therefore assigns him a role in the revolutionary political enlightenment of the German public sphere. However, the fulfillment of this mission, as Heine was acutely aware, was fraught with seemingly insurmountable obstacles.

While Heine refers to the portion of the draft he sends to Christiani as chapter two of this text, it is likely that the material in question is actually what eventually becomes chapter fourteen in the final version of *Ideas: The Book Le Grand*. This speculation is based on the probability that what ultimately finds its place as chapter thirteen of the published text—the chapter in which Heine deals with questions of history, mocks the Germans' pedantic drive toward systematic exposition, and finally gives a self-parodistic account of the "system" his "ideas" are to follow (see *Ideas*, 284–87; *206–9*)— represents the first chapter of the draft entitled "Ideas on History." This title, at any rate, succinctly describes the content of this portion of Heine's text, and since chapter fourteen necessarily follows on chapter thirteen, picking up where the prior section left off and embellishing the notion of "ideas" presented there, it most likely constitutes the "second" chapter of the "Ideas on History" that Heine sent to Christiani. Now, my speculations on the historical genesis of this text are not proffered in the interests of a simple philological reconstruction of the *Ur-Ideas*, the initial draft of *The Book Le Grand*. On the contrary, this philological question is pertinent for the interpretation of Heine's text, for if my reconstruction is correct, it indicates that this critical attack formed the initial focus of this work. The target of this assault, moreover, is not so much the political reality of the Restoration period as it is the dominant intellectual conditions in the German public sphere and, given this milieu, the status of the serious writer with a political mission. One of the driving impulses behind the composition of *Ideas*, then, was Heine's wish to analyze the dilemmas of politically engaged authorship in Restoration Germany.

As early as May of 1826 Heine expressed his intention to exploit the second volume of *Travelogues* as a medium for denouncing the miserable circumstances of the free-lance writer, circumstances that conditioned the crises Heine himself experienced as author. To Varnhagen von Ense he expressed his concerns in the form of doubts about his own future as a writer. "I'm . . . concerned not merely because of the miserable economy in our literature, where one is so easily out-winged by the insignificant in the judgment of the public, but also because I will speak ruthlessly about such misery in the second volume of *Travelogues*; I will wield my whip and incur the eternal damnation of those who shape public opinion" (*HB* 1: 260). This ruthless condemnation of a literary "economy" in which the trivial outpaces the substantial finds its concrete expression in chapter fourteen of *The Book Le Grand*, chapter two of the draft entitled "Ideas on History."

Heine clearly has doubts about whether his new literary undertaking can reckon with success: he fears that his critical incursions will be repulsed by precisely those determiners of public opinion whose role he would like to usurp. On the other hand, the diffidence he voices concerning his future as writer stands in stark contrast to the almost cocky confidence he expresses in the previously cited letter to Wilhelm Müller following the publication and successful reception of this work. In addition, Heine's remarks to von Ense make clear that it is through this very specific lens—that is, by condemning the "miserable economy" of literature—that Heine focuses his critique of contemporary sociopolitical ills in Germany.

Heine recognized that his impulse toward critical ruthlessness and his ambition to become a popular author whose books were widely bought and read did not jibe well with one another. He experienced the contrariness of these two drives as a conflict between free expression in the service of political emancipation and forced slavery to the ideologically nurtured tastes of the reading public. Expressed in economic terms, he realized that in the literary marketplace of Restoration Germany the political use-value he sought to lend his literature was at odds with the commercial exchange-value of his texts as literary commodities.[23] This is the aporia constitutive of the "miserable economy" of literature that Heine set out to lambaste in *Ideas: The Book Le Grand*. However, this work goes far beyond the simple exposition of this critical analysis; indeed, its conception derives from Heine's attempts to reconcile this conflict between "service" and "servitude." In *Ideas*, then, he sought to develop a literary practice that would appeal to the institutionalized horizon of the German literary public sphere and to the demands of the literary marketplace, while at the same time allowing him to condemn these very institutions.

Chapter fourteen of *Ideas* has commonly been taken as a programmatic exposition of Heine's satirical method, his knack, as he describes it, for living off the foolishness of his contemporaries. Heine transforms, as he expresses it with characteristic wit, these "capital fools" into "capital" by writing about their folly (*Ideas*, 292; *213*), and he thanks God for letting him work in the "vineyard" of the world where fools flourish like grapes: "I only need gather the grapes, press them with my feet, squeeze them, barrel them, put them in the cellar, and I then have the clear heavenly gift" (*Ideas*, 295; *216*). Remaining within the realm of the culinary imagery he so likes to exploit, he goes on to compare his satirical method with the preparation of food. "And although fools do not exactly fly roasted into my mouth but run at me rather raw and not even half-baked, still I know how to turn them on a spit, stew them and pepper them until they are tender and tasty" (*Ideas*, 295–96; *216*). The culinary metaphors are strategically appropriate in the context of Heine's plight as free-lance writer, for it is the conflict between writing as bread-winning occupation and as medium of revolutionary-political service that shapes his personal dilemma. The question, however, is whether we can simply take his portrayal of his satirical abandon at face value, or whether we must not, in fact, view it as an ironic simplification of the very complex relationship that obtains between satirical writer, the object of his satire, and the public that feeds him by purchasing the satirical product. If we take his metaphors as accurate analogies for his satirical method, then we would have to conclude that his satirical target and the source of his sustenance—that is, his reading, purchasing public—are identical. If this is the case, then it does not augur well for the economic success of his satirical venture. Not even Heine's contemporaries were masochistic enough to purchase and read books that shamelessly ridiculed them. This suggests that in the interest of the exchange-value of his literary commodity, Heine either had to camouflage his satire—at which point it would, strictly speaking, cease to be satire at all—or package it together with literary palliatives more to the liking of his prospective readers. Heine himself was clearly cognizant of this problem, since, as we have seen, he expressed skepticism about his future as a writer in anticipation of public reactions to the excoriating satirical onslaught contained in *Ideas*. Pure satire represents a questionable, perhaps even self-defeating tactic for the writer who is financially bound to the very public he would satirize. What artist, to draw a relevant analogy, could openly mock his patron and still expect to enjoy the fruits of patronage? As literary-critical program, then, blistering satire interferes both with Heine's need to appeal to his "patrons" as well as with his desire to effect the broad dissemination of his revolutionary "ideas." Indeed, far from providing an adequate solution to the aporia of the service artist as Heine conceived it, satire merely threatens to aggravate this already intractable dilemma.[24] Consequently, the satirical program expressed in chapter fourteen of *Ideas* must itself be read as Heine's satire of any such naive critical project. Such overt critique cannot effectively accomplish critical service because it ignores the fact of the writer's servitude, his economic and political dependence on the indulgence of the reading public.

Heine himself was cognizant of the inherent weakness of a program that practices such merciless satire. The overly lavish self-praise he heaps upon his satirical penchant is simultaneously undercut by a pervasive tone of skepticism. For example, despite his boast that he will never run out of satirical "capital" and that his economic outlook consequently is superb, his actual material poverty is painted in the bleakest of terms. "You see, madame, I can use everybody, and the city directory is actually the inventory of my property. And I consequently can never go bankrupt, for I would transform my creditors [*Gläubiger*] themselves into sources of income. Moreover, as already stated, I really live very economically—damned economically! For instance, while I write this I am sitting in a dark, gloomy room on Dismal Street" (*Ideas*, 293–94; 214). Heine ironizes his own commentary by contrasting the potential wealth of satirical objects with the tangible poverty of his lifestyle. Indeed, his willingness to exploit even his "Gläubiger"—the word alludes both to Heine's "creditors" as well as his "faithful," those who "keep the faith" with him—hints that his financial desperation is so great that he would not stop at exploiting even those who have remained true to him as author. Moreover, he freely admits that he would trade the fortune he possesses in satirical property for fortune in the lottery (*Ideas*, 289; 211). Free-lancing satire, in other words, by no means brings the free-lance writer substantial financial returns; and while the satirical use-value of Heine's public may have been great indeed, the economic exchange-value of the satirical product was nonetheless not great enough to guarantee him a solid livelihood.

Still, Heine could not completely neutralize his satirical-critical penchant, and he believed that the second volume of *Travelogues*, but especially *Ideas*, testified to his own incorrigible lack of restraint. Fearing dire political consequences as a result of his critical candor, Heine left for England on the very day the collection was published. From London he wrote in self-castigation to Friedrich Merckel: "Despite my better insights, I will never be able to give up perpetrating stupid pranks, that is, expressing liberal viewpoints." And he continues with the query, "I'm curious to hear from you whether some government did not take offence at my book" (*HB* 1: 309). To be sure, Heine's most immediate fear is that this volume will elicit grievous political repercussions, and given the ruthless persecution directed against critics of the sociopolitical order during this period, his fears were legitimate. But he recognized that the Restoration public was wholly intimidated and co-opted by the forces of political oppression, and this caused him to view persecution by the reading public as well as by the government as emanating from a single source. Heine's understanding of his plight as writer is always conceived against this repressive political backdrop, so that the misery of literature and the misery of political life in the Restoration are inseparable: persecution by political authorities and rejection by the reading public are just two sides of the same problem. Thus the misery of the contemporary writer, as depicted in the fourteenth chapter of *Ideas*, can be read as a structural homology for the misery of general sociopolitical existence in Germany during this period.

Heine's images betray that the writer's forced reliance on the reading, purchasing public manifests itself in a reflex of (feigned) devotion with which he curries its favor. Recalling the Horatian maxim that an author should withhold his manuscripts from publication for nine years, Heine pronounces its impracticality for the present age, in which the author must either publish or perish.

But we, we unlucky latecomers, live in a different era. Our art patrons have entirely different principles: they believe that authors and medlars flourish best if they lie for a period of time on straw; they believe that the dogs would not be fit for hunting metaphors and thoughts if they were fed too well; and if they nonetheless occasionally feed a poor dog, then it is the wrong dog who least deserves the scraps: for example, the dachshund who licks hands or the tiny Italian toy spaniel who knows how to cuddle up into the lady's perfumed lap or the patient poodle who has learned a practical trade and can fetch and carry, dance and drum. (*Ideas*, 290; 212)

Only those writer-dogs who kowtow to the will of their masters can hope to reap reward; yet it is these obsequious creatures, according to Heine, who least deserve favor. The equation of writers with dogs provides more than just an ironic commentary on the lowly social status of literati: this metaphor also evokes all those images of dependence, faithfulness, and slavishness commonly associated with canines. The portrayal of the writer as one who must fawn to win his meager keep stands in glaring contrast, once again, to Heine's celebration of the method of satirical exploitation presented in the same chapter. Indeed, far from living luxuriously off the foolishness of his patrons, according to this account the author must ingratiate himself to these fools to receive even a few meager scraps. The patrons of literature view authors as mere "hunters" after metaphors and thoughts, as hounds who lead their masters to this titillating intellectual prey. Under these socioeconomic conditions, writers are demoted to the position of performers who will stoop to anything just to please their lord and master, the bourgeois public.

Up to this point Heine appears to offer no level on which this demeaning appraisal of the place and posture of the writer can be reconciled with his valorization of satire and of the engaged author as the resounding voice of political emancipation. However, careful scrutiny of the final words in the cited passage divulges a subtle interpretive clue that points in the direction of a resolution. The list of canine activities Heine cites as the required responses to the demands of the new Maecenas, "fetch and carry, dance and drum," represents a rather curious assemblage. This enumeration begins with activities commonly associated with canines ("fetch and carry"), but when Heine completes this list with the addition of "dancing" and "drumming," he seems to rupture the confines of his conceit, since these are occupations not commonly attributed to dogs—except, perhaps, in the circus. This technique of misalliance is frequently employed by Heine in this text as a humorous device; however, in this instance it presents much more than a simple incongruous juxtaposition designed to make the reader laugh. As humorous exaggerations, these elements both underscore the absurdity of the comparison and, since they designate activities primarily attributed to human beings, reinforce the human tenor that lurks behind the metaphorical vehicle. Moreover, dancing and drumming are connected by means of alliteration. But their connection actually goes much deeper, since these two activities typically symbolize for Heine subliminal levels of communication, the covert expression of what cannot be overtly stated. Thus Heine's dancing bear in *Atta Troll: A Midsummernight's Dream* (1841), for example, has a symbolic function equivalent to that of the drummer Le Grand in *Ideas*. Including drumming and dancing in this enumeration of canine activities hence has two very significant functions: on the one hand, these elements serve to recall the symbol of the drum that is central to this text and thereby link the remarks from this chapter with the narrative sequences that deal with Napoleon and the drum major Le Grand; on the other hand, they allude to a possible connection between the assignments of Heine's writer-dogs and the pedagogical mission Le Grand pursues through the nonverbal medium of his drum. In what way might drumming, as practiced by Le Grand, offer an alternative to the slavishness otherwise demanded of the writer? To answer this question it is necessary to examine the function of Le

Grand's drum and assess its relevance as a cipher for the textual practices Heine himself deploys in this text.

As the "spirit of language," as Heine terms it (*Ideas*, 270; *194*), Le Grand's drumming represents that undiluted message for whose expression concrete words are either inadequate or inappropriate. In this sense the rhythmic communication of Le Grand's drum becomes the symbol for a transparent, immediate language that bypasses the arbitrary signs of verbal expression. The drum, then, takes on the significance that natural signs possessed for the eighteenth century, preserving a semiotic otherness similar to that which Schiller ascribed to the "signifying stone" of art. By drumming out specified rhythms, Le Grand is able to communicate the meaning of concepts such as "liberté," "egalité," and "bêtise" to his pupil Heine, who, at this young age, does not yet understand French. Moreover, he also employs his drum as an accompaniment to his verbal history lessons, permitting Heine to comprehend the meaning underlying his incomprehensible words. "I did not, of course, understand the words he spoke," Heine comments, "but since he constantly drummed while speaking, I knew what he wanted to say. This is basically the best teaching method" (*Ideas*, 271; *195*). Now, the substance of Le Grand's lessons is profoundly revolutionary: he introduces his pupil to the abstract ideals and concrete history of the French Revolution. More importantly, Le Grand exploits a language calculated to guarantee his student's receptivity to these foreign ideas, and he thereby overcomes any spontaneous bias his German pupil might harbor against them. The art of drumming, then, represents a form of covert speech that evades both internal-psychological and external-political censors: it symbolizes, in short, a communicative strategy that circumvents the forces of systematic distortion by subliminally transmitting truths that cannot be formulated overtly in verbal expression.

Heine is Le Grand's pupil in a double sense: not only does he absorb the content of Le Grand's lessons, but he also assimilates Le Grand's teaching method, appropriating it for his own revolutionary-pedagogical discourse. "Is drumming an inborn talent, or did I develop it at an early age? In any case, it is rooted in my limbs, in my hands and feet, and often involuntarily manifests itself. Involuntarily" (*Ideas*, 272; *196*).[25] Heine's repetition of the adverb "involuntarily" has the ironic effect of calling this very involuntariness into question: his insistent reassurance smacks of a cover-up that attempts to disguise an acutely purposive act behind the mask of accident. At any rate, he goes on to relate an incident from his student days in which his feet "involuntarily" drummed out a protest to the antiliberal sentiment of a lecture he was attending: "These poor mute feet, incapable of expressing their humble opinion in words, strove to make themselves understood by drumming, and they drummed so loudly that I consequently really got into trouble" (*Ideas*, 273; 196). The muteness of Heine's feet, of course, reflects the muteness forced upon him by political circumstance, and drumming becomes the symbol for what Heine elsewhere called the "esoteric" level of communication, that latent significance that lies below the manifest content of verbal expression.

The pertinence of Heine's theoretical distinction between "esoteric" and "exoteric" layers of signification for the textual structure of *Ideas* has often been noted. As a rule, however, this overlaying of a deeper, "esoteric" political message with a superficial, innocent, "exoteric" narrative, a strategy I will call double-tracking, has been viewed only as a tactic that allows Heine to smuggle his oppositional political ideas past the agencies of governmental censorship. Although I do not wish to deny the validity of this argument, it is significant to recognize that it ignores the problematic—the miserable economy of literature—that for Heine himself was of central importance in *Ideas*. Only when viewed in the context of Heine's dilemma as service writer does the deeper relevance of this strategy come into relief, elucidating how he experiments with double-tracking as a potential literary-aesthetic solution to the "misery" of literature. Caught between supplication before the (literary and political) tastes of his readership and the drive to revolutionize its (literary and political) attitudes, he exploits double-tracking as a textual construction that permits him to appeal and criticize at once: he sneaks an esoteric message of political emancipation past the resistant psychic censors of his audience by packaging it in an innocent exoteric guise. What I want to suggest, then, is that this technique is not so much employed to ensure that Heine's text reaches the reading public by evading governmental censorship, but to circumvent their psychic defense mechanisms and hence guarantee its acceptance *by* this reading public. Double-tracking is the strategy Heine develops so that as service writer he might "fetch and carry, dance and drum" at one and the same time: it makes it possible for him to serve up biting critique while ostensibly playing the role of the docile writer-dog concerned solely with the entertainment of his masters.

Although satirical invective is the modus of Heine's critique, this satire only becomes marketable—is only "bought" by the audience, who is simultaneously the satirized object—when it is mollified through its fusion with another technique with which it shares a family resemblance: humor. The satiric and humorous elements in *The Book Le Grand* hence exist in a relationship of necessary reciprocal interdependence. This interaction between humor and satire in Heine's works has too often been misunderstood, primarily because it has been assumed that these two discursive modes are either incompatible or antagonistic. Thus Heine's often silly witticisms are frequently interpreted as the neutralizers of his satirical attacks. Consequently, those who perceive in him the Romantic self-ironist tend to highlight the function of humor, while those who prefer to see in him the politically engaged intellectual commonly play down its significance.[26] The antagonism between "Heine the Romantic" and "Heine the engaged artist" thus finds its textual counterpart in the interplay between ironic humor and critical satire. However, a careful reading of *The Book Le Grand* makes evident that, far from canceling each other out, Heine's Romantic and political personae and their respective discursive styles are bound together in a dialectical interaction of mutual enhancement. The double-tracking of humor and satire reflects the division between Romantic love poet and revolutionary writer that traverses Heine's subjectivity. But what sets Heine apart is his own recognition of his—and his audience's—divided subjectivity, as well as his attempt to exploit textual strategies that, on the one hand, are coherent with this insight and, on the other, attempt to mend this rift.

Heine's humoristic facade is the *conditio sine qua non* of his satirical critique: it represents that structure of appeal without which his critical observations could never reach their target. Without the candy-coating of humor, Heine's public could never be expected to swallow the bitter pill of his reprehension. It is only when perceived against the backdrop of what I have termed the crisis between service and servitude that the relationship of mutual necessity obtaining between the humoristic and satirical elements in Heine's writing comes into relief. Failure to highlight this crucial dilemma tends to obscure not only this stylistic issue, but also gives us a skewed conception of the impact of official censorship on Heine's writing. Although state censorship undoubtedly played a significant role, the problem of those psychic censorship agencies internalized by the reading public posed a much greater and more subtle dilemma for the writer who measured success in terms of *e*ffective and *a*ffective reception. The interaction of esoteric and exoteric textual levels is a strategy developed primarily as a solution to this practical problem, which threatened to undermine Heine's emancipatory and pedagogical mission.

Heine's most plastic description of the interplay between exoteric and esoteric levels of significance, which is found in the *Journey from Munich to Genoa* (1830), published in the third volume of *Travelogues*, appears at first glance to belie this hypothesis. Here Heine explains the functioning of these two communicative layers on the example of the opera buffa, which he calls "that marvelous genre that accords to humor the freest room for play" (*HW*

2: 352). Reminiscent in this respect to the drum in *Ideas*, the opera buffa is depicted as the only communicative medium in which the Italians, suffering under the political oppression of their Austrian occupiers, can express their suppressed desires for political liberation. "Poor oppressed Italy is forbidden to speak," Heine notes, "and it is permitted to express the sentiments of its heart only by means of music." He goes on to describe how the melodies and pantomime of the opera buffa conceal both the Italians' love of freedom and the animosity they harbor for their foreign rulers. "That is the esoteric meaning of the opera buffa. The exoteric sentries in whose presence it is sung in no way fathom the significance of these joyful stories of love—of love's tribulations and love's teasings—under which the Italians conceal their most deadly thoughts of liberation, just as Harmodius and Aristogiton concealed their dagger in a myrtle wreath" (*HW* 2: 353). This passage is often cited as evidence that the exoteric level is a disguise intended to hide the esoteric message from external political authorities, here concretized as the Austrian "sentries." Yet there are important differences between the situation of the Italians and that of Heine's fellow Germans. First of all, Heine portrays the Italians as united in their desire for political liberation, while he perceives the Germans to be united only in the resigned acceptance of their own (self-)subjugation. Moreover, the Italians are repressed from without by a foreign power, whereas the Germans are repressed from within—that is, by indigenous political masters. The Italians, as externally tyrannized insiders, exploit the double-tracking of the opera buffa to ensure that the Austrian sentries, the oppressive Others, remain outside of the society they rule. In the case of Germany, however, the Other responsible for political tyranny is the Germans themselves: the line between insiders and outsiders is drawn through the native population, as well as through the subjectivity of each individual. In the psychological sphere this self-division manifests itself as a struggle between the id and the superego, between spontaneous, self-emancipatory drives and the self-repression of these drives by the agency of psychic control, which represents an introjection of the politically oppressive Other.[27] Addressed to the self-repressed German public (sphere), Heine's exoteric and esoteric textual levels are consequently not aimed at "foreign" oppressor and "native" victim of oppression, but rather at separate roles inscribed within the self-divided German subject, which is at once both the oppressed victim and the (self-)oppressing master.

We must take a closer look at Heine's conception of the interplay of esoteric and exoteric levels in the opera buffa if we wish to discover the specific relevance of this model for *Ideas*. It is obvious, first of all, that the opera buffa represents an artistic technique that exploits humoristic abandon to conceal the "knife" of political revolt. More specifically, however, this art form hides this latent threat in a very particular manifest content: behind the mask of *love* stories, tales of love's "tribulations" and "teasings." Heine amplifies by describing "a comic duet in which he played the enamored old man and she his mocking young amante" (*HW* 2: 351). This description supplies the essential clue to the connection between the structure of the opera buffa and that of *Ideas*: it is beneath the exoteric mask of the traditional story of unrequited love for a married woman that Heine hides the political scalpel with which he hopes to dissect German Restoration society. In *Ideas* Heine enciphers into the exoteric drama of the spurned lover an esoteric tale about how the Germans consistently reject the advances of their political liberators. In other words, he exploits the typically Romantic paradigm of unrequited love, which is structured around wooing and its rejection, to suggest parallels between the role of the spurned lover and that of the repudiated political emancipator, on the one hand, and of the disdained service writer, on the other. The epigraph that introduces three separate chapters of *Ideas* (chapters one, two, and twenty) serves as a simplified paradigm of this pattern of entreaty and rejection. "She was lovable, and he loved her. He, however, was not lovable, and she did not love him.—Old Play" (*Ideas*, 248, 250, 308; *174, 176, 227*).

It is probably no coincidence that this paradigm is presented as epigraph on three different occasions, for it manifests the underlying structure that characterizes three relationships: exoterically, of course, the relationship between Heine as would-be lover and "madame" as the loved woman who rejects his advances; in the exoteric political domain, the relationship between Heine as would-be liberator and the oppressed public who abjures his emancipatory politics; and in the dimension of literary reception, the relationship between Heine as would-be service writer and the readership that disdains the serious message of his text. The narrative structure of the work concretizes this relationship of wooing and rejection, moreover, in the dialog between the suitor-narrator who woos and the madame-reader who rejects his advances. The analogical linkage of the political and literary-receptive subtexts to the exoteric level of the conventional love story operates with such a careful parallelism that any shifts in the relationship concretized in the interaction between the narrator and madame are indicative of shifts in the respective political and literary relationships for which it stands. The tale that Heine relates throughout *Ideas* is thus a threefold tale of the "unshed tear" (*Ideas*, 248; *174*), the story of his inability to win madame's sympathies for any of his solicitations. To be sure, madame does eventually shed this tear (*Ideas*, 305; *225*), and I will examine the significance of this event later in my analysis.

Heine's initial meditations on the esoteric and exoteric levels of signification are recorded in a letter to Friedericke Robert from October 1825. Here it is the structure of the Aristophanic comedy, specifically *Birds*, to which this pattern is applied.

However, there lies a more profound meaning in this poem [*Birds*]; and while the exoteric cacklers (i.e., the Athenian loud-mouths) were delightfully amused by fantastic figures and pranks and jokes and allusions . . . , the esoteric reader (e.g., myself) discovers in this work an immense worldview: I see in it the god-defying insanity of human beings, a true tragedy, and all the more tragic since that insanity is ultimately victorious and holds happily to its delusion that its city in the clouds really exists. (*HB* 1: 232)

Interestingly enough, Heine was apparently not the only esoteric reader of Aristophanes in Germany at this time, for Hegel employed strikingly similar arguments to praise Aristophanes' plays, which he took to be exemplary for dramatic comedy. In his *Lectures on the History of Philosophy* (1822–31), Hegel commented:

[Aristophanes] was no common . . . buffoon who simply ridiculed the most holy and superb things and who merely handed over and sacrificed everything to the wit of his derision in order to make his fellow Athenians laugh. Indeed, everything has a much deeper foundation: his jests are grounded in profound seriousness. . . . It is a miserable wit that is insubstantial, that does not rest on contradictions that lie in the subject matter itself: Aristophanes was no bad joker.[28]

Hegel goes on to summarize his comments in this generalized and pointed remark: "If the subject matter is not contradictory in itself, then the comedy is superficial, ungrounded."[29] And elsewhere Hegel indicates that the earnestness underlying the comic in Aristophanes' plays is essentially political. "If I had to cite authorities on the role of the not-merely-humorous in comedies, then I would refer above all to Aristophanes; in most of his plays, which to us seem primarily farcical, the primary interest is informed by the most bitter seriousness, namely by *political* seriousness, and in all seriousness."[30] Both Hegel and Heine conceive Aristophanes' comedies in terms of an exoteric humorous-comic edifice that is erected on a tragically serious foundation. Hegel sees the humor of such comedy arising immediately out of contradictions in the subject matter addressed; Heine views the comic as a disguise for a powerful worldview that is steeped in the recognition that the sane is always outmaneuvered by the insane.[31] Heine conceived *The Book*

Le Grand as an Aristophanic comedy cast into narrative form.[32] The fundamental "tragedy" of such a literary enterprise—the tangible proof that insanity and ignorance always reign supreme—expresses itself in the irony
that, as Heine remarks, Aristophanes' (and, by extension, Heine's) fellow citizens devour the humorous facade but fail to see beyond it into its tragic
ground. Thus Heine was aware that his own humor, which was intended to
serve as a palliative to help his readers recognize their own tragic situation
and respond accordingly, could have the opposite effect of blinding his audience to the seriousness of his appeal. The success of his political program
depended totally on his ability (or failure) to achieve this delicate balance
between wit and sobriety.

In the same letter to Friedericke Robert, continuing the remarks cited
above, Heine lends the appellation "irony" to this intermingling of comedy
and tragedy.

Precisely that is the irony that always constitutes the primary element of tragedy.
The most monstrous, horrible, and frightening things, if they are not to be unpo-
etic, can only be portrayed in the checkered cloak of the ridiculous, reconcilingly,
as it were. That is why in *Lear* Shakespeare has the most dreadful things be spoken
by the fool; that is why Goethe chose the form of a puppet play for the most frightful material, for *Faust*; that is why the even greater poet (Friedericke would say "the
primeval poet"), namely our Lord, mixed in a good dose of jocularity with all the
horror scenes of this life. (*HB* 1: 233)

In this passage, Heine attempts to define irony as a specific poetic practice.
To be sure, his invocation of God as the master "ironist" smacks of metaphysical inevitability; but this allusion in fact represents his own ironic appeal to the authority of a deity—who is specifically conceived as the primeval
poet—to underwrite the authenticity of his own "ironic" literary program.
As a metaphysical worldview—as opposed to a literary-aesthetic program—
ironism evokes political resignation,[33] and nothing could be farther from
Heine's intent in this period of his life, a period in which he is increasingly
embracing new forms of literary-political activism. In this transitional phase
of his artistry Heine was concerned principally with the evolution of a literary aesthetics that could adequately express his ironic double vision and
effectively transmit it to his readership. The Aristophanic comedy as he (and
Hegel) interpreted it provided a model for such a literary practice. Like Hegel, Heine perceives historico-political, not metaphysical, circumstances as
the basis for the fissured foundation underlying the comic. Insofar as Heine's
poetic practice merely reproduces in its own textuality the sublime and
ridiculous of sociopolitical reality, his poetics in the *Travelogues* can be termed

mimetic. But perhaps we should designate this literary practice as hyper-mimesis, since it attempts not only to realistically reflect the exoteric surface of the objective sociopolitical life-world, but to penetrate to its otherwise unseen, esoteric core. Indeed, it is by playing off these two dimensions against each other, and thereby exploiting his own ironic perspicacity, that Heine unmasks the sociopolitical reality of the Restoration in all its absurdity. For Heine this absurdity derives from the essential historical regress embodied in the reconstruction of the pre-Napoleonic world atop the ruins of the progressive Napoleonic empire he so admired.

It is significant that the definition of poetic irony found in Heine's letter to Friedericke Robert finds its way in almost unaltered form into chapter eleven of *The Book Le Grand*.

Du sublime au ridicule il n'y a qu'un pas, madame! But life is basically so fatally serious that it would be unbearable without such a connection between the pathetic and the comic. Our poets know that. The most horrible images of human madness are shown to us by Aristophanes only in the laughing mirror of wit. Only in the doggerel of a puppet show does Goethe dare to utter the great pain of the thinker who comprehends his own nothingness, and Shakespeare puts the gravest indictment about the misery of the world into the mouth of a fool who is anxiously rattling his cap and bells.

They all learned it from the great primeval poet who in his thousand-act world tragedy knows how to drive humor to the utmost, as we see every day. (*Ideas*, 282; 204–5)

Heine goes on to make explicit reference to the political sphere by mentioning the supplanting of Napoleon by the Bourbons as an example of this "one step" that separates the sublime from the ridiculous (*Ideas*, 282; 205). Moreover, these comments occur in the text immediately after the demise of Napoleon has been narrated, and Heine transfers this contrast between the pathetic and the comic immediately into his text when he remarks that upon finishing the chapter on Napoleon, a woman came to his door asking him to remove her husband's corns (*Ideas*, 283; 205). This seemingly insignificant addendum, which appears to be included simply to heighten the humorous effect of this passage, actually focuses Heine's damning commentary on the banality of this new reality. Heine ironically portrays himself as someone who has been demoted from the sublime position as historian of the Napoleonic age to the ridiculous role of someone whose only productive act is the removal of his neighbor's corns. The farcicality of this image gives vent to Heine's personal frustration, implying that authorship has become a totally trite occupation: instead of performing major critical surgery on Restoration society, Heine is only able to apply his critical knife to the most banal of affairs. The narration of this episode, with which the chapter concludes, thus has the important function of evoking once again the "miserable" situation of the free-lance writer and linking it with the political malaise of the Restoration. Moreover, it provides a paradigmatic example of just how skillfully Heine double-tracks the humorous and the critical in this text, disguising his sometimes bitter reproaches behind an ironic wit that at times blends into the farcical.

The Book Le Grand is structured around a series of dichotomous relations that operate on various levels of the text: esoteric-exoteric; reason-folly; tragedy-comedy; sublime-ridiculous; critical-pandering; appeal-rejection; service-servitude. This entire complex is held together by the overriding duality between writer and reader, textually manifest in the narrative form in which Heine addresses madame. This communication is not verbal, not face to face, but scriptive, passing through the medium of the very text of Ideas itself. Heine calls attention to the act of composition at two points in the narrative: in both the eleventh and fourteenth chapters, that is, in those chapters that contain his self-reflective deliberations on the humorous and satiric strategies constitutive of the compositional poles that structure this dichotomous text (see Ideas, 283, 294; 205, 214). Ideas thus is structured around the ambiguous temporality common to epistolary communication. Although he projects madame as present and their interaction as immediate, Heine yet stresses that this communication passes through the temporal deferral and spatial distance of the textual medium. Madame's presence, therefore, is in fact nothing other than her presence to mind for Heine as he composes his text, and she is present to his mind specifically as the reader of this work.

If madame is inscribed into Ideas as its reader, then by examining the interaction between the narrator and madame we can draw inferences about the relationship between author and reader, between literary practice and its envisioned (ideal) reception, that Heine projected for this work. The relationship between Heine as narrator and madame as reader manifests precisely that tension between service and servitude, appeal and rejection, that is concretized in Heine's recurrent epigraph. Heine exploits the Romantic motif of unrequited love as a kind of parable that can be applied to the relationship between the service writer and his reader. This explains, among other things, why Heine projects his reader as a madame rather than a sir, or as both madame and sir, as Laurence Sterne had done in Tristram Shandy, the novel from which Heine culled this technique.[34] The image Heine adopts to depict the dependence of the writer on his public, we discovered, is that of the obedient, well-trained canine. In one of its aspects, Heine's relationship to madame is characterized by just such slavish pandering. In its exoteric manifestation, of course, this servility is expressed through the language of love and courtship: Heine as writer assumes the role of the devoted lover; madame as reader exploits this devotion to assert her position of mastery. Heine underscores this metaphorical connection, thereby alluding to his role as the submissive writer-lover, when he ironically identifies himself with madame's dachshund. "When I arrived in Godesberg, I sat down again at the feet of my beautiful friend, and near me lay her brown dachshund, and we both looked up into her eyes" (*Ideas*, 301; *221*). The "beautiful friend," as we subsequently learn (*Ideas*, 306; *225*), is none other than madame herself. We recall that in the scene discussed earlier the dachshund is mentioned as a particularly obsequious species of dog (see *Ideas*, 290; *212*). In the cited passage, Heine depicts himself at the feet of madame, in the conventionalized pose of the smitten lover found so often in the tradition of *Minne*, in Petrarchan portrayals, as well as in Heine's own Romantic poetry; but he ironically undercuts this idolatry by comparing it with the posture of a particularly fawning breed of dog, a connection he reiterates by way of emphasis just a few lines later.

In chapter seventeen, where the story of the meeting with the "beautiful friend" in Godesberg is continued, this conflation of the motifs of devoted courtship and canine toadying becomes even more prominent. Heine again plays on images drawn from *Minnesang* and Petrarchan poetry—in this case a description of the admired woman's hand—then radically subverts his own staged idealization by means of derisive exaggeration. "It was a lovely hand, so tender, transparent, perfumed, brilliant, sweet, soft, loving—really I must send to the apothecary for twelve shillings' worth of adjectives." This idealization is further shattered when Heine relates the disciplinary function this hand performs: "And she often struck me on the mouth with all five [fingers]" (*Ideas*, 303; *223*). The beauty of this beloved hand is thus directly linked with an overt act of violence whose purpose is control and mastery over the obsequious suitor. Heine highlights this disciplinary aspect by exposing in further ironies the "manipulative" character of this hand. "Having been thus hand-polished [*manupoliert*], I firmly believe in animal magnetism. But she did not strike hard, and when she struck I always deserved it for some godless turn of phrase; and as soon as she had struck me, she at once repented it and took a cake, broke it in two, and gave half to me and the other half to the brown dachshund" (*Ideas*, 303; *223*). The humor and critical acerbity of this passage turn on the verbal play in Heine's neologism *manupoliert*, which fuses the combined form of the Latin word for hand (*manu*) with the verb *polieren*, meaning "to polish"; but *manupoliert* ("hand-polished") plays on the participle *manipuliert* ("manipulated"), thereby invoking the manipulations characteristic of the imperious will to domination guiding the actions of this "beautiful hand." The reference to magnetism, furthermore, expresses a backhanded jab at the inanity of such a fatal attraction in which loving devotion is exploited by the loved one for her/his own self-empowerment. However, recalling that Heine elsewhere designates the plight of the writer as the difficulty of winning his daily bread, this passage underhandedly reveals precisely what makes this attraction so fatal: the hand of reproach is the same hand that feeds Heine cake. His servility to madame is defined by this dialectic of punishment and reward that replicates the process of behavior modification by which the will of animals is broken and they are "persuaded" to obey. Thus it is no coincidence that Heine must share this morsel of food with madame's loyal dog.

This last example bears witness to the extraordinarily subtle and skillful way in which Heine weaves the esoteric problematics of service writing and political emancipation into the exoteric layer of his text, associating certain thematic complexes with particular recurrent images. There is a pervasive method to the ostensibly digressive madness of Heine's discourse in *Ideas*: underneath this hodgepodge of witticisms, aperçus, free associations, and literary allusions there is a carefully constructed ideational network that transmits Heine's political and literary messages. Thematically the disintegrative discourse of *Ideas* is held together by the motif of unrequited love, while structurally it is cemented by the narrative interchange between author-narrator and madame-reader. The task of the esoteric reader is to follow Heine's complex intratextual allusions and put together the "deeper" significance lurking behind the exoteric surface of this Romantic love tale. The misery of Heine's fatal attraction for—that is, his economic and political dependence on—a public who answers his "affection" with castigation and manipulation is exposed by means of the analogy to the torture of the devoted lover who is manipulated and exploited by the object of his affections. Early in the text Heine comments on the veritably masochistic manner in which maltreatment fans the flames of love, again playing on romanticized notions of love's dependencies. Relating to madame the story of a relationship from his youth, Heine remarks: "I would certainly have fallen in love with her had she been indifferent toward me; but I was indifferent toward her, because I knew that she loved me. Madame, if anyone wishes to be loved by me, they must treat me *en canaille*" (*Ideas*, 259; 184). When read as an exoteric encodation of Heine's relationship to his reading public, this admission expresses the double-edged problematic of Heine's situation as a service writer: as long as he must woo his readership, they will be able to lord over him, extracting literary and political compromises; however, if he once wins the devotion of his readers, he can treat them *en canaille* and dish out incisive critique. Heine apparently believed in the truth of this maxim, since, we recall, he took the popular success of the *Travelogues* as a signal that he was now in total control of his readership (see *HB* 1: 290, 315–16). This is the wish-fulfillment dream of the service writer: that his critical voice will be liberated from the chains of public servitude.

The pattern of nonmutuality in love relationships also supplies a damning commentary on the sociopolitical atmosphere of Restoration Germany. In this historical epoch, Heine implies, human relations in general are marked by an interaction in which maltreatment provokes love and love calls forth maltreatment. This perversity is a symptom of a world out of kilter, one in which love is interpreted as nothing but an exploitable dependence. Thus it is the power of domination wielded by the *domina* that Heine highlights throughout *The Book Le Grand*, and it quite naturally calls up the relationship between rulers and ruled in Metternich's Germany. Extended into the sociopolitical realm, this structure of nonmutuality points to the paradox that the German authorities can ensure the devotion of their subjects by treating them as brutally as possible. In fact, for Heine this is the ultimate conundrum of the Restoration: the more the bourgeois public is oppressed, the more it submits to its oppressors.

Up to this point I have stressed the narrator's subordination to madame, interpreting it as a reflection of the servitude of the service writer vis-à-vis his readers and of the submission of the Restoration public to its tyrannical rulers. This relation of subordination, however, is offset by the inverted relationship in which the narrator is superior to madame. Now, if the analogy between the exoteric structure of nonmutual love and the esoteric literary-receptive and sociopolitical dimensions of the text holds up, then those parts of the narrative in which the narrator has the upper hand over madame would mark the points at which Heine both wins over his public and effects the critical emancipation of his oppressed fellow Germans. The narrator asserts his ascendancy in subtle ways throughout the text: in the tone of condescension with which he consistently addresses madame, for example, and in the ironic refrain "Madame, you really have no idea" (*Ideas*, 249, 267, 285, 288; *175, 191, 207, 209*), in which he alludes to her vast ignorance. Indeed, the narrator persistently attempts to cast madame-reader in the role of a disciple who stands to gain from his experience and wisdom. "She" is thus portrayed as a "woman" who has led a sheltered existence, collecting her knowledge not first-hand from life itself, but second-hand through literature (*Ideas*, 249; *175*). Furthermore, he treats her as someone who is so gullible and naive as to take his obvious fictions—for example, his claim that he is the Count of Ganges (*Ideas*, 256; *182*)—for fact. In this sense madame is the descendant of those naive readers whose errors Schiller discloses in *The Robbers*: like them, she takes texts at their face value rather than reflectively contemplating their deeper significance and drawing inferences from them about her life-world. Madame represents, in short, the paradigmatic exoteric reader. The purpose of Heine's literary "wooing" is to transform her, through her hermeneutical interaction with the text of *Ideas*, into an esoteric reader, and it is especially here that we come to perceive the extent to which Heine carries forward the project Schiller initiated in *The Robbers*.

The challenge Heine sets for himself in *The Book Le Grand* is daunting, indeed: he seeks to exploit a meager margin of (authorial) superiority and authority to effect (politically) progressive transformations in madame-reader. Heine employs this text as a medium for revolutionizing his reading audience by dismantling the mechanisms of its collective repressive superego. If, as I have proposed, this process of curative reception is inscribed into the interrelationship between the narrator and madame, then we should be able to find evidence that she undergoes a metamorphosis in which her resistance to the narrator and his political message breaks down and her intrapsychic breach begins to heal. The symptoms of such a transmogrification manifest themselves as the mutually therapeutic effect that Heine's narrative has on both suitor-narrator and madame-reader.

In the exoteric story of *Ideas* the liberating effect of Heine's narration is enciphered into the motif of the unshed tear. This motif is associated with the "Old Play" in which Heine himself claims to have played the "leading part" (*Ideas*, 248; *174*), and it runs throughout the text. The sole purpose of Heine's narrative, in fact, is the evocation of this tear from that one woman—madame herself—who did not weep when he first played this tragic role (see *Ideas*, 248; *174–75*). In chapter eighteen, when Heine finally arrives at the point of relating what he terms "the real story" of his work (*Ideas*, 304; *224*), he narrates the tale of unrequited love between a "knight"— Heine himself, as he later admits (*Ideas*, 306; *225*)—and Signora Laura. Now, this story—the allusion to Petrarch can scarcely be overlooked—represents but one more manifestation of the paradigm embodied in the "Old Play" and retold in various forms throughout *Ideas*. This time, however, Heine's narrative has the desired effect: "Vous pleurez, madame?" Heine then asks (*Ideas*, 305, 306; *225*), signaling that the text has reached its denouement. The weeping of this previously unshed tear signals the breakdown of madame's resistance to the narrator's solicitations. Given the paradigm of the necessary nonmutuality of love on which Heine insists throughout, the winning of madame's sympathies necessarily must effect a reversal in the power structure of their relationship: the narrator-author has gained a position of dominance and can presumably steer the relationship in whatever direction he pleases. Hence the gradual liberation of the narrator is reflected in his gradual empowerment over madame as lover and reader. As a result, it is only after madame has wept the unshed tear that Heine can exploit his superior knowledge and decipher for her all the enciphered love relationships that his narrative has presented (*Ideas*, 306–7; 225–26). This revelatory unriddling models for madame the act of decoding that she must now complete: it points her down the road that will lead from the exoteric level of the text to its esoteric meaning. Only after madame has displayed sympathy for the narrator, and thereby given testimony to her openness to him and his tale, can she be introduced to the text's hidden meanings without the danger that she will rebel against and censor this latent significance. Only at this point, in short, has the ground been fully prepared for her successful transformation from exoteric to esoteric reader.

This dimension of affective reception can be traced in the theme of memory and remembering that is woven into Heine's narrative. The therapeutic effect of the act of narration for both parties resides in the fact that this interaction liberates repressed memories. Over the course of Heine's narration, madame progressively recalls that she herself is the "beautiful friend" from Godesberg who figures so centrally in his tale; and it is this process of recall that elicits the previously uncried tear. Reciprocally, madame as audience stimulates the narrator's memory so that as his story develops, he gradually recalls central experiences from his youth. As we will see, Heine ultimately attributes to this mnemonic therapy a distinctly political significance.

The role of the reader as stimulus to the narrator's memory is first developed in chapter five. Here we are told that in his childhood conversations with "beautiful Johanna"—yet one more manifestation of the madame-persona—Johanna reminds him of names he has forgotten: "In such happy hours I told her stories from my childhood, and she listened earnestly to me, and curiously enough, when I could not recall the names, she reminded me of them" (*Ideas*, 259; 185). Only after Johanna supplies Heine with the name of "little, dead Veronica" (*Ideas*, 260; 185) does he possess the password that will open the vault of his childhood memories, including those relating to the march of the conquering French troops into Düsseldorf. "And now that I have it [the name Veronica] again, my earliest childhood wants to bloom into memory again; and I am again a child playing with other children in the palace courtyard at Düsseldorf on the Rhine" (*Ideas*, 260; 185). With this, the necessary precondition for the narration of the next five chapters, those dealing with Le Grand, Napoleon, and the ideals of the French Revolution, has been fulfilled: only now can the subliminal political dimension enter the narrator's consciousness and thus rise—at least temporarily—to the exoteric surface of the text. In these five chapters Heine describes the glory of Napoleonic rule as a brief interlude, which, with the advent of the Restoration era, is then mysteriously eradicated from history as well as from his memory.

Heine was psychologically astute enough to recognize—decades before the theories of Freud—that amnesia can result from external oppression or self-repression, and in *Ideas* he identifies the political dispassion of his own Romantic phase as the product of just such repression. His youthful vitality represents a veneer that plasters over a dead spot in his own existence, and in this sense he is a true child of the Restoration, in which "everything looked so dead and yet so fresh as salad growing in a graveyard" (*Ideas*, 278; 201). Characteristic of this historical epoch, Heine suggests, is a divergence between its fresh appearance and its factual backwardness, a fundamental split between illusion and substance. The sociopolitical world itself, so it seems, is divided by a rift between exoteric facade and esoteric essence. Heine responds to this moribund reality by retreating into the internal world of books: "And I became so smart," he comments, "that I forgot all the old games and fairy tales and pictures, and little Veronica and even forgot her name" (*Ideas*, 280; 202). His inability to remember the "dead Veronica" stands in for that political forgetfulness into which the "dead Napoleon" falls in the period of the Restoration, a connection suggested by the associative inter-twining of these two figures throughout this chapter. Heine implies that the political suppression of Napoleon during the Restoration parallels the re-pression of his personal memories from this historical era: the Napoleonic empire has been so completely eradicated that even personal, nonpolitical memories of this period have been wiped from his mind. The thoroughness of this amnesia bears witness to the effectiveness of the oppressive sociopo-litical measures instituted in the age of Metternich. This gap in Heine's memory would have remained permanent if it had not been filled in by the one person who kept the memory of the dead emperor alive: Le Grand, who beats out a memorial to Napoleon on his drum.

Le Grand's drum, we noted, symbolizes the esoteric level of communi-cation in the strategy of double-tracking that Heine employs in this text. But this drum also functions as a mnemonic device, stimulating recall of the re-pressed past in so effective a manner that Heine is able to picture it again "vividly" (*Ideas*, 274; 197). After the death of Le Grand, the rhythms of his drumming, which are etched into Heine's subconscious, keep the memories and the ideals of the emperor alive; and these rhythms force their way "involuntarily" to the surface whenever Heine feels most threatened by the oppressiveness of Restoration society (*Ideas*, 272; *196*). When he articulates these rhythms, of course, Heine takes over Le Grand's role as guardian over and stimulator of those memories that have been forcibly repressed. As Le Grand's pupil, Heine seeks to transfer this mnemonic function to the text of *The Book Le Grand* itself: the purpose of his narrative, then, is to revitalize for the Restoration public the dead memories of the Napoleonic era. However, to accomplish this, Heine, like Le Grand, must employ the technique of double-tracking to bypass the repressive mechanisms—both externally concretized and psychically internalized—that have caused this repression in the first place. Thus the hidden political agenda of Heine's text is brought into the reader's consciousness much in the same way that Heine's memories of the Napoleonic era are brought back into his consciousness. This means that *Ideas* is specifically conceived with this affective purpose in mind, with the intent of eliciting specific perlocutionary responses in its readers by means of those illocutionary acts concretized in the communicative interaction between narrator and madame. Both communicative transfers, that between Le Grand and Heine and that between the author-narrator and the inscribed reader of *Ideas*, establish a therapeutic exchange that opens onto a process of anamnesis, of political-historical consciousness-raising. The narrative situation of the text describes a dialectical interchange of reciprocal recall: just as the focus on the reader stimulates the narrator's recollection, his narrated recollections stimulate her memories, completing the circle of this mutually liberating hermeneutical interaction.

The healing process depicted in *The Book Le Grand* reflects the metamorphosis Heine himself was undergoing as a writer at the time of the text's composition. He made no secret of the fact that this text contained explicitly autobiographical characteristics (see *HB* 1: 286, 293), and the historical past it invokes is tightly intertwined with his personal experiences. In its autobiographical dimension, *Ideas* relates Heine's conversion from the Romantic obsessions of his youth to his active political engagement with the ideals of the French Revolution. This conversion is represented in the text as the education the narrator receives at the hands of the drum major Le Grand. When in chapter five Heine abandons the fictive persona of the Count of Ganges, this act symbolizes the jettisoning of those fictions characteristic of his Romantic past, a process that has been likened to that of a snake shedding its skin.[35] During this Romantic period, Heine tells us in chapter five, women were his sole interest, and he did not concern himself with political issues (*Ideas*, 258; *183*). It is certainly no coincidence that this was a time when women fawned over him (*Ideas*, 258–59; *183–84*). However, once the memories of the Napoleonic era transmogrify him from a Romantic love poet into a service writer, these fortunes in love, emblematic of his fortunes as a writer, are erased.

One scene from *The Book Le Grand* gives an especially plastic depiction of Heine's political conversion. Recalling the entrance of the French troops into his home town of Düsseldorf, which as a child he observed from a perch atop the statue of the Prince Elector, Heine allegorically represents his abandonment of the Germanic political past and his welcoming of the French reforms as the "letting go" of his hold on the statue of the Prince Elector that supports him.

And while I myself shouted *"Vivat!"* I held fast to the old Prince Elector. And that was necessary, for I really became dizzy. It already seemed to me as if the people were standing on their heads, because the world whirled around; the Prince Elector with the full-bottomed wig nodded and whispered, "Hold fast to me!" and only as a result of the cannon fire that now started did I come to my senses and slowly climb down from the Prince Elector's horse. (*Ideas*, 265; *190*)

Heine emblematizes here what he will later call his change of allegiances from the party of the fools, to which he by nature belongs, to the party of reason (*Ideas*, 297; *217*). The topsy-turviness of the world represents a humorous literalization of the French Revolution; and Heine's initial reluctance to let go of the Electoral Prince bespeaks the general reluctance of the conquered Germans to assimilate in any but the most superficial ways the new political order. But Heine ultimately ignores the admonition that he "hold fast" to the symbol of the historical past, and with this he expresses his resolve to accept and disseminate the revolutionary ideas of the new age. *Ideas* tells the story of how this political resolve, which is forcibly repressed in the era of the Restoration, ultimately resurfaces in Heine's consciousness, resulting in his decision to dedicate himself as a service writer to the liberation of these repressed political ideals, and thus to the emancipation of his self-repressed fellow Germans.

Heine's text goes far beyond the mere narration of this conversion: it is programmatically structured in such a way as to penetrate those psychic agencies responsible for this political repression and effect a similar conversion in its readers. Heine exploits structures and motifs characteristic of his Romantic past as vehicles that permit him to expose his political ideals and give expression to his damning critique of the retrograde political reality in which he and his contemporaries live. In one respect, his aim is simply to re-present the emancipatory ideals of the French Revolution by encoding them into an ostensibly simple autobiographical tale; but the affective purpose of his narrative is to call forth in his readers, by stimulating their own recollection of the Napoleonic era, a transformation from political complacency to political activism similar to the one *Ideas* relates. In this sense *The Book Le Grand* formulates Heine's plea to his German contemporaries that they follow his example and abandon their Romantic "perversity," replacing it with the passion for self-liberation and the desire for a revolutionary future.

Ideas: The Book Le Grand manifests the rich and complex texture of a narrative created by a divided subject for divided subjects. Exploiting a counterpoint between concession and rebellion, humor and satire, Romantic love story and the political tale of conversion to revolutionary politics, and exoteric and esoteric textual dimensions, Heine attempts to discover a mode of literary production that can extricate him as author from the dilemma of the oppositional writer, who is trapped between the drive for literary-political service and servitude to a politically (self-)repressed public. Viewed from the perspective of textual reception, Heine goes well beyond the simple portrayal of a personal crisis, attempting to formulate in the hermeneutic interaction between divided text and the divided consciousness of its projected readers a kind of literary-hermeneutical therapy that will tip the scale of bourgeois Unhappy Consciousness in the direction of emancipatory political resolve.

Romanticism, Revolutionary Literature, and the Public Sphere

To provide a literary-historical and sociological horizon against which Heine's literary accomplishment in *Ideas* comes more clearly into focus, it is necessary both to examine that self-overcoming of literary Romanticism with which he symbolizes his transformation from "minnesinger" to political bard, and to assess its implications for his conception of the relationship between service literature and the bourgeois public sphere. Heine's complicated relationship to the phenomenon of literary Romanticism has been one of the most debated questions in Heine scholarship.[36] While Romanticism remains throughout his life a central concept in both his historical understanding and his literary focus—from the defense of Romanticism in the early essay entitled "Romanticism" (1820) to the crusade against Romanticism in *The Romantic School* (1833–35) and his return to Romantic poetry later in life—Heine's evaluation of this literary movement is characterized by profound ambivalence. The *Travelogues* evolve precisely on the cusp between

Heine's early defense of Romanticism and his searing critique in the 1830's. In this sense they are transitional works for Heine in two important respects: they mark the formal-aesthetic transition from poetry to journalistic prose, on the one hand, and the shift in Heine's evaluation of the political implications of Romantic literary conceptions, on the other.

In a central passage near the conclusion of *The Romantic School*, Heine associates Romantic literature with the regressive political conditions in Germany, contrasting attitudes there with those prevalent in France.

The writers who pulled medievalism out of its grave in Germany had other aims [than comparable writers in France] . . . , and the influence they were able to exercise on the general public endangered the liberty and happiness of my country. The French writers had *only artistic interests*, and the French public sought only to satisfy its suddenly awakened curiosity. . . . Alas, in Germany it is different. Perhaps just because in Germany medievalism is not completely dead and putrefied, as it is in France. German medievalism is not lying mouldered in its grave; on the contrary, it is often animated by an evil spirit and steps into our midst in bright, broad daylight and sucks the red life from our hearts. (*Romantic School*, 494–95; 124–25; emphasis added)

Because the French Romantic writers pursued purely artistic interests, Heine asserts, their attitudes represented no significant sociopolitical threat for the French public sphere; by contrast, however, literary Romanticism in Germany is intimately associated with general public attitudes. Now, we can scarcely help but notice that Heine's articulation of the relationship between aesthetics and politics in this comment contradicts the position he takes elsewhere: French writers are commended here for exactly that aesthetic autonomy for which Heine denounced Goethe and the Kunstperiode, while German Romanticism is attacked because it merges literature with the life-world. But it is not so much the literary program of Romanticism that Heine criticizes here as its backward political program. Romanticism for Heine is fundamentally a literature of affectivity, and as such it stands in contrast to classicism; but nonautonomy and effect on "the great mass of people," he recognizes, do not necessarily mean that literature will be implemented in an *emancipatory* project. Indeed, his denunciation of Romanticism for its politically regressive impact marks his awareness of the perilous consequences that emerge out of what Walter Benjamin would later diagnose as the aesthetification of politics.[37] But the appropriation of aesthetic semblance for the purposes of ideological retrenchment is merely the negative side of a coin upon whose obverse is stamped the impression of an emancipatory politicized aesthetic. The deautonomization of literature, in other words, serves as the ground in which both the politically affirmative products of the culture industry and the critical literature of revolutionary design take root. For Heine the devolution of Romanticism into a politically affirmative and restorative movement focuses the hazards of deautonomization. His critique of Romanticism thus is not directed at its aesthetic substance, but at its co-optation by the forces of repression.

As a passage from his "Confessions" indicates, Heine considered in retrospect that his struggle against the Romantic sensibilities of the German public sphere was successful, although he admits, thereby ironizing this accomplishment in typical fashion, that he himself was later revisited by Romantic sentiments. "Despite my campaigns aimed at the extermination of Romanticism, I myself always remained a Romantic—to a greater degree, in fact, than even I suspected. After I had dealt the death blows to the sensibility for Romantic poetry in Germany, I myself was again seized by an infinite longing for the blue flower in the dream-land of Romanticism" (*HW* 6/1: 447). Heine's purpose in the period of his campaign against Romanticism, as his words bring out, was its extermination in the German public sphere. Because he held literary Romanticism responsible for the dissemination of "sensibilities" that, to his mind, helped breed the political complacency and resignation characteristic of the Restoration public, Heine could view his campaign against Romanticism as a fundamentally political struggle.

This association of artistic tendencies and general public proclivities presupposes an intimate interconnection between the institution of literature and the German public sphere. This assumption, in turn, calls forth the corollary that the reshaping of literary sensibilities has the potential to effect modifications in the political attitudes of the general (reading) populace. Thus Heine's attack on the retrograde worldview of literary Romanticism stands in for his critique of the backward-looking historical gaze of Restoration Germany. Consequently, in *The Romantic School* he accuses the Romantic writers of working "hand in hand with the aims of the governments" toward the suppression of Napoleon and the ideals of the French Revolution, and he indicts them for swimming "with the current of the time" (*Romantic School*, 379–80; 22). Curiously enough, however, at approximately the same time (1834), he expresses a diametrically opposed view of the politics of Romanticism, describing it as a "revolution in art which even now is not at an end and which started with the struggle of the Romanticists, the mutinies of the Schlegel brothers, against the ancient classical regime" (*History of Religion*, 619; 224). The contradiction between these two assertions is only apparent, for although Heine identifies with the attack of the early German Romantics on classicism, he senses that this originary revolutionary impulse

somehow dissipates and that Romanticism ultimately joins forces with tra-
ditionalism. His denunciation of Romanticism thus must be considered as
an attempt to rescue its initial revolutionary-critical purpose. At the same
time, of course, his critique of Romanticism is also self-critique of that Romantic persona he assumed in his early poetic works. *Ideas*, as we have seen,
both portrays this self-transcendence and seeks to project it into the dimension of reader reception.

Heine's critical appropriation of Romantic conventions in *Ideas* is of interest because of the implications it holds for his conception of the relationship between literary practice and praxis in the socialized life-world. His
diagnosis that the sociopolitical ills of Restoration Germany are reflected in
the popularization of conventions common to Romantic literature hints at
a firm belief in literature's function in the socialization processes responsible for the ideological education of the bourgeois public. Rather than simply espousing oppositional doctrines, revolutionary literature must therefore revolutionize the aesthetic practices of institutionalized literature. Thus
the burgeoning political significance of literature and literary criticism in the
Vormärz, for which Heine's criticism of the Romantics in *The Romantic
School* is but one of the most prominent examples, is grounded in the recognition that literature possesses the potential to alter the conventions and
structures of society at large. Service literature for Heine is conceived in
terms of intervention in those structures of the institution of literature that
reflect the restorative principles dominant in the public opinions of the period. Although he takes quite seriously the role of literature in the process
of *Bildung*—of cultivation and formation—he also recognizes that re-for-
mation must often take the form of de-formation. *Ideas*, the text that most
explicitly manifests his turn to a literature of revolutionary political re-for-
mation, thus operates with principles of critical de-formation and re-appro-
priation: its revolutionary literary discourse re-forms the apolitical language
of late Romanticism to recapture the historical purpose of the originary Romantic revolt. Heine's critical appropriation of the motif of unrequited love
for his assault on the perverse lovelessness of his contemporaries thus represents his attempt to return to and revive the originary revolutionizing potential inherent in early Romanticism.

Heine firmly believed that *Ideas* successfully rehabilitated and revitalized
Napoleon and the ideals of the French Revolution in the German public
sphere.[38] But it would be a mistake to try to extrapolate either from the tactics of the *Travelogues* or from the programmed literary-hermeneutic therapy of *Ideas* a theoretical model for the articulation of an effectively revolutionary literature per se. Indeed, Heine's strategy of revolutionizing the pub-

lic sphere by means of the political refunctionalization of structures inherent in the dominant institution of literature represents a response to very specific historical conditions: the existence of a potentially emancipatory *literary* public sphere, one in which the institution of literature is yet closely bound up with public discourse. This interconnection is the condition of possibility of Heine's revolutionizing discourse in the *Travelogues*. Now, Heine himself was to abandon this model shortly after his move to Paris and his experiences of the July Revolution in 1830, turning to journalism as a much more direct form of engaged writing. The strategy of revolutionizing the literary public sphere by restructuring its discourse from within necessarily becomes obsolete as soon as this public sphere is perceived to have undergone that structural transformation, identified by Jürgen Habermas, in which it loses its emancipatory impulse and takes on instead an ideological character—when it begins, in other words, to concern itself primarily with the protection of bourgeois class interests rather than with the realization of a common good.[39] The shift that occurs in Heine's writing strategies from the popularized literature of the *Travelogues* to the critical journalism of the 1830's and beyond stems from his insight into this fundamental transformation in the bourgeois public sphere. This shift is accompanied by a reconception of his reading public: if the *Travelogues* are addressed to an educated bourgeois elite who possess the potential of becoming esoteric readers, the journalistic writings of the subsequent period abandon this tactical sophistication and attempt to drive home their political critique in a more open and direct manner, thereby addressing a greater cross section of the German public. The strategy employed in *Ideas* is thus relevant only prior to Heine's recognition of the historical devolution of the bourgeois literary public sphere into an ideological fortress concerned with the preservation of bourgeois class interests, and his shift in strategies in the early 1830's helps us locate this transformation as a historical phenomenon.

This historical circumscription of Heine's literary-revolutionary practice in *Ideas* can be elucidated by contrasting the conceptual strategies of his attack on the institution of art with those pursued by the historical avant-garde as described by Peter Bürger.[40] This comparison is especially illuminating because of certain similarities between the textual strategies operative in Heine's *Travelogues* and those followed by the avant-garde artists. Heine's texts share with the aesthetic tactics of this later artistic movement, for example, the dismantling of the organic work-character of the artistic product, the loose, aleatory principle of textual construction, and the intrusion of elements of life-praxis into the aesthetic work.[41] Despite this apparent congruence of textual practices and the shared conceptual project of an open offensive against the idealist aesthetics of autonomy, Heine's position with regard to textual *reception* could scarcely be more at odds with the stance adopted by the avant-garde. Because the Heine of the *Travelogues* still conceived the role of the political writer in terms of the exploitation of emancipatory-utopian potentials inherent—if temporarily repressed—in the bourgeois public sphere and the institution of literature, he could view his political project as a recapturing and reassertion of this repressed liberational power. Thus he did not find it necessary either to abandon completely or to destroy the institution of art; rather, he sought its reoccupation by writers and aesthetic programs dedicated to progressive emancipatory politics. Heine's exploitation of conventions of Romantic literature reflects this reoccupation of institutionalized literature. Once he has infiltrated the institution, however, and won the support of the reading public by appealing to their institutionalized literary sensibilities, he attempts to exploit this position as insider to redirect public sentiment toward political engagement for emancipatory politics.

Where Heine infiltrates and appeals, the avant-garde explodes and affronts. Given the historical (d)evolution of the institution of art into the primary ideological organ of the bourgeois public sphere, Heine's strategy was no longer an option for avant-garde artists. From their perspective, those who infiltrated the institution would simply be co-opted and their critical potential neutralized by its integrative force. With the transformation of the institution of art from a bastion of liberation to a stronghold of bourgeois class interests, the emancipatory potential of the literary public sphere evaporates. Believing that the bourgeoisie lacked any spark of emancipatory power, the avant-garde turned against its own public, launching a frontal attack on the institution of art and affronting the aesthetic sensibilities of the patrons who subscribed to its tenets. The paradox of this strategy, of course, is that by situating itself radically *outside* the institution of art and establishing itself as an absolute aesthetic Other, the avant-garde unwittingly replicated the elitism and autonomy characteristic of the institution it was assaulting. Heine, by contrast, was able to occupy and exploit a position *inside* the ruling institution of art. His manipulation of Romantic literary conventions was accomplished in the belief that by manipulating the aesthetic sensibilities of a reading public socialized in part by this institution, he could help recover its repressed historico-political revolutionary mission. Instead of attacking the institution of art, Heine exploited it by appropriating and refunctionalizing its discourse.

The revolutionary literary-aesthetic practices Heine follows in the *Travelogues* represent an important historical station in the evolution of a socially relevant critical aesthetics. An understanding of these strategies and their operation provides us with insights into the historical possibilities and impossibilities of a literature that seeks to couple literary-aesthetic revolution with political revolt in the sociopolitical realm of life-praxis. Heine's example demonstrates especially well that the political-revolutionary potential of literature can only fully be comprehended when revolutionizing textual practices are viewed in the context of historically determined conditions of textual reception in the public sphere. Thus only after we have recognized—to play on Hegel's famous dictum—the *pastness* of Heine's politico-aesthetic practices in *Ideas*, their reliance on particular historically determined parameters that regulate both the productive and receptive horizons of the hermeneutical dialectic, have we truly comprehended their literary-historical significance.

CHAPTER FIVE

The Madness of Civilization

Carnivalization, Spectatorship, and the Critique
of Enlightenment in Büchner's 'Woyzeck'

> In their existing organization, monopolizing science and remaining thus out-
> side social life, the *savants* form a separate caste, in many respects analogous
> to the priesthood. Scientific abstraction is their God, living and real individu-
> als are their victims, and they are the consecrated and licensed sacrificers.
> —Mikhail Bakunin

IN THE fragmentary novella *Lenz*, a literary elaboration on Pastor Oberlin's
account of the incipient madness of the poet Jakob Michael Reinhold Lenz,
Georg Büchner evinces a fascination for the disposition of the schizophrenic.
"Meanwhile his condition had become even bleaker," he writes of Lenz, "all
the peace . . . was gone; the world he had wished to serve had a gigantic
crack, he felt . . . a terrible void and yet a tormenting anxiety to fill it" (*BW*
I: 97–98; 156). There can be little doubt that this remark represents Büchner's
projection of his own crises and his experience of a ruptured world into the
figure of Lenz. The tension between desperate hope and an all-pervasive
sense of futility, which is characteristic of his Lenz, reflects Büchner's own
pendulation between the will to positive sociopolitical change and passive
resignation to the seeming unalterability of the human condition. His tornness between critical engagement and metaphysical fatalism mirrors in augmented fashion that tornness his contemporary Heinrich Heine lamented,
and it underscores the disjunctive subjectivity experienced by critical intellectuals in Restoration Germany.

Because of this apparently irreconcilable conflict in his intellectual biography, Büchner, like Heine, was destined to become a wound for German
cultural history. Although Büchner was only discovered at the end of the
nineteenth century by the Naturalists, who admired him as a significant precursor of their own socially critical dramatic realism, subsequent genera-

tions have tended to situate him in the Schopenhauerian tradition of metaphysical pessimism. As in the case of Heine, for Büchner it is senseless to attempt to unravel these two ostensibly contradictory intellectual tendencies, for they exist in a necessary dialectical relationship. Indeed, it is their indefeasible intertwining that constitutes Büchner's character and stamps him as a classically divided bourgeois intellectual, rent by the tendency toward resigned accommodation with and critical resistance against bourgeois ideology and practice. Reinhold Grimm is hence correct when he asserts the relevance of the Gramscian dictum, "pessimism of the intellect, optimism of the will," for Büchner's philosophical position, an attitude in which, in Grimm's words, "knowledge and bitter insights, resulting in paralyzing nihilism, are countered over and over by an untiring determination to revolt against all injustice, oppression, and misery."[1]

Büchner's critical resolution is most concretely realized in the revolutionary political manifesto *The Hessian Messenger* (1834), which he composed with Friedrich Ludwig Weidig. Opening with the provocative injunction, "Peace to the huts! War on the palaces!" (*BW* 2: 35; 41), this treatise exposes the corruption of the Hessian government and implores the populace to mount a revolt against its exploiters. But to give a complete picture of Büchner's intellectual temperament it is necessary to cite in conjunction with this revolutionary manifesto his well-known remarks to his fiancée, written at about the same time as *The Hessian Messenger*, in which he bemoans the "terrible fatalism of history."

I studied the history of the Revolution. I felt as if I were crushed under the terrible fatalism of history. I find in human nature a horrifying sameness [*entsetzliche Gleichheit*], in the human condition an inescapable force, granted to all and to no one. The individual merely foam on the waves, greatness sheer chance, the mastery of genius a puppet play, a ludicrous struggle against an iron law: to recognize it is our utmost achievement, to control it is impossible. . . . The word *must* is one of the curses with which man has been baptized. The dictum, "It must needs be that offenses come; but woe to that man by whom the offense cometh"—is terrifying. What is it within us that lies, murders, steals? (*BW* 2: 425–26; 260)

The dialectical hinge on which Büchner's equivocation between revolutionary action and historical fatalism turns is concretized in the phrase "horrifying sameness" ("entsetzliche Gleichheit"): *Gleichheit*, or "equality," the preeminent political ideal of the Revolution, is here condemned as a uniformity that flattens all difference into identity. In Büchner's first play, *Danton's Death* (1835), the omnipresent image of the guillotine symbolizes this horrible equality that "republicanizes" by "swinging its sickle over all our heads" (*BW* 1: 51–52; 99). For Büchner, the bourgeois ideal of equality has already devolved into that form of leveling equivalence, into the tyrannical logic of identities, that Adorno would later associate with the negative underside of the bourgeois episteme. Büchner's sense of "horrifying sameness" thus expresses the reversion of bourgeois emancipatory ideals into an ideology of control and mastery, projecting it as a metaphysical principle, similar to Schopenhauer's notion of the will, that operates beyond—or at the very heart of—the human subject itself.

In *Danton's Death* Büchner embodies in St. Just and Robespierre—two figures who, like Odoardo Galotti in Lessing's *Emilia Galotti*, commit murder to defend bourgeois virtue—the philosophy of a deranged enlightenment that exploits emancipatory ideas as tools for human oppression. St. Just gives voice to this ideologically tainted brand of enlightenment when he remarks: "Nature follows its laws serenely and irresistibly; man is destroyed when he comes in conflict with them. . . . I ask you now: should moral nature in its revolutions be more considerate than physical nature? Should not an idea be permitted to destroy its opposition just as well as a law of physics?" (*BW* 1: 45; 93). As the empirical sciences reduce nature to irrevocable, often brutal laws, so, too, the intellectual and moral criteria that govern human interaction become ironclad regulations that demand absolute conformity: whatever resists this order is uncompromisingly destroyed. The realm of culture, traditionally conceived as that which elevates humanity above nature and its absolute dictates, carving out a margin of relative freedom in the world of blind necessity, now becomes a mere reflex of this necessity. Instead of opposing natural determinism, culture itself fatalistically mimics nature's superiority over humanity. Here we witness the culmination of the bourgeois tragedy whose inception we traced in Lessing's *Emilia Galotti*: violence against and mastery over human subjects are legitimated by an appeal to the very virtues and principles that ostensibly constitute the progressive, emancipatory core of bourgeois ideology.

For Kant, as we have seen, this narrowing of reason into purposive rationality represented a mere "misuse" that could be prevented and corrected, while in Lessing's *Emilia Galotti* and Schiller's *Robbers* instrumental reason already appears as a potentially destructive undercurrent that threatens to hollow out the ideals of bourgeois rational society. In Büchner's thought this critical recognition has advanced to the point at which instrumentalized rationality becomes a universal, quasi-metaphysical force, and "enlightened" human beings its mindless pawns. In *Danton* Büchner depicts the absolutization of bourgeois reason as a dissemination of the rhetoric of destruction throughout revolutionary France: all its citizens, not just the Revolution's leaders, are shown obeying and/or exploiting the dictates of a cruel logic to justify violence against their fellow human beings. Appealing to the wretched masses, one citizen argues with pseudosyllogistic reasoning: "You have hunger pains and they [the aristocrats] have gas pains, you have holes in your jackets and they have warm coats, you have calluses and they have velvet hands. Ergo: you work and they do nothing; ergo: you earn it and they steal it; . . . ergo: they are thieves and must be killed" (*BW* 1: 14; *63*). Empirical observation and the rationale of syllogistic logic combine to segregate an oppressed we from an oppressing Other, and to underwrite violence against this Other once it is identified. The repetition of the causal particle "ergo" marks the inexorable ruthlessness and mindlessness of this logic. The misuse of reason hinted at by German thinkers at the end of the eighteenth century becomes such a dominant and all-encompassing principle in Büchner's world that it takes on the inevitability of a metaphysical doctrine. The "inverted world" becomes the seemingly irreversible norm of intellectual, socioeconomic, and natural existence under the sociopolitical and epistemic conditions of the German Restoration. Büchner's sense of desperation at the omnipresence of this perverted reason marks him as a significant precursor to the critical theoreticians of the Frankfurt School, whom he antedates by a century.

We should note at this point that Heine does not fit the framework of this intellectual-historical outline; he remains an uncritical advocate of enlightened reason and unflinchingly pursues the ideals of the bourgeois revolution, never succumbing to that critical skepticism about Enlightenment thought that in his contemporary Georg Büchner already develops into full-fledged pessimism. In this sense Heine represents—if we ignore the personal resignation inherent in his late poetry—one of the last firm believers in Enlightenment ideals in Germany, and his literature manifests a last gasp of enlightened optimism. This optimistic thrust is especially in evidence in *The Book Le Grand*, in which he gives a psychological-therapeutic twist to the pedagogical recovery project Schiller sketched in *The Robbers*. In his *Travelogues* Heine still believes himself able to take "healthy" human reason as an intrinsic standard whose just governance over human affairs has merely been repressed due to extrinsic sociopolitical factors; as a result, he can still conceive *Ideas* as a text which, functioning as a psychic liberator, is capable of intervening in this repression and bringing the German populace back to its senses. For Büchner, by contrast, any such project is futile and misguided. Thus, despite their close historical contemporaneity, their shared "tornness," and their mutual critical rejection of the sociopolitical conditions of Restoration Germany—from whose political persecution both literally had to flee—there is a significant difference in their critical outlooks and their literary-aesthetic programs.

Unfortunately, Büchner only provides us with very sparse theoretical re-

flections on his own literary aesthetics and its critical function; for that reason, we can only sketch a bare outline of his theoretical horizon, first by examining his occasional reflections on art and literature, and second by ex-
trapolating from his dramatic practice. This second task I will attempt to accomplish by examining Büchner's last literary work, the fragmentary drama
Woyzeck (1836–37).

Büchner's Aesthetics: The Dialectic of Mimesis and the Dialectic of Enlightenment

Scholarly accounts of Büchner's aesthetic attitudes have commonly concentrated on two discussions on art that find their way into his literary texts.
In both instances Büchner places into the mouths of fictionalized characters—Camille in *Danton's Death* and Lenz in the novella that bears his
name—vehement diatribes against idealism in art (see *BW* 1: 27, 86–88; *85–86*,
146–48). It is true that Büchner attacks the artificiality of idealist representations, contrasting these "wooden puppets" with the flesh-and-blood characters presented by realist aesthetics, which he valorizes. But Büchner's own
aesthetic conceptions were hardly as simple and schematic as all this; indeed,
even these ostensibly straightforward reflections on aesthetic issues indicate,
when scrutinized carefully, that he was well aware of the aporias inherent
in the representational practice of mimetic realism.[2] In *Danton's Death*, for
example, Danton counters Camille's assault on idealism by attributing to
the painter Jacques-Louis David, the realist artist who documented the
events of the Revolution, a "cold-bloodedness" that, in its depiction of the
victims of Revolutionary justice, seeks to capture in art "the last spasms of
life" (*BW* 1: 37; *86*). To be sure, Büchner practiced a radical form of documentary realism in his own literary texts, all of which, with the exception
of the comedy *Leonce and Lena* (1836), were based on actual historical accounts. But Büchner's Danton criticizes precisely such historical mimesis,
accusing it of viewing the human life-world with cold callousness. In Lenz's
discourse on art, similarly, realism, although set above idealistic portrayal,
is nevertheless compared to "a Medusa's head" that transforms nature into
lifeless stone and thus implicitly replicates the transgressions of a "lifeless"
idealism (*BW* 1: 87; *147*). At best, then, these formulations merely adumbrate
a self-contradictory aesthetic stance that simultaneously valorizes and criticizes Büchner's own realistic method. This self-critical reflex is an index of
his awareness that the "cold-blooded" mimesis of realistic aesthetics is always already entangled in the dialectic of enlightenment: mimetic re-presentation preserves the represented object, but at the price of turning it into

lifeless matter. This insight distinguishes Büchner from most of those practitioners of bourgeois realism in Germany who postdate him, and it links
him with the (self-)critical sagacity of more recent critics of enlightened
thought. The self-ensnarement of realistic aesthetics in the principles of an
alienating purposive rationality—its reliance on the positivistic scientism of
empirical investigation—forms the central aporia of Büchner's artistic theories.

Aside from these theoretical reflections embedded in literary texts, Büchner's most direct and salient comments on literary aesthetics can be found
in his correspondence. It is no coincidence that his two most detailed discourses on method evolve out of the drive to set his own literary endeavor
apart from that pursued by Heine, Gutzkow, and the other writers of Young
Germany, with whom Büchner's name came to be associated. In a letter to
his family written in January 1836, he firmly repudiates any connection to
this band of infamous literary renegades. "*I by no means belong to the so-
called 'Young Germany,' the literary party of Gutzkow and Heine,*" he emphasizes. He continues by explaining what he sees as this movement's fundamental failing, and this leads him to distinguish his own literary practice
from theirs.

Only a complete misunderstanding of our social conditions could lead these people to believe that a complete transformation of our religious and social ideas
would be possible through our current literature [*Tagesliteratur*]. . . . I'm going my
own way and staying in the field of drama, which has nothing to do with all of these
disputes; I draw my figures as I see fit in accordance with nature and history, and I
laugh about people who want to make me responsible for the morality or immorality of these characters. (*BW* 2: 451–52; *283*)

The "misunderstanding of our social conditions," of which Büchner accuses
Heine, Gutzkow, and their followers, boils down to their failure to perceive
the absolute hegemony of those epistemic and sociopolitical circumstances
that they naively believe they can vanquish by means of mere "Tagesliteratur," that genre of popularized literary-revolutionary text characteristic of
these authors. It is not the potential of a critical literature per se that Büchner calls into question, however, but simply the specific literary-critical practice of Young Germany. Indeed, the recognition informing Büchner's critique is akin to that recognition made by Heine himself, which ultimately
convinced him to turn away from literature and embrace critical journalism
instead. Büchner realizes that the bourgeois literary public sphere possesses
no liberational potential, and that the emancipatory ideals of the Enlightenment have become, in the words of his Danton, a "citadel of reason" (*BW*
1: 62; *109*), a fortress of ideological oppression. This reversion, which Jürgen

Habermas identifies as one of the fundamental structural transformations in the history of the bourgeois public sphere,[3] marks the ultimate dialectical regression of enlightenment into myth, that is, of bourgeois revolutionary-emancipatory ideals into a protectionist ideology.

Büchner takes differences in their sociopolitical conceptions as the basis for distinguishing his literary practice from that of Young Germany. This sociopolitical divergence precipitates two literary-aesthetic juxtapositions: that between idealism and realism as literary methods, on the one hand, and that between narrative and drama as literary genres, on the other. Thus, in this letter Büchner champions his own literary practice as a naturalistic realism that conceives its characters as documentary records copied from nature and history, implicitly contrasting this with the utopian, idealizing designs pursued by the Young Germans. Moreover, he contrasts favorably his own dramatic procedure with the specifically narrative literature of Heine and Gutzkow: drama, he maintains, has no hand in the petty and senseless "disputes" in which their narrative discourse engages.

Büchner formulates his personal disavowal of the literary tactics of Young Germany once more in a letter to Karl Gutzkow himself. Now, it is significant that Gutzkow attempted to establish himself as Büchner's literary mentor.[4] Indeed, in a letter from March 1835 Gutzkow appeals to his would-be disciple to "carry on the idea-smuggling of freedom as I do: wine is camouflaged in the straw of novellas, nothing appears in its natural dress." And he justifies this literary subterfuge by maintaining: "I believe one can be of more use in this way than if one runs blindly against guns that are by no means only loaded with blanks."[5] Some months later in a letter to Gutzkow, Büchner formulates what reads like a rejection of this summons to literary *imitatio*.

By the way, in all honesty it seems to me that you and your friends didn't exactly take the most sensible path. Reform society through *ideas*, through the *educated* classes? Impossible! Our times are purely *materialistic*; if you had ever worked along more directly political lines, you soon would have come to the point where reform would have stopped on its own. You will never bridge the chasm between the educated and uneducated classes.

I'm convinced that the educated and prosperous minority, as many concessions as it might desire for itself from the authorities, will never want to give up its antagonistic attitude toward the masses. And the masses themselves? For them there are only two levers: material poverty and *religious fanaticism*. Any party that knows how to operate these levers will conquer. (*BW* 2: 455; *286*)

One can scarcely imagine a more succinct and pointed repudiation of the pedagogical project of the German Enlightenment than that formulated by

Büchner in this passage. If Heine's *Ideas* represents a paradigmatic manifestation of the will to reform society by means of "ideas" and through the educated literary elite, Büchner's aesthetics is founded on an insight into the political futility—the historical "pastness"—of such a program. Büchner no longer has faith that the bourgeois educated class has the will to disseminate its own sociopolitical and economic advantages among the entire population, and thus he throws into question the entire trickle-down theory of the German Enlightenment's philosophical-historical "education of the human race," the belief that the unrestrained free flow of information in the (bourgeois) public sphere ultimately guarantees enlightenment to all. Since revolutionary change can no longer be effected through the bourgeoisie, Büchner believes one must look to the uneducated masses; however, they are not moved by "ideas"—at least not in the philosophical sense—but only by material deprivation and religious fanaticism. Thus Büchner seems to deny—as did Hegel, although for totally different reasons—that, under the given historical conditions of Germany in the first half of the nineteenth century, literature can accomplish effective critical-political service. However, he also denies that Hegel's idealist dream of regulated historical change through philosophical (self-)reflection can ever be realized.

Given the collapse of the Enlightenment pedagogical project, we might justifiably ask, is there any critical purpose left for literature whatsoever? Since it seems obvious that Büchner did not intend his plays to be mere realistic mirrors, but composed them with a pervasive critical intent, we can only speculate about the kind of social function he thought this literature could perform. Although Büchner gives no direct answers to these questions, he does point us in certain directions. For one thing, he makes clear that the audience addressed by a revolutionary-critical literature must be the uneducated classes. Thus he envisions the conditions of literary reception in a radically different manner than do Heine and Gutzkow. This explains in part his rejection of narrative texts, consumed as commodities and absorbed in a process of privatized reading, in favor of the immediate, communitarian performance of drama. However, if Büchner believes that the only "levers" for revolutionizing the masses are "poverty" and "religious fanaticism," then we must ask what potential relationship drama, as he conceived it, has to these levers. Although it certainly cannot ratchet up the actual poverty of the masses, dramatic portrayal can perhaps bring this poverty to critical reflection, throwing it into relief by means of aesthetic representation. Realism, thus understood, would be the aesthetic counterpart of materialism and would serve to re-present and thus deepen the audience's awareness of the material relations governing society. In this aspect, drama for Büchner continues the project of self-reflection and consciousness-raising inherent in critical enlightenment, with the important difference, however, that it addresses itself to an entirely different public, to the uneducated masses.

Of course, for Büchner this modified project of enlightenment is never separable from the critique of enlightenment, just as for him documentary realism is always already entangled in the life-extinguishing abstraction of a mimetic representation that substitutes aesthetic signs for real objects, thereby turning them into "lifeless stone." On the other hand, dramatic spectacle certainly has been—and can be—exploited for the cultivation of religious fanaticism. In this respect, dramatic presentation embodies a mythic dimension that stands over against the critical spectatorship of enlightenment: it exhibits what one might call a demagogic purpose. These two aspects of the dramatic spectacle—reflective spectatorship and mythic pageantry—merge in Büchner's dramatic practice, especially in the drama *Woyzeck*. Büchner's literary-aesthetic practices thus reflect what Adorno identifies as the ineluctable dilemma of modern art, its tension between enlightenment and myth. Adorno could be describing Büchner's aesthetics when he writes: "The dilemma of art between regression to real magic and surrender of the mimetic impulse to thinglike rationality helps formulate art's law of motion; this dilemma must not be done away with." According to Adorno, it is the very irreconcilability of these two principles that defines art as a form of "rationality criticizing itself without being able to overcome itself."[6] Büchner's *Woyzeck* is a text produced by this aesthetic dialectic between magic (spectacle) and mimesis to thinglike rationality (reflective spectatorship), and as such it manifests the ultimate aporia of Unhappy Consciousness: the dilemma that rational critique of enlightenment is fundamentally implicated in the very rationality it would criticize.

Critical diagnosis of enlightenment has constantly been plagued by the paradox that the critique of enlightened thinking necessarily finds itself entangled in those very forms of thought it would assail. From the "fragments" of Friedrich Schlegel through the aphoristic philosophizing of Friedrich Nietzsche to the self-sublating critical discourse of Max Horkheimer and Theodor Adorno in their *Dialectic of Enlightenment*, the attack on enlightened rationality has consistently found it impossible to operate *on* the structures of this reason without operating *with* these structures themselves.[7] In all these instances the rigidity of formal logic is fractured by its staged collision with the irrational, the metaphorical, the aesthetic. But for the contemporary exemplars of this critique of enlightenment—and here I would place Büchner's name beside those of Nietzsche, Horkheimer, and Adorno—this paradox takes the form of an inescapable aporia that threatens to undermine the entire critical project before it can even be formulated.

At the very beginning of *Dialectic of Enlightenment*, Horkheimer and Adorno note that under the given sociopolitical conditions, criticism of these circumstances is inevitably doomed to fall into affirmation. They refer to this paradoxical reversal as the "metamorphos[i]s of criticism into affirmation," a "sickness" they describe as follows: "It is characteristic of the sickness that even the best-intentioned reformer who uses an impoverished and debased language to recommend renewal, by his adoption of the insidious mode of categorization and the bad philosophy it conceals, strengthens the very power of the established order he is trying to break."[8] The central thesis of this work, of course, is that enlightenment, although it originally provided the means for the emancipation of humanity from the obscurity of myth, ultimately reveals itself to be a more insidious form of myth itself. "False clarity," they write, "is only another name for myth."[9] In this critical text Horkheimer and Adorno confront this paradox, taking on the arduous task of initiating a critical salvage operation intended to help rescue enlightenment from itself by freeing its original emancipatory moment from the dialectical reversal into enslavement. Their own method, not surprisingly, is itself a dialectical one; for what Horkheimer and Adorno refer to as their petitio principii, the recognition that their critique of enlightenment is grounded in a belief in its emancipatory power,[10] manifests itself as an attempt to turn the critical reflection of enlightenment back upon itself and thereby set in motion a process of self-reflective correction. Thus, they distinguish their own project from that of conservative critics of civilization by claiming "the issue is not that of culture as a value. . . . The point is rather that the Enlightenment must consider itself [*muß sich auf sich selbst besinnen*]."[11] Their own self-conscious application of the "mode of categorization" characteristic of enlightened rationality hence has a double purpose: it permits them, first of all, to take a first step toward this self-reflective folding of enlightenment back upon itself; and second, it allows them to turn the necessity that critique of enlightenment can only be carried out on enlightenment's own terms into their own methodological virtue. They thus attempt to exploit their own critical dilemma as a methodological in-road that makes effective critique possible.

Jürgen Habermas has coined the phrase "performative contradiction" to describe the circular critical strategy pursued by Horkheimer and Adorno in *Dialectic of Enlightenment*.[12] With this expression, Habermas characterizes a critical double-move whereby in the very moment critique is advanced, its impotence is simultaneously acknowledged. Performative contradiction thus manifests a tactic coherent with that critical desperation resulting from the recognition that the immediate sociopolitical environment begs denunciation, but has such ascendancy that contradiction seems futile at best, and counterproductive at worst. Performative contradiction, in other words, represents the last resort of critical reflection when confronted with the hegemony of bourgeois purposive rationality and the realization that it is itself implicated in this reversion of reason into myth.

Büchner's thought evolves out of his own perception that a merciless sociopolitical critique of Restoration Germany is as necessary as it is futile. As early as 1833 he wrote in a letter to his parents:

Young people are accused of using violence. But aren't we in an eternal state of violence? Because we were born and raised in a prison, we no longer realize that we're trapped in a hole with fettered hands and feet and with gags in our mouths. What do you call a *lawful state*? . . . Supported by raw military might and by the stupid conniving of its agents, this law is *eternal, brute force*, insulting justice and good sense, and I will fight *tooth and nail* against it wherever I can. If I do not take part in whatever has happened or might happen, I do so neither out of disapproval nor out of fear, but only because at the present time I regard any revolutionary movement as a futile undertaking. (*BW* 2: 416–17; *250*)

These remarks, written a year before the publication of *The Hessian Messenger*, indicate clearly that Büchner's uncompromising resistance to the given sociopolitical conditions was held in check by his sense that under these circumstances all revolt was in vain. Throughout Büchner's correspondence there are many similar commentaries which demonstrate that, although he himself was poised for all-out attack on Restoration society, he nevertheless held out little hope for positive change.[13] *The Hessian Messenger* represented for him a kind of experiment in revolutionary action intended to test the political climate in Germany, and its results corroborated his hypothesis that conditions in Hesse were far from ripe for political revolt. Indeed, the *Messenger* provides a paradigmatic example of that kind of critique which, by justifying the intensification of repressive countermeasures against would-be revolutionary destabilizers, ends up ultimately affirming and aggravating those very circumstances it strives to undo. Such self-negating critique, although it concedes its own critical impotence, simultaneously recognizes that the only alternative to this impossible opposition is silent affirmation of the status quo. Like Horkheimer and Adorno, then, Büchner found himself caught between the drive to critical assault and the necessity of its self-retraction. In his dramatic practice he develops a response to this dilemma that resembles the performative contradiction practiced by these later critics in *Dialectic of Enlightenment*.

Although Büchner's position as practicing natural scientist might at first glance seem to indicate a partisanship that would make him an unlikely critic of scientistic reason, there is in fact evidence which indicates that it was precisely Büchner's experiences as natural scientist that permitted him to arrive relatively early at critical insights into the alienating and reifying tendencies inherent in empirical positivism. Indeed, he participated as historical and disciplinary insider in those watershed developments in the evolution of the natural sciences into knowledge-disciplines that transpired early in the nineteenth century,[14] and it is well known that he responded with skepticism to the turn from holistic science to the purposive-rational scientism that was then coming into prominence. In *Knowledge and Human Interests*, Habermas outlines the historical transformation that occurs in the nineteenth century when scientific positivism supplants epistemology as the dominant scientific discourse. With this event, according to Habermas, transcendental-logical inquiry into the conditions of possibility of knowledge is cut off and replaced by the dogmatic methodological self-affirmation of positivism. "By making a dogma of the sciences' belief in themselves," Habermas maintains, "positivism assumes the prohibitive function of protecting scientific inquiry from epistemological self-reflection." Positivism, in other words, "is philosophical only insofar as is necessary for the immunization of the sciences against philosophy."[15] For Habermas this development has two significant corollaries: first, it gives rise to the jettisoning of the thinking subject as the point of reference in systems of knowledge; second, it replaces the displaced subject, once conceived as the ground of all knowledge, with the formal structures of logic and mathematics—that is, with methodology.

Even in its most superficial aspects, Büchner's academic career appears as a rejection of this tendency toward the "immunization of the sciences against philosophy"; for in his post at the University of Zurich he lectured not only on narrowly scientific topics, but on the history of philosophy as well. Indeed, Büchner's philosophical and scientific interests work together as mutually supplementary positions, and this protected him against what Habermas indicts as the flattening of epistemology into methodology. Unhappy Consciousness thus manifests itself in Büchner's thought as the dialectical interaction between philosophical self-reflection and methodological positivism.

In the scientific treatise "On Cranial Nerves," Büchner criticizes what he calls the "teleological" direction of scientific investigation on three different accounts: first, he accuses it of a materialism that views the organism merely as "a complex machine" (*BW* 2: 291); second, he attacks the circularity of its methodology; and third, he indicts its tendency to abstract completely from the traits of any individual organism to establish an artificial, general model. This criticism should not be read as evidence of Büchner's sympathies for the Romantic "philosophy of nature," as some scholars have suggested;[16] instead, it should be viewed as his rejection of scientistic positivism, whose encroachment upon the natural sciences Büchner was beginning to sense. To the "teleological" method Büchner juxtaposes what he terms the "philosophical" view. Taking an idealist rather than a materialist standpoint, this method denies that natural phenomena are guided by any overriding purposiveness and seeks instead to discover "fundamental laws for the total organization" of any organism (BW 2: 292). Now, one can scarcely overlook that this valorization of an idealistically grounded natural science at the expense of materialist positions is at odds with Büchner's aesthetic conceptions, which reverse this hierarchy, lauding materialism and vehemently assailing aesthetic idealism. This provides us with a first indication that the opposition between idealism and materialism is just as insufficient for a proper understanding of Büchner's view of scientific methodologies as it is, as we have seen, for the apprehension of his aesthetic standpoints. Indeed, his methodological reflections in "On Cranial Nerves" go well beyond this simple dichotomy. It has generally been overlooked, for example, that Büchner divides the "philosophical" view into two subcategories; and to better understand Büchner's views it is essential that we follow his arguments as he develops this distinction.

The "philosophical" method is unified by its search in all individual beings for "the manifestation of a primordial law [Urgesetzes], a law of beauty that develops the highest and purest forms by following the simplest sketches and lines" (BW 2: 292). However, this search, according to Büchner, has traditionally led in two very different directions.

The question about such a law led quite naturally to the sources of thought by which the enthusiasm of absolute knowledge has always let itself be intoxicated: the intuition of the mystic and the dogmatism of rational philosophers. Upon critical consideration one must deny that it has ever been possible to build a bridge between the latter and the life of nature that we perceive immediately. A priori philosophy still lingers in a desolate desert; there is an immense distance that separates it from fresh, green life. (BW 2: 292–93)

Büchner submits even the philosophical method, to the extent that it adheres to the "dogmatism of rational philosophers," to an excoriating critique. Whereas he previously denounced the teleological method for its abstractionism, its methodological circularity, and for confusing cause and effect, he now castigates the philosophical position, grounded in a priori rules of reason, for its distance from nature, its sterility, its desolate artificiality. It is instructive to recall the words with which in his *Aesthetics* Hegel laments the "distress of the present time" that he makes responsible for the disappearance of art: "Intelligence," Hegel maintains, "itself subserves this distress, and its interests, in sciences which are useful for such ends alone, and it allows itself to be seduced into confining itself to this desert."[17] Both Hegel's critique of scientific knowledge for its narrowing into purposive disciplines and Büchner's attack on a scientific method that operates on the basis of a priori laws of reason culminate in the metaphor of a dry, sterile desert, infinitely far from the fertility and vitality of the life such knowledge claims to comprehend. But Büchner radicalizes Hegel's critique to the extent that Hegelian idealism itself also falls under the "dogmatism of rational philosophers" that he lambastes. Be that as it may, the common ground between Büchner's attack on the teleological method and his critique of a priori philosophizing is the rejection of methodologies that jettison individual traits in favor of abstractions and formal principles.

Unfortunately, Büchner does not pursue the second option open to the philosophical method, the alternative of mystical insight, which he juxtaposes to a priori knowledge; as a result, we can only speculate about what he might have had in mind. The juxtaposition itself suggests that this intuitive comprehension represents for him a positive value. Perhaps his suppression of any explanatory commentary is a symptom of his own concessions to that scientific dogmatism he opposes, since we can assume that a defense of the "intuition of the mystic" would certainly have undermined the authority of this scientific tract in the eyes of Büchner's scientist colleagues. At any rate, the reference to mystical intuition implies that Büchner envisions a mode of perception that somehow combines empirical observation with perspicacious divination, thereby arriving at a mode of scientific understanding that balances the particular and the general, concrete facts and overriding hypotheses. Such a conception would align Büchner with two prominent German poet-scientists of the preceding generation: Georg Christoph Lichtenberg, who promoted an aphoristic method of investigation intended to counter the prejudice of a priori rules and dogmatic systems; and Goethe, whose investigation into the metamorphosis of plants Büchner himself cites as exemplary of that search for a "law of beauty" underlying the multiplicity of individual phenomena (see *BW* 2: 293).

Büchner's distinction between mystical intuition and the dogmatic rules of a priori philosophy rings strikingly similar to the dichotomy between natural and arbitrary signification in which Enlightenment thinkers formulated their critique of bourgeois epistemic structures. In both instances immediate perception (*Anschauung*) and intrinsic relations are placed above formal logic, arbitrary conventions, and a priori laws. Although Büchner never directly addresses the semiotic questions underpinning this problematic,[18] there is nevertheless a definite homology between his critique of dogmatic thought-structures that abstract from concrete phenomena and his persistent critique of language and rhetoric. Thus, whereas Büchner emphasizes that his historical investigations into philosophy acquainted him with "the wretchedness of the human spirit" (*BW* 2: 450; *282*), he similarly indicts the "technical language" ("Kunstsprache": literally, "artificial language") of philosophical discourse for its remoteness from the human concerns it purports to address, vehemently asserting that "for human affairs . . . one should find human expressions" (*BW* 2: 421; *256*). Here again, Büchner castigates philosophical discourse for its distance, its alienation from the profoundly "human affairs" it aims to represent. What he essentially demands is a mode of discourse that possesses some intrinsic, natural, or motivated relationship with the states of affairs it relates, and in this sense his wistful vision of authentic philosophical expression is wholly in line with the hopes Lessing and Schiller attached to the use of natural signs. What Büchner bemoans, in the final analysis, is that philosophical discourse operates with a semiotic system based on arbitrary signs, rather than with natural or "magical" signs that immediately and intrinsically relate to their signifieds. In this sense, what he laments is nothing other than that philosophizing is always already accomplished in the name of enlightenment, whose condition of possibility, as Horkheimer and Adorno point out, is that epistemic system structured around the arbitrariness of the sign, a system that "puts an end to the superstitious fusion of word and thing."[19] The transformation of the human life-world by the victory of instrumentalized reason plays a central role in Büchner's first drama, *Danton's Death*, and this problematic reappears in *Woyzeck*, his last literary text, this time focused specifically as a critique of scientistic positivism. The fragments that constitute the text of *Woyzeck* constantly circle around those issues that Horkheimer and Adorno would later identify as the dialectic of enlightenment.

The Dialectic of Enlightenment in *Woyzeck*

Like *Danton's Death*, *Woyzeck* must be considered first and foremost a documentary drama. The medical account dealing with the case of the historical Woyzeck, written by the physician Johann Christian August Clarus, constitutes the source from which Büchner compiled the information for his dramatic portrayal.[20] However, this document provided Büchner with much more than a mere source from which he culled factual information for his own rewriting of the historical events; indeed, what probably struck him most about this affidavit was not so much the pitiable existence led by Woyzeck himself as the haughty and callous demeanor of Clarus's "scientific" deliberations on his case. Clarus held final responsibility for ascertaining whether the historical Woyzeck could be considered mentally competent at the time he murdered his lover, Frau Woost. Despite considerable evidence that contradicts his judgment, Clarus established Woyzeck's sanity, arguing primarily that this crime derived from the perpetrator's inability to control his animal passions. When he rendered this medical opinion, Clarus pronounced Woyzeck accountable for his crime, and he thereby essentially signed his death warrant.

Büchner's worst suspicions about the inimicality of scientistic reasoning to tolerant and charitable human interrelations take on concrete form in the dispassionate and heartless manner in which Clarus passes judgment on Woyzeck. In this affidavit Büchner came across a particularly grotesque example of the exploitation of scientistic methodologies as a tool for the oppression—and ultimately for the elimination—of one human being by another: in reading this document, Büchner becomes a witness to the reversion of enlightened reason into myth and mastery. As a result, Büchner's principal concern in his dramatic rendering of this historical documentation is not so much the character of the historical Woyzeck himself as the manner in which Clarus represents this figure. In other words, it is Clarus's narrative itself, as a symptom of what Horkheimer and Adorno call the "false clarity" of enlightenment thinking, that Büchner seeks to aesthetically reproduce in *Woyzeck*. The aim of these dramatic fragments, then, is to provide a critical reflection of the "dogmatism of reason" that makes itself manifest in Clarus's affidavit. Büchner accomplishes this by reinscribing Clarus's scientistic testimony in a dramatic spectacle that critically recontextualizes its logical mechanisms, thereby disclosing the calculating inhumanity that underwrites his idealizing conception of human nature. This aesthetic strategy develops on the basis of a double-move: on the one hand, Büchner confronts the cold objectivity of the gaze with which Clarus scrutinizes his "object" with the humanizing gaze of dramatic spectatorship; on the other hand, he exploits grotesque inversions of Clarus's hierarchical understanding to uncover and satirize the logical inconsistencies in his rationalizations. Büchner's goal is to turn Clarus's scientistic rationality back upon itself, employing this self-reflection as a tactic of critical revelation. The "performative contradiction" of *Woyzeck* resides in the fact that Büchner must appropriate Clarus's enlightened methodology in the aesthetic structure of this drama to critically lay bare its insidious fusion of enlightenment and myth.

Given Büchner's acute sensitivity to language and his penchant for humoristic puns, wordplay, and neologisms, he could scarcely have overlooked the irony that in the instance of August Clarus *nomen* is indeed *omen*: Clarus's report on the Woyzeck case is grounded in the tacit assumption that rational "clarity" is unquestionably "august." In the preface to his deposition Clarus himself stresses that his deliberations are motivated solely by "love of truth";[21] but his one-sided, obviously prejudicial handling of this case belies this assertion, exposing this love of truth as nothing but a willfully manipulative interpretation of the facts. Indeed, even a cursory reading reveals that the supposed objectivity of Clarus's investigation rests on a specific set of values that are bound up with his own social station as part of the educated class. Given this social position, it comes as no surprise that he privileges reason over emotion, education over ignorance, and freedom of the will over natural and social determination. Clarus's "love of truth" thereby reveals itself to be grounded in the major tenets of bourgeois ideology, and it is on the basis of these ideologically entrenched values that he condemns Woyzeck.

The primary ideal of this ideological worldview is the repression of irrational, animalistic passions by the rational faculties. Clarus diagnoses as the motivation behind Woyzeck's act of murder *"the preponderance of passion over reason."*[22] What he criticizes in Woyzeck, in short, is the failure successfully to civilize and hence repress his nature. In his reflections Clarus asserts so absolutely the dominance of reason over passion that his attitude vis-à-vis Woyzeck ultimately betrays that cold-blooded objectivity Büchner so brilliantly twists into caricature in his portrayal of the Doctor in his dramatic rendering (see *Woyzeck* H4, viii, 64–65; *237–38*).[23] Throughout his deliberations Clarus consistently valorizes "freedom of the will" and "the free use of reason,"[24] as does Büchner's Doctor in *Woyzeck*; and he passes sentence on Woyzeck by measuring him as flesh-and-blood being against these abstract idealizations of human nature. Although these principles may indeed be appropriate to Clarus himself, they are certainly out of touch with the reality of Woyzeck's social station and material poverty. In his dramatization of the Woyzeck case, Büchner plays out this ideological confrontation in the conflict between the Captain and Woyzeck. When the Captain condemns Woyzeck for his "immorality," Woyzeck's line of defense is to cite his poverty and assert his subservience to the demands of nature (*Woyzeck* H4, v, 62; *207–8*). Both the Captain and Clarus take as their point of departure a rationalized and dogmatic conception of the human being grounded in the optimistic principles of Enlightenment thinking, and they employ it as an ideal standard that then allows them to condemn as unfit—and thereby sentence to death—those who, like Woyzeck, do not measure up. Human nature is forced to conform to the a priori laws that govern their ideological vision of an abstract and denatured human being.

Ultimately there is a bitter irony inherent in this censure of the historical Woyzeck, one that certainly was not lost on Büchner. If Clarus had simply ruled that Woyzeck was insane, if he had determined, in his words, that "the deranged notion had taken *exclusive* control over [Woyzeck's] reason,"[25] then he could have declared Woyzeck unaccountable for his actions and thus spared his life. But Clarus insists that Woyzeck is not incapable of reasoned thought; nor has his free will been taken hostage by aberrant obsessions. Woyzeck's sin is an unpardonable infraction against the use of divine reason, and this explains for Clarus why he "arrives at false judgments and conclusions, at errors and prejudices."[26] In other words, what Clarus attacks in Woyzeck is precisely a deficiency in his capacity to reason, a lack that stems from the perverting influence of the irrational and subjective—of prejudice, error, and false judgment—on Woyzeck's free will and his free use of reason. Woyzeck embodies for Clarus a dangerous imperfection in the clarity of august reason. Clarus could have accepted Woyzeck if he had proven to be entirely insane, because as the absolute Other of reason insanity represents no threat to the sublime logic of bourgeois purposive rationality; but as hybrid between reason and unreason, as this "confusion of subjective sensations with objective ideas,"[27] Woyzeck undermines the very integrity of reason itself by threatening to overturn the central relationship on which it is founded: the distinction between the subjective and the objective. This is one of the seminal points at which Büchner picks up Clarus's argument and transforms it into a constitutive element of his critical dramatic reproduction. In the carnival scenes of *Woyzeck* (h1, i and ii, 31–32; 226–27; h2, iii, 46; 203–5), Büchner presents precisely such hybridizations of man and animal, reason and passion, thereby throwing into critical relief Clarus's one-sided insistence on the abstract purity and dominance of humanity's rational faculty.

Clarus justifies his condemnation of Woyzeck by segregating prejudice, the nemesis of enlightened reason, from insanity as absolute and unmasterable nonreason. "Prejudice and insanity are distinguishable by the fact that the former derives either merely from a *limitation in the means* to correct one's ideas and gather knowledge and experience, or from indolence in the use of these means," whereas characteristic of insanity is that "the deranged notion . . . intervenes in all the operations" of reason and thus clouds the victim's judgments.[28] Obviously, what Clarus objects to is the "limita-tion" of Woyzeck's "means"—that is, his underprivileged status in society, his lack of formal education, his poverty. These are the qualities that define for him Woyzeck's "moral degeneracy."[29] But if we step outside the circular chain of Clarus's logic, submitting it, as Büchner obviously did, to critical scrutiny, his censure of Woyzeck takes on the character of an unwitting con-demnation of the socioeconomic order responsible for Woyzeck's "limited means," and by extension of the very enlightened logic that structures and legitimates this order. What this critical reading of Clarus's affidavit brings to light, moreover, is that those very qualities Clarus condemns in Woyzeck form the basis for his own rational judgments: the enlightened ideology that indicts Woyzeck demonstrates its own grounding in a specific set of preju-dices, false judgments, and errors. Indeed, if Woyzeck's "coldness" and "feel-inglessness" are the conditions of possibility for his murder of Frau Woost, as Clarus believes,[30] then the same applies for Clarus's execution of Woyzeck. The very evidence that enables Clarus to brand Woyzeck as a murderer, in other words, is replicated in Clarus's murderous reflections on Woyzeck—with the important difference, however, that what he lambastes in his social inferior as the infiltration of reason by passion is glorified in his own person as the quintessence of healthy reason. Consequently, when Clarus passes judgment on Woyzeck as a curious hybrid of reason and un-reason he also implicitly passes judgment on his own perversely hybridized reason. Although it appears to him that with the decapitation of Woyzeck the ominous infection of reason by unreason has been forestalled, in fact the contagion triumphs by dressing its own instrumentalized rationality in the imperial robes of reason itself. When read through this critical lens, the Clarus report is disclosed as the self-perpetuation of that "false clarity" in-dicted by Horkheimer and Adorno in *Dialectic of Enlightenment*. Clarus's af-fidavit, as the paradigmatic textual concretization of bourgeois enlightened discourse, exemplifies that merging of myth and enlightenment—the re-version of enlightenment to myth—that these later critics of bourgeois so-ciety identify as the historical turn of bourgeois civilization against itself.

Clarus represents a false enlightenment in one further significant respect: in his report he advances the pedagogical argument that the punishment of Woyzeck will serve as a disciplinary example from which the uneducated masses will derive an important lesson. Already in his preface Clarus justi-fies his judgment in the Woyzeck case by pointing to the potentially bene-ficial effects that his execution, when considered as a disciplinary-pedagog-ical example, could have on the masses: "May it be profoundly impressed upon the next generation of our youth at the sight of this bleeding criminal, or at the very thought of him, that laziness, gambling, drunkenness, illegal stilling of sexual desire, and bad company can unwittingly and gradually lead to criminality and the gallows."[31] For Clarus, Woyzeck stands as the negative example of all those vices so abhorrent to enlightened bourgeois society, and he exploits the ritual of Woyzeck's public execution as a kind of moralizing example-story: the condemnation of prejudice, viewed as a grotesque hybridization of reason and superstition, becomes a tool for the moral disciplining of the underprivileged masses. Reckoning with the perverse "curiosity" ("Schaulust": literally, "lust for viewing") with which these "degenerate half-humans," as Clarus derogatorily calls them,[32] will view Woyzeck's execution, he imagines the transformation of this sadistic spectatorship into an enlightened gaze: identifying with the punished offender, those who witness this act of state-authorized violence will learn to subordinate their passions to the dictates of reason. Significantly, Clarus understands the pedagogical effect of this spectacle in a manner consonant with the aesthetics of catharsis propagated by theoreticians of drama in Germany during the Enlightenment. Thus, he anticipates that this pedagogical spectacle will initiate a process of purification in which those passions that constitute the dark underside of life—in fact, the essence of life itself—will be gradually eradicated, leaving only that sterile, idealized "desert" of a moral and enlightened humanity. Clarus's abstract measuring-stick for human value thereby doubles as the rod of discipline. Given Clarus's exploitation of this aesthetics of pity in the disciplinary spectacle of Woyzeck's death, it seems unlikely that Büchner, otherwise so critical of Clarus's approach, would have conceived *Woyzeck* in the context of this dramatic tradition, as has often been maintained.[33] I will return to this point when examining the development Woyzeck undergoes in Büchner's dramatic fragments.

Büchner's caustic satirization of Clarus in the figure of the Doctor presents but the most obvious evidence that he read this affidavit in a manner approaching the reading sketched here. Indeed, the fallout of such a critical reading irradiates throughout most of the scenes Büchner composed for this play. To chart the traces of Clarus's false clarity as the formative impulse behind the aesthetic structure of Büchner's text, I will concentrate on two issues: carnivalization, and questions of spectatorship and the enlightened gaze. The centrality of these two motifs for Büchner's conception of *Woyzeck* is demonstrated by the fact that they form the focus of the carnival or festival scenes (*Woyzeck* h1, i and ii, 31–32; 226–27; and h2, iii, 46; 203–5), which were the very first episodes Büchner composed for this play. Their importance is further underscored by the fact that these scenes are among the only ones Büchner planned to use in all versions of the drama.[34]

Büchner's representation of carnival in *Woyzeck* serves a number of relevant functions. As a spectacle addressed to the uneducated masses whom he saw as the motor of revolutionary social change, his festival scene reproduces the pedagogical pageant Clarus hoped Woyzeck's execution would become. In this scene Büchner portrays his own characters exhibiting the *Schaulust* of "degenerate half-humans" that Clarus so disdained. This, in turn, gives a first indication that Büchner intends to exploit such spectatorship for the spectacle of *Woyzeck* as drama. Moreover, this scene picks up the principles defended by Clarus in his affidavit, but simultaneously distorts them by projecting them through the lens of the carnivalesque. This episode thus marks Büchner's initial critical confrontation with the medical affidavit on which his play is based, and it thereby points to the fundamentally documentary and thus polyphonic nature of the drama itself.

Woyzeck is constructed in terms of the confrontation of two discourses, as the challenge of Clarus's ideological worldview by Büchner's critical reading, and in this sense the very conception of the play betrays a fundamental feature of carnival, defined as a site "where two texts meet, contradict, and relativize one another."[35] According to Mikhail Bakhtin, whose views Julia Kristeva represents in this quotation, carnival names that place at which authority and ideology are transgressed, where the high and the low, the institutionalized and the repressed, change places or are fused. Thus, carnival is constructed around two reflexes: hierarchical inversion and grotesque hybridization.[36] The festival with which Büchner begins the composition of *Woyzeck* consciously introduces that hybrid of reason and unreason that is anathema to Clarus's idealizing rationality, and it consequently signals, in the words of Bakhtin, the "temporary suspension, both ideal and real, of hierarchical rank," thereby opening onto "a special type of communication impossible in everyday life."[37] Now, as the one institutionally legitimate site at which the overturning and destabilization of authoritative values can be enacted, carnival possesses a significant ideology-critical potential in that it helps to maintain and revitalize oppositional views. On the other hand, some critics have objected that as licensed insurrection, carnival can also function as a societal safety valve which, by allowing for the controlled release of repressed critical drives, ultimately contributes to the stabilization of the status quo. Both of these potentials inhere in the mechanism of carnival, and the question of its oppositional or restorative impact therefore becomes a function of how it is exploited.[38] In the carnival scenes of *Woyzeck* Büchner attempts to capitalize on the critical potentials that derive from an introduction of those ascendant societal values represented by Clarus in a context that overturns their hierarchical dominance: when Clarus's ideological precepts are placed in the mouth of the Barker at the fair, they are subjected to the ridicule of the spectators who view Büchner's drama.

The speech of the Barker, which turns on the hybridizing fusion of human and animal, reason and nature, is calculated to mock Clarus's idealizing valorization of the first term in each of these dichotomies.

Gentlemen! Gentlemen! Look at this creature as God made it: he's nothing, nothing at all. Now see the effect of art: he walks upright, wears coat and pants, carries a sword! . . . Ladies and gentlemen, here is to be seen the astronomical horse. . . . Show your talent! Show your beastly rationality! Put human society to shame! Gentlemen, this animal that you see here . . . is a member of all learned societies, is a professor at our university. . . . That is beastiognomy. Yes, that's no brutish individual [*viehdummes Individuum*], that's a person! A human being, a beastly human being, but still an animal, a *bête*. (*The horse behaves improperly.*) That's right, put *société* to shame. You see, the beast is still nature, unideal nature! . . . Observe his power of reason! He can calculate, but he can't count on his fingers. (*Woyzeck* h1, ii, 31–32; 226–27)

Clarus's idealized vision of the human being is confronted here with "unideal nature," animals dressed as humans and trained to perform characteristically human acts. Büchner appropriates such performances, which in fact were a traditional element of the fair, to expose the artificiality of Clarus's distinction between culture and nature. Culture, the Barker proposes, is nothing but a veneer pasted over nature, so that even animals can become human by assuming their outward dress. The obverse of this proposition, of course, is that beneath its cultured guise humanity—Clarus included—is nothing but brute nature. In the Barker's speech bourgeois individuality is mocked as a "brutish individual"—the assonance of the German words "viehdummes Individuum" gives this grotesque fusion an almost farcical tinge—and the majesty of human reason is called into question when it is attributed to a horse that can "calculate" but cannot count on its fingers. Reason, the Barker's words suggest, cannot see the trees for the forest: it can make abstract calculations, but it has no connection to the physicality of fingers and thus has lost sight of the concrete life-world.

This carnival scene forms an important nexus that ties together both the major themes and the characters of *Woyzeck*. The Barker, as trainer of these human animals, appears as the carnivalized counterpart of Clarus: both comment, from a position of implied superiority, on grotesque hybridizations of man and beast, reason and nonreason. But if both the Barker and Clarus embody the dialectic of enlightenment, in its carnivalized manifestation its paradoxicality is thrown into critical relief. Even the Barker's language, with its curious admixture of everyday dialect and foreign words, and in its creation of humorous neologisms like "beastiognomy," represents a grotesque hybridization that both imitates and parodies the language employed by Clarus in his affidavit. This same language is characteristic of the Doctor and the Captain who appear later in the play, and this is but one of the many indications that these figures are also parodistic renditions of Clarus. Even the horse, whom the Barker describes as a "professor" and a "member of all learned societies," both mocks Clarus and explicitly anticipates the figure of the Doctor, who is also referred to as "professor." Büchner prefigures the ironies inherent in the character of the Doctor and the Captain by introducing them in their carnivalized forms, and this sets the stage for a critical recognition that will expose them as "degenerate half-humans" who, if anything, are more beastly than those simpletons like Woyzeck whom they treat as beasts. Moreover, by putting the carnival on stage, Büchner inscribes this inherently spectatorial event into a greater dramatic spectacle, and this doubling enhances the critical reflectivity of Büchner's audience. In other words, with the carnival scene Büchner attempts to recreate the self-ironization and self-condemnation of reason he recognized in the Clarus report by contextualizing it in the fair booth and putting it on display in all its innate grotesqueness for his dramatic audience to witness. The spectacle of Woyzeck's execution, which Clarus had sought to turn to disciplinary-pedagogical ends, is replaced by a pedagogical spectacle that puts in question the supremacy this august clarity claims for itself. This carnivalization thus paradigmatically manifests Büchner's attempt to aesthetically appropriate Clarus's enlightened gaze and turn it against enlightenment itself.

The operation of this revelatory doubling can best be exposed by examining the dual functions of the Captain and the Doctor. Within the context of the world on stage—that is, viewed from the perspective of Büchner's character Woyzeck—these figures represent the noncarnivalized counterparts of the human animals at the fair: they are authorities who must be respected and taken seriously, even if their attitudes appear to be self-contradictory. But viewed from the perspective of the dramatic spectator, they appear simply as further carnivalized manifestations of a perverse reason, and thus both their authority and its rational substructure are called into question. The fact that the critical functioning of *Woyzeck* for Büchner's own spectators depends heavily on the depiction of these characters explains why their roles increase steadily with each successive version of the drama. Moreover, since the Captain and the Doctor are alter egos of Clarus, their increasing importance indicates how the specter of Clarus came more and more to dominate Büchner's conception of this play.

In the interaction between the Captain and Woyzeck, the former extols those same societal values that Clarus holds dear, and he exploits them to reaffirm his superiority over Woyzeck as his social subordinate.

CAPTAIN: I fear for the world when I think about eternity. Activity, Woyzeck, activity! Eternal, that's eternal, that's eternal—you realize that, of course. But then again it's not eternal, it's only a moment, yes, a moment. . . . Woyzeck, you always look so upset. A good man doesn't act like that, a good man with a good conscience. Say something, Woyzeck. What's the weather like today?

WOYZECK: It's bad, Cap'n, bad—wind.

CAPTAIN: I can feel it, there's something rapid out there. A wind like that reminds me of a mouse. *(Cunningly.)* I believe it's coming from the south-north.

WOYZECK: Yes, Cap'n.

CAPTAIN: Ha! Ha! Ha! South-north! Ha! Ha! Ha! Oh, are you stupid, terribly stupid. *(Sentimentally.)* Woyzeck, you're a good man, a good man—*(With dignity.)* but Woyzeck, you've got no morality. Morality—that's when you are moral, you understand. It's a good word. You have a child without the blessing of the church, as our Reverend Chaplain says, without the blessing of the church—*I* didn't say it.

WOYZECK: Cap'n, the good Lord isn't going to look at a poor little kid only because amen was said over it before it was created. The Lord said: "Suffer little children to come unto me."

CAPTAIN: What's that you're saying? What kind of a crazy answer is that? You're getting me all confused with your answer. (*Woyzeck* H4, v, 61–62; *207*)

The discourse of the Captain is nothing but empty verbiage devoid of any essential meaning, but it nevertheless bristles with power. On the one hand, he merely spouts ideologically charged slogans, as when he repeats the words of the Chaplain; but when Woyzeck responds by quoting the Bible, the Captain is taken unawares and thrown into confusion. On the other hand, his language tends towards the purely formulaic, falling either into tautology ("Morality—that's when you are moral") or consciously applying contradiction ("south-north") to trap his dialogic partner. Tautology allows him to lend credibility to his opinions by propping them up with false logic, while contradiction is deployed as a strategy allowing him to play up Woyzeck's stupidity and, by extension, assert his own intelligence, thereby reinforcing the hierarchy that governs their interaction. His values, moreover, are identical to those Clarus cherishes: activity, virtue, intelligence—although ironically, he himself evinces none of these. Later in this same scene, moreover, he explicitly champions that suppression of instinctual drives that Clarus stresses in his affidavit.

If the Captain embodies thoughtless formalism and vacuous ideals, the Doctor embodies that "dogmatism of reason" that Büchner criticized for its barrenness, highlighting the gulf that separates it from organic life. The scene "The Professor's Courtyard" choreographs the reifying gaze of the Doctor by positioning him on the roof with a view over his students' heads and into the neighboring garden.

Gentlemen, I am on the roof like David when he saw Bathsheba, but all I see is underwear on a clothesline in the garden of the girls' boarding house. Gentlemen, we are dealing with the important question of the relationship of subject to object. If we take only one of the things in which the organic self-affirmation of the Divine manifests itself to a high degree, and examine its relationship to space, to the earth, to the planetary system—gentlemen, if I throw this cat out of the window, how will this organism relate to the *centrum gravitationis* and to its own instinct? (*Woyzeck* h3, i, 55; *223*)

As the Doctor's own comparison brings to light, his distanced gaze does not fall upon the beauty of Bathsheba, who, in the biblical tale to which the Doctor alludes, aroused King David's lust; rather, it reveals only the women's undergarments hanging in the next garden. The Doctor as empirical scientist becomes, by contrast to the biblical King David, a kind of voyeur who finds his pleasure in the distanced observation of women's underwear. The demystifying gaze of reason is thereby equated with alienation from the carnal world and its passions; it displays a perverse obsession with empty signs that tantalizingly refer to, but simultaneously occult, the world of the flesh. But there are further significant implications in the Doctor's comparison. On the most obvious level, by identifying himself with King David he performs an act of shameless self-aggrandizement. But by means of this allusion he unwittingly also transfers to himself the negative attributes of the biblical figure: King David, we recall, arranged in a treacherous manner to have Bathsheba's husband Uriah killed so that he himself might take possession of her. Thus, the Doctor's attempt at self-glorification unintentionally reverts to a damnation of his enlightened gaze as perverse voyeurism, on the one hand, and as a surreptitious and cunning will to possession and mastery, on the other. This negative aspect is further highlighted by the Doctor's language. The bombast and exaggerated complexity of his discourse scarcely veil his desire to perform a rather adolescent and cruel experiment: he intends to throw a cat out the window to observe its response to the *centrum gravitationis*. Here Büchner once more turns the enlightened gaze back upon itself, revealing the empirical scientist's obsession with observation as but one manifestation of that *Schaulust* with which Clarus believes illiterate "half-humans" will view Woyzeck's execution.

For the cat the scene ends happily: thanks to the Doctor's mania for details, he is so distracted by the lice in its fur that it manages to escape. But here the action takes a potentially fatal turn for Woyzeck, who becomes a substitute for the cat as experimental object.

DOCTOR: Woyzeck, wiggle your ears for the gentlemen; I meant to show it to you
  before. He uses two muscles. Come on, hop to it!
WOYZECK: Oh, Doctor!
DOCTOR: You beast, shall I wiggle them for you, or do you want to do as the cat?
  So, gentlemen, this represents a transition to the donkey. (*Woyzeck* h3, i, 56;
  223–24)

Structurally this episode replicates the carnival scene, with the Doctor taking the place of the Barker, Woyzeck that of the human animal, and the students that of the spectators at the fair. Woyzeck's hybridization of human and animal traits is scientifically demonstrated when he wiggles his ears like a donkey. However, the Doctor must intimidate Woyzeck to persuade him to perform: he threatens to make him "do as the cat," that is, to throw him out the window. Throughout this scene, Woyzeck is reduced to nothing but a mere experimental substitute for the escaped cat, with whom, from the Doctor's alienated perspective, he is identical insofar as he performs an identical function. Horkheimer and Adorno identify this principle of infinite substitutability as one of the fundamentals of scientistic reason. "An atom," they remark, "is smashed not in representation but as a specimen of matter, and the rabbit does not represent but, as a mere example, is virtually ignored by the zeal of the laboratory."[39] The Doctor's alienating gaze recognizes no differences among empirical samples: all objects in the life-world are reduced to mere examples, cases to be observed and studied without sentiment or emotion, each instance replaceable by any other. All matter becomes nothing but the potential victim of an obscene thirst for knowledge that suspends all human emotions to ensure the objectivity of its observations. "No, Woyzeck, I'm not getting angry," the Doctor at one point assures his human guinea pig, "anger is unhealthy, unscientific" (*Woyzeck* H4, viii, 65; 210). For Horkheimer and Adorno, the principle of fungibility manifest in experimental science marks a major point of intersection between enlightenment and myth. Experimental science, in their opinion, universalizes the "specific representation" characteristic of mythic thought so that representation "is exchanged for the fungible—universal interchangeability,"[40] thereby reducing all substance to function. Universal fungibility and logical formalism are two sides of the same phenomenon to the extent that both abstract from all that is individual, collapsing it into the eternally same by making it either the proxy for an abstract idea or a mere placeholder in a formal structure.

These two characteristics of scientistic positivism are concretized in *Woyzeck* in the Captain's empty-headed formalism and the Doctor's reifying reduction of all living things to specimens.

The scene "The Professor's Courtyard" does indeed pose, to cite the words of the Doctor himself, "the important question about the relationship of subject to object"; and the answer it gives is that this relationship is defined by manipulation, mastery, and violence. The Doctor establishes himself as the all-controlling instrumental subject who lords over animal and human "objects" alike by virtue of the superior perspective of his enlightened gaze. A modern version of the myth of Medusa, this positivistic outlook strips all life of individual worth by universalizing it into the exemplar of some abstract hypothesis. Alienating distance, its founding principle, institutes an objectivity that guarantees the subject mastery over the lifeworld. Thus the Doctor is in full command of Woyzeck's bodily functions; when he calls his subordinate "Subject Woyzeck," he by no means grants him subjectivity, but only defines Woyzeck's subjugation, as scientific "subject," to the arbitrary will of the Doctor, who will continue to treat him as nothing but "an interesting case" (*Woyzeck* H4, viii, 65; *211*).

In the carnival scene, as well as in the figures of the Captain and the Doctor, Büchner represents to his audience the return of enlightenment to myth, or the atavism of myth in enlightenment. This dimension of his drama hence can be read as an elaboration of the second of the two critical theses proposed by Horkheimer and Adorno in *Dialectic of Enlightenment*: "Enlightenment reverts to mythology." However, the portrayal of this regression of enlightenment to myth in the instrumentality of bourgeois rationality is but one of the moments of Büchner's drama, the other being that moment described by the first of Horkheimer and Adorno's critical theses, which asserts: "Myth is already enlightenment."[41] The magic power of myth, in their view, derives from mimesis, and the transition from myth to enlightenment occurs when mimesis is replaced by *ratio*. But in this *ratio*, mimesis—myth itself—is retained: "Only consciously contrived adaptation to nature brings nature under the control of the physically weaker. The *ratio* which supplants mimesis is not simply its counterpart. It is itself mimesis: mimesis unto death."[42] However, it is not only to nature that the weaker must adapt, but also to the authoritarian structures of human society. This is the course pursued by Woyzeck in Büchner's drama: he opts to adapt to those principles of subjective mastery modeled for him by the Captain and the Doctor and turn these principles against others, thereby establishing himself as a mastering subject. In other words, he follows the path of mimesis, or of what I will call mimetic adaptation, which can be characterized as the assumption and application of those very attitudes by which Woyzeck himself is oppressed. Woyzeck's rational mimesis—his mimetic assimilation of purposive rationality—does in his case indeed become a mimesis unto death.

For August Clarus, as we have seen, Woyzeck's murder of Frau Woost represents the failure of enlightenment to completely master nature. What I want to suggest is that when we critically overturn Clarus's privileging of reason, as Büchner indicates we should, then this act of violence ceases to signify the failure of enlightenment and instead marks its insidious victory. When Woyzeck commits murder, this is an index of his desire to appropriate the will to purposive-rational mastery, and it is in this sense that this character embodies the attempted coming-to-enlightenment of myth. Now, to make this claim is not to deny that Woyzeck is first and foremost a victim of oppression.[43] However, it is precisely because of the severity and seeming inescapability of this oppression that Woyzeck turns to the last-ditch strategy of mimetic adaptation to the structures of instrumental mastery, recognizing this as the only feasible way to effect his own liberation.

In *Woyzeck* instrumentalized subjectivity is depicted as a reflex of the reifying gaze of purposive rationality: the subject is constituted as such at that moment when nature comes to be viewed as objective other, as a non-subjective, manipulable object. This self-empowerment of the human subject by means of mastery over nature and over other human beings is by no means limited to the figures of the Captain and the Doctor. Most of the characters in Büchner's play attempt to appropriate the authoritative perspective of enlightenment to establish themselves as mastering subjects. Büchner points to the universality of this drive to self-empowerment, showing that it is not—or at least no longer—the property of a specific social class that employs it to regulate interclass relations. The scene portraying the verbal scuffle between the Doctor and the Captain, for example (*Woyzeck* h2, vii, 50–53; *239–40*; cf. also H4, ix, 66; *211*), demonstrates how these attitudes govern intraclass relations as well. Büchner stresses that each of these characters deals with the other in a manner absolutely parallel to his treatment of Woyzeck. The Captain admonishes the Doctor, as he does Woyzeck, that "a good man" does not "run like that" (h2, vii, 50; *239*), while the Doctor considers the Captain to be nothing but "a most interesting case" (H4, ix, 66; *211*). The laws of abstraction, substitution, and reification are thus shown to be universally applied principles in human intercourse; their ubiquity bespeaks the incipient preeminence of an instrumentalized reason that recognizes no human subject that transcends its own abstract laws. In addition, the face-off between Captain and Doctor demonstrates that this struggle for domination is carried out primarily as a discursive contest. On this level, as well, the interaction of these two characters replicates the one each carries on with Woyzeck. To be sure, in their verbal sparring with Woyzeck, the Captain and the Doctor have the additional advantage that if pressed, they can pull rank on him by appealing either to their superior position in the social hierarchy or to their superior knowledge. We have already observed, for example, how in the debate on morality he has with the Captain, Woyzeck skillfully trumps his superior officer's appeal to the authority of "our Reverend Chaplain" by citing the Bible itself (see *Woyzeck* H4, v, 61–62; *207–8*). The Captain responds by stepping outside the discursive battle lines: insisting on his own unquestionable knowledge and authority, he declares Woyzeck's statement to be confused nonsense. Thus, the Captain answers Woyzeck's invocation of Holy Scripture by maintaining the preeminence of enlightenment over myth: he occupies a position that establishes himself as the instituter of rational meaning and proceeds to deny that Woyzeck's remark is meaningful. The Captain's tactic thus represents the quintessential defensive maneuver of enlightened reason: whatever falls outside the narrow confines of the logic by which it establishes significance is branded as "senseless" and "metaphysical"—in other words, it is reduced to myth.

The socially subordinate characters in Büchner's drama learn to adapt to, and to adopt, the techniques used to oppress them. The assimilative process by which myth becomes enlightenment is paradigmatically exemplified in the "sermon" of the First Apprentice.

FIRST APPRENTICE (*preaches on the table*): Yet when a wanderer stands leaning against the stream of time or gives answer for the wisdom of God, asking himself: Why does man exist? Why does man exist?—But verily I say unto you: how could the farmer, the cooper, the shoemaker, the doctor exist if God hadn't created man? How could the tailor exist if God hadn't given man a feeling of shame? How could the soldier exist, if men didn't feel the necessity of killing one another? Therefore, do not ye despair, yes, yes, it is good and pleasant, yet all that is earthly is passing, even money eventually decays.—In conclusion, my dear friends, let us piss crosswise so that a Jew will die. (H4, xi, 68–69; *214*; cf. also h2, iv, 47–48; *236–37*)

This speech subtly interweaves myth, superstition, prejudice, and the alienating posture of enlightenment. The Apprentice borrows his overall discursive style from the Bible, of course, thereby invoking, as does Woyzeck, the authority of Judeo-Christian myth. With the abasement of the physical, empirical world that is characteristic of Christian doctrine, the Apprentice intermingles a capitalist ideology of socioeconomic exploitation that views creation as nothing but the means to profit. This seamless dovetailing of Christian and bourgeois ideologies brings out their essential compatibility, a similarity that Max Weber would later identify and analyze. The Apprentice ignores, significantly, the communitarian, utopian aspect of Judeo-Christian myth; he simply exploits the authority of its discourse to lend conviction to the call to aggression against the Jews with which his sermon concludes. Myth and discursive logic, unreason and reason, merge in this sermon only to culminate in more persuasive and brutal forms of superstition and prejudice. We become witnesses here to the operation of the process called "displaced abjection":[44] the victim of oppression finds relief by assimilating the structures under which he suffers and turning them against others whom he can thereby define as his subordinates. This appropriative mechanism is rendered scenically in this episode by the Apprentice's assumption of a position atop the table, which affords him symbolic superiority over his audience. In this posture he replicates the pose taken up by the Doctor when he lectures to his students from the roof in the scene "The Professor's Courtyard." The Apprentice thus emblematically assumes the position characteristic of the alienating, reifying gaze of enlightenment to "preach" his sermon of aggression. This monolog thus underscores the essential compatibility of reason and myth, rationality and superstition, indicating how their hybridization produces hierarchical exploitation, reification, and discursively legitimated violence. It thereby exemplifies that process of mimetic assimilation by which myth appropriates enlightenment strategies of empowerment.

The Jews play the same role in the Apprentice's drive for self-empowerment that Marie ultimately plays in Woyzeck's impulse toward self-assertion. Büchner stresses this parallelism by placing the sermon of the Apprentice in counterpoint to Woyzeck's observation of Marie dancing with the Drum Major, both episodes occurring at the same time and place and included in one and the same scene.

WOYZECK *stands at the window.* MARIE *and the* DRUM MAJOR *dance past without seeing him.*

MARIE *(dancing by)*: On! and on, on and on!

WOYZECK *(chokes)*: On and on—on and on! *(Jumps up violently and sinks back on the bench.)* On and on, on and on. *(Beats his hands together.)* Spin around, roll around. Why doesn't God blow out the sun since everything rolls around fornicating, man and woman, man and beast. (H4, xi, 68; *213*)

Woyzeck's position as nonparticipating observer who, peering through a window, witnesses the sexually explicit interaction of the dancing couple without himself being observed, brings him into alignment with the voyeurism of the Doctor's enlightened gaze. Woyzeck quite literally assimilates the Doctor's distanced, reifying perspective, and the volte-face this effects in his attitudes is signaled when he assumes a position of moral self-righteousness to condemn the world for its licentiousness. In his debate with the Captain, Woyzeck had defended his own relationship with Marie against the charge that it was illicit by appealing to the irrepressible drives of nature (H4, v, 62; 208); now, however, he attacks this natural drive as fornication, entreating God to unleash destruction upon these grotesque hybridizations of "man and beast." Woyzeck, the one-time defender of nature against morality and reason, now shifts sides and promotes, as do the Captain and Clarus, the repression of nature in the name of virtue and human purity.

The main distinction between the acts of mastery perpetrated by the Captain and the Doctor and Woyzeck's murder of Marie is simply that society sanctions such actions in the former case as the legitimate wielding of authority, but condemns them in the latter as a threat to civilization and its authoritarian reason. The murder of Marie follows logically upon Woyzeck's assumption of the reifying gaze and his condemnation of impure and immoral humanity. This deed, as Büchner portrays it, is not a crime of passion, as Clarus maintained; on the contrary, it takes on the character of a basic act of purposive rationality. The murder of Marie is a violent and reifying crime against nature that testifies to the dialectical entanglement of enlightenment with myth, and as such it reflects the crime Clarus himself perpetrates against the historical Woyzeck. It is here that we perceive most profoundly how Büchner maneuvers enlightenment into a position of self-reflection in which it is forced to confront its own mythic and barbarous underside. Moreover, since with the murder of Marie Woyzeck both destroys, to paraphrase his own words, the only thing he has in the world (see h2, vii, 52; 240) and also ensures his own death, it exposes the self-destructive reflex that is part and parcel of the fusion of enlightenment and myth, reason and non-reason, a reflex constitutive of bourgeois epistemic structures and their respective sociopolitical and socioeconomic practices.

Horkheimer and Adorno argue that magic and myth give way to enlightenment at that moment when arbitrary signs, which mediate between a meaning-attributing subject and a meaningless object, supplant the natural affinities among beings in the world. The subject-object distinction that this semiology institutionalizes always already implies the establishment of a hierarchy of power and mastery.

The world of magic retained distinctions whose traces have disappeared even in linguistic form. The multitudinous affinities between existents are suppressed by the single relation between the subject who bestows meaning and the meaningless object, between rational significance and the chance vehicle of significance. On the magical plane, dream and image were not mere signs for the thing in question, but were bound up with it by similarity or names.[45]

The universal validity of instrumental reason is predicated on the absolutization of a semiotic relation structured around arbitrary signs; it is this relation, as the basis of bourgeois enlightened thinking, that underwrites the principles of substitutability and exchange constitutive both of scientistic positivism and of bourgeois socioeconomic practice. In this sense, the hypotheses of Horkheimer and Adorno are coherent with the theories of Foucault and Baudrillard, who identify a semiotic-epistemic paradigm shift as the rift that separates the enlightened bourgeois world from its historical antecedents. Critical bourgeois intellectuals such as Lessing and Schiller could still hope that this transformation was reversible, that "the representative or signifying function of language" could "find its way back," as Foucault expresses it, to the "raw being" of iconicity,[46] or that the "emancipated sign," as "common denominator of the real world toward which no one has any obligation," could be retrotransformed into the "obliged sign," to cite Baudrillard's formulations.[47] For Horkheimer and Adorno, however, as well as for Büchner, there is no refuge from the arbitrary, emancipated, nonobliged sign. In *Woyzeck*, Büchner portrays the hegemony of this epistemic formation in terms of the necessary assimilation of its reifying structures by his protagonist.

The hypothesis that Woyzeck's murder of Marie manifests the coming-to-enlightenment of myth in terms of the appropriation of a subject position that allows the manipulation of objects can be corroborated by examining the way Woyzeck's relationship to signs changes over the course of the drama. Already in the first scene of the second draft of the play, Büchner depicts Woyzeck as someone obsessed with the interpretation of the book of nature. In this scene—which is retained with minor alterations in the final manuscript—Woyzeck and Andres are in an open field outside of town cutting branches. "Yeah, Andres, it really is—this place is haunted. Do you see that shining stripe there across the grass, where the toadstools are growing? That's where heads roll at night; once somebody picked one up, thought it was a hedgehog. Three days and two nights, and he was dead. (*Softly.*) It was the Freemasons, I figured it out" (h2, i, 43; 233; cf. H4, i, 57; 201). Both characters feel uneasy in this open field, alone with nature and far away from the city, the protective shield of human culture; but for Woyzeck, in particular, the natural world has become an uncanny and accursed place bristling with uninterpretable signs. Nature appears to him neither as a nourisher nor as a legible text, but as an unfathomable and demonic power. This anxiety is not merely a symptom of Woyzeck's incipient insanity; on the contrary, it reflects his waxing alienation from the life-world. Already at the beginning of the dramatic action, then, Woyzeck is positioned at the hinge between myth and enlightenment. He is caught in a phase of epistemic transition similar to the conflict of semiologies experienced by the bourgeois subject decades earlier: nature no longer constitutes for him an immediately comprehensible hieroglyph, but it has not yet been systematized into a taxonomy of legible signs, as it has for the Doctor, for example. In other words, Woyzeck no longer participates integrally in nature, but neither is he (yet) an instrumental subject who rules over it on the basis of meaning-attributions made possible by arbitrary signs. However, this scene provides two indications that Woyzeck will ultimately move in the direction of becoming a mastering subject. First, he ascribes the illegible signs he perceives in nature to the Freemasons, thus implying an awareness that they might actually be man-made, culturally determined significations. The secrets of the Masonic brotherhood represent for Woyzeck the secrets of that enlightened reason the Doctor and Captain possess, but from which he is excluded. It is this exclusion from the fraternity of reason, he realizes, that makes him "terribly stupid" and thus an object to be manipulated by those who have attained enlightenment. Second, and as if in response to this recognition, Woyzeck and Andres flee at the close of this scene out of the open field back into the security of the army barracks. They thus seek refuge, paradoxically, behind the walls of the very cultural institution responsible for their oppression, indicating that they recognize its power to rescue them from the incomprehensible dangers of nature. It is consistent with this that Woyzeck turns to the Doctor to discover the key for an understanding of these indecipherable signs: the Doctor, after all, has proven himself to be an expert at the interpretation of such signs as pulse and heartbeat, and he is even able to interpret Woyzeck's urine. "The toadstools, Doctor. There—that's where it is. Have you seen how they grow in patterns? If only someone could read that" (H4, viii, 65; *210*; cf. h2, vi, 50; *238*). Ironically, the Doctor regards Woyzeck's obsession with signs in nature—which, in fact, merely reflects the Doctor's own positivistic fetish to interpret similar signs—as an aberration. He thereby provides a critical metacommentary of sorts on his own attitudes. At any rate, Woyzeck understands that the Doctor is not prepared to initiate him into the mysteries of the enlightened hermeneutics that is the basis of his intellectual superiority.

Only after he becomes aware of Marie's act of adultery does Woyzeck develop into a meaning-attributing, mastering subject. This evolution is pictured in the scene in which he confronts her with her sin (h2, viii, 53; *241*; H4, vii, 63–64; *209*). The first thing Woyzeck notices about Marie in this moment is her beauty, and this is already an indication that under his gaze she is being transformed from a human being into a mere beautiful object that can be possessed. "Behind male admiration of beauty," Horkheimer and Adorno argue, "lurks always . . . the barbaric obscenity with which strength greets weakness in an attempt to deaden the fear that it has itself fallen prey to impotence, death, and nature."[48] At the same time, however, Woyzeck is surprised that Marie's sin is not written across her face. He then begins to seek the sign of this sin as a blemish on the face of Marie's beauty: "You've got a red mouth, Marie. No blister on it?" But ultimately he identifies Marie's beauty itself as the sign of her sin: "Marie, you're as beautiful as sin" (H4, vii, 63; *209*). This reading, the attribution of the signification "sin" to Marie's beauty, legitimates for Woyzeck his mastery over her: the murder of Marie, and the resulting elimination of her beauty, becomes identical for him with the destruction of her sin. The mechanism of displaced abjection permits Woyzeck to overcome his own societal impotence by taking charge over Marie; he thereby displaces the oppression he senses in the sociopolitical, economic, and natural environment into a relation of domination by the male subject over the female object. Violence against this female object provides the ultimate proof that the male subject possesses and controls it.

Throughout this scene, which depicts his coming-to-subjecthood as the coming-to-mastery over Marie, Woyzeck evinces his reliance on the sense of sight. Scrutinizing Marie with the same intensity with which the Doctor examines his specimens, Woyzeck remarks: "Hm! I don't see anything, I don't see anything. Oh, I should be able to see it; I should be able to grab it with my fists" (H4, vii, 63; *209*). By linking "grabbability" and "fists" to the evidence procured by infallible vision, Woyzeck draws a connection between the irrefutability of Marie's visually perceived sin and the consequence of violence against her. This association exposes the link between the reifying gaze of the purposive-rational subject and the manipulative aggression against the object that falls under its purview.

Woyzeck evolves with a certain inevitability into a (bourgeois) subject who masters the empirical life-world by exploiting the reifying, alienating gaze of positivistic reason. Read in the manner I have proposed, Büchner's play is anything but a tragedy of jealousy. But neither is it simply a tragic tale about the consequences of poverty and social inequality. Sketched into these fragments, and especially into the figure of Woyzeck, is an allegory of the tragedy of enlightenment, of the presence of enlightenment in myth and the reversion of enlightenment back to myth. "Myth turns into enlightenment, and nature into mere objectivity. Men pay for the increase of their power with alienation from that over which they exercise their power. Enlightenment behaves toward things as a dictator toward men. He knows them in so far as he can manipulate them."[49] With these words Horkheimer and Adorno adequately summarize the tendencies Büchner depicts in *Woyzeck*. The bitter paradox of enlightenment's empowerment over nature is expressed in Woyzeck's becoming-dictator-over, and consequent destruction of, the only significant "object" in his life. In this, however, Woyzeck is no longer an individual; paradoxically, it is his becoming-individual as purposive, would-be bourgeois subject that makes him identical with all the domineering characters in the play. All those who exist in this fictional world, to a greater or lesser degree, have either assumed the standpoint of enlightenment, the position of a purposive, meaning-attributing subject that stands over against a world of manipulable objects, or are in the process of assimilating this posture. If there is resignation in this drama, then it is resignation to the inevitable victory of bourgeois purposive rationality—which is simultaneously the inevitable victory of mythic barbarism in the guise of technical mastery. Büchner prefigures the resignation that Horkheimer and Adorno will sense a century later when confronted with the reality of European fascism. Indeed, the world evoked in Büchner's dramatic fragments, a world of prejudice, violence, and rationally legitimated terror, is decidedly proto-fascistic. Nevertheless, Büchner's resignation, like that of Horkheimer and Adorno a century later, is a resignation of protest, a resignation that criticizes despite its recognition that all critique is futile. Büchner displays, to express it in all its paradoxicality, a resignation of defiance that refuses to abandon the search for an escape from the aporia of an enlightenment that is dialectically intertwined with myth.

Büchner's *Woyzeck* expresses the paradox of this critical posture as a performative contradiction. Taking as his point of departure Clarus's perversely enlightened condemnation of the historical Woyzeck, Büchner attempts to translate this scientistic discourse into a drama that performs both the narrated events of the source as well as the moralizing stance of the original narrator. In other words, the disciplinary-pedagogical gaze propagated by Clarus is itself subjected to critical scrutiny—to the potentially carnivalizing gaze of dramatic spectatorship. Büchner seeks to prepare his audience to apply such a carnivalizing, hierarchy-inverting strategy by introducing these bourgeois values in the grotesque, inverted world of carnival. In this way he hopes to develop in *Woyzeck* a dramatical re-presentation of the case of the historical Woyzeck that can exploit the unconscious ironies of Clarus's report and turn this ironic gaze back upon itself. This dramatic appropriation of Clarus's objectifying gaze—which is, in the final analysis, the object of Büchner's critique—marks the performative contradiction of this work. With this critical appropriation of objectified observation as dramaturgical technique, Büchner breaks with the aesthetics of affect otherwise dominant in bourgeois drama; he creates for the theater a pedagogical technique that assimilates the alienated, reflective gaze characteristic of bourgeois scientistic reason to turn it back on itself in self-reflection and thereby expose the proliferating infection of mythic barbarism inherent in this purposive rationality. In terms of Büchner's own aesthetics, this critical doubling reflects his own skeptical interrogation of the practical paradoxes of that realistic technique he defends in his theoretical deliberations, and it thus marks the precarious position of the divided subject at this crucial historical juncture. The paradox of enlightenment and of realist aesthetics of representation coincide to the extent that only by turning them against themselves, as Büchner does in *Woyzeck*, can humanity be rescued from their alienating web.

In this second historical station of Unhappy Consciousness we have observed how bourgeois (self-)critique battles desperately to assert itself in the face of its final repression under the hegemony of purposive rationality. I have examined texts whose innovative aesthetic structures derive from the struggle to conquer a last critical stronghold for protecting the internal voice of opposition against the bourgeois epistemic formation and its representative economic and sociopolitical practices. In the third historical station of the divided subject, to which I will now turn, this repressed emancipatory drive insistently returns, only to be forcefully repressed once more. In the literature produced by the divided subject in the next historical configuration I will investigate, aesthetic innovation arises not out of protest against the bourgeois epistemic formation, but precisely out of the attempt to repress once and for all this oppositional drive and collapse the dialectic of bourgeois critical subjectivity into the monolithic and monotonous structure of blind affirmation.

The Return of the Political Repressed
and the Aporia of the Bourgeois Subject

CHAPTER SIX

The Hermeneut(r)ic(k) of the Psychic Narrative

Freud's "Uncanny" and the Political Unconscious
in Hofmannsthal's 'A Tale of the Cavalry'

> Psychoanalysis is that spiritual illness for which it believes itself to be the cure.
> —Karl Kraus

Interiorization and Bourgeois Counterpolitics

In his interpretation of the expressionist film classic *The Cabinet of Dr. Caligari* (1919), Siegfried Kracauer discloses the narrative innovation introduced by director Robert Wiene as a technique whose purpose is the effacement of a subversive political critique. By projecting Hans Janowitz's antiauthoritarian screenplay as the psychotic vision of an insane narrator, Wiene effectively neutralizes its originary political dimension.[1] This psychic framing has two significant components: first, by portraying the narrated events as the imaginings of an individual subject, Wiene interiorizes and privatizes them; second, by disclosing the cinematic text's deviations from the viewers' normal perceptions of empirical reality as the distortions of a deranged psyche, he alienates the narrated events from the audience's experience of its own sociopolitical life-world. These same two processes are also at work in a particular subtype of narrative fiction that came into prominence during the heyday of literary modernism in Austria and Germany between the fin de siècle and the First World War. In what follows I will associate such psychotexts with the ambivalent semantic field marked off by the German words *heimlich* and *unheimlich*, as sketched by Sigmund Freud in his essay entitled "The Uncanny" (1919).

In this essay Freud concerns himself with a definition of the "uncanny" as a specific type of eerie and anxiety-ridden experience, and his working hy-

pothesis is that "the uncanny is that class of the frightening which leads back
to what is known of old and long familiar." He proceeds to demonstrate the
validity of this theory by beginning with an examination of the German
word *unheimlich*, which he considers to be the negation of the word *heimlich*. "The German word '*unheimlich*' is obviously the opposite of '*heimlich*'
('homely'), '*heimisch*' ('native')—the opposite of what is familiar; and we are
tempted to conclude that what is 'uncanny' is frightening precisely because
it is *not* known and familiar."[2] Now Freud, in fact, believes that just the opposite of this seemingly obvious supposition holds true—that the uncanny
evolves as a fear precisely of what is known and familiar. To justify this ostensibly counterintuitive proposition, which seems to contradict the logic
of language itself, Freud sets about probing the very different significations
attributed to the German word *heimlich*. *Heimlich* means "belonging to the
house, not strange, familiar, tame, intimate, friendly, etc.," and as its opposite, *unheimlich* would thereby signify the nonhomey, nonfamiliar, noninti-
mate, or alien.[3] But *heimlich*, as Freud points out, is a peculiarly ambiguous
word, since it also has a second primary definition that is the exact antithesis to the first. In this semantic constellation *heimlich* signifies not the familiar, but rather what is "concealed, kept from sight, so that others do not get
to know of or about it, withheld from others."[4] As the negation of this signification of *heimlich*, *unheimlich* would then signify the unconcealed, the un-
withheld, thereby allowing Freud to conclude that "everything is *unheimlich*
that ought to have remained secret and hidden but has come to light."[5] Thus
the semantic circuit of the words *heimlich* and *unheimlich* describes a complex force-field of significance in which each term possesses diametrically
opposite significations and hence ultimately overlaps with its own negation.
"What interests us most . . . is to find that among its different shades of
meaning the word '*heimlich*' exhibits one which is identical with its opposite, '*unheimlich*.' What is *heimlich* thus comes to be *unheimlich*."[6] After investigating some examples of the divergent uses of these two words, Freud
finally arrives at the following conclusion: "Thus *heimlich* is a word the
meaning of which develops in the direction of ambivalence, until it finally
coincides with its opposite, *unheimlich*. *Unheimlich* is in some way or other
a sub-species of *heimlich*."[7] If *heimlich* denotes both the private and the secret, then *unheimlich* signifies the nonprivate and the no-longer-secret; it thus
signals for Freud the return to consciousness of what has been forgotten.[8]
As verbal sign, the word *unheimlich* refers to a reflex that Freud conceives as
one of the fundamental mechanisms at work in the psychic economy: the
ineluctable return of the repressed. It is typical for Freud's expository procedure, of course, that he explores language to draw inferences about the

phenomena it signifies. But the essay "The Uncanny" is a remarkable work if only because here Freud assumes the role of the literary critic, attempting to prove his hypothesis about the uncanny by examining its concretization in, and receptive transmission through, particular uncanny works of literature. Moreover, he explicitly associates the uncanny in literature with a pe culiar mode of narrative text. Throughout these analyses I will refer to such uncanny fictional texts as "psychic narratives" or "narratives of the psyche."

The novel narrative technique of psychic narratives operates in a manner coherent with the semantic ambivalence Freud uncovers in the words *heimlich* and *unheimlich*. In the present chapter my aim is to demonstrate that such texts, which came into special prominence among Freud's Austrian and German contemporaries, perform a function similar to the cinematic innovations introduced by Wiene into *Caligari*: they obscure and repress an originary revolutionary political sentiment by interiorizing or privatizing it as psychic deviation, that is, by rendering this political impulse *heimlich*, simultaneously "private" and "secret." On the broadest plane this mechanism corresponds to that general bourgeois inclination toward a privatization of the political, a tendency that has formed one overriding focus of these investigations. During its nascent phase in the eighteenth century, as Reinhart Koselleck demonstrates,[9] this privatization of the political bespeaks the attempt on the part of the ascendant bourgeoisie to occupy a moral-political high-ground wholly segregated from the political corruption it associated with, or projected onto, the absolutistic state. This autonomy from quotidian sociopolitical realities was supposed to guarantee that the bourgeoisie, uncompromised by these corrupt circumstances, would be able to formulate and implement an effective revolutionary-utopian political program. In Schiller's *Robbers* we examined the mechanics of this move toward privatization of sociopolitical opposition as the voluntary repression and submersion of resistance, its displacement from the overt to the covert. This tendency corresponds to the shift from dramatic to narrative forms of literature and to the privatized conditions of literary reception offered by the process of reading. In Heine's *Ideas: The Book Le Grand* this making-private and making-secret of political revolt attains narrative codification in the strategy of double-tracking, in which the private-secret, esoteric message of political (self-)emancipation is disguised behind an innocent, exoteric narrative. The hermeneutical liberation of this "secret" meaning in the process of reading—its *unheimlich* desecretization, as it were—constitutes the literary-receptive correlative of this political liberation. Until Heine, at least, then, privatization still retains an oppositional moment, bespeaking resistance to the existing structures of public life. In the innovative psychic narratives that represent one of the major literary-aesthetic accomplishments of High Modernist literature, privatization no longer contains this emancipatory kernel; on the contrary, the aim of the narrative innovation introduced by these texts is precisely to repress this bourgeois revolutionary impulse once and for all. We will investigate the operation of this (self-)repressive narrative mechanism on the example of Hugo von Hofmannsthal's short story *A Tale of the Cavalry* (1898), a text that displays in paradigmatic fashion the repressive occultation of political rebellion characteristic of the bourgeois subject at this historical station.

Commentators on Hofmannsthal's *Tale of the Cavalry* have seldom failed to note the psychic, dreamlike texture of this narrative, and it has frequently been associated with the character of the uncanny. I would like to begin my analysis by distinguishing a group of often closely interrelated traits that describe the narrative principles constitutive of *A Tale of the Cavalry*, while keeping this characterization general enough to allow it to serve as an anatomy of that subset of fictional texts that I term narratives of the psyche. (1) Psychic narratives tend to focus almost exclusively on one central character; other figures derive their significance wholly on the basis of their interrelations with this anchor character, who functions as a kind of hub around which the fictional events revolve. (2) These narratives are "ex-pressionistic" in the literal sense of the word; that is to say, external narrated events (and even secondary characters) take on the quality of projections emanating from, or shaped by, the perceptions and understanding of the anchor character.[10] (3) This projection of interior psychic states into the fictional world remains partly obscured by the fact that this world itself seems on the surface to comprise an objective, factual documentation of "realistic" events. This documentary texture, however, is ruptured by phantasmagoric, "uncanny" occurrences out of keeping with its factual tone. Due to this intermixture of the subjective and the objective, the psychically determined and the empirically given, the text takes on the character of a manifest dream in which all figures, objects, and events become ciphers that seem to refer symbolically to a latent psychic significance. (4) Constitutive of these narratives is the confrontation and interpenetration of two distinct narrative styles. The framing context is constructed as an objective third-person narration that reads much like a documentary report. At certain hinge points, this narrative frame reverts almost imperceptibly into narrated monolog, the recounting of events as perceived or imagined in the eyes and mind of the anchor character. The dovetailing of subjective and objective that is operative on the level of fictional events is thus reiterated and buttressed by the intermingling of subjective and objective narrative styles. (5) The reader's perspective on the narrated events is identical with that of the anchor character: it is through his/her eyes, and thus through his/her psyche, that the narrated events are mediated to us as readers. Figural narration, in other words, is the dominant narrative mode of such texts; but this internal perspective is masked by the objective narrative framework, as well as by the application of third-person narrative diction. (6) The key to the coherence of these narratives is exploitation of what Dorrit Cohn calls "narrated monologue" (often designated with the German phrase *erlebte Rede*) or "narrated perception," which consists, as she succinctly defines it, in the "transformation of figural thought-language into the narrative language of third-person fiction."[11]

It has come to be widely accepted that the vigorous evolution of European fiction in the nineteenth and early twentieth centuries turns on a curious paradox: the marked "inward turn" or subjectification of modern fiction is accompanied—indeed, made possible—by a growing objectification in narrative technique. Commenting on this paradox, Cohn notes that "precisely those authors who . . . most decisively abandoned first-person narration (Flaubert, Zola, James), instituting instead the norms of the dramatic novel, objective narration, and unobtrusive narrators, were the ones who re-introduced the subjectivity of private experience into the novel: this time not in terms of direct self-narration, but by imperceptibly integrating mental reactions into the neutral-objective report of actions, scenes, and spoken words."[12] Narrated perception is one of the prominent symptoms of this paradoxical intertwining of subjectification and objectification. Hans Robert Jauss has attempted to assess the repercussions of this fictional technique for an aesthetics of reception by referring to Flaubert's trial on the charge of immorality for *Madame Bovary*.[13] Flaubert's acquittal is predicated, as Jauss explains, on the legal defender's ability to decouple authorial convictions from the figural perspective that advances the immoral views the prosecution believed attributable to Flaubert himself. The technique that made this confusion of authorial and figural values possible, of course, is extensive use of narrated perception, and Flaubert's defense was based on a stylistic analysis that exposed this device as a narrative sleight of hand that camouflaged the subjective views of a fictional character behind objective narrative diction. Unaccustomed to this technique, Flaubert's readers, according to Jauss, reacted to it with "an alienating uncertainty of judgment."[14] As an aside, it is worth noting that it is just such incertitude that for Freud is typical of the sentiments evoked in the readers of uncanny literature,[15] and this point of coherence indicates the significant overlap between uncanny psychic narratives and narrated monolog as fictional technique. Now, Jauss is concerned solely with the potentially beneficial receptive ends effected by this uncertainty of judgment: viewing it as evidence that Flaubert's readers were forced by the narrative trick of this text to confront and question their own bourgeois morality, he interprets it as a critically productive narrative strategy. But Jauss's conclusion is somewhat one-sided and perhaps too optimistic, since the condition of possibility of the reader's hermeneutical uncertainty, on the most general level, is a privatization of the criteria of reception: Flaubert's readers are indeed decoupled from patterns of reception shaped by communitarian ethics and bourgeois moral codes, but at the price of being grounded more firmly in a bourgeois ideology that suspends public, transpersonal values by reducing them to private-secret (*heimlich*) affairs of the internal self. The interiorization of narrative, its privatization and subjectification by means of its increasing focus on the figural psyche, corresponds to a privatization and subjectification of the act of reading, as well. The coupling of literary realism to subjectification, the hallmark of modernist narratives, thus marks an internalization of the real, its "psychification," as it were; and this, in turn, suggests that reality in the "realistic" fiction of literary modernism is always only *perceived* reality, filtered through the psychic lens of a privatized bourgeois consciousness. The evolution of the novel as a quintessentially bourgeois literary form hence can be viewed as a literary-institutional development that buttressed the tendency toward privatization in bourgeois consciousness. The privatization of literary reception that accompanies this transformation can be conceived as a further dimension, situated specifically in patterns of reader-response, of what Lucien Goldmann identifies as the homology between the forms of novelistic fiction and the structures of individualistic bourgeois society.[16]

Recent sociohistorical critiques of Freud's psychoanalytical project have diagnosed the privatizing and mythifying tendencies of his thought in terms of the displacement of sociopolitical tensions into the internal realm of bourgeois consciousness. Freud's development of psychoanalysis as a positive science betrays a paradoxical interdependence of subjectification and objectification homologous to the development of modern narrative.[17] Situating Freudian psychotheory in the socioeconomic context of bourgeois society, sociopsychologists have attempted to show, for example, that Freud's theory of Oedipal conflict employs the myth of the primal scene to shift an antagonism of class hierarchies into the internal realm of the bourgeois family.[18] Within the narrower context of the cultural-historical milieu of turn-of-the-century Austria, Carl Schorske has revealed the "counterpolitical ingredient in the origins of psychoanalysis," its tendency to reduce politics "to an epiphenomenal manifestation of psychic forces."[19] He ascertains that the seminal theses of Freudian psychoanalysis evolve as displacements of historical and sociopolitical issues. In addition, he argues that the hermeneutical procedure Freud employs in *The Interpretation of Dreams*, the work that marks his methodological breakthrough, is formulated as an interpretive practice that underwrites and legitimates this supplanting of public, sociopolitical concerns by private and personal sentiments.

Schorske's interpretive methodology merits closer scrutiny because the mechanics of interpretive overturning that it models has affinities with the aims of the hermeneutical project I want to outline in the present chapter. Seeking essentially to out-Freud Freud, he reads the dream analyses from *The Interpretation of Dreams*, which ostensibly reveal the very mechanisms by which psychic material is repressed, themselves as symptoms of a pervasive psychic repression. Schorske thereby critically discloses the censorship of unconscious political desires as the condition of possibility of Freud's theoretical-methodological breakthrough.[20] Turning Freudian interpretive strategies against Freud's own interpretations, Schorske models a practice that, to the extent that it undoes Freud's own hermeneutics, can be labeled a counterhermeneutics or a hermeneutics of resistance. What his critically resistant investigation discovers as the moving force behind Freudian interpretive procedures is a political unconscious, to employ Fredric Jameson's phrase: the disclosures of depth-hermeneutics are unmasked as strategies of concealment whose purpose is the effacement of social or political sentiments that are at odds with bourgeois consciousness. Viewed from this critical perspective, Freud's procedure of decoding public elements in dream texts as signifiers for private signifieds appears itself as a process of encodation: he semioticizes, so to speak, the historico-political sphere to efface it; that is, he transmutes political and public signifieds in the manifest text into signifiers that refer to private and personal significations in the latent dream content.

Schorske's metainterpretation focuses on Freud's analysis of his so-called Revolutionary Dream, whose etiology Freud himself traces back to an encounter, rife with subversive political implications, with Count Thun, the Austrian minister president.[21] Witnessing the Count exploit his political and social position to procure a cabin on a train, Freud spontaneously and "unconsciously" reacts to this assertion of privilege by humming the subversive aria from *The Marriage of Figaro*, and the incident evokes in his mind, by Freud's own admission, "all kinds of insolent and revolutionary ideas."[22] The "inadvertent" humming of this implicitly rebellious melody is strikingly reminiscent of the episode in Heine's *Book Le Grand* in which the narrator relates how his feet and hands "inadvertently" drum out the rhythms of those revolutionary tunes that his mouth, muted by the oppressive sociopolitical circumstances of Restoration Germany, are forbidden to sing (*Ideas*, 272; *196*). However, in his interpretation of the dream incited by this incident, Freud expunges entirely these unconscious rebellious sociopolitical sentiments by substituting his own father, the representative of authority in the narrow sphere of the bourgeois family, for Count Thun, the representative of sociopolitical authority and privilege. This hermeneutical tactic permits Freud to interpret his dream of political rebellion as an act of symbolic revenge against his biological father.[23] Whereas Heine's literary-aesthetic strategy in the *Travelogues* sought to sublate—to cancel yet preserve—precisely such an esoteric political message by camouflaging it behind an exoteric narrative, Freud's aim is to extirpate this seditious sentiment. Freud's tactic thus signals an act of secondary political self-repression that hermeneutically undoes, as it were, the literary-therapeutic effect Heine sought to achieve in the dimension of textual reception. Schorske's hermeneutically resistant reading of Freud's dream analysis short-circuits this secondary displacement of the politically charged manifest dream text into a privatizing latent dream content.

My purpose in what follows is to demonstrate that a hermeneutics of resistance patterned after the interpretive practice Schorske employs is appropriate for reading the uncanny psychic narrative *A Tale of the Cavalry*, composed by Freud's Austrian contemporary and fellow liberal bourgeois, Hugo von Hofmannsthal.[24] I hope to show that this narrative encourages readers to semioticize sociopolitical elements in the manifest text, reading them, in accordance with Freudian interpretive strategies, as signifiers of a latent, psychically repressed, and private signified. My point is that the hermeneutical provocation constitutive of this text is in fact a hermeneu*trick*: it manifests an attempt to divert interpretive attention away from particular subversive political impulses essential to the very constitution of the text itself. Similar to what Schorske's reading of the *Interpretation of Dreams* reveals about the covert mechanism of concealment disguised behind Freud's apparent hermeneutical disclosures, if we step outside the interpretive guidelines Hofmannsthal's narrative of the psyche encourages us as readers to apply, the interpretive steering mechanisms embedded in the text can be shown to perform the function of an oblique political censorship. As in Schorske's analysis, application of this counterhermeneutic to *A Tale of the Cavalry* both discloses revolutionary political desires as the driving force behind the text and exposes the attempt to disguise and repress this political unconscious as the source of its sophisticated literary-aesthetic strategies. The innovative, uncanny narrative structure of Hofmannsthal's text thus is a product of this drive to conceal its originary sociocritical impulse.

The "Uncanniness" of Freud's Hermeneutics

Freud's essay "The Uncanny" suggests its relevance to this investigation on a number of different levels. First, an element of the uncanny is constitutive of psychic narratives in general and Hofmannsthal's *A Tale of the Cavalry* in particular, both on the plane of narrated events and in the dimension of reader reception. Second, the dialectic of the terms *heimlich-unheimlich*, as sketched by Freud in the opening section of this essay, and his association of the *unheimlich* with the return of the repressed, with the disclosure of something that should have remained hidden, proves especially fruitful when applied to *A Tale of the Cavalry*. But this dialectic is manifest in Freud's essay on the uncanny itself: by construing the uncanny in terms of the psychologically personal and the private, Freud is secretly (*heimlich*) suppressing its underlying sociological correlatives. A hermeneutical overturning is thus necessary to render Freud's deliberations *unheimlich*, to reveal what they seek to conceal. Most important, however, is that in this essay Freud places himself explicitly in the role of a literary critic, reaching his understanding of the uncanny on the basis of an analysis of the mysterious short story "The Sandman" (1817), written by the German Romantic author E. T. A. Hoffmann. Freud treats this narrative as a text that paradigmatically embodies what he conceives as the literary uncanny, and the interpretive practice he employs in his analysis supplies a kind of model for the hermeneutical response that uncanny narratives evoke for readers schooled in the tenets of Freudian psychoanalysis. Finally, in his conclusion to this essay Freud outlines what amounts to an aesthetics of reception for the literary uncanny, attempting to specify the textual components required of an uncanny text if it is to successfully transfer its uncanny effect to its readers.

In a brief metacommentary on the compositional strategies he pursued while writing the essay "The Uncanny," Freud concedes that in structuring his narrative account he found it necessary to reverse the sequence of the steps his analytical procedure actually followed. "Let me also add," he remarks, "that my investigation was actually begun by collecting a number of individual cases, and was only later confirmed by an examination of linguistic usage. In this discussion, however, I shall follow the reverse course."[25] Taking this admission as a clue that will help unravel the analytical strands that constitute Freud's essay, my counteranalysis will reverse his reversal, beginning with his attempts in the final section of this treatise to elucidate the receptive effect of the uncanny. Here Freud seeks to account for the fact that in some (literary) texts uncanny occurrences on the level of narrated events fail to communicate the sense of the uncanny to the reader, while in other instances the sensation of the uncanny experience portrayed in the fic-

tional world is transferred immediately into the dimension of reader reception. Traditional fairy tales, he notes, typically relate uncanny occurrences
that fall outside our empirical perceptions of the world, but these texts rarely
cause us as mature readers to share the sense of the uncanny as experienced
by the fairy-tale figures themselves. Two conditions commonly absent in
the fairy tale, he concludes, must be fulfilled if the uncanny fictional text is
to evoke an uncanny receptive effect: first, the fantastic event must be embedded in a context of seemingly factual, objective narration; second, the
reader's perspective must be consonant with that of the fictional character
who experiences the uncanny occurrence.[26]

What Freud describes as the textual devices prerequisite for the reception
of the uncanny in literature thus coincides with two fundamental practices
of the psychic narrative: the clash of objective and subjective styles and gravitation toward figural narration. The hermeneutical provocation of the uncanny text derives, for Freud, from the reader's inability, predicated on the
disjunction of subjectivizing and objectivizing narrative tendencies, to blend
these disparate textual elements into a coherent sense. Freud's literary uncanny and what I have termed the narrative of the psyche thus overlap on
at least two crucial points of literary technique; but in addition, they are coherent with regard to the character of their resulting hermeneutical provocation and its receptive effect. According to Friedrich Schleiermacher, one
of the founders of modern hermeneutical theory, the two fundamental rules
of interpretive textual understanding are: "I am understanding everything
until I encounter a contradiction or nonsense"; and "I do not understand
anything that I cannot perceive and comprehend [construiren] as necessary."[27]
The logical contradictions and rifts in narrative consequence typical both of
Freud's uncanny and of the psychic narrative constitute just such challenges
to our patterns of hermeneutical comprehension, and they thereby provoke
an uncommonly furious hermeneutical activity in those readers who try to
precipitate a unified latent sense out of their manifest textual inconsistencies.

In the literary analyses contained in this essay Freud responds to this hermeneutical provocation, and it is instructive to examine the precise character of his interpretive response. Commenting on Hoffmann's "The Sandman," Freud remarks on the pervasive equivocality between the fantastic
and the realistic that sets the entire tone of this narrative. "It is true," he
comments, "that the writer creates a kind of uncertainty in us in the beginning by not letting us know, no doubt purposely, whether he is taking us
into the real world or into a purely fantastic one of his own creation."[28] For
the psychologist E. Jentsch, whose early work on the uncanny Freud takes
as his jumping-off point, this insecurity in judgment forms the very essence

of the uncanny. However, Freud takes issue with this assertion, pointing out that this uncertainty, while present at the text's inception, is ultimately dissolved: our own indecision disappears as soon as we recognize, over the course of reading "The Sandman," "that [the author] intends to make us, too, look through the demon optician's [Coppola's] spectacles or spy-glass."[29] In other words, our interpretive uncertainty with regard to Hoffmann's text evaporates once we, stepping outside the figural perspective, become aware that the narrative forces us to observe events through a distorted lens, an optic to which the text's ostensible inconsistencies can be attributed. Here we can scarcely overlook the obvious analogy between the narrative trick Freud discovers in "The Sandman" and the framing technique Wiene introduces into *Caligari*: in a strikingly similar way, the denouement of this film arrives, and our uncertainty as viewers ends, when the narrated events are exposed in the concluding scenes as the imaginings of the insane narrator whose perspective we as viewers have up to this point unwittingly shared. For Freud, however, the uncanny aspect of Hoffmann's text—and his observation applies to *Caligari* as well—is not dispelled with the dissolution of this uncertainty, and he takes this as persuasive evidence that the uncanny is not grounded merely, as Jentsch proposed, in the sensation of intellectual insecurity.

Having debunked Jentsch's theory, Freud sets about establishing an alternative explanation for the effect of the uncanny. Returning to the interpretation of Hoffmann's short story, he focuses on the obsessive fear harbored by the protagonist Nathaniel that he will lose his eyes. Freud calls upon his psychoanalytic experience to help solve the riddle of this obsession. "A study of dreams, phantasies and myths has taught us that anxiety about one's eyes, the fear of going blind, is often enough a substitute for the dread of being castrated. The self-blinding of the mythical criminal, Oedipus, was simply a mitigated form of the punishment of castration."[30] Although for us today in the age of anti-Oedipus Freud's maneuver may perhaps seem all too familiar, it still merits careful analysis. He begins by reaching out beyond the text itself to his clinical experiences, which "often enough" reveal that in diverse narratives the eyes must be read as displaced or repressed signifiers for the penis and that the fear of blindness is a symbolic index of the castration complex. Freud stresses the general methodological principle that underwrites this association by invoking what he refers to as the "substitutive relation [*Ersatzbeziehung*] between the eye and the male organ which is seen to exist in dreams and myths and phantasies."[31] Although this "substitutive relation," which I will henceforth call substitutional displacement, may, in fact, be a relationship confirmed by Freud's clinical experience, it clearly constitutes a specific hermeneutical strategy. Freud arbitrarily—that is, by going outside the text and appealing to experiences derived from his clinical practice—isolates the element "eyes" in Hoffmann's text and treats it as a privileged signifier that refers to the infantile experience of fear of castration. Once this substitutional displacement has been accomplished, he is able to provide an interpretation of Hoffmann's text in which all its elements fall neatly into place, forming a coherent sense. It is this interpretive move, the reliance on substitutional displacement, that allows Freud to solve the mystery of the uncanny: the *unheimlich*, he concludes from his analysis, derives from the recollection of infantile experience, and the effect of the uncanny springs from the return of this forgotten-repressed material to the (semi)conscious mind of the writer in the process of composition and to that of the reader in the act of reading. Following this logic, it would then seem to be the shared psychic paradigm of the Oedipal complex that forms the link permitting the receptive transfer of the uncanny from writer to reader.

It is necessary at this point to draw some connections between the literary analysis Freud provides here and the methodology he pursues in the interpretation of his Revolutionary Dream, a hermeneutics whose counterpolitical mechanism Schorske so convincingly exposes. It is by no means coincidental, first of all, that in *The Interpretation of Dreams* Freud relates his Revolutionary Dream as an example intended to illustrate that infantile material is one of the primary sources of dreams: the section under which this interpretation appears is headed "Infantile Material as a Source of Dreams." When in the process of his interpretive analysis Freud admits that, for the sake of discretion, he must be less than complete in his revelations, he justifies his omissions with a statement that reveals the way his procedure is overdetermined by the aim to demonstrate that infantile material comprises a cardinal source of dreams: "I will merely pick out the elements leading to the two childhood scenes *on whose account alone I embarked upon a discussion of this dream.*"[32] In other words, it is Freud's desire to demonstrate the centrality of infantile experience as a principal source of dreams that motivates the interpretive moves which write sociopolitical resentments out of his analysis of the Revolutionary Dream. This same purpose, of course, underpins his investigation of the uncanny in Hoffmann's "The Sandman," and in this instance, as well, his hermeneutical tactics—his substitutions, inclusions, and exclusions—are deployed as means that will help him arrive at this preordained conclusion. In the dream analysis this makes it possible for him to banish the "insolent and revolutionary ideas" of the manifest dream text by reducing them to "rebellion against my father."[33] In this instance, it is the fermenting protest against sociopolitical givens that, reduced by substitutional displacement to infantile experience, is effaced and repressed. In the specification of the uncanny derived from his interpretation of "The Sandman," on the other hand, it is judgmental uncertainty, that is, the very equivocation constitutive of the divided bourgeois subject, that Freud is at pains to dismiss, and he once again deploys the hermeneutical strategy of substitutional displacement to effect this subrogation. As we will see, however, this equivocation uncannily resurfaces as the return of the repressed in Freud's investigation of the uncanny.

If Freud's tactic of substitutional displacement is exposed as a mechanism of concealment by which certain unacceptable motives are censored and effaced while being replaced by others more in line with his analytic aim, the question arises as to what alternative interpretive procedure might be followed by a counterhermeneutics that seeks to resist his strategy and expose what it willfully obfuscates. Freud himself suggests *ex negativo*, as it were, the key to such a counterinterpretive practice in the sections of the essay "The Uncanny" that follow his interpretation of Hoffmann's story. Freud seems not to have found his association of the uncanny with the recollection of infantile complexes to be entirely convincing, and as a result of certain second thoughts, he sets about examining the phenomenon of the doppelgänger in a further tale by Hoffmann to track down a possible second source of the uncanny. This second complex capable of unleashing the sensation of the uncanny, he maintains, is the revitalization of overcome primitive convictions.[34] This second thesis represents but a logical supplement to the first insofar as it associates the state of primitiveness with the "childhood" of mankind and thus mythically expands the proposition that the recurrence of infantile experience motivates the uncanny, projecting this conception into the developmental, philosophic-historical conception of the human race that forms the cornerstone of bourgeois historical understanding. However, to arrive at this expanded hypothesis, Freud finds it necessary to identify the doppelgänger, his example for a resurrection of overcome primitive convictions, with the splitting-off from the ego of a self-critical agency, what here is termed the ego-critique and would later become known as the authoritarian superego. The primitive image of the doppelgänger, Freud explains, comes to be invested with new, more relevant significance when it reasserts itself in the cultured mind. "The idea of the 'double' . . . can receive fresh meaning from the later stages of the ego's development. A special agency is slowly formed there, which is able to stand over against the rest of the ego, which has the function of observing and criticizing the self and of exercising a censorship within the mind, and which we become aware of as our conscience."[35] He continues by associating the doppelgänger with those elements of the ego that are rejected by the superego or ego-critique. Curiously enough, however, he then goes on to assert a secondary interpretation of the double, one that stands in diametrical opposition to the first, claiming that aside from representing those personal wishes repressed by means of self-censorship, it can also embody drives whose realization has been prevented due to circumstances *external* to the subject itself and thus are independent of its psychic economy. "But it is not only this latter material, offensive as it is to the criticism of the ego, which may be incorporated in the idea of a double. There are also *all the unfulfilled but possible futures* to which we still like to cling in phantasy, *all the strivings of the ego which adverse external circumstances have crushed.*"[36] The projected double thus is characterized by a functional ambivalence, representing both a mechanism of self-critique that represses desires unacceptable to the ego and serving as a reminder of those unrealized desires whose fulfillment has been frustrated by adverse circumstances external to the individual. This fundamental waffling marks the point at which the problem of intellectual equivocation, banished in the opening sections of Freud's essay, comes back ultimately to haunt it.

To be sure, this ambivalence could be resolved if we were to read into this early essay the hypothesis Freud articulated some years later, according to which the repressive superego represents nothing other than the introjection of external authority into the individual's psyche itself, an internalization that then takes the form of that self-critical mechanism known as the "conscience."[37] Although this would allow us to identify external and internal censorship, it does not ultimately dispel the functional ambivalence Freud circumscribes; for in the final analysis, the two aspects of the doppelgänger phenomenon as he describes them signify nothing other than distinct reactions by the individual to *external* oppression, one submissive and deferential—its incorporation as self-critique—the other recalcitrant and rebellious—resentful indictment of external oppression. In the aspect of self-critique, on the one hand, the double signifies the individual's identification with and acceptance of externally imposed authoritarian constraints; but as the representation of unfulfilled potentials, on the other hand, it sides with the individual's own ego-potential *against* these limitations, and as such it is the ineradicable mark of a violently repressed revolutionary-utopian desire. The doppelgänger as conceived by Freud thus incorporates those countervailing drives whose interaction we have traced throughout our investigations as the constitutional poles of self-divided Unhappy Consciousness: it focuses into a single image the bourgeois subject's conspiratorial collusion with the forces of sociopolitical critique and its simultaneous accession to the demands of the very sociopolitical regime it secretly (*heimlich*) opposes.

In its incarnation as the doppelgänger, however, the dialectical reciprocity of Unhappy Consciousness is exposed as a system of absolute ambivalence. Hugo von Hofmannsthal's psychic narrative *A Tale of the Cavalry*, whose uncanniness emerges to a large part out of its extensive exploitation of the doppelgänger motif, tells the story of this ambivalence between submission and rebellion, portraying it as a fatal equivocation that leads ultimately to the demise of the bourgeois subject itself. Hofmannsthal's protagonist Anton Lerch thus represents a historical station of the divided subject in which the canceling out of its antithetical urges ceases to mark a system of dialectical interpenetration and signals instead an absolute self-antagonism in which bourgeois subjectivity itself is canceled out: mutual dialectical subl(im)ation reverts to enfeebling, ultimately self-destructive equivocality.

Before turning to our interpretive inquiry into Hofmannsthal's text, we must return for a moment to the literary-critical procedure Freud follows in his essay "The Uncanny." Freud's essay itself, I wish to propose, supplies clues to an interpretive methodology that would provide a counter-hermeneutical alternative to substitutional displacement. In his attempt to forge a link between infantile material and primitive psychic states as the two sources of the uncanny—in his desire to align, in effect, his analysis of Nathaniel's obsessive fear of loss of his eyes in "The Sandman" with his reflections on the doppelgänger—Freud is forced to appeal to bourgeois philosophic-historical conceptions and draw the metaphorical analogy between the life of the soul characteristic of the human child and that of primitive peoples as the "infancy" of humankind.

However, there is a much more obvious connection between fear for one's eyes and the doppelgänger phenomenon as he defines it, a connection that Freud either overlooks or suppresses. There is, after all, a rather direct and palpable filiation between the eyes, the organs of observation whose projected loss causes anxiety, and Freud's identification of the double in its self-critical aspect as an agency of repressive self-observation. This clear interconnection gives rise to the critical question: why does Freud ignore the metonymic link between eyes and the psychic agency of self-observation and ego-critique, opting instead to metaphorically displace the central image from "The Sandman" by reading it as a signifier for penis? Wouldn't the metonymic link between eyes and the self-observing agency of ego-critique, after all, have provided him with a convincing basis on which he would be able to associate and identify the two manifestations of the uncanny he examines? Indeed, it seems likely that it is precisely this plausible interrelation that Freud wanted to avoid; for it is only by way of the detour that passes, through the practice of substitutional displacement, from eyes to penis that he is able to establish the resurgence of infantile material as a source for the experience of the uncanny. Moving metonymically from eyes as the organs of observation to the phenomenon of ego-critique and self-observation would have the undesired effect of collapsing his first thesis about the sources of the uncanny into his second one, thereby effectively writing infantile material out of his theory. Such a solution seems both more logically consistent and simpler than the conclusion at which Freud arrives, since instead of forcing him to postulate two distinct if related sources for the uncanny—the return of repressed infantile material and the reminiscence of overcome primitive states of the soul—it would allow him to propose a single, unified cause. The fact that Freud circumvents this more elegant and manifest conclusion indicates just how much was at stake for him in his attribution of the uncanny to the return of infantile experience. In the broader scheme of his psychoanalytical project, of course, this attribution allows him to confirm in his investigations of the uncanny his fundamental belief that psychic disturbances have their origin in unovercome infantile material—that is, in experiences like the "primal scene," which inscribe the conflict between the individual and the community in the narrow space of the bourgeois family—rather than conceiving this antagonism as one between individual utopian-political desire and its sociopolitically imposed (self-) repression. But on the broader level of interpretive methodology, the metonymic procedure that I am suggesting also has the side effect of marginalizing the tactic of substitutional displacement that is so central to Freud's entire psychoanalytic project.

In the specific case of the analyses presented in the essay "The Uncanny," the hermeneutical tactic of substitutional displacement permits Freud to stress intrafamilial factors as responsible for the functional ambivalence he associates with the experience of the uncanny, playing down the sociopolitical dimension to which his investigation of the doppelgänger reluctantly yet insistently alludes: the waffling of the divided subject between self-identification *against* oppressive external authority and identification *with*—internalization of—this authority in the form of (self-)repressive measures. Freud's own ego-critique, as it were, is occupied with the marginalization of this unexpungeable yet (politically) unacceptable variety of the uncanny, an uncanny predicated on the return to consciousness of externally suppressed potentials, of utopian possibilities—the "fantasy" of radically other "possible futures" than those sanctioned by the sociopolitical circumstances realized in bourgeois society. The mark of Freud's own divided bourgeois subjectivity manifests itself in the interpretive effort expended to undermine and thwart his own critical sociopolitical insights.

I have already alluded to the interpretive-methodological inference that can be drawn from our critical examination and put into practice in an analysis of *A Tale of the Cavalry*. If in his interpretation of "The Sandman" Freud proceeds metaphorically, substitutively displacing a principal element of Hoffmann's text by designating it as a symbolic signifier that refers to a signified whose relevance is established on the basis of his clinical experience, a counterhermeneutics that seeks to reveal the censoring mechanism at work in this method and uncover what it attempts to conceal must operate metonymically, connecting elements in the text on the basis of their conceptual or intratextual correlations. Instead of occulting elements of the manifest text by replacing them with extra-textual signifieds, this counterpractice takes the text at its word, so to speak, seeking elucidation on the basis of interrelations suggested by its very textuality. In other words, the aim is not to break through the manifest text of Hofmannsthal's story by decoding it in terms of latent symbolic meanings, but rather to scrutinize it for those intratextual relationships that contribute to its structuration *as text*, reading these structural relationships as hermeneutical clues. Although this may at first blush sound like a plea for a return to the formalism and text-immanence of New Criticism, this is certainly not my intention at all. My point is merely that symbolic understandings that define the text's significance by moving along the vertical axis of metaphorical substitution fall victim to distortions and concealments executed by the text itself: they succumb to textual sleights of hand that attempt to steer reception away from the text's own political unconscious. Given that the receptive guidance system of the text, which encourages vertical metaphorical decoding, constitutes an interpretive ruse, a counterhermeneutical practice that aims to uncover the mechanics of this textual deception and make its political secrets *unheimlich*, "un-secret," must proceed horizontally and metonymically. When applied to Hofmannsthal's *A Tale of the Cavalry*, this methodology belies the claim that sociocritical interpretations of this text are purely hypothetical because they cannot be derived through text-immanent investigation.[38] On the contrary, what my interpretation will demonstrate is that it is only on the basis of careful intratextual analysis that we can penetrate to the *political* unconscious of Hofmannsthal's uncanny narrative.

The Political Unconscious in Hofmannsthal's *A Tale of the Cavalry*

Hofmannsthal's *A Tale of the Cavalry* has given rise to furious hermeneutical activity in the postwar era, making it one of the few stories that can compete with Kafka's texts in terms of the quantity and variety of interpretive commentaries.[39] Yet at first glance this animated critical debate seems out of keeping with the relatively simple plot-line of this story. Anton Lerch, an Austrian cavalry sergeant on active duty in Italy during the revolutionary upheavals of 1848, participates in the suppression of the Italian rebels. Over the course of the day's events narrated in this tale, he runs into a woman with whom he was acquainted in his youth and is suddenly overcome with irrepressible drives for sexual and military conquest. After capturing a horse from an enemy officer during a skirmish and returning to his squadron, Lerch is shot down by his commanding officer, Baron Rofrano, when he refuses to give up this prize booty. The story ends without supplying any definitive explanation of Rofrano's action, and critical examinations of the text have consistently sought to discover what motivates the ostensibly senseless and cold-blooded execution of Sergeant Lerch.

It is the seemingly unmotivated and exaggerated nature of Rofrano's act of violence against one of his fellow, if subordinate, officers that lends this story the character of a riddle; and this enigma crystallizes around two questions, formulated by one of the earliest commentators on this story, to which interpretive analyses have continually attempted to provide answers: "Why does Sergeant Anton Lerch have to die? Why must he die in this way?"[40] Although a plethora of solutions to this riddle have been proposed, these tend to fall more or less into three general categories. One body of critics solves this puzzle by appealing to psychological issues, claiming that Lerch's death results, for example, from his inability to accept his own split personality, because of his own human-sexual failings, or as the result of a displaced Oedipal complex that forces him to challenge his superior officer, who represents an embodiment of the father-figure. A second set of interpreters cites metaphysical causes as the driving force behind Lerch's murder, arguing that his sacrificial elimination effects a cathartic purification of the entire cavalry squadron, that his death symbolizes flight from the empirical realm and advancement into a mythic "beyond," or that he simply has become the all too human victim of inscrutable transcendental powers. Finally, a third and much smaller group of interpreters locates the motives behind Lerch's liquidation in a sociological problematic, viewing his murder as the suppression of a desire to transgress social hierarchies or situating it in a class conflict between Lerch and his aristocratic superior, Baron Rofrano.

The first two types of readings abstract completely from the explicit sociohistorical context of Hofmannsthal's story, either interiorizing the struggle that results in Lerch's death by understanding it solely in terms of his own intrapsychic strife, or mystifying it by conceiving Lerch as the innocent prey of unnamed metaphysical authorities. But even those interpretations that focus their attention on matters of social antagonisms tend to play down the revolutionary political dimension of the story, the events of the 1848 revolution that form its historical backdrop and set the entire plot in motion. Thus the receptive history of *A Tale of the Cavalry* exhibits a general tendency toward the marginalization of these sociohistorical elements fundamental to its constitution. This displacement or repression of the political, typical of the scholarly response to this text, is given paradigmatic expression by one critic who maintains that although *A Tale of the Cavalry* "may express idealistic political sentiments, . . . the real beauty of the story lies in the technical brilliance of the style and in Hofmannsthal's archetypal vision."[41] In a similar vein, a second commentator declares: "One can think as one will about the external events, about the doubtlessly present social-critical elements, and even about the crass disciplinary action of the Captain; the true content of [*A Tale of the Cavalry*] resides in its atmosphere."[42] The political (under)tone of Hofmannsthal's tale has commonly struck its interpreters as particularly *unheimlich*, as something that had better been left undisclosed and whose centrality to the text must therefore be denied or at least minimized. Consequently, they have incessantly responded by attempting to conceal this political moment behind questions of aesthetic form, mythic vision, "atmosphere," or psychological conflict. My aim, therefore, is to develop an interpretation that does justice to the formal-structural makeup of the text, paying heed to its character as "psychic narrative," while yet taking into account the sociopolitical outcroppings that form the woof of its textual fabric. Although I do not wish to deny that the story depicts a fundamentally psychic conflict, I will argue that this psychic struggle must be conceived as the internalization of sociopolitical desires and antagonisms, as their introjection into an ambivalent doppelgänger that "doubles" as the embodiment of unrealized revolutionary-utopian potentials and (self-)repressive superego. The narrative structure of Hofmannsthal's text reflects this sociopsychic conflict in its own textual mechanics as a struggle between the assertion of rebellious sociopolitical opposition and repressive countertactics that seek to efface this irrepressible political drive. The overt references to the revolutionary events of 1848 comprise the remainder of this incompletely repressed revolutionary political desire: they mark the return of the repressed, the *unheimlich* as the surreptitious resurgence of what the (self-)censoring superego of the narrative would prefer to keep private and secret (*heimlich*).

Precious little is actually known about the origin and composition of *A Tale of the Cavalry*. First published in December of 1899, it is clear only that Hofmannsthal began work on this story in July of 1898. On the twenty-third of that month he wrote to his friend and fellow poet Leopold von Andrian: "If I am at all capable of writing prose, then I will write a short tale of the cavalry based on Radetzky's campaign in 1848."[43] The story was probably conceived, and major parts of it written, on the previous day, July 22, 1898, since it is on this day fifty years earlier—July 22, 1848—that the narrated events of the fictional account take place. Now, it is perhaps no coincidence that it was at almost exactly this same time that Freud dreamed his Revolutionary Dream; and the numerous points of contact between Freud's dream text, his interpretive analysis, and the motifs and structures of Hofmannsthal's story suggest the possibility that their recollections and fictive (dream) elaborations stem from similar topical-historical stimuli.

In his dream Freud projects himself back into the events of 1848, imagining himself in the role of the Austrian revolutionary student leader Adolf Fischhof. He explains this historical fantasy by claiming that the fiftieth anniversary celebrations of Kaiser Franz Joseph, who came to power in 1848 on the heels of that year's revolutionary movements, caused these historical events to become especially present to his mind. Although he admits that this fantasy finds its immediate motivational impulse in his own subversive reaction to the encounter with Count Thun at the train station on the day of the dream, Freud nevertheless consciously discounts the revolutionary implications of the manifest dream text. The language by which he effects this subrogation of the political is worthy of analysis, since it "uncannily" reveals how precisely those revolutionary events Freud obstinately tries to suppress leave their indelible traces in his own unconscious. "This revolutionary phantasy, however, which was derived from ideas aroused in me by seeing Count Thun," Freud writes, "was like the façade of an Italian church in having no organic relation with the structure lying behind it."[44] The simile of the church facade, of course, is intended to illustrate the arbitrariness of the semiotic relationship that obtains between manifest dream text and latent dream content: the manifest text as signifier relates to the latent meaning as signified in the same manner as a mere facade relates to the organic structure of a building. One wonders, however, why Freud specifies that the churches to which his metaphorical vehicle refers must be Italian, since in Freud's native Vienna, as throughout Austria in general, it was not uncommon, in the wake of the Counter-Reformation, for Baroque facades and ornamentation to be grafted onto churches from earlier architectural periods. Freud thus had plenty of opportunities to witness this architectural phenomenon elsewhere than in Italy. Now, as we know, the struggle of the Italians for liberation from despotic Austrian rule was emblematic of the nationalist battles that wracked the Austro-Hungarian monarchy during the revolution of 1848, and it is in the context of the Italians' struggle for political emancipation that Hofmannsthal embeds the story of Anton Lerch. Fifty years later, in the summer of 1898, when Freud and Hofmannsthal were composing their (dream) texts, the Austrian empire was again being ravaged by similar nationalist struggles for liberation, and the political climate in Vienna was marked by parliamentary chaos, vehement demonstrations, and general revolutionary turmoil.[45] The adjective "Italian," itself wholly superfluous to Freud's metaphor, invokes this political tension by inadvertently recalling the Italian struggle for liberation in 1848; it thereby marks in Freud's own language the clandestine return of the political repressed—it is the index, in short, of the *unheimlich* content that Freud's self-interpretation seeks to render *heimlich*.

Freud's Revolutionary Dream and Hofmannsthal's *A Tale of the Cavalry* share more than just a similar date of origin: both are responses to the political turmoil of Austria in 1898, responses that explicitly contextualize this reality in the revolutionary events of 1848. Both texts, moreover, attempt to gloss over and repress the traces of this historico-political impetus. Finally, as my interpretive analysis will elucidate, both protagonists, Freud's dreamself and Anton Lerch, express their repressed sympathies for the political rebellion so objectionable to their bourgeois sensibilities by means of an unconscious personal identification with the oppressed revolutionaries themselves. The ambivalent structure of both texts, their uncanny melding of the sociopolitical and the psychological, of public and private issues, replicates the political ambivalence of their protagonists and their authors, alike. In the case of both texts, author and protagonist refuse to accept the revolutionary implications that spring from their political unconscious, and the narratives themselves bear the traces of this political repression.

If there is one feature that especially stands out in Hofmannsthal's protagonist Anton Lerch, then it is acute, ultimately debilitating ambivalence. Investigating the meanings of the word *heimlich*, we recall, Freud characterized its semantic field in terms of an unstable ambivalence: "Thus *heimlich* is a word the meaning of which develops in the direction of ambivalence, until it finally coincides with its opposite, *unheimlich*."[46] The ambivalence that begins to take possession of Anton Lerch after his squadron's ride through Milan and the subsequent meeting with Vuic, a woman with whom he had passing acquaintance as a young man, is closely bound up with the various semantic nuances of the words *heimlich* and *unheimlich*. This connection manifests itself most concretely in the motif of the doppelgänger, which plays a central role in the signifying network of the text. Just as Freud gives an ambivalent interpretation of the doppelgänger, viewing it both as the representation of the psychic agency of self-critique and as the manifestation of precisely those unfulfilled desires and potentials this authoritarian conscience represses, in Hofmannsthal's text the double signals both political repression and the return of this repressed, and in this sense it is indeed the concrete token of the *unheimlich*.

After a morning of successful skirmishes, Baron Rofrano leads his cavalry squadron through the unprotected town of Milan. It is here that Lerch gets his first taste of an ambivalent secret-private "homeyness": the civilian existence of Milan presents itself in the form of "the bare arms of unknown [female] beauty," on the one hand, and in the guise of "pallid, cursing figures slipping into house-doors," on the other (*Tale*, 40; *323*). Both of these descriptions evoke a complex relationship in which exposure and concealment hold each other in check; in each, the homey is shot through with an air of the unknown or the secretive. The "bare arms" of "unknown" women are indicative of a sexual enticement in which what is most intimate, most private and secret, is alluringly exposed. Similarly, the "pallid, cursing figures" that disappear behind "house-doors" represent this fusion of revelation and concealment, turned from the sexually alluring to the mysterious and suspect. These two emotions, enticement and suspicion, significantly prefigure Lerch's perceptions when he meets Vuic later the same day, and they ultimately become the structuring principles of the fantasy that this chance meeting triggers.

Lerch recaptures this fleeting sensation of an enticing-suspicious, secret-private homeyness when he halts to attend to his horse and registers in detail the scene at the house at which he pauses.

Hardly had [Lerch] raised the second white-socked hoof of his bay to inspect the shoe when a door [of the house] leading straight into the front of the entry actually opened to show a woman, sensual-looking and still not quite past her youth, in a somewhat dishevelled bedgown, and behind her a sunny room with a few pots of basil and red pelargonium in the windows, while his sharp eyes caught in a pierglass the reflection of the other side of the room, which was filled with a large white bed and a papered door, through which a stout, clean-shaven, elderly man was just withdrawing. (*Tale*, 41; *323–24*)

In this moment Sergeant Lerch, who absorbs the most minute details of this scene, lives up to the designation of his military title as "Wachtmeister," which when translated literally means "master of observation." He indeed proves himself in this passage—as he does throughout the story, in fact—to be a master observer from whose "sharp eyes" no detail can escape scrutiny. The "dishevelled," "sensual-looking" woman he now perceives reembodies the sexual allurement of the "bare arms" espied during the ride through Milan, while the "elderly man" glimpsed in the mirror while he "withdraws" behind a rear door reinvokes the suspicious "figures slipping into house-doors" that Lerch likewise witnessed during this march earlier in the day. This intriguing allurement is further augmented by the captivating if simple details of this petit bourgeois household and the private-secret life of the civilian that it conjures up. Recognizing in this woman the at one time more youthful Vuic, Lerch promises to return after the present military campaign and make her house his quarters; and as he rides on, rejoining his squadron, he succumbs to a series of fantasies that amplify on this encounter.

In this vision Lerch imagines himself as part of a "civilian life of peace still irradiated by war, an atmosphere of comfort and pleasant brutality with no officer to give him orders, a slippered life with the hilt of his sabre sticking through the left-hand pocket of his dressing-gown" (*Tale*, 42; 325). The "comfort" ("Behaglichkeit") that Lerch envisions overlaps completely with the definition Freud cites of the *heimlich* as the homey: "the enjoyment of quiet content, etc., arousing a sense of agreeable [*behaglicher*] restfulness and security as in one within the four walls of his house."[47] But what is particularly remarkable about Lerch's fantasy is the manner in which it merges this "privacy" and "homeyness" with the distinctly "public" and "unhomey" paraphernalia of the soldier. Commentators have tended to interpret this curious intermingling of the artifacts of bourgeois comfort with the weapons of war as indicative of Lerch's desire to transfer the commandeering authority of the military officer over to his own self-contained bourgeois private sphere. However, the text supplies no concrete evidence that would support this speculative hypothesis, and it seems more likely that this hybridization of the private and the public bespeaks the waffling of Lerch's allegiances, an ambivalent double-identification with both his soldier and his civilian personae. As my analysis will reveal, however, this fusion of civilian and military life holds yet a deeper significance, since—far from representing a mere displacement of Lerch's desire for military empowerment into the sphere of bourgeois private life—it metonymically recalls the warlike-homey character of the enemy revolutionaries, the Italian militiamen fighting to free their homeland, whose struggle for liberation requires them to bear military arms while still wearing the garb of their civilian existence.

The text inconspicuously hints at Lerch's surreptitious sense of personal identification with the rebellious citizens whose insurrection he is charged to suppress by establishing a network of subtle intratextual allusions that connect the substance of the Sergeant's wish-fulfillment daydream to the military encounters experienced earlier in the day. The battles of that morning found Lerch's company pitted against "irregular" militiamen ("Frei-scharen") (*Tale*, 40; 322) who, side by side with regular soldiers of the Italian military, fight a war of self-liberation against their Austrian overlords. Re-minded by the chance meeting with Vuic of his own youth, Lerch begins to establish associative links between his past and the activities of these "youth-ful" and "handsome" irregulars who are "irregularly armed" and wear "strange headgear" (*Tale*, 39; 321–22). When in his fantasy Lerch later imag-ines himself clothed in civilian dress yet armed for war, he projects himself into the role of these "irregular" soldiers, whose outward appearance man-ifests similar incongruities. In effect, he identifies with these rebels, envi-sioning himself as their fellow revolutionary. This identification signals the return to awareness of those dreams of personal liberation and "possible fu-tures" whose repression is symbolized by Lerch's subordination to the strict hierarchical order of military life. However, even when they are freed from Lerch's political unconscious, these repressed desires cannot enter his con-scious mind without first being arraigned by his authoritarian superego and subjected to the process of a transmogrifying self-censorship. The confla-tion of these utopian political desires with the sexual lust for Vuic is one of the symptoms of this censorship, as are Lerch's outwardly incongruous as-sociation of his rebellion against the bourgeois order with the objects of bourgeois comfort and his obsessively avaricious fascination with wealth and personal reward. The (self-)censor's tactic is as obvious as it is effective: the unacceptable political desire, which as desire cannot simply be trace-lessly squelched, is transmuted into desires that bourgeois morality overtly condemns but covertly sanctions: into monetary, territorial, and sexual dreams of empowerment. These various visions of self-empowerment, in other words, do not form the crux of Lerch's motivations; instead, they rep-resent epiphenomenal manifestations, distorted by the superego's vigilant self-disciplining, of a utopian drive for sociopolitical liberation and self-enti-tlement.

It is consistent with this that the fantasies that creep into Lerch's mind af-ter his experience at Vuic's house center on the clean-shaven man rather than on the woman herself. The fact that Lerch only glimpses this man in a mirror, rather than perceiving him immediately, implies that this specular image reflects a self-projection engendered by Lerch's fantasy. This male Other, with whom Lerch presumably must compete if he expects to take possession of Vuic and occupy her house, hence is no empirical being, but the Other of Lerch himself, and as such this episode marks one of Lerch's principal encounters with his doppelgänger. This figure does not represent an alter ego, as one might first suspect, but rather reflects—literally—Lerch's growing ambivalence. Combining the clean-shavenness of youth with Lerch's "elderly" physiognomy, this figure, explicitly identified as "something between"—a "Mittelding": literally, an "in-between thing" (*Tale*, 42; *325*)—"mirrors" the debilitating equivocation of Lerch's simultaneously repressed and repressive self.

The fact that this character is positioned in a house door, as we have seen, aligns him with the "pallid figures" that disappeared behind house doors as the squadron rode through Milan earlier that same day; and like them, the clean-shaven double represents that suspicious yet alluring homey-secrecy circumscribed by the oppositional semantic field of the word *heimlich*. In Lerch's fantasy this character hence becomes associated not only with Vuic's home, but with secret political complots that take place in "suspicious houses." "The clean-shaven man was now a somewhat servile companion . . . , now he was hard pressed and had to pay blackmail, was involved in many intrigues, was in the confidence of the *Piedmontese*, was *Papal* cook, procurer, owner of *suspicious houses* with gloomy pavilions for political meetings, and swelled up into a huge, bloated figure from which, if it were tapped in twenty places, gold, not blood would pour" (*Tale*, 42; *325*; emphasis added). The transmogrifications Lerch's clean-shaven double undergoes over the course of this fantasy bear testimony to the workings of the superego's censorship. As a "servile companion" associated with questionable underground political movements, this phantasm symbolizes Lerch's repressed political persona; but as the vision progresses, the double takes the form of a money-bag that disguises this repressed wish for political self-empowerment behind a thirst for riches. At the same time, in a semantic shift that counters this censorship mechanism, the double is also transformed from a companion in the political underground to a conquerable object. As the political suspect is transformed into a billowing money-bag, so Sergeant Lerch's enemy ceases to be the poor Italian revolutionaries it is his duty to suppress and becomes rather his wealthy aristocratic superior officer Baron Rofrano. Plundering this money-bag, Lerch avenges himself symbolically on the effigy of that person whom he unconsciously identifies both as his socioeconomic oppressor and his sociopolitical master. This metamorphosis of the double, then, marks both the repressive censorship of Lerch's political rebelliousness and the insistent return of this repressed drive for political insurgency.

The semantic elements that I have highlighted in the quoted passage are similarly subtle indicators of the return of this repressed political unconscious, and they thus play a role that parallels Freud's inclusion of the adjective "Italian" in his metaphor of the church facade. This passage functions as a structural nexus which, on the basis of intratextual allusions, refers backward to the suppressed rebellions of the morning and thereby subtly links these events. This linkage reveals the repressed revolutionary-political undercurrent that unconsciously motivates Lerch's pursuits, demonstrating how in his fantasy he latches onto and reiterates certain elements from the morning's military adventures. One of his squadron's first actions, for example, was the arrest of "a wayfarer . . . whose very guilelessness and insignificance aroused *suspicion*. Sewn into the lining of his coat he was carrying detailed plans of the greatest importance relating to the formation of *irregular* corps [*Freikorps*] . . . and their liaison with the *Piedmontese* army" (*Tale*, 39; *322*; emphasis added). I have highlighted the three words in this passage that link this episode with Lerch's phantasmagoric vision. The adjective "suspicious" ties this wayfarer to the "suspicious houses" owned by Lerch's clean-shaven double in his guise as political conspirator. The word *frei* ("free") that makes up the first element in the compound noun "Freikorps" stresses that these "irregular" civil troops both serve "freely"—that is, voluntarily—and that they are involved in a struggle for their own political freedom. Both these qualities set them apart from Sergeant Lerch, whose problematic "Dienstverhältnis"—his difficult relationship with his own servitude to the authority of his superiors during his many years of military service—is referred to twice in the text (*Tale*, 42, 47; *325, 331*). But as we have seen, in his imagination Lerch unconsciously identifies with the "irregular" nature of these "free" rebels. Finally, the adjective "Piedmontese," which also cropped up in Lerch's fantasy as an attribute of his clean-shaven double, underscores the link between this doppelgänger and the political conspiracy of the rebellious Italians, which Sergeant Lerch must uncover and crush. This verbal link between the captured conspirator and the self-projections with which Lerch invests his doppelgänger underscores his secret-private (*heimlich*) identification with the self-liberating revolutionaries and thereby marks the *unheimlich* return of his repressed drive for self-emancipation. Moreover, if this conspirator arouses suspicion primarily because of his "guileless and insignificant" behavior, then the ostensibly guileless actions of Sergeant Lerch become the index that he himself is politically suspect. It is this recognition by Captain Rofrano that motivates his otherwise seemingly inexplicable murder of the outwardly "guileless and insignificant" Anton Lerch. Rofrano comprehends that, like the captured rebel who has secret plans sewn into the lining of his coat, Sergeant Lerch has secret rebellion against his superior officer and the repressive political authority he represents sewn into the very text(ure) of his psychic constitution.

Immediately following the capture of this conspirator, Lerch and his squadron are involved in another military confrontation with the rebels, and once again elements from the description of this event leave their traces in Lerch's fantasy vision. In this encounter the squadron takes prisoner twenty-seven rebels who are identified as "Neapolitan *irregulars* [*Freischaren*] under *Papal* officers" (*Tale*, 40; *322*; emphasis added). Like the attribute "Piedmontese" associated with the insurgents in the previous passage, the adjective "Papal" links these enemy officers to Lerch's double in his guise as "Papal cook" (*Tale*, 42; *325*). Furthermore, these Papal officers lead a band of "Freischaren," irregular and "free" militiamen who, like the "Freikorps" mentioned in the prior episode, implicitly fight voluntarily in the cause of their own political liberation.

Certain qualities are consistently associated with the rebel militiamen against whom Sergeant Lerch does battle: as a rule, they are young and handsome, and display the vitality and potency of early manhood. For example, the enemy officer whom Lerch kills—and whose captured horse becomes the bone of contention between him and Rofrano, ultimately calling forth Lerch's assassination—has "a young, very pale face" (*Tale*, 46; *329*). Similarly, in another of the skirmishes that takes place early in the day, Lerch and his troops surround and capture eighteen students who are characterized as "handsome young men with white hands and long hair" (*Tale*, 39; *322*). The references to whiteness, hands, and hair employed in conjunction with these "*suspicious* figures" (*Tale*, 39; *321*; emphasis added) will return in the meeting with Vuic as traits of this woman herself, just as the "beautiful villa" in the vicinity of which these students are first sighted recurs in the later episode demoted to the status of the petit bourgeois household. Now, Vuic herself, we recall, is a figure whom Lerch associates with his own youth; and when he lends her the attributes of his youthful enemies, he reinforces his perception that she—and by logical extension he himself—is "still not quite past her youth" (*Tale*, 41; *323*). Still, Lerch is aware that Vuic, like both Lerch himself and his clean-shaven double, is a curious "Mittelding," "something in-between" youth and elderliness, between the fleshy corpulence of middle age and the "full yet slender figure" (*Tale*, 41; *324*) she once possessed. Vuic and the young rebels thus remind Lerch of his own lost youthfulness, of a time when he envisioned for himself "future possibilities" for his own development, potentials distinct from the course his actual life has followed.

Lerch's anxiety about these lost potentials is concretized, on the one hand, in the signs of aging, in the "stout" and "elderly" man he recognizes in his doppelgänger (*Tale*, 41; *324*), and, on the other, as the melancholy, wistful identification with his youthful and rebellious enemies. Lerch thus projects himself as competing personae when he conjures up his doubles: he identifies both with his own free and rebellious youth, of which the young revolutionaries remind him, and with his aging, repressive self as Sergeant Lerch. These two personae coincide with the contrasting facets of the doppelgänger as conceived by Freud, and they point to the inimical confrontation between the contrary impulses of Lerch's divided subjectivity. As "Wachtmeister," master *self*-observer, Sergeant Lerch manifests that critical self-observation and self-mastery characteristic of the repressive and authoritarian superego. But as the symptom of his seditious identification with the youthful revolutionaries, the double also serves as the reminder of the unrealized potentials and desires of his adolescence, drives that were squelched by his capitulation to sociopolitical subordination, represented concretely in his duty as a soldier.

It is through their association with the problematics of youthfulness and sexuality that the revolutionary political nature of Lerch's desires is concealed from his own consciousness. Now, the text of *A Tale of the Cavalry* itself, as psychic narrative, reflects the repressed-repressing subjectivity of its protagonist; and since the story's readers share his figural perspective, they are also subjected to the censorship mechanisms that efface the political moment in Lerch's self-understanding. My critical reading thus attempts to assume a standpoint outside the psychotext that constitutes this story to uncover these mechanisms of concealment and see through to the text's political unconscious. One of the primary hermeneutical ruses the text deploys to censor its own political unconscious is the association of Lerch's drive for sociopolitical liberation with the melancholy and futile attempt to recapture the vitality and sexual prowess of youth. Given this context, the fact that Lerch's pistol misfires when he later rides through the mysterious village appears to take on a specific sexual-symbolic significance (*Tale*, 44; 327): the text encourages us to read the pistol as a phallic symbol, and its misfiring as a symptom of Lerch's sense of his own aging and his anxiety about incipient sexual impotence. If we were to follow Freudian interpretive strategies here, as the uncanniness of this psychic narrative suggests we should, we would turn "pistol" into a privileged signifier that could be effaced and replaced by the signified "penis." This would then lead us to interpret the encounter with Vuic and Lerch's desire of sexual conquest as an attempt to recapture the youth she represents for him. However, what the metaphorical substitution of penis for pistol displaces is precisely the metonymic associations of the misfired pistol with the aberrance of Lerch's military existence, on the one hand, and with the "misfiring" of those revolutionary political desires he harbored in his youth, on the other. In this context the misfiring pistol refers to Lerch's failure to turn his pistol into a weapon for his own emancipation, as the young revolutionaries do. As my analysis has shown, Lerch's suppressed desire as political insurgent only makes itself known through careful examination of the metonymic connections and intratextual allusions that mark the return of what the (psychic) text otherwise represses. Only when we resist the temptation to interpret *A Tale of the Cavalry* symbolically, concentrating instead on a reading based on these metonymic, intratextual patterns, are we able to penetrate to its deep-structural political unconscious.

In his eerie experiences of the uncanny village, in which Lerch encounters his doppelgänger as his own mimetic reflection (see *Tale*, 43–45; 326–28), we can once again trace the allusive metonymic chains that emanate from the nexus passage describing Lerch's fantasy about his clean-shaven double. This village attracts Lerch's attention because it is "enticing and suspicious" ("auf verlockende Weise verdächtig") (*Tale*, 43; 325), and it thus embodies for him the suspicious allurement of the private-secret (*heimlich*) that has caught his fancy throughout the day's adventures. The tension inherent in this enticing suspiciousness, which bespeaks a kind of morbid curiosity mingled with anxiety, aptly characterizes the double bind of Lerch's repressive-repressed psychic condition. Lerch is enticed, of course, by the hope of realizing the dream of conquest formulated in his fantasy about the clean-shaven double. Augmenting this vision with concrete images, Lerch pictures himself entering into the village and taking an enemy general by surprise. "So inflamed was [Lerch's] imagination that it swelled to the hope of surprising in the village some ill-defended enemy general, or of winning some other great prize" (*Tale*, 43; 326). Lerch's desires are not disappointed, since in a sense he does indeed encounter the enemy officer of whom he dreams as he is about to leave the village: however, this enemy officer appears in the guise of Sergeant Lerch himself. Riding out of the village, Lerch becomes aware of "a man of his own regiment, a sergeant riding a bay with white-socked forefeet." Aware that the only horse in the company matching this description is his own, Lerch spurs his horse on to meet the mysterious figure. "And now, as the two horses . . . placed the same white-socked forefoot on the bridge, the sergeant, recognizing with starting eyes his own wraith, reined in his horse aghast" (*Tale*, 45; 328). In this final confrontation the doppelgänger once again manifests the double nature of Lerch's enemies. On the one hand, he encounters again the rebellious revolutionary in himself, the "owner of suspicious houses" whose rooms are the site of oppositional political assemblies; on the other hand, he comes face to face with the oppressive enemy he has introjected into his own subjectivity—with the authoritarian "Wachtmeister" who represents his own self-repressive superego.

Aroused by the impressions evoked at Vuic's house, the otherwise re-pressed, secret-private (*heimlich*) rebellious persona of Lerch's youth is momentarily left unguarded: the master (self-)observer lets down his vigilance, and this results in the *unheimlich* return of this repressed sociopolitical de-sire. This revelation is immediately repressed anew, so that Lerch's subjec-tivity is caught up in a constant internal struggle between the (re)assertion of a seditious drive for sociopolitical opposition and the violent self-disci-plining of this mutinous wish. The identifying mark of Lerch's Unhappy Consciousness is his fatal ambivalence, his existence as a "Mittelding," a con-dition scenically portrayed throughout the uncanny scene in the mysterious village: Lerch rides explicitly through the *middle* of this town; the bloody battle between two rats, themselves representative of Lerch's self-destruc-tive dualistic subjectivity, takes place before his eyes in the *middle* of the street; and he sees a "dirty white bitch"—but another embodiment of Lerch himself—try to bury the bone that distinguishes her from the pack of the mangy dogs in which she runs in the *middle* of the street (*Tale*, 44; 326–27). This insistent association of Lerch with the ambivalent "in-between thing" he perceives in the reflection in Vuic's mirror culminates after his execution at the hands of Baron Rofrano when he falls *between* the two horses, the bay of "Wachtmeister" Lerch and the iron-gray captured in his triumph over the youthful enemy rebel (*Tale*, 48; *331*). The victory that brings this horse as booty appears to be the fulfillment of Lerch's persistent and enticing fantasy of conquest: he encounters the sought-after enemy, slays him, and makes off with a splendid horse as his reward. But even this triumph is an expres-sion of Lerch's ambivalence. When he fulfills his military duty by slaying this officer, he appeases his authoritarian superiors—both Captain Rofrano and his own superego—by symbolically slaughtering his own youthful re-belliousness. However, he simultaneously counters this act of compliance when he takes possession of the slain officer's horse and stubbornly refuses to relinquish it. This action bespeaks Lerch's rebellious desire to supplant the enemy officer, to take over his revolutionary function as he takes charge of his horse. Thus Lerch's victory over this enemy once again signals both the moment of his own political (self-)repression and the return of this re-pressed rebellion in the form of identification with the conquered enemy in his role as (self-)liberator.

Lerch's inability to choose between the alternatives of subordination or rebellion drives the conflict characteristic of bourgeois subjectivity to the extreme of a debilitating equivocation. This self-negating equivocation ulti-mately brings on the death of Lerch as bourgeois subject. In the moment immediately prior to his execution by the superior officer whose authority he stubbornly if only passively resists, Lerch is still struggling to suppress the "bestial anger" against his (self-)oppressor and uphold the facade of the submissive subordinate.

While Anton Lerch's steady, unflinching gaze, flashing now and then an oppressed, doglike look, seemed to express a kind of servile trust born of many years of service, his mind . . . was flooded with visions of an *alien ease*, and *from depths in him unknown to himself* there rose a bestial anger against the man before him [Captain Rofrano] who was taking away his horse, a dreadful rage . . . such as only can arise, in some *mysterious* fashion, through years of *close companionship*. (*Tale*, 47–48; *330–31*; emphasis added)

Lerch can neither capitulate by freeing the captured horse, as his superior officer has ordered him to do, nor act in accordance with his insolent anger: his internal struggle expresses itself in the constantly subdued "flashing" of this repressed bestiality across his forcefully composed face. The "rage" that "mysteriously" wells up in Lerch is directed not (only) against Captain Rofrano, but also against the "Wachtmeister" himself, the authoritarian egocritique with which Sergeant Lerch is only too familiar on the basis of their "years of close companionship." Lerch's psychic self-repression, moreover, has its sociopolitical correlative in the military actions of Baron Rofrano: since, as his name indicates, Rofrano is himself Italian, his campaign against his fellow Italians' struggle for political liberation must be seen as an overt act of brutal political (self-)repression. It is through the internalization of this sociopolitical conflict that Lerch's subjectivity is constituted as a self-destructive system of ambivalent, counterpositional, and mutually inimical impulses. As bourgeois subject, Lerch makes this sociopolitical problematic *heimlich*: he privatizes and interiorizes it by integrating it into his own psychic constitution, and he conceals it or makes it secret by disguising its seditious sociopolitical character.

Confirming once more the metonymic, intratextual network that weaves the structural fabric of this text, Lerch's concluding meditations reiterate a final time impressions formulated in his afternoon fantasy. The feeling of "alien ease" ("fremdartige Behaglichkeit") that he senses just before he is slain recalls the "atmosphere of comfort [*Behaglichkeit*] and pleasant brutality with no officer to give him orders" first evoked by the scene at Vuic's house (*Tale*, 42; *325*). The oxymoronic phrase "alien ease" drives home the semantic instability of this vision of "homeyness," linking it with the semantic ambivalence of the word *heimlich*. Lerch's desire for a "homeyness" free of the submissive service to an oppressive-repressive, external-internal Other must remain *heimlich*; when it flickers "now and then" back to consciousness as the irrepressible return of the repressed, it is immediately choked back into the depths of his unconscious by a renewed and more violent act of repression. Despite the fact that in the encounter with Vuic he had recognized the power of "the word, once spoken" (*Tale*, 42; *324*), Lerch now allows himself to be executed in a "moment of mute insubordination" (*Tale*, 48; *331*).

With Lerch's execution, the rebellion brewing in the collective political unconscious of Rofrano's squadron is squelched, and the mechanisms of repression—both sociopolitical and psychic—come away victorious. The same holds true for the historical events that form the backdrop of Hofmannsthal's story: the political upheavals of the 1848 bourgeois revolutions failed, except on the surface, to realize the emancipatory ideals under whose banner these struggles took place. If we take Lerch's ambivalent struggle as representative of the sentiments of the revolutionaries of 1848, then *A Tale of the Cavalry* suggests that the failure of this bourgeois-liberal revolution must be attributed to divided commitments on the part of the would-be rebels themselves: their attempts to become revolutionary masters in their own homes were frustrated from within, by their own compelling need to master this rebellious impulse by submitting it to an authoritarian self-critique. Divided within and against themselves, the attempts of these bourgeois revolutionaries to attain (self-)emancipation were doomed to failure from the very outset. This observation, moreover, is valid mutatis mutandis for Hofmannsthal, for his contemporary Sigmund Freud, and for the crumbling institution of bourgeois liberalism as paradigmatically manifest in the Austria of 1898. In the case of Hofmannsthal, who after the turn of the century developed into a conservative ideologue of bourgeois culture, one could speculate that *A Tale of the Cavalry* represents the artistic product in which he cathartically worked through and successfully jettisoned his own youthful resistance to the precepts and practices of bourgeois liberalism.[48] Read in this manner, the death of Hofmannsthal's protagonist Anton Lerch signals the final sellout of bourgeois self-critique, the ultimate capitulation and self-subjugation of the bourgeois subject to its own alienating and repressive ideology.

In Schiller's Karl Moor we witnessed how this self-critical resistance to the bourgeois epistemic formation attempts to salvage its utopian potential by going underground, withdrawing entirely from the domain of bourgeois sociopolitical and economic praxis; a century later this self-repressed bourgeois resistance-movement reappears, a kind of ghost who, as the *unheimlich* return of the repressed, haunts Hofmannsthal's Anton Lerch. His execution, which results from "mute insubordination," projects the brutal extermination of this utopian impulse as the triumph of acquiescence and conformity over critical resistance, thus spelling the end of bourgeois Unhappy Consciousness as a dialectically structured subjectivity. The rescue operation designed to protect the ideality of the bourgeois subject from the reification and violence wrought by its own social practices hence only stalls its ultimate demise as critically self-reflective consciousness. What comes after Anton Lerch can no longer be called a "subject" in this dynamic sense, since it represents the flattening of the dialectic between rebellion and capitulation into the monotony of submission to the sociopolitical, socioeconomic regime of bourgeois practice. In this sense, Hofmannsthal's narrative anticipates by more than fifty years the eradication of the subject that is philosophically codified in Foucault's declaration of the end of (bourgeois) man and the general banishment of the subject by post-structuralist theory as an ideological chimera.

What defines Hofmannsthal's *A Tale of the Cavalry* as an especially remarkable text is not simply the way in which it prefigures the historical demise of the bourgeois subject; rather, its uniqueness is grounded in its capacity as narrative to recreate and transmit in its own aesthetic structure the self-repressive struggle that culminates in the collapse of Unhappy Consciousness. If the eviscerating ambivalence of Anton Lerch's subjective (un)consciousness operates along lines of the dynamic tensions circumscribed by the terms *heimlich* and *unheimlich*, then this dynamic forms the mechanism that structures the textuality of *A Tale of the Cavalry* itself. This text embodies a self-equivocating signifying practice in which certain (political) significations are censored and repressed, made *heimlich*, in the very moment they uncannily resurge from the political unconscious. The text itself thus aesthetically replicates the repression it portrays—indeed, it portrays this repression only insofar as it mimics it in its own textual composition and transfers its mechanics into the sphere of reader reception. The readers of Hofmannsthal's narrative are subjected by the text itself to the same repression of political opposition to which its protagonist himself succumbs. This hermeneutrick, as I have called it, functions by encouraging us to interpret the text symbolically, displacing public, sociopolitical signifieds by reading them as signifiers for private, intrapsychic complexes. To evade this hermeneutical ruse one must pursue a counterhermeneutics which, instead of interpreting on the basis of substitutional displacement as Freud did in the interpretation of his Revolutionary Dream, traces the text's internal network of intratextual allusions and metonymic associations. Viewed from this perspective, the revolutionary narrative strategy of Hofmannsthal's text is revealed to be the product of a pervasive repression of resistant political desires. The elimination of this oppositional impulse paves the way for the (d)evolution of the bourgeois subject into the submissive agent of bourgeois hegemony. To the extent that this text, as narrative of the psyche, aesthetically invokes and receptively transmits this act of (self-)repression, it furthers and underwrites this process. In this sense the characteristically High Modernist literary-aesthetic structure it embodies reflects an eradication of critical resistance that serves the ends of bourgeois political reaction.

The literary-aesthetic procedure modeled in *A Tale of the Cavalry* is generally associated with the mature writings of Franz Kafka, in which the same technique is also paradigmatically manifest. Although it has often been assumed that Kafka perfected the psychic narrative in *The Judgment* (1912),[49] we have seen that this technique attained fruition over a decade earlier in Hofmannsthal's short story. To make this assertion is not to detract from the genius of Kafka's literary accomplishments, but only to assert a particular historical consonance that links Hofmannsthal and Kafka as two contemporaneous bourgeois authors who experienced from within the collapse of bourgeois liberalism in Austria. In the next chapter we will work out the points of contact between *A Tale of the Cavalry* and Kafka's *The Judgment*, stressing the overlap between literary technique and the aesthetic repression of bourgeois self-critique. If Hofmannsthal's narrative projects the demise of the bourgeois subject as self-reflective consciousness, Kafka's story both confirms this diagnosis and provides an insightful analysis of the aporias of the divided subject at this historical station.

CHAPTER SEVEN

Infinite Commerce

The Aporia of Bourgeois Subjectivity
in Kafka's 'The Judgment'

> The irrationality of the rational system comes to light in the psychology of the ensnared subject.   —Theodor W. Adorno
>
> We are no longer a part of the drama of alienation; we live in the ecstasy of communication.   —Jean Baudrillard

Kafka's Bourgeois Writing Table: Literature Between
Autonomy and Social (Self-)Disciplining

More than any other German modernist writer, Franz Kafka represents the aporetic instantiation of a schizoid bourgeois subjectivity torn between the fantasies of the autonomous individual and the alienating structures of the bourgeois world. Kafka himself diagnosed his self-division in terms of the conflict between his wholly personal and obsessively private literary pursuits and the mercilessly insistent demands of his public existence, concretized especially in his hated career as juristic bureaucrat in a state-run insurance agency. To his intermittent fiancée Felice Bauer, he remarked that he was destined to be "pulverized" and "torn apart" by the antagonism between the office, the symbol of conformity to bourgeois life, and writing, the ultimate expression of creative autonomy (*Letters to Felice*, 407, 412–13; 275, 279). As I have shown in the chapters on Lessing and Schiller, the ideological precepts of institutionalized bourgeois literature, which valorize artistic "genius" and the absolute autonomy of the literary work, evolve, on the one hand, as a form of opposition against the reduction of bourgeois thought to purposive rationality, and, on the other, as a protest against the submission of the literary work to the (d)evaluative commercial mechanisms of the bourgeois marketplace. This dialectical tension between commodification and autonomization reaches its zenith in Kafka's literary conceptions, where the mystery of literary creation is constantly played off against the

real economic and social demands of bourgeois socioeconomic and discursive practice. In his reflections on the act of writing, Kafka gives in to that
tendency, so common among bourgeois artists, to mystify and idealize the
act of creation. In a remark from one of his notebooks, for example, he valorizes writing as "a form of prayer" (*Hochzeit*, 348; *312*); and in a letter to Max
Brod from 1922, he describes writing as a "reward for serving the devil," as
a descent down "to the dark powers" of creativity (*Letters*, 384; *333*). These
appeals to the divine or demonic power of creativity find their dialectical opposite in Kafka's pervasive reluctance to publish his works: subjecting his individualistic literary texts to the laws of circulation in the bourgeois public
sphere threatens both to corrupt their aesthetic purity and to undercut the
individuality of the writer who produces in the isolation of a monadically
private world. Given this, it comes as no surprise that Kafka continually insisted that the moment of creative production was the only one that was of
any significance to him as writer. Kafka's well-known request to Max Brod,
his friend and literary executor, that he destroy all of Kafka's extant manuscripts upon his death is but the most extreme manifestation of this absolute
privatization of the literary creation.

Kafka's perceived antagonism between the requirements of bourgeois existence and the absolute solitude he viewed as the necessary precondition
for literary creativity is further concretized in the ambivalence and perverse
indecision with which he approached the planned marriage to Felice Bauer.
For Kafka, marriage represented the ultimate submersion of the individual
in the stream of bourgeois life; marriage was, as he described it, "the most
social of acts" (*Letters to Felice*, 598; *423*), and as social act it by definition came
into fundamental conflict with the absolute isolation he required for his writing. In the letter to Felice's father in which he asks for his daughter's hand
in marriage, Kafka sabotages his own petition by including an excoriating
self-critique that stresses his own unsuitability for a life of bourgeois responsibility. This self-condemnation culminates in the assertion: "I am nothing but literature and can be nothing but literature" (*Diaries*, 318; *229*). In
Kafka's self-understanding, literature, the scriptive emancipation of what he
called "the incredible world inside my head" (*Diaries*, 306; *221*), is absolutely
inimical to immersion in the socialized bourgeois life-world. In a letter to
Felice written in 1913, he attempts to elucidate the diametrical opposition
between writing and all forms of social intercourse by describing his ideal
writing situation as that of a cellar-dweller, completely isolated from empirical events. "I have often thought that the best mode of life for me would
be to sit in the innermost room of a spacious locked cellar with my writing
things and a lamp" (*Letters to Felice*, 250; *156*), he asserts, citing such condi-

tions as the prerequisite for true creativity. And a few months later he further restricts these conditions, claiming that the seclusion his writing demands is not that of "a hermit . . . , but like the dead. Writing in this sense," he continues, "is a sleep deeper than that of death" (*Letters to Felice*, 412; 279).

Despite these programmatic assertions, Kafka's literary texts do not betray that absolute autonomy from social discourse and intercourse about which he fantasized. Indeed, these dreams of literary independence represent utopian counterimages that project his longed-for escape from a debilitating participation in the bourgeois world. Kafka's literature arises out of the struggle between this vision of absolute autonomy and the frightful but often wistfully coveted dependence on the patterns of a bourgeois existence. Kafka's writing comes into being precisely at this fault-line in his own subjectivity: it is the rubble of a bourgeois subject "pulverized," to use Kafka's own word, by the friction between the private and the public, between autonomy from and submission to bourgeois life praxis.

One of Kafka's earliest extant letters, sent to his friend Oskar Pollak in August of 1902, describes the act of writing as a process structured by a dialectic between creative abandon and its spontaneous physical disciplining. With characteristic ironic humor, Kafka portrays this disciplining mechanism as a constituent part of the "bourgeois writing table" at which he sits and writes.

I sat at my fine writing table. You don't know it. How could you? You see, it's a writing table disposed to bourgeois respectability that is intended to educate. Where the writer's knees usually are, it has two horrible wooden spikes. And now pay attention. If you sit down quietly, cautiously at it, and write something with bourgeois respectability, then all's well. But look out if you become excited, if your body quivers ever so slightly, for then you inescapably feel the spikes in your knees, and how that hurts. I could show you the black-and-blue marks. And what that means to say is simply: "Don't write anything exciting and don't let your body quiver while you write." (*Letters*, 11; 3)

This passage provides us with some insights into Kafka's own view of his socialization as bourgeois writer, insights that are otherwise obscured by the mystifying deliberations about writing he formulated later in his life. Especially significant is Kafka's identification of the disciplinary function of his "writing table" with the educational procedures of bourgeois society, for this is the first expression of a problematic he confronts in various forms throughout his life. All creative inspiration, as the mark of social impropriety, is exorcized from the "respectable" bourgeois literary product by means of physical coercion directed against the writing subject. Kafka projects the writer as someone who succumbs to the educational demands of bourgeois

society by internalizing its disciplinary strategies: even in the ostensibly autonomous, private sphere where he sits at his "bourgeois writing table," the
author is subjected to mechanisms of bourgeois (self-)mastery. On the other
hand, the author experiences within himself a creative energy that excites
him, egging him on to transgress the bounds of bourgeois respectability.
Thus for Kafka, the circumstances of the bourgeois writer are defined by a
principal antagonism between inspired creativity and its violent (self-)disci-
plining.

In this chapter I will investigate the operation of this dialectic in the short
story *The Judgment* (1912), the text that marks Kafka's breakthrough to his
mature literary style. In this text the dialectic of creativity and its disciplining
manifests itself in the suppression of certain rebellious sociopolitical fantasies
that helped shape the initial conception of this story. This dialectic is inscribed, moreover, into the fictional world of *The Judgment*, which, in the juxtaposition of its protagonist Georg Bendemann and his alter ego, the mysterious "friend" in Russia, depicts the dilemma of the bourgeois subject in
terms of an aporetic choice between total assimilation of the rationalizing,
reifying structures of bourgeois socioeconomic and discursive practice, or
uncompromising withdrawal from bourgeois social and commercial circulation into the impotent isolationism of nonpraxis. In this configuration, self-
critique of the bourgeois epistemic formation—even in the paradoxical form
of performative contradiction as practiced by Büchner—is no longer possible: critical subjectivity collapses either into the authority-oriented personality or escapes into free-floating, disseminal, private intellectualism.

One peculiarity of Kafka's *The Judgment* is that, like Hofmannsthal's *A Tale
of the Cavalry*, this text reproduces the aporetic choice of its protagonist on
the level of literary reception, as well. As even the most cursory glance at
the effective history of *The Judgment* indicates, this text channels the hermeneutical energy of its readers into two primary yet antithetical directions.[1]
Biographical positivism, armed with the insights of Freudian psychoanalytic
theory, comprises one major interpretive tack scholars have pursued.[2]
Grounding the fictional world in biographical facts culled from Kafka's life
documents, this interpretive current privatizes Kafka's narrative, reading
it—much in the manner that Freud read his Revolutionary Dream—as a psychotext that can be reduced to significations attached to conflicts in the bourgeois family. Such interpretations merely replicate the ideological self-mys-
tification of autonomous and private creativity to which Kafka himself succumbed, projecting problems with profound sociopolitical implications as
the productive crisis of a mysteriously tortured, if infinitely creative, individual. This biographical tendency has largely conditioned Kafka criticism,

in which—to apply the words with which Mikhail Bakhtin criticizes the biographical direction of Rabelais scholarship—"a 'faulty' biographism prevails, in which social and political events lose their direct meaning and sharp implications, are minimized, blunted, and become mere facts in the author's own life story. They remain at the level of everyday trivialities."[3] Where positivistically oriented psychobiographical interpretations of *The Judgment* dissolve the signifying structures of the text into narrow biographical reference, the second predominant interpretive direction takes an opposite approach, insisting on the multivalent textual economy of Kafka's narrative.[4] Such critics tend to view this text as a self-reproducing, labyrinthine set of semiotic operations that stands radically outside the sociological and ideological domains. But such valorizations of *The Judgment* as a paradigmatic (post)modernist text simply recast the doctrine of aesthetic autonomy into the discourse of modern semiotics, and they thereby perpetuate that ideological mystification of the creative process that Kafka himself perpetrated.

Kafka's championing of the creative process as an irrational, transintentional act is nowhere more clearly in evidence than in his reflections on the composition of *The Judgment*. He firmly believed that with the creation of this narrative he achieved a creative breakthrough, and the intense concentration and absorption that produced this text became for him the acid test of successful writing. In an often cited diary entry from September 23, 1912, written right after he finished composing *The Judgment*, Kafka described with overweening enthusiasm the immediacy and spontaneity with which this story was composed in one tremendous creative outpouring.

This story, "The Judgment," I wrote at one sitting during the night of the 22nd-23rd, from ten o'clock at night to six o'clock in the morning. . . . The terrible effort and joy about how the story developed before me, as if I were advancing through water. . . . How everything can be said, how for everything, for the strangest fancies, there waits a great fire in which they perish and rise up again. *Only in this way* can one write, only with such coherence, with such a complete opening of the body and the soul. (*Diaries*, 293–94; *212–13*)

The metaphor of the total "opening" of body and soul encapsulates the modernist theory of spontaneous creativity, familiar from the aesthetic programs of artists from the Romantics through the symbolists up to John Cage's practice of "automatic" creation. This theory champions a form of artistic production in which all rational constraints are bracketed so that the unconscious can speak in a clear and undistorted voice. Kafka's Austrian contemporary Sigmund Freud, drawing on remarks by Friedrich Schiller, defended just such a view of unconscious creativity in *The Interpretation of*

Dreams, employing it as a strategic means for justifying his methodological principle of free association as an analytical process capable of rendering "the 'unintentional' ideas to 'intentional' ones." According to Freud this procedure raises unconscious ideas to the level of consciousness without their being subjected to the distortive repression they otherwise suffer as they pass from the unconscious into the conscious mind. Following Schiller, Freud designates this process in terms of reason "relaxing its watch upon the gates."[5] Reformulated into the terminology Freud would later develop, this thesis defines creativity as those moments in which the superego, the psychic censor that stands between the drives of the unconscious and the ego's consciousness, relaxes or shuts down its censorship mechanisms and allows unconscious images to enter the conscious mind in a relatively pure and unaltered form.

The general coherence between Kafka's description of the spontaneous "opening of body and soul" that produced *The Judgment* and modernist theories of the aesthetic process, on the one hand, and Freud's conception of artistic creativity, on the other, has lent support to the position that Kafka's breakthrough to his own peculiar form of literature emerges when he first learns to let down his rational guard, allowing his inherent creativity to flow and thereby gaining direct access to the images that populate his unconscious.[6] The connection to Freud's theory of creativity is lent credibility, moreover, by Kafka's own remarks that "thoughts about Freud" crossed his mind while composing this story (*Diaries*, 294; 213). Indeed, this conception of Kafka's creative process has become so ingrained in Kafka scholarship that to call it into question is to challenge a primordial law of Kafka scholarship. Be that as it may, my hypothesis is that Kafka's literary breakthrough is not so much predicated on an "opening" to his unconscious as it is on the mechanism of repression that is triggered once this opening occurs. My point will be that *The Judgment* does not comprise an uncensored text that involuntarily welled up in and flowed out of Kafka's unconscious in that September night, but rather that it is the product of a struggle between these unconscious impulses—impulses that have a decidedly sociopolitical character—and their repressive disciplining by the censoring superego.

Evidence in support of this hypothesis can be found in the very same diary entry in which Kafka applies the metaphor of the "opening" to describe the creation of *The Judgment*; for in this passage he also employs strikingly different images to portray this creative process. He writes, for example, of the "terrible effort" this writing cost him, comparing it with the struggle of "advancing through water," thereby hinting that this exertion derives from the attempt to move against the floodwaters of the unconscious. That the creative process is more one of dialectical conflict than of an unhindered flow of ideas is confirmed when Kafka shifts the metaphorical vehicle from the basic element of water to that of fire: the "strangest" ideas, Kafka maintains, perish and are resurrected, are consumed and transfigured, in the conflagration that marks the act of literary creation. If we lend credence to these images, *The Judgment* is not born as a simple emergence, as an "opening" that gives access to the unconscious, but rather as an interactive give-and-take between those "strange ideas" produced by the unconscious and their consuming transformation—that is, their repressive distortion and sublimation. Far from being a simple unconscious release, then, the creative mode Kafka describes is structured as a dialectical sublation in which unanticipated "fancies" are simultaneously canceled yet preserved. In other words, Kafka's ideal of literary creativity must be imagined as a kind of palimpsest in which the spontaneous writing of the unconscious is overwritten and transformed by the writing machine of the repressive agency of censorship, the authoritarian superego.

Now, it is not insignificant that this creative struggle is, in fact, much more akin to the conception of dream production and the functioning of the dream-work that Freud presents in the theoretical section of *The Interpretation of Dreams* than it is to the theory of spontaneous creativity that he upholds in the initial methodological discussion of this same work. This discrepancy in Freud's position derives from the fact that in his methodological discussion he is intent upon defending the paradoxical notion of an intentional (conscious) grasp of unintentional (unconscious) ideas, since this is the only way he can legitimate his own procedure of reflectively interpreting the unconscious images of dreams. Artistic creativity serves him here as a model that demonstrates the viability of this paradox. In the case of Kafka, however, the creative act resembles more the dialectic of unconscious opening and repressive distortion that Freud later describes as characteristic of the dream-work.

In the analyses of Hofmannsthal's *A Tale of the Cavalry* and Freud's Revolutionary Dream, I argued that these narratives make certain revolutionary-political moments essential to their constitution appear marginal or superfluous to an interpretive understanding of the text. On the basis of a hermeneutical counterpractice I exposed how these texts, unable wholly to eradicate these sociopolitical moments without suspending their own condition of possibility, seek at least to render them *heimlich*, both secret and private. Essential to the character of these narratives, however, is the fact that their political unconscious proves irrepressible, and their uncanny quality derives from the *unheimlich* return of this repressed sociopolitical message. The same mechanism is operative in Kafka's *The Judgment*, a text which, like Hofmannsthal's *Tale of the Cavalry*, follows the paradigm of what I have called a psychic narrative. Reporting to Felice Bauer in a letter from June 1913 about his aims when he first conceived *The Judgment*, Kafka claims: "When I sat down to write, after a Sunday so miserable I could have screamed . . . , I meant to describe a war; from his window a young man was to see a vast crowd advancing across the bridge, but then the whole thing turned in my hands into something else" (*Letters to Felice*, 394; 265). Kafka's original intention to portray a war—that is, a specifically sociopolitical conflict—somehow gets away from him, turning into "something else" during the process of composition. To be sure, conflict remains the central focus of Kafka's text; but instead of occurring in the sociopolitical domain, it manifests itself as an Oedipal struggle, the battle between father Bendemann and his son, as each vies for supremacy over the other. The sociopolitical struggle Kafka identified as the impulse behind the composition of *The Judgment* is thus reinscribed in the purely psychological realm: like the sociopolitical content of Freud's Revolutionary Dream, it is displaced into the private sphere of the bourgeois family. This displacement, however, fails wholly to eradicate the sociopolitical moment from Kafka's text: it returns, with the uncanny insistence of the repressed, as the association of Georg's friend in St. Petersburg with the revolutionary events in Russia. All the semantic tensions Freud associated with the terms *heimlich* and *unheimlich* are mapped onto the relationship between Georg, the son who remains home and becomes a successful businessman, and the friend, a kind of prodigal son who has "run off the rails" in an alien land (*Judgment*, 53; 77). If Georg's offensive against the father represents the sublimation of revolutionary impulses, an interiorization that renders them *heimlich*, both secret and private, then the association of the Petersburg friend with the sociopolitical upheavals in Russia marks the *unheimlich* return of this repressed political unconscious, its deprivatization and desecretization. But the terms *heimlich* and *unheimlich* apply to Georg and his friend, his repressed alter ego, even in their literal meanings: Georg, as the son who remains home, is also *heimlich* in the concrete sense of "homey," whereas the friend, who leaves home to live in an alien environment, is quite literally *unheimlich*, alienated and "unhomey."

Material evidence of the mechanism that represses the sociopolitical impetus behind *The Judgment* can be gleaned from a study of the manuscript. Characteristic of Kafka's compositional style is that his texts are put down on paper in the original act of writing with such precision that deletions or major revisions are a rare occurrence, and this is no less true of *The Judgment*. But it is precisely the cleanness of his manuscripts that makes deletions stand out, and in this case there is an especially noteworthy instance of a sentence expunged in the original process of composition. This occurs in the part of the text describing the plight of Georg's friend in Russia, who is depicted standing among the ruins of his ransacked business. "Lost in the vastness of Russia he [Georg] saw him [the friend]. At the door of his empty, plundered warehouse he saw him. Among the wreckage of his showcases, the slashed remnants of his wares, the falling gas brackets, he was just barely still standing. {A trampling tumultuous mob of people marched past in waves}" (*Judgment*, 64; *85*). In the manuscript, Kafka crossed out the final sentence of this passage, which I have enclosed in braces.[7] This sentence is significant insofar as it suggests that the destruction of the friend's warehouse results from the rampages of a revolutionary mob. Moreover, this marching mob recapitulates precisely that image that Kafka identified in the aforementioned letter to Felice as the original conception for the entire story. This act of erasure, then, is one concrete manifestation of the moment of repression in the dialectic of inspiration and self-disciplining that informs Kafka's creativity. When Kafka deletes this sentence, he eliminates the sociopolitical cause underlying the demolition of the friend's commercial enterprise, with the result that the destruction of his "showcases" and "wares" is mystified, made to appear either as an inexplicable act of God, or as the result of his personal failure.

Although the sociopolitical impetus behind *The Judgment* is subjected to severe acts of repression, it is nevertheless not entirely banished. This repressed political content finds its way back into the text when Georg recounts for his father the stories about the revolutionary events in Russia that the friend related on his last visit home. "He [the friend] told us on that occasion the most incredible stories of the Russian Revolution. For instance, when he was on a business trip to Kiev how during a riot he saw a priest on a balcony who cut a broad cross in blood on the palm of his hand, then held up this hand and appealed to the mob" (*Judgment*, 62; *83*). It is no coincidence that throughout the receptive history of *The Judgment* this passage has proven to be one of the most problematic and inscrutable of the entire text.[8] Although most interpreters choose simply to ignore it, those who confront the hermeneutical provocation presented by this passage tend to understand it symbolically, viewing in the priest's actions either an act of religious martyrdom that prefigures Georg's sacrificial suicide at the conclusion of the story, or identifying him as a symbolic reconstitution of the father-figure. Yet it is likely that this anecdote alludes to an actual historical occurrence, the so-called Bloody Sunday massacre in St. Petersburg, which occurred on January 22, 1905.[9] On this date a crowd of workers, led by the priest Gregory

Gapon, marched to the square in front of the Winter Palace, where they were met by Czarist soldiers, who fired upon them, killing or wounding several hundred. It would come as no surprise if Kafka, who in 1905 was a twenty-two-year-old student who avidly read writings by such Russian anarchists as Kropotkin and Bakunin (see *Diaries*, 323, 466; *233, 333*) and attended meetings of the Czech anarchist circle in Prague,[10] registered in his memory the events of Bloody Sunday. The text itself gives a number of indications, at least, that this passage refers to this concrete historical event. The most obvious of these is that Kafka explicitly mentions the Russian Revolution, of which Bloody Sunday represents a primary event. It is noteworthy, in addition, that Kafka wrote *The Judgment* on what he described as "a Sunday so miserable I could have screamed" (*Letters to Felice*, 394; *265*) and that it is specifically on a Sunday morning that Georg Bendemann's story takes place. The congruity of these temporal references suggests a link between the revolutionary event of Bloody Sunday, the framing narrative of Georg Bendemann's Sunday encounter with his father, and Kafka's own situation on the "miserable Sunday" on which this story was written. Finally, Georg's friend lives in St. Petersburg, the historical site of the Bloody Sunday massacre. To be sure, in Georg's recounting, the event is displaced from Petersburg to Kiev; but this transposition is nothing but one more manifestation of those repressive censorship mechanisms that seek to obscure this allusion to an act of overt sociopolitical rebellion. However, this repressive mechanism is only partially successful, for the mob ("Menge") exhorted by the Priest in this scene is the counterpart of the crowd ("Menschenmenge") that was central to Kafka's initial conception of this story, and it is this very same mob of people ("Volksgetümmel") that appears in the sentence stricken from the passage that describes Georg's vision of his friend standing among the ruins of his warehouse. Like this repressed sentence, the Bloody Sunday scene directly links Georg's friend to the revolutionary masses by making him into a historical witness who later tells the story of their rebellion.

Such concrete historical references are a rarity in Kafka's fiction. But it is precisely the general paucity of such allusions to the historico-empirical world that underscores the significance of this passage for *The Judgment*. In Hofmannsthal's *A Tale of the Cavalry* and Freud's Revolutionary Dream, as we have seen, a similar reference to revolutionary historical events becomes the index of the repressed political unconscious. Their texts attempt to cover over these sociopolitical allusions by diverting hermeneutical attention into a metaphorical axis, seducing interpreters into producing symbolic readings. This is the case for *The Judgment*, as well, and as a result, interpreters of this text have commonly succumbed to a hermeneutrick that is similar to the one we examined in our discussion of *A Tale of the Cavalry*. Like Hofmannsthal's story, Kafka's text distracts hermeneutical energy away from the sociopolitical outcroppings that mark its political unconscious. My counterhermeneutics, which attempts to circumvent this hermeneutical ruse, will begin by reinscribing the psychological and biographical aspects of Kafka's narrative in the sociopolitical sphere. The theoretical horizon of this sociological reinscription is supplied by sociocritical conceptions of the bourgeois family as an institution of socialization and ideological indoctrination. This will permit me to approach the Oedipal conflict in *The Judgment* as a manifest content that has latent sociopolitical underpinnings, namely the authority-orientation imbued in the subject by the disciplinary process of bourgeois socialization.[11] From here I will move to an interpretation of Kafka's narrative, an analysis that, as in the examination of *A Tale of the Cavalry*, will pursue the intratextual links in Kafka's story to turn out the *unheimlich* political unconscious that this psychic narrative attempts to repress.

Kafka's Socialization and the Web of Bourgeois Ideology

Louis Althusser's definition of ideology as "the imaginary relationship of individuals to their real conditions of existence" suggests that ideology represents a kind of fictionalizing elaboration on existing social conditions. To accept this, however, is, according to Althusser, not tantamount to conceiving ideological fictions as mere masks, lacking any substantial relation to the real circumstances they seek to disguise. On the contrary, ideology as Althusser conceives it is structured around a tension between concealment and revelation, an interaction reminiscent of the dialectic of repression and its insistent return that constitutes the structural core of *unheimlich* narratives of the psyche: the very act of representation with which ideology attempts to disguise social reality—to make it *heimlich*—also hints *ex negativo*, as it were, at the fundamental structures of this social reality, thereby simultaneously rendering them *unheimlich*. Althusser calls this dialectical reflex the "illusion/allusion" structure of ideology. "While admitting that [ideological 'world outlooks'] do not correspond to reality, i.e. that they constitute an illusion," he elaborates, "we admit that they do make allusion to reality, and that they need only to be 'interpreted' to discover the reality of the world behind their imaginary representation of that world (ideology = *illusion/allusion*)."[12] Especially significant in Althusser's definition is his insistence on the role of critical interpretation in uncovering the allusions to the real embedded within ideology's illusions. In what follows I will attempt to exploit such a strategy of critical interpretation in my examination of Kafka's life documents, pursuing those allusions that point beyond the private-secret (*heimlich*) concerns of the bourgeois family to their ground in the realm of socioeconomic reality. In the essay "Authority and the Family" (1936), Max Horkheimer sketches the theoretical framework necessary for such a sociological grounding of relations within the bourgeois family. Horkheimer demonstrates that the structures of authority and submission practiced in interactions within the bourgeois family reflect in microcosm the mechanisms of domination operative in bourgeois society as a whole. As the principal educational institution of society, the family is charged with the function of reproducing in the emerging generation those character traits required for the smooth functioning of the socioeconomic machine.[13] The qualities Horkheimer cites as typical of "authority-behavior"—that is, of the "authoritarian" character trained to affirm and subordinate himself/herself to external authority[14]—overlap in many respects with the conspicuous characteristics of Kafka's personality.

Portraying the relationship between the bourgeois family and the institutions of bourgeois society as a whole, Horkheimer remarks that conditions in the family are strategically adapted to circumstances in the sociopolitical life-world. Characteristic of the ideological nature of bourgeois subjectivity, however, is that this interconnection necessarily remains opaque to the authority-oriented bourgeois individual.

Brutal oppression in social life makes for strictness in the exercise of educational authority, and restrictions on power and domination in public life are reflected in a more tolerable discipline within the home. Yet the bourgeois child of recent centuries regarded his socially conditioned dependence on his father as the consequence of a religious or natural state of affairs. The experience that paternal power was not underived occurred to him usually only in case of extreme conflict.[15]

Horkheimer mentions a series of points that I want to take up in the context of Kafka's social and familial existence: the parallel between sociopolitical repression and bourgeois familial education, as well as its converse, the analog between sociopolitical or socioeconomic impotence and surrender to parental authority; the tendency of the bourgeois child to "metaphysicalize," so to speak, his/her dependence on the patriarch by viewing it in terms of religious or natural laws; and the ideologically conditioned incapacity of the authority-oriented individual to strip the veil from power relationships in the family and perceive behind them the operation of larger sociopolitical mechanisms.

Corroborating Horkheimer's assertion that the ideological function of

the bourgeois family is to (re-)create a specific form of human consciousness, Habermas has maintained that the mode of subjectivity specific to the
bourgeois period has its "home, literally, in the sphere of the patriarchal con-
jugal family."[16] The hypostatization of the bourgeois family as a private
realm, independent of those socioeconomic and political relations at work
in society at large, Habermas maintains, is essential to its very constitution.
"Although there may have been a desire to perceive the sphere of the family
circle as independent, as cut off from all connection with society, as the domain of pure humanity, it was, of course, dependent on the sphere of labor
and of commodity exchange."[17] The bourgeois conception of the patriarchal
family and its component individuals as the exponents of "pure humanity"
forms an ideological reflex whose purpose is the concealment of socioeconomic dependencies; it obscures, in other words, what we might call the
synechdochic relationship between patriarchal family and the bourgeois socioeconomic domain. Not only is the family an integral part of the socioeconomic world, but it mirrors in its own matrix of personal interactions the
relationships of domination and submission constitutive of society at large.
It is specific to the character of a subjectivity trained to display authority-behavior that it is ideologically myopic and thus unable to perceive the synechdochic connection between, for example, submission to the authority of the
father and subservience to sociopolitical domination. Kafka's often vehement diatribes directed against the father who, as bourgeois patriarch, mu-
tilated his son's personality by subjecting him to especially harsh educational
measures, must be viewed in the context of these theoretical recognitions.[18]

Kafka's "Letter to His Father" (1919) is central to an understanding of his
authority-oriented character. Scholars have commonly noted, of course, that
Kafka's portrayal of the relationship between himself and his father sheds
considerable light on the interactions between Georg and father Bendemann
in *The Judgment*. For the most part, however, "Letter to His Father" has been
narrowly construed as psychological testimony that confirms the Oedipal
strife between Franz and his powerful father, Hermann. In fact, however,
this letter is a significant sociohistorical document insofar as it records in
painful detail the socialization mechanisms at work in a representative bourgeois family at the turn of the century. Similarly, while *The Judgment* has often been counted among the many texts of German Expressionism in which
the revolt of sons against the father plays a prominent role,[19] the connection
between such filial rebellion and the tyranny of sociopolitical institutions
has often been overlooked. Yet Kafka's "Letter to His Father" resembles in
many respects the critique of the often violent discipline and arbitrary
tyranny endemic to German educational institutions frequently voiced in

the literature of this period.[20] As an indictment of those bourgeois educational methods, which Kafka held responsible for the destruction of his authentic personality, "Letter to His Father" is not a unique document among
his writings. Indeed, it represents but one major offensive in a series of critical attacks Kafka directed against his upbringing at home and in school.
Scattered among his letters, diaries, and notebooks from throughout his mature life, these texts constitute a massive critique of a brand of social disciplining whose purpose, as Kafka saw it, was the eradication of all his unique
and individual traits. These materials document Kafka's recognition that in
bourgeois society the family and the school function, as Althusser claims,
as the primary institutional apparatuses charged with the reproduction of
acceptable socioeconomic subjects: they coerce the bourgeois individual into
submitting to the socioeconomic order of production, and they train it to
manipulate the rules of the dominant ideology, thereby enabling the individual to become an agent of societal repression.[21] Kafka's attempts to extricate himself from this process of ideological (self-)disciplining involved
him in an internal conflict that left indelible scars.

Kafka's first denunciation of the process of ideological indoctrination inflicted upon him by his bourgeois education is expressed in a series of
sketches recorded in his diary in 1910.

> When I think about it, I must say that my education has done me great harm in
> some respects. I was not, as a matter of fact, educated in any out-of-the-way place,
> in a ruin, say, in the mountains—something against which in fact I could not have
> brought myself to say a word of reproach. In spite of the risk of all my former teach-
> ers not understanding this, I should prefer most of all to have been such a little
> dweller in the ruins . . . ; even though I might have been weak at first under the
> pressure of my good qualities, which would have grown tall in me with the might
> of weeds [Unkraut]. (Diaries, 14; 15)

Although this reproach lacks specificity, its critical thrust is focused into a
group of poignant metaphors. The positively charged image of the ruin-
dweller who develops in total isolation from society suggests that Kafka's
critique is directed at the general socialization processes that occur in civilization at large, rather than any particular institutions such as school or family. Such generalizing indictments of the civilizing process, of course, are
commonplaces in the cultural criticism of the fin de siècle, evident, for example, in the writings of Richard Wagner, Friedrich Nietzsche, and Oswald
Spengler and culminating some years later in Freud's *Civilization and Its Discontents* (1930). It is probably no coincidence that Kafka's image of the ruin-
dweller anticipates his later conception of the writer as a "cellar-dweller"

who is totally insulated from any contact with society, and this filiation suggests that for Kafka literary creation is not so much an asocial as an antisocial activity, a pursuit explicitly formulated as a counter to the socializing mechanisms of bourgeois society.

In Kafka's 1910 diary sketch the protest against the process of culturation is also registered in the valorization of the weed as a symbol of those elements of the personality that manage to escape cultivation. Kafka's identification of the "good qualities" of the individual with the uncultivated plant—the "Unkraut"—focuses the conflict between nature and culture into the negating prefix "un." This prefix marks the civilized world's condemnation of everything that serves no useful function in its structured intercourse. Now, it is significant that Kafka frequently associates the prefix "un" with the antisocial protagonists of his stories. In *The Metamorphosis* (1913), Gregor Samsa must undergo a metamorphosis into an "*ungeheueren Ungeziefer*," a "horrible bug" (*Erzählungen*, 71, emphasis added; *CS*, 89) to flee from his hectic life as a traveling salesman; and Georg's renegade friend in *The Judgment* is described as "*un*satisfied and *un*able to do anything about his *un*satisfaction" ("*un*zufrieden und *un*fähig, diese *Un*zufriedenheit jemals zu beseitigen") (*Judgment*, 56–57; 79; emphasis added).[22] In both these instances the negative prefix represents a censorious judgment passed on the eccentric individual from the perspective of the civilized world. Kafka's ruin-dweller, who chooses existential uncertainty over the stability of the social system, thus is a forerunner of Georg Bendemann's alienated childhood friend, who leaves home and family and subjects himself to the socioeconomic "*un*certainty" ("*Un*sicherheit") (*Judgment*, 55; 78; emphasis added) of political conditions in Russia. Georg, who remains at home and assumes the family business, submits voluntarily to the civilizing process and becomes its most representative advocate. It is only when seen through his ideologically entangled perspective, which by means of figural narrative techniques we as readers share throughout most of *The Judgment*, that the utopian escape of the friend appears as a form of *un*achievement.

The centrality of this problematic for Kafka in these early years is underscored by the fact that he returns to and revises this germinal sketch about the ruin-dweller no less than five times (see *Diaries*, 14–17, 685–91; 15–21). As these drafts develop, they also become more specific, naming parents, teachers, relatives, and others as the practitioners of an educational terror whose aim is to enforce upon the individual absolute conformity to specified societal norms. When he accuses these educators of trying to "make another person out of me" and thus of "having spoiled a good, beautiful part [of me]" (*Diaries*, 687; 17–18), Kafka attacks the eradication of all individual

differences in the name of total adaptation to the authority-behavior required by the social system. As we will see, in the figure of Georg Bendemann, Kafka plays out in his literary imagination the fate of the ideologically indoctrinated subject who submits and adapts absolutely to the bourgeois status quo.

In a longer reflection found among his posthumous papers and presumably written in 1916, Kafka lashed out once more against his upbringing, specifically identifying home and school as the sites in which all individuality is
broken as the subject is coercively sub-jected to institutionalized standards
and norms.

> Every human being is peculiar, and by virtue of his peculiarity, called to play his
> part in the world. . . . So far as my experience went, both in school and at home
> the aim was to erase all trace of peculiarity. In this way they [teachers and parents]
> made the work of education easier, but also made life easier for the child, although,
> it is true, he first had to go through the pain caused him by discipline. (*Hochzeit*,
> 227–28; 201)

Kafka explicitly links the socialization process of educational institutions
with his upbringing in the family, portraying both as processes of violent
disciplining aimed at a kind of sociological *Gleichschaltung*, the compulsory
elimination of any traits peculiar to the individual. This critique clearly arises
out of his perception of a contradiction between a bourgeois ideology that
valorizes individuality and a bourgeois practice that is bent on the elimination of all nonconformative "peculiarities." To be sure, Kafka concedes that
such socialization mechanisms are part of a long-term strategic plan whose
results are presumably beneficial both for the individual and for the social
totality: they enhance the adaptability of the child to the challenges of the
natural and social environment, an adaptability that increases his/her
chances of survival and minimizes the possibility of future conflicts.

In "Authority and the Family," Horkheimer notes that the reflex of subordination to social structures is intended to protect the best interests of the
subordinated. Indeed, as Max Weber argues in *The Protestant Ethic and the
Spirit of Capitalism*, such (self-)disciplining constitutes the condition of possibility for economic progress and individual success under the capitalist regime. However, the conformity-enforcing socialization whose aim is the
emancipation of humanity from natural determination slips, through the
momentum of its own internal dialectic, into a more severe and limiting
form of determination: mastery over nature is accomplished only at the
price of self-mastery, the self-inflicted disciplining of the human subject by
other human subjects. "Mastery over nature is linked to the introjected vi-

olence of human beings toward other human beings, to the introjected violence of the subject over its own nature."[23] This reflex marks the dialectic of enlightenment that is situated in the very core of bourgeois socialization practices. The demise of Georg Bendemann in *The Judgment* is intimately bound up with this dialectical reversion of the civilizing process into a disciplinary instrument turned against the cultivated subject. In Georg's fate we witness how successful adaptation to the norms of bourgeois socioeconomic exchange leads inexorably to the self-destruction of bourgeois critical subjectivity.

Kafka's response to the coercion of his family upbringing is a sword that cuts two ways: it instills in him a deep-seated resentment of the family, a resentment Kafka conceives as elemental to his entire existence (see *Hochzeit*, 229; *203*); but it also sets in motion a process whereby the disciplinary measures under which he suffers are systematically introjected, so that external compulsion ultimately gives way to violently repressive self-castigation. This ambivalent double-reflex, which points both to Kafka's empathy with the potentials of his nonsocialized, eccentric selfhood and to his identification with the authority that disciplines and squelches these utopian potentials, reflects the same equivocation Freud associated with the symbol of the doppelgänger. The process of introjection in which the authoritarian superego is constituted always results in the paradox that the subject is divided by conflicting loyalties to the spontaneous drives of the ego, on the one hand, and to the principles of socialization, on the other. Consistent with this is Kafka's assertion in "Letter to His Father" that his divided subjectivity derives from his internalization of the conflict between him and his father, its absorption into his own psychic constitution (see *Letter/Father*, 192; *65*).

Kafka's characteristic self-hatred derives in large part from this introjection of the violent disciplinary mechanisms practiced by his father, Hermann Kafka, the archetypal bourgeois patriarch. The fantasies of self-mutilation and suicide so prevalent both in Kafka's fiction and in his self-reflections in letters and diaries are testaments to the crass internalization of these tyrannical punishment mechanisms. The writing machine in *In the Penal Colony* (1915), which inscribes into the convict's flesh the command he has transgressed, is perhaps the most plastic concretization of this brutal process of introjection. In a sketch from his miscellaneous notebooks, Kafka finds another striking image for the internalization of externally threatened punishment. "It was as though someone were touched, simply by way of warning, with a fagot that was not intended to hurt him, and he then undid the bundle, drew the individual tips of the twigs into himself and began pricking and scratching his inner being according to a plan of his own, while the other person's hand was still calmly holding the other end of the fagot" (*Hochzeit*, 230; *204*). Kafka graphically depicts the development of the super-ego as the internalization of external coercion and authority in the form of brutal self-subjugation. As Kafka's conceit suggests, this introjected disciplinary structure possesses the virtue of relative efficiency: the threat alone of physical violence suffices to convince the authority-oriented individual to take up the weapon wielded by external authority and turn it against himself/herself. Kafka employs a closely related image to depict this process of introjection in one of his aphoristic texts, as well: "The animal wrests the whip from its master and whips itself in order to become master, not knowing that this is only a fantasy caused by a new knot in the master's whiplash" (*Hochzeit*, 42; *37*). This aphorism stresses an aspect of this problematic that is particularly relevant to Georg Bendemann: the relationship, namely, between self-disciplining and the attempt to achieve a position of mastery over others.

In "Authority and the Family" Horkheimer portrays the subsumption of physical violence into the psychic apparatus of the individual subject as a primary reflex of the socialization process.

> Yet the whole psychic apparatus of members of a class society . . . serves in large measure only to interiorize or at least to rationalize and supplement physical coercion. The so-called "social nature" of man, his self-integration into a given order of things, . . . is essentially reducible to the memory of the acts of force by which men were made "sociable" and civilized and which threaten them still if they become too forgetful.[24]

The authority-oriented personality produced by this process is characterized by insecurity, diffidence, guilt, weakness, and indecision—all qualities prominent in Kafka's character. Horkheimer stresses the memorializing function of physical coercion, the exploitation of pain to brand a memory into the disciplined subject. In *On the Genealogy of Morals* (1887), Nietzsche refers to this operation that produces the agency of the conscience as the "making of memory."[25] According to this view, the entire civilizing process is built upon a mnemotechny structured around the infliction of physical suffering. The greater the punishment, the deeper the mnemonic brand penetrates into the psyche of the disciplined subject and the less likely he/she is to forget the lesson it marks.

Kafka documents the procedures of just such a disciplinary mnemotechny in "Letter to His Father," in which he relates one particularly "memorable" event, the so-called pavlatche episode, citing it as a particularly crass example of his father's tyrannical educational practices. Kafka recalls how as a very young child he whined once during the night for a drink of water; father Hermann responded to this plea by dragging his son out of bed, carrying him out onto the balcony ("Pavlatche"), and locking him outside. Kafka recounts how the incommensurability of this senselessly severe punishment to his innocent request came to represent for him the unfathomability of his father's tyrannical authority.

> What was for me a matter of course, that senseless asking for water, and the extraordinary terror of being carried outside were two things that I, my nature being what it was, could never properly connect with each other. Even years afterwards I suffered from the tormenting fancy that the huge man, my father, the ultimate authority, would come almost for no reason at all and take me out of bed in the night and carry me out onto the *pavlatche*, and that meant I was a mere nothing for him. (*Letter/Father*, 167; 17)

Kafka relates this episode "as typical of [Hermann Kafka's] methods of bringing up a child and their effect on me," and he comments further: "I dare say I was quite obedient afterwards at that period, but it did me inner harm" (*Letter/Father*, 167; 17). But this occurrence represents more than simply a case of punishment senselessly out of proportion with the alleged crime. Pleading for water, Franz merely appeals to the father to fulfill his role as family provider; the father, however, responds to this plea not in his guise as loving nourisher, but instead in his alter ego as the overpowering, violent, and inscrutable disciplinarian. As Horkheimer points out, these two roles of the bourgeois paterfamilias inherently dovetail, since the father's superior position within the family derives fundamentally from his function as material provider.[26] Hermann Kafka, as Kafka explains elsewhere in the "Letter," never tired of reminding his children of the self-sacrifices he made in his role as family provider. Franz is thus made to feel guilty about his resistance to the social conformity demanded by the father, who, skillfully exploiting the pathos of the martyr, accuses his son of ingratitude for the "high and handsome" lifestyle made possible by the fact that the father, through his selfless toil, relieves him of any "material worries" (*Letter/Father*, 162; 7). The horror Kafka associates with the pavlatche episode thus derives essentially from the contradiction between these two principal roles of the father: the child witnesses his elder undergo an unpredictable Dr. Jekyll-Mr. Hyde transformation that transmogrifies the loving provider into the ruthless and all-powerful "ultimate authority."

According to Horkheimer, awe of the physical strength of the father is strategically instilled in the bourgeois child to ensure his/her inscription in and submission to this perverse (inter)relationship between paternal love and the child's respect for (paternal) authority. "When the child respects in his father's strength a moral relationship and thus learns to love what his reason recognizes to be a fact, he is experiencing his first training for the bourgeois authority relationship. The father thus has a moral claim upon submission to his strength, but not because he proves himself worthy of respect; rather he proves himself worthy by the very fact that he is stronger."[27] The lesson engraved into and under the child's skin is simply that "might makes right"; the father's physical supremacy appears to the child as a symptom of his authority, whereas in fact it is its condition of possibility. The child thus perceives the power of the father as a god-given or natural fact, and this calls forth a fatalistic acceptance of the mystery of the father's boundless superiority, a preeminence that appears to be underwritten by his empirical stature.[28] When viewed in the context of the pavlatche episode, this theory goes a long way toward explaining Kafka's sense that he was "weighed down" by his father's "mere physical presence" (*Letter/Father*, 168; 19). Moreover, it elucidates Kafka's tendency, on which he remarks in "Letter to His Father," to mystify his elder, inflating him into a larger-than-life figure. "For me you took on the enigmatic quality that all tyrants have whose rights are based on their person and not on reason," he baldly admits (*Letter/Father*, 169; 21). In Kafka's experience of father Hermann and his tyrannical demands, the purportedly rational system of a socializing education discloses its irrational underside: the riddle of the father's power bears witness to the fundamental irrationality underpinning the structures that produce bourgeois love as authority-behavior. Bourgeois (paternal) love thus is exposed as an Eros "that is bureaucratic, judiciary, economic, or political,"[29] and respect for the father always already signals obeisance before the sociopolitical authority he represents.

Kafka's insight into the bourgeois family as an institution that furthers a perverse socialization process designed to reproduce absolutely conformist authority-oriented subjects stayed with him throughout his life. In a series of letters he sent to his sister Elli in 1921 regarding the education of her son, Felix, Kafka insists on the damaging impact of education in the family and advises that Felix be sent away to school (see *Letters*, 339–47; 290–97). In the course of this correspondence he refers to Jonathan Swift's assertion in *Gulliver's Travels* that the education of a child should never be entrusted to the family. Kafka then goes on to define "real education"—as opposed to "family education"—as "the quiet, unselfish, loving development of potentialities of a growing human being or merely the calm toleration of the child's independent development." He then continues:

The essential difference between true education and family education is that the first is a human affair, the second a family affair. In humanity every individual has his place or at least the possibility of being destroyed in his own fashion. In the family, clutched in the tight embrace of the parents, there is room only for certain kinds of people who conform to certain kinds of requirements and moreover have to meet the deadlines dictated by the parents. If they do not conform, they are not expelled . . . but accursed or consumed or both. (*Letters*, 344–45; *295*)

Implicit in Kafka's distinction is the exclusion of the bourgeois family from the domain of humanity, and this represents a significant break with the identification, fundamental to bourgeois ideology, of the family sphere with that essential humanism responsible for nourishing the development of the autonomous subject. However, the very fact that Kafka is able to segregate the authoritarian structures of the family from those that determine society at large indicates that his thought is still caught in an ideological web that mystifies the interconnections between patriarchal and sociopolitical authority. Totally bracketed out of this dichotomy between the "human" and the "familial" are the sociopolitical and economic mechanisms governing human interactions in the bourgeois life-world.

There is at least one point in his correspondence with Elli, however, when Kafka seems to perceive that what he terms the "cage of the grown ups" (*Letters*, 339; *290*) does not exist in a total social vacuum. Referring again to Swift, he remarks: "Besides, Swift knows how to qualify his dictums and holds that it is not absolutely necessary to remove the children of poor people. For the world presses in upon the poor, their working life cannot be kept at a distance from their hut . . . , and so there is no place there for the oppressive, poison-laden, child-consuming air of the nicely furnished family room" (*Letters*, 347; *297*). The oppressive educational measures that Kafka experienced are recognized as determinants bound up with class and economic status and predicated on an isolating circumscription within the private sphere of the bourgeois family. Only in the families of the poor does an intimate and necessary—that is, a not yet ideologically obscured—connection obtain between the operations of the "working life" and the principles that structure interactions in the family. In the bourgeois family such interconnections between the socioeconomic realm and the domain of the patriarchal family remain hidden behind an ideological facade. Conformity to those norms dictated by the patriarch is not (yet) clearly perceived as the price of socioeconomic mastery.

It is questionable whether Kafka's insights into the problematic socialization of the child in the bourgeois family would have attained this clarity

without the guidance of Swift, since with the exception of these remarks to
Elli his thoughts on this issue move stably within the orbit of bourgeois ideology. This is demonstrated most clearly by his general tendency, despite
the recognition that he has been shaped by the socializing strategies of the
family patriarch, ultimately to ascribe his own tortured subjectivity to metaphysical—metaeconomic, metasocial, metaempirical—causes. One example of this tendency to fatalistically "metaphysicalize" the relations of the
patriarchal family as the necessary and unalterable conditions inherent to
life itself can be found in a passage from a letter to Felice written in October 1916.

Any relationship not created by myself, even though it be opposed to parts of my
own nature, is worthless; it hinders my movements, I hate it or come near to hat-
ing it. . . . Yet, I am my parents' progeny, am bound to them and my sisters by
blood. . . . Thus they [his parents] deceive me, and yet I cannot rebel against the
laws of nature without going mad. So again there is hatred, and almost nothing but
hatred. (*Letters to Felice*, 729–30; *525*; cf. also *Diaries*, 514–15; *371–72*)

Kafka mystifies the relationships among the members of the patriarchal family by interpreting the bonds forged by social necessity as "blood" bonds that
tie the child to his/her parents. The socially conditioned dependence of the
child on the authority of the patriarch thus appears to spring from a natural
state of affairs.[30] The moment this bond is perceived as an absolute natural-
moral law, any infraction against it becomes literally unthinkable: it is irrational insofar as it lies beyond the ideologically instituted limits of bourgeois
rationality. Kafka implicitly recognizes that one must jettison the intellec-
tual-moral baggage of the bourgeois order if one is to rise up against its principles; and he indicates, moreover, that he, at least, no matter how much he
might desire such a rupture, remains incapable of taking this final step. This
unfulfilled sociopolitical desire is subsequently rechanneled and sublimated
into the austere demand for a literature whose hallmark is that autonomy
Kafka himself as bourgeois subject could never attain.

The fact that Kafka's critiques of the civilizing process either stop with
an indictment of the patriarchal family or, when he aims past this primary
target, are deflected by the conceptual armor of metaphysical hypostatiza-
tions such as "nature" and "blood," testifies to his ineluctable ensnarement
in the web of bourgeois ideology. Kafka's reaction to this predicament is as
typical for him as it is for authority-behavior in general: he attributes all
those failures forced upon him by external circumstance to his own insufficiencies and failings. Remarks he makes in a letter to Felice from April 1913,
just a few months after the composition of *The Judgment*, exemplify this ten-

dency to condense the frustrations he felt toward his environment into self-blame, turning this vague social enmity against himself. "I go about in a state of pointless despair and rage," he writes, "not so much against my environment, against my destiny, against that which is above us, but only and passionately against myself, against myself alone" (*Letters to Felice*, 356; 236). According to Horkheimer, precisely this reversion of potential societal critique into self-castigation is decisive for the formation of the authority-oriented character. "For the formation of the authority-oriented character it is especially decisive that the children should learn, under pressure from the father, not to trace every failure back to its social causes but to remain at the level of the individual and to hypostatize the failure in religious terms as sin or in naturalistic terms as deficient natural endowment."[31] The enormous guilt and overriding diffidence characteristic of Kafka's personality mark him as the product of a "successful" bourgeois education: he is paradigmatically authority-oriented in Horkheimer's sense.

The socialization of son by father, as Horkheimer points out in "Authority and the Family," is the central relationship in which the scepter of patriarchal authority is passed from one generation to the next. As an instructional procedure that condenses a centuries-long civilizing process into a few short years, this educational policy necessarily relies on the persuasive force of coercion.

The development of every human being from self-centered infant to member of society is, despite all modifications, essentially an abbreviated repetition of a thousand-year-long civilizing process which is unthinkable without an element of coercion. But it makes a difference whether this coercion is the spontaneous reflection in the father-son relationship of the prevailing social contradictions or proves rather to be a provisional relationship which is eliminated as the individual grows and moves out into the larger society.[32]

Although this condensed civilizing process is unthinkable without disciplinary violence, the fundamental question becomes whether this discipline is carried out in the interests of blind conformity to the status quo, or whether it leaves room for the development of those potentials unique to the given individual. Horkheimer believes the former to be the case for the authoritarianism of the bourgeois family; and Kafka confirms this view when he writes to Elli: "These are the two educational methods, born of selfishness, employed by parents: all gradations of tyranny and slavery. . . . But these are two frightful educational methods, two anti-educational methods, suited to stamp the child back into the ground from which it sprang" (*Letters*, 346; 296).

Horkheimer perceives as an alternative to this impasse a dialectical reci-

procity between socially enforced demands for conformity and the nurtur-
ing of those eccentricities endemic to each individual; such a dialectical
openness holds out the promise of a progressive compromise in which the
integration of the individual into the social fabric is accompanied by individual modifications of its very texture. Such a progressive dialectic has no
place in Kafka's understanding of his own development; nor is it anywhere
manifest in the fictional worlds portrayed in Kafka's literature. Indeed,
Kafka's most (in)famous protagonists—from Josef K. in *The Trial* (1914–15),
to K. in *The Castle* (1921), to Georg Bendemann in *The Judgment*—tend to pursue a course of strategic adaptation to the very structures responsible for
their alienation. Kafka's heroes thus act in accordance with the recognition
that power and mastery are attained only on the basis of careful conformity
to bourgeois society's rationalizing practices. In short, they recognize, as
Horkheimer expresses it, that "one travels the paths to power in the bourgeois world not by putting into practice judgments of moral value but by
clever adaptation to actual conditions."[33] Success in the bourgeois world accordingly requires the jettisoning of moral scruples—morality is retained
solely as an ideological mask—and the strategic appropriation and manipulation of authorial mastery in the service of a surreptitiously violent self-
empowerment. This is precisely the formula for success that Georg Bendemann pursues—initially with great success—in *The Judgment*. The failure of
this quintessential project of bourgeois self-empowerment is one of the paradoxes on which this story turns. This defeat, as my interpretation will demonstrate, passes judgment—this is one of the many implications of the
story's title—on the inherent abstraction of bourgeois interhuman and commercial exchange.

In my examination of Büchner's *Woyzeck*, I argued that to escape his own
societal oppression and attain to a degree of self-empowerment, Woyzeck
pursues a strategy of mimetic adaptation to the very principles that bring
about his own oppression. This tactic of mimetic adaptation, characteristic
of the authority-oriented behavior of the bourgeois subject, is also practiced
by Georg Bendemann in Kafka's *The Judgment*. In reflections on the relationship between sociology and psychology, Theodor Adorno elaborates on
the inevitable reification of the bourgeois subject that results from such
strategic adaptation to the reified conditions of bourgeois life.

The mechanism of adaptation to reified conditions is simultaneously the reification of the subject itself: the more faithful it becomes to reality, the more it becomes
a thing, the less it actually lives, the more senseless its entire "reality" becomes. . . .
The subject is divided into the machinery of social production extended into its inner being, and an undissolved remainder that, as an impotent reserve sphere, de-

generates into a curiosity over against the rapidly proliferating "rational" component.[34]

Adorno's words adequately describe the strategy pursued by Georg Bendemann and the consequences it calls forth. Georg responds to the oppression
of the bourgeois patriarchal world by appropriating its own oppressive rationality and turning it against his father, the aging patriarch. The price of
this tactic, as Adorno notes, is an ineluctable splitting of the subject into a
reified agent that has internalized the dominant societal modes of production and an "undissolved remainder" of human subjectivity. This mimetic
reproduction of the specific rationality of bourgeois socioeconomic production thus describes a process of self-reification by which the subject assimilates itself to the real. What remains after completion of such mimetic
adaptation is a remnant of creative human (bourgeois) subjectivity that cannot be reduced to the common denominators of instrumental reason and
abstract identity-logical exchange. This "impotent reserve sphere" represents the final outpost of the imaginary, of utopian difference in a world otherwise (self-)subjected to the order of the symbolic. In the bourgeois life-
world, where only mimetic adaptation can pave the way to self-empowerment, this utopian reserve is strangled off from the rationality of bourgeois
exchange; it atrophies into that curious and unfathomable, irrational ec-
centricity personified in *The Judgment* by Georg's friend in Petersburg. As
Georg's alter ego, the friend marks the "undissolved remainder" that is left
over when Georg opts for the strategy of mimetic adaptation. In this story
Kafka thus portrays the historical development of the bourgeois subject as
a dead end that leads inexorably to compulsory conformity to the reifying
structures of bourgeois thought and socioeconomic practice. Creative subjectivity survives only as a curiosity, an eccentric remainder that is totally
desocialized and hence condemned to absolute sociopolitical and economic
impotence.

Georg Bendemann and the Curse
of Unhappy Consciousness

Kafka's short story *The Judgment* prototypically manifests the entire spectrum of features characteristic of the psychic narrative: the narrated events
turn on the perceptions of the anchor character, Georg Bendemann, and figures such as the father and the friend primarily embody projections of his
consciousness; figural narration is the dominant narrative mode of the text,
so that readers unwittingly experience events predominantly through

Georg's psychic lens; this subjective orientation is couched behind the objective fictional diction of narrated monolog, which joins seamlessly with a framing narrative structured as an omniscient and objective report. In addition to fulfilling these structural criteria, *The Judgment* also contains thematic elements that link it to Hofmannsthal's *A Tale of the Cavalry*. Central among these is the motif of the uncanny doppelgänger, a motif that assumes concrete form in Kafka's story as the split in Georg Bendemann's subjectivity between Georg the successful merchant and his alienated, commercially unsuccessful friend.[35] As in Hofmannsthal's narrative, the semantic ambiguities and equivocations characteristic of the text of *The Judgment* mirror the dichotomous, self-repressive subjectivity of the anchor character. In some respects, however, Kafka's tale is more complex than Hofmannsthal's. This added complexity is attributable to two phenomena. First, although Georg's subjectivity forms the hub of the narrated events, it is the father, functioning as the common bond linking the self-alienated halves of Georg's divided subjectivity, who comprises the structural matrix of the story. The uncanny element enters into *The Judgment* when the text's center of gravity shifts from the figural center (Georg) to the structural center (the father). This occurs in the episode that details the confrontation between Georg and his father. Moreover, *A Tale of the Cavalry* displays a monolinear plot structure composed of a single sequence of temporally and causally intermotivated occurrences, whereas *The Judgment* divides, somewhat unevenly, into two plot strands which, on closer examination, prove to be merely two perspectives on a single plot: the narrative of Georg's growing success stands over against the failures of the father and the friend. But as the development of the story indicates, Georg's success is inherently tied to the father's and the friend's failures, and the text reaches its denouement when Georg's position of apparent superiority over the other characters is reversed.

Georg Bendemann, whom Kafka characterizes simply as "a young merchant" (*Judgment*, 53; 77), is a representative figure for Kafka's early fiction of the years from 1911 to 1913, in which characters bound up with the sphere of bourgeois commerce are common elements. Essential to Gregor Samsa, the protagonist of *The Metamorphosis*, for example, is the fact that he works as a traveling salesman; and Kafka's protagonist Raban from the fragmentary early novel "Wedding Preparations in the Country" (ca. 1907–8) expresses both fascination with and admiration for the existence of commercial travelers: "They must not stay long anywhere, for everything must be done fast, and they must always talk only about their goods. With what pleasure, then, one can exert oneself in an occupation that is so agreeable!" The agreeability of this occupation derives from the fact that its practitioners, as "people who had been concerned with goods since their youth," are integrated in a communicative-commercial network that affords them a secure basis for all interhuman relations (*Hochzeit*, 22–23; *CS*, 63–64). Raban perceives the world of bourgeois commerce as a sphere in which the abstract exchange of commodities and signs provides the ultimate frame of reference for human intercourse. Himself standing outside this community grounded in commodification, Raban is an early analog of Georg Bendemann's Petersburg friend. Unlike this friend, however, Raban views with a certain envy the "successful" exchanges of communicative signs and commodities in which salespeople participate. By contrast, the merchant Georg Bendemann experiences the world of abstract exchange from within, and Georg projects the envy characteristic of Raban onto the unintegrated, "unsuccessful" friend in Petersburg. This shift in Kafka's early fiction from a figural perspective located outside the world of bourgeois commerce ("Wedding Preparations") to one situated inside that world (*The Judgment* and *The Metamorphosis*) forms one of the principal conditions on which his aesthetic breakthrough is predicated.

Writing in the *Spectator* in 1711, Joseph Addison defined the role of the merchant at the inception of bourgeois mercantile capitalism in the following way. "[Merchants] knit Mankind together in a mutual Intercourse of good Offices, distribute the Gifts of Nature, find Work for the Poor, add Wealth to the Rich, and Magnificence to the Great."[36] According to this definition, the merchant has a variety of significant functions in society: as the increaser of wealth and magnificence he represents the motor behind the accumulation of both material and symbolic capital; merchants, moreover, are interlocutors between the wealthy and the poor insofar as they mediate between capital and the mass of impoverished workers; they further stand between man and nature, distributing nature's fruits—although not necessarily distributing them equally, as Addison himself implicitly admits; and they comprise, finally, the basic stitch that "knits" humankind into a coherent social fabric. Examining the central role merchants play in the bourgeois epistemic order, Foucault lends Addison's arguments a semiotic-discursive cast by identifying the merchant's mediative function as the guarantee for the eternally open interplay of commercial and discursive exchange. Merchants, Foucault suggests, perform a function in the bourgeois commercial network wholly analogous to that of abstract signs in symbolic communication, on the one hand, and to that of money in the exchange of commodities, on the other: they operate as that third element which, abstracting from the concrete and individual characteristics of any two objects, mediately links them in a binding and meaningful—that is, profitable—

interrelation.³⁷ Such mediation, in other words, is the condition of possibility of interconnectedness in a structural network that makes the natural world meaningful, gives commodities an exchange-value, and lends communicative signs their signification. The merchant Georg Bendemann is shown throughout Kafka's narrative to be a full participant in the abstractive logic of this epistemic order.

It falls to the father, in the very breath in which he condemns his son to death by drowning, to give a description of Georg's divided character. "An innocent child, yes, that you were, truly," he says to Georg, "but you were even more truly a devilish human being" (*Judgment*, 67; 87). With this declaration the father essentially identifies Georg and his friend as the two sides of Georg's own schizoid personality: the "friend from [Georg's] youth," whose face is familiar to him "since childhood" (*Judgment*, 53; 77) is none other than Georg's persona as "innocent child," while the "devilish human being" manifests itself in Georg the successful merchant. Indeed, Georg's business success is predicated precisely on the repression or marginalization of that "innocent" aspect of his personality represented by the friend. The "peculiar relationship of correspondence" ("besonderes Korrespondenzverhältnis") (*Judgment*, 56; 79) that links Georg and his Petersburg friend refers not only to the fact that they correspond with one another—that is, that they maintain epistolary communication—but suggests, as well, that they correspond *to* one another as alter egos. The "peculiarity" of this relationship is grounded in its repressive nature. The discourse Georg employs in his epistolary correspondence with the friend is rife with the half-truths, distortions, and manipulations he uses to rationalize this act of violent (self-)repression, which is the price of his commercial success.

Georg's mimetic simulation of patriarchal authority, his assumption of the seat of economic and discursive power, makes itself evident in his psychic text in the form of calculative dissimulations and strategic rationalizations. These (self-)deceptions express themselves as semantic equivocations that expose the latent "devilish" motivations underlying the manifest layer of Georg's "innocent" intentional consciousness. One of the primary verbal complexes that discloses this web of deceptions is formed by the semantic interplay of a particular set of etymologically related words: the noun *Erfolg* ("success"), the verb *erfolgen* ("to occur" or "to result from": literally, "to succeed upon"), and the verb *folgen* ("to follow"). These three signifiers comprise the ideological glue that holds together Georg's self-understanding as "successful" ("erfolgreicher"; literally, "rich with success") merchant. In his self-reflections, Georg brazenly boasts about his multiple accomplishments: in the economic sphere, his business sales have increased over the last two

years to five times their previous volume, while in the social domain this incipient prosperity is mirrored in his engagement to Frieda Brandenfeld, "a
girl from a well-to-do family" (*Judgment*, 56; 79). The fact that Frieda is "well
to do" is not coincidental; it is likely, in fact, that the financial advantage
Georg will gain from this filiation forms his primary motivation, since when
he mentions her in the letter to his friend her wealth once again figures as
her central characteristic (see *Judgment*, 57; 80). The liaison with Frieda thus
is but a strategic move in the game of economic mastery Georg plays, and
as such she becomes a symbol of the financial success that distinguishes
Georg from his unsuccessful friend. In his deliberations about what he, the
paragon of success, could possibly write to a friend "who had obviously run
off the rails" (*Judgment*, 53; 77), Georg considers advising him simply to return home and follow the example set by his successful friends, that is, by
Georg himself. "Should one advise him to come home . . . ? But that was as
good as telling him, and the more kindly the more offensively, that all his ef-
forts hitherto had miscarried, that he should . . . come back home . . . , that
only his friends knew what was what and that he himself was just an old
child who should follow [*folgen*] the example of his successful [*erfolgreichen*]
home-keeping friends" (*Judgment*, 53–54; 77–78). Georg gives an unwitting
commentary on the hidden aggression that underpins the double-speak he
employs in his correspondence with the friend when he notes that as his
words become "more kind" they also become all the "more offensive." What
he thereby suggests is that lurking behind the verbal guise of concern and
careful solicitude for his friend is nothing other than the desire to denigrate,
wound, and offend him. Furthermore, in the advice he imagines himself giving the friend, he unwittingly betrays his own formula for success: staying
home and following, that is, imitating, the model of success patterned in the
bourgeois patriarchal family. The semantic resonance between the words *er-
folgreich* ("successful") and *folgen* ("to follow") draws a causal connection between mimetic adaptation to the authoritarian behavior of the patriarch and
socioeconomic success in the bourgeois world.

   The importance of signifiers related to the principle of *Erfolg*, the concept
that is central to Georg's self-understanding, is confirmed when, acting on
his resolve to report his engagement to the friend, Georg once again employs a word that subtly underscores the relationship between this marriage
and Georg's success. "And in fact he did inform his friend, in the long letter
he had written that Sunday morning, of the effected [*erfolgte*] engagement"
(*Judgment*, 57; 80). It is difficult to render this semantic play in English translation, of course; but what is significant in this passage is Georg's use of the
attributive modifier *erfolgte*, a form derived from the verb *erfolgen*, when he

relates his engagement. On the surface this word simply signifies that this bond has been "concluded," "realized," or, as I have translated it above, "effected"; but it simultaneously conjures up the social and economic success, the *Erfolg*, that this marriage promises Georg. The semantic undertone of Georg's report is thus calculated to play up—"the more kindly, the more offensively"—precisely those successes that define Georg's position of superiority vis-à-vis the friend.

These examples give us a first inkling of how Georg's messages to the friend are structured around semantic tensions between the manifest and latent content of his discourse. The double-edgedness of Georg's communicative signs, in fact, is fundamental to the correspondence he carries on with the friend. Georg admits that their relationship is a superficial one, lacking any real substance, when, after recounting the complex deliberations that have dissuaded him from being open and honest with the friend about his own good fortunes, he identifies the overriding paradox of their "correspondence": "If one wanted to keep up the correspondence with [the friend] at all," he asserts, "one could not send him any real news, even of the sort that one would frankly tell to the most distant acquaintance" (*Judgment*, 54; 78). By admitting that he cannot relate to this alter ego as he would to even the most distant acquaintance, Georg implicitly denies that their relationship deserves the name of friendship, at all. The father must be credited with critical insight into this discrepancy; for when he asks his son, "Do you really have this friend in St. Petersburg?" (*Judgment*, 60; 82), he is not so much expressing doubt about the existence of Georg's alter ego as empirical being as he is questioning whether the relationship Georg maintains with this second self can accurately be designated as one of friendship.[38] Indeed, the relationship between Georg and his "friend" remains purely formal and abstract: it is an empty line of communication over which—so Georg imagines, at least—no significant information ever passes. In fact, however, Georg's ostensibly insignificant signs are replete with subliminal messages: he exploits the superficial "relationship of correspondence" to the friend as a means for abasing and repressing this "unsuccessful" alter ego, thereby empowering his merchant persona. Georg upholds a communicative link with the "friend" only to transmit what the father perceptively calls his "lying little letters" (*Judgment*, 64; 85), those signs, significant in their insignificance, that help him to assert and legitimize the ascendancy of the "devilish human being" over the "innocent child."

Georg's exploitation of double-speak to couch significant subliminal messages behind ostensibly insignificant signs is paradigmatically manifest in his unwitting announcement to his friend of his impending marriage.

Yet Georg had no desire to let his friend know about his business successes [*Erfolgen*]. . . . So Georg confined himself to writing his friend about unimportant occurrences such as collect at random in one's memory when one idly thinks things over on a quiet Sunday. . . . And so it happened to Georg that three times in fairly widely separated letters he had told his friend about the engagement of an insignificant man to an equally insignificant girl, until in fact, quite contrary to Georg's intention, his friend began to show some interest in this remarkable event. (*Judgment*, 56; 79)

Georg begins this deliberation by citing his refusal to notify the friend of his own business successes. However, he then goes on to describe how a similar attempt to withhold from the friend information about his engagement by supplying him with stories about "unimportant occurrences" and "insignificant" people unwittingly attracts the friend's attention. Georg's communication with the friend thus turns on a functional dialectic in which concealment reverts to revelation. Georg's "correspondence" with the friend, in short, circumscribes the tension inherent in the terms *heimlich* and *unheimlich*: although attempting on the level of manifest content to keep his successes secret, Georg simultaneously discloses them in the latent undertones of his language. Thus it is precisely by trying not to remark on his engagement that he makes it into a "remarkable event." The unconscious yet systematic nature of these *unheimlich* slips is brought out by the "random" way they occur to Georg as he "idly" reflects, as well as by certain grammatical constructions that stress his role as a passive agent ("And so it happened to Georg."). It is coherent with Freudian theory, of course, that the unintentional bears the mark of a deeper intention: it points to Georg's desire to boast about his own success and mockingly condescend to his failed friend from his own position of socioeconomic preeminence.

Georg's essentially "devilish" character is brought out by the implication that his own financial successes are inherently connected to other people's disasters. Thus the boom in Georg's business is casually related to the death of his mother, an event that "hit [the father] harder" than it did Georg (*Judgment*, 60; 82). Georg essentially exploits the weakness the mother's death occasions in the father, and Georg's awareness that he stands to profit from this new state of affairs once again finds expression in the semantic equivocations attached to the verb *erfolgen*.

The friend had certainly been informed of the decease of Georg's mother, which had occurred [*erfolgt*] about two years ago, . . . and had expressed his sympathy in a letter with a dryness that led one to conclude that the grief caused by such an event could not be imagined in an alien land. Since that time, however, Georg had applied himself with greater determination to the business as well as to everything else. . . . Perhaps since her death his father had become less aggressive, although he was still active in the business . . . , but at any rate, during those two years the business had developed in a most unexpected way. (*Judgment*, 55; 78–79)

Georg presents the co-incidence of his mother's decease with his own "un-expected" financial successes as wholly serendipitous; but the resonance of the word *Erfolg* in the verb *erfolgen* suggests that these two occurrences are in fact related by a structure of necessary suc-cession. If Georg concentrates on the business with "greater determination" after his mother passes, then this does not bespeak an attempt to work through or distract himself from his sorrow; rather, it indicates his eagerness to take advantage of an adver-sary—the father—who has become "less aggressive" due to grief over his wife's death. Georg sees the death of the mother not as a personal tragedy, but as a business opportunity that he can—and does—mercilessly exploit. This is likely what the father is referring to when he later claims that "cer-tain unpretty things" took place following the mother's death (*Judgment*, 60; 82). Moreover, the "dryness" with which, according to Georg's perception, the friend responded to news of his mother's death is really nothing but a projection of Georg's own remorselessness onto his alienated alter ego.

Georg Bendemann perceives the world as a closed system containing a finite amount of wealth and power; whatever gains he is to make hence must come at the expense of others. The death of the mother, the old age and grief of the father, the failure of the friend: Georg makes all these de-plorable circumstances into stepping stones on the way to his own self-em-powerment. This world, in which the competition for might is as merciless and violent as are those who possess it, is the universe of the father(s) in a twofold sense: first, Georg inherits the business that his father developed, and with it he assumes the economic might and concomitant authority of the bourgeois patriarch; second, Georg replicates in his own behavior that bureaucratized Eros, that hypocritical *caritas*, typical of the authoritarian pa-triarch who camouflages his will to power behind the mask of the self-sac-rificing provider. I have documented Kafka's insights into such a self-serv-ing Eros in my analyses of the relationship between father and son he de-picted in "Letter to His Father" and in his other miscellaneous commentaries on bourgeois education. What he despises in Hermann Kafka is precisely that reflex in which the martyrdom of the provider who sacrifices himself for his dependents is exploited to enhance this relation of dependence. For the bourgeois patriarch, love is nothing but a method for guaranteeing the slavish gratitude of his subordinates: he holds it as a promissory note that binds them to him in a relationship of infinite indebtedness. Georg Bendemann's sin is the assimilation of this bureaucratized Eros, and when he calls out before falling to his death, "Dear Parents, I have always loved you, all the same" (*Judgment*, 68; 88), he is neither lying nor acting out a role, as has sometimes been presumed;[39] rather, to the extent that he has merely appropriated and mimetically replicated that rapacious behavior that in the patriarchal family and the world of bourgeois commerce is passed off as "love," Georg has indeed "loved" his parents all along.

The double-edged semiotic practice that Georg deploys against his friend represents a strategy of self-repression in which his utopian alter ego is banished from his conscious life. Georg's ascendancy to the seat of bourgeois socioeconomic power can occur only on the basis of this repressive self-aggression that is grounded in an ambiguous signifying practice. This same semiotic mechanism, however, dominates the struggle between father and son as well, and in this instance it is the mark of aggression against external enemies rather than against the enemy in oneself. This conjunction of internally and externally directed hostility reflects the linkage of "the introjected violence of human beings over other human beings to the introjected violence of the subject" identified by Habermas and other representatives of the Frankfurt School as one of the primary tendencies of bourgeois thought and socioeconomic practice. Both Georg and his father are typical representatives of this covertly violent worldview, and they relate to each other throughout the text as mutual competitors and adversaries.

Georg hints at the commonality that joins the two Bendemanns when he notes that since the death of the mother he and his father have lived "in a common household" ("in gemeinsamer Wirtschaft") (*Judgment*, 55; 78). The German phrase implies not merely that they participate in a joint household, but that they share a common economic base ("Wirtschaft"), as well. As such, this phrase alludes to the fact that when Georg begins asserting himself more actively in the family business, he and his father enter into competition for dominance in the business that is their "common" ground. Although Georg goes to great lengths to portray his and his father's common existence as a sentimental familial bond, his thoughts unwittingly betray a degree of estrangement that belies this feigned emotional attachment.

He went . . . into his father's room, which he had not entered for months. There was in fact no need for him to enter it, since he interacted [*verkehrte*] with his father daily during business and they took their lunch concurrently [*gleichzeitig*] in a restaurant; in the evening, to be sure, each took care of himself as he saw fit, yet even then they usually sat together for a while in their common [*gemeinsamen*] living room, each with his own newspaper—unless, as was most frequently [*am häu-*

figsten] the case, Georg was with friends, or most recently, visiting his fiancée. (*Judgment*, 58; *80–81*)

In these deliberations Georg unconsciously exposes the antipathy for his elder that is disguised behind a self-deluding vision of family harmony. Although he overtly stresses the intercourse he maintains with his father and the "common" ground of their private lives, he simultaneously admits that he has not visited his father's room "for months." He justifies this fact with the remark that he and his father interact daily in the business, and this claim underscores that their common *Wirtschaft* is indeed more economic than familial in nature. To be sure, even this assertion is later contradicted by the father, who maintains that Georg, playing the role of the busy boss who can't be bothered, "locks [himself] away in [his] office" whenever he is at work (*Judgment*, 63; *85*). Besides, Georg's reflections themselves contain glaring contradictions, as when he claims, on the one hand, that he and his father "usually" sit together evenings, while on the other hand admitting that he in fact is "most frequently" either with friends or with his fiancée: Georg would have to be much more than just a divided subject to be at home with his father and away with friends and fiancée at one and the same time. But this is only the most obvious place in which the text of Georg's self-reflections exposes the mendacious rationalizations that constitute its fabric. At best, it seems, the lives of Georg and his father run along parallel tracks that intersect only in their common *Wirtschaft*: they do not each lunch *together* in a restaurant, but only *concurrently* ("gleichzeitig," not "gemeinsam," as one would expect); each admittedly cares for himself independently in the evening, but even in the "common" ("gemeinsames") living room, where each is occupied with his own newspaper, there is no genuine social intercourse. The interactions between father and son are thus infrequent and insubstantial; since the death of the mother they have merely coexisted, enmeshed in a covert struggle for ascendancy. *The Judgment* tells the story of how this secret (*heimlich*) battle comes into the open, eventually evolving into unsecret (*unheimlich*), open warfare.

The verb *verkehren*, which occurs in the cited passage, constitutes a nodal point of significations similar to the one that crystallizes around the word *Erfolg* and its derivatives. As verb, *verkehren* means literally "to have intercourse" or "to traffic," with all the attendant connotations these phrases have in English, from the sexual, to the commercial, to the implications of social discourse, and finally to traffic and to networks of communication. The noun derived from this verb, *Verkehr*, is the final word of *The Judgment*: "At that moment there passed over the bridge an infinite traffic-commerce-communication-intercourse [*unendlicher Verkehr*]" (*Judgment*, 68; 88). This sentence, which immediately follows the narration of Georg's leap to his death from the bridge, provides him with a fitting testimonial; for throughout the story, Georg has highlighted his active *Verkehr*, designating it as the quality that distinguishes him from both his father and his friend. Where Georg has intercourse with friends and business acquaintances, the father sits home alone and the friend wastes away in a foreign country; whereas the promise of sexual intercourse is invoked by his attachment to Frieda, the father's partner is deceased and the friend is condemned to remain a bachelor; whereas his business has taken an unexpected upturn, the father has become "less aggressive" and the friend faces financial ruin. Indeed, it is by playing up the various connotations of the word *Verkehr* that Georg segregates his successes from the failures of the friend.

Now [the friend] was carrying on a business in St. Petersburg, which had flourished to begin with but had long been going downhill. . . . So he was wearing himself out to no purpose in a foreign country. . . . By his own account he had no real connection with the colony of his fellow countrymen out there and almost no social intercourse [*keinen gesellschaftlichen Verkehr*] with native families, and so he was preparing himself for permanent bachelorhood. (*Judgment*, 53; 77)

Georg's summary of the friend's abortive attempts to establish "connections" in an alien world traverses much ground, beginning with his commercial failure, moving from there to his social isolation, and concluding with the implicit sexual abstinence of the bachelor. The common element linking the friend's failure on all these fronts, the economic, the social, and the sexual, is his lack of *Verkehr*. By contrast, Georg, tied into a far-reaching network of interpersonal and economic connections, flourishes in business, in social and sexual intercourse, and even—in his own mind, at least—in the intercourse with his father: he enjoys, in short, a veritably "infinite intercourse."

Georg's aim in the covert war against his father is to displace his elder, who, as patriarch, occupies the center of this network of infinite commercial-sexual-social-discursive intercourse. He goes about this by attempting to initiate a total reversal of their roles. When he imitates the paternal care of the father for his child by undressing his elder and placing him in bed, Georg symbolically usurps the patriarchal role while demoting his father to the position of a helpless child. He attempts to underwrite this role reversal when he recommends that he and the father exchange rooms. Of course, Georg makes this suggestion under the pretense that his own room is light, while the father's is quite dark, and thus he once again camouflages his will to domination under the guise of self-sacrificing martyrdom and loving concern typical of the patriarchal provider. Once again, moreover, Georg's insidious drive to mastery is exposed by a telling semantic equivocation. "We'll switch rooms," Georg tells his father, "you can move into the front room and I'll move in here. You won't notice the change. . . . Come, I'll help you undress-move out [*Ausziehen*], you'll see I can do it. Or would you rather go into the front room at once. . . . That would be the most reasonable thing" (*Judgment*, 61; 83). This passage turns on the pun on the word *Ausziehen*, which means either "to undress" or "to move out." As this ambiguity suggests, Georg's careful "undressing" of the father masks the drive to "move him out"; it thereby marks the *unheimlich* return of Georg's concealed will to self-empowerment. This scene further concretizes the hypocrisy inherent in Georg's very being by exposing the discrepancy between his words and his actions: even while he is in the process of "undressing" his father and putting him to bed in the back room, he maintains that it would be most "reasonable" if his elder would move out immediately. But Georg's ambiguous signs are not simply the index of a Freudian slip that reveals the latent desire behind his manifest statements; instead, they represent a calculative manipulation intended to assert the "reasonableness" of his shrewd will to power. Within the subtext of his discourse, Georg essentially asks the father for permission to displace him; and when he insists "You'll see, I can do it," he attempts to lend his takeover bid credibility and inevitability.

Now, the father, himself an expert in the manipulation and interpretation of equivocal signs, understands only too well the provocation that lurks behind the manifest sense of Georg's remarks: he easily penetrates Georg's discursive smokescreen since, as he haughtily asserts, "a father doesn't need to be taught how to see through his son" (*Judgment*, 64; 85). As this scene develops, the father demonstrates his own facility in the deployment of cunning semiotic traps. First pretending to accede to his son's offensive by letting himself be undressed and carried to bed, he then launches his counter-attack by posing a seemingly innocent question.

"Am I well covered up [*zugedeckt*] now?" asked the father, as if he were not able to see whether his feet were properly tucked in or not.

"So you find it snug in bed already," said Georg, and tucked the coverings [*Deckzeug*] more closely around him.

"Am I well covered up [*zugedeckt*]?" asked the father once more, seeming to be strangely intent upon the answer.

"Don't worry, you're well covered up [*zugedeckt*]."

"No!" cried his father, . . . threw the cover [*Decke*] off with a strength that made it unfold completely, and sprang erect in bed. . . . "You wanted to cover me up

[*zudecken*], I know, my little fruit, but I'm far from being covered up [*zugedeckt*] yet."
(*Judgment*, 63; 84)

This verbal exchange, which draws its vitality from the functional ambiguities inscribed in the word *zudecken*, forms the denouement of *The Judgment*,
marking the juncture at which the uncanny ruptures the hitherto placid narrative surface and steers the plot in a radically different and unforeseen direction. The German verb *zudecken* means "to cover up" in the sense of "to
tuck in"; but it also signifies "to cover over," both in the abstract sense of "to
conceal" and in the concrete sense of "to bury." The centrality of this verb
in the quoted passage is indicated by the fact that it occurs five times, as well
as by its further resonance in the nouns *Deckzeug* ("bed coverings") and *Decke*
("cover," or "blanket"). The father cunningly counters Georg's semiotically
inscribed power play by contriving one of his own, which is vastly more
complex and rhetorically charged than that of his son. His victory demonstrates clearly that he is the true master of ambiguous signs, while Georg is
but his fumbling apprentice. However, the potency of the father's cunning
play on words does not merely derive from the fact that he outmaneuvers
Georg by beating him at his own game; it is grounded, instead, in the fact
that his double-speak also provides a self-reflexive metacommentary on the
occultation of intersubjective violence implicit in this discursive tactic itself.
Thus the father "uncovers" Georg's cover-up by disclosing the real motivation behind the son's solicitous "tucking in" as a will to "bury" his elder, to
put him in the grave so that Georg can rule the networks of infinite com-
merce-communication-intercourse (*Verkehr*) without challenge. The text emblematically represents the characters' opposing drives to "cover" and "uncover" this will to mastery in their distinct handlings of the (bed)cover:
Georg tucks it more completely around the father, reinforcing through this
gesture his covert desire to cover him over; the father, in turn, undoes this
act by throwing off the cover with such force that it "unfolds completely."
This complete unfolding of the cover metaphorically depicts the disclosure
of Georg's cover-up, and as such it is the concrete emblem of the *unheimlich*
in this story. The uncanny breaks into the text—and into Georg's psyche—
at the moment when his secret wish to displace the father is rendered un-
secret. This disclosure lays bare the "devilish" manipulator covered over by
Georg's pretense to being an "innocent child." This recognition, which is accompanied by the violence characteristic of the return of the repressed, in
turn drives Georg to fulfill of his own volition the sentence passed on him
by the father.

It is no coincidence that the drowning of Georg Bendemann, who does battle with his father to establish himself as master over the networks of *un-endlicher Verkehr* made possible by the bourgeois epistemic formation, is itself drowned out by the infinite traffic-commerce-intercourse on these very networks. It is tempting to conclude from this that Georg simply fails in his hostile takeover attempt and is justifiably punished by the victorious father. But if this is the case, we are led to ask, what justification does the father have to pass judgment on his most perfect offspring, on the "little fruit" who so exactly emulates the principles inherent in his own patriarchal authority? In doing so, is he not implicitly condemning himself and his own socioeconomic and semiotic practices, which, after all, Georg has simply imitated? The fact that as Georg runs from his father's room to carry out his death sentence he hears the sound of the father collapsing on his bed (*Judgment,* 67; 83) seems to suggest that the father's condemnation of his son ought to be interpreted as a self-condemnation of these two quintessential representatives of bourgeois infinite commerce. It is important to note here that one further signification is attached to the word *Verkehr*: "inversion" or "perversion." The world dominated by infinite *Verkehr* is an infinitely *verkehrte Welt,* an "inverted world" in the Marxian sense, and the double-demise of the Bendemanns at the end of the story seems to pronounce a critical judgment on the self-destructive tendency endemic to this "perverted" order of bourgeois *Verkehr.*

But the conclusion of *The Judgment* is more complex than this interpretive hypothesis suggests, since it confronts us with the apparent paradox that although the proxies of the inverted world of bourgeois commerce perish, its infinite *Verkehr* survives as the story's last word. Viewed within the context of the structural economy of *The Judgment,* this suggests that those subjects who regard themselves as the masters of the abstract and systematic networks of bourgeois *Verkehr* turn out instead to be the dispensable pawns of an absolute and autonomous system. Read in this way, *The Judgment* tells the story of the revenge of bourgeois ideology on the subjects who perpetrate it: it is not the ideologically hypostatized bourgeois subject that turns out to be absolute and autonomous, but the inhuman system that this myth of the autonomous subject is intended to mask. The "subjects" of the commercial world, the two Bendemann merchants, are portrayed ultimately as the victims of a structurally autonomous discursive-commercial traffic that operates simultaneously through and beyond their individual subjective consciousnesses. Georg and his father are disclosed to be "sub-jects" only to the extent that they are mercilessly sub-jected to and sub-jugated by the order of the symbolic, the mediative structures of inter(ex)change that drive the infinite *Verkehr* of the "verkehrte Welt." This is a universe of total alienation and reification, of abstractions, connections, and "relations of correspondence." Kafka thus diagnoses as the inevitable end station of the bourgeois episteme a "postmodern condition" in which the subject has relinquished all creativity and oppositional force and capitulated absolutely to the structures of infinite commerce. Here the desubjectivized human being is subjected unrelentingly and mercilessly to the demands of a self-administered system. In this sense the "infinite commerce" with which *The Judgment* concludes anticipates the anonymously administered worlds Kafka depicted in detail in his later novels, *The Trial* and *The Castle*.

Despite the fact that infinite *Verkehr* literally has the last word in *The Judgment*, there is yet another horizon in the story suggesting that the supremacy of commerce-intercourse-discourse is not the text's sole statement. The ultimate (self-)entrapment of the bourgeois subject and its devolution from active subject to passive agent only tells the story of one aspect of Georg Bendemann's schizoid personality; the narrative about the marginalized friend in Petersburg, Georg's "unsuccessful" alter ego, gives a different but no less pessimistic perspective on this life-world. I have suggested that the friend represents what Adorno terms the impotent "reserve sphere" of utopian resistance that atrophies into a mere curiosity when the subject mimetically adapts to the reifying structures of bourgeois socioeconomic and discursive practice. In this sense, the friend not only embodies everything Georg must repress to become a successful agent in the infinitely productive semiotic and economic order of bourgeois exchange, but also everything bourgeois society in general represses to achieve its socioeconomic supremacy. According to Horkheimer, in the bourgeois family this marginalization of utopian impulses is concretized in the suppression of the mother and the noncoercive, humanitarian love characteristic of the mother-child relation.

In bourgeois civic life . . . common concerns always had an essentially negative character, being mainly concerned with the warding off of dangers. But common concerns took a positive form in sexual love and especially in maternal care. The growth and happiness of the other are willed in such unions. A felt opposition therefore arises between them and hostile reality outside. To this extent, the family not only educates for authority in bourgeois society; it also cultivates the dream of a better condition for mankind.[40]

The dual mission of the bourgeois family corresponds to the dual structure of the divided bourgeois subject. Horkheimer implicitly identifies the negative character of bourgeois civic concern with the world of the fathers, the authoritarian relations concretized in the father-son relation and mirrored in bourgeois commercial intercourse. On the other hand, he associates its positive aspect, its dream for a human condition that is better than the one actualized in the existing conditions of the bourgeois life-world, with sexual communion and the mother-child bond. In his view, women represent an antiauthoritarian moment to the extent that they embody a "reservoir" from which one can draw "to resist the total dehumanization of the world."[41] In the bourgeois family, the love modeled in the mother-child relation hence provides a utopian alternative to the egocentric, bureaucratized Eros of the paternal tyrant. Evidence that Kafka recognized this utopian otherness of the feminine is documented in "Letter to His Father," where he identifies his mother as the voice of reason amidst the babble of the father's tyranny: "In the maze and chaos of my childhood," he writes, "[mother] was the very prototype of good sense and reasonableness [*Vernunft*]" (*Letter/Father*, 182; 47).

In the world of the *The Judgment*, the positive form of communitarian interchange associated with the love-bonding typified by the mother and sexual love has been totally suppressed: Georg's mother is deceased, the friend is doomed to bachelorhood, and Georg's sexual union with Frieda has been reduced to a commercial venture, a connection that promises socioeconomic benefits.[42] To the marginalization of the feminine in the universe of infinite commerce corresponds the banishment of the friend, who similarly embodies that "reservoir" of resistance against the "total dehumanization"— the total desubjectification—at work in the world of infinite bourgeois commerce. The text underlines this connection of the friend's estrangement to the mother's death by establishing each of them as the causal factors that initiate Georg's period of thriving socioeconomic success: they mark the point in his life at which Georg becomes motivated to apply himself "with greater determination to the business as well as to everything else" (*Judgment*, 55; 78). In the existence Georg pursues, this reservoir of resistance against the authority of the patriarchal world runs dry: positive communitarian interests are purged from bourgeois socioeconomic practice, and the "devilish" side of the divided subject, the impulse to capitulate to and mimetically adapt the reifying structures of bourgeois socioeconomic and discursive practice, wins out over the "innocent" core of utopian resistance to and self-critique of the bourgeois epistemic formation.

In *The Judgment*, the friend is the only figure who escapes the annihilation of the subject by the autonomous structures of infinite commerce. This suggests that Kafka's story may harbor a utopian perspective, a faint hope that the creative subject has not (yet) been totally eradicated in the postmodern world of late capitalism. The survival of the friend as a potential reservoir of utopian resistance is related to one of the most paradoxical and seemingly inexplicable aspects of Kafka's tale: the tendency of the father, the model for patriarchal authoritarian behavior, to gravitate toward the utopian perspective represented by the deceased mother and estranged friend. The text brings out the father's association with the utopian reserve Georg has repressed in his own subjectivity by highlighting his devotion to his dead wife—who, significantly, is identified throughout the text solely by means of her role as "mother"—and by claiming he has formed an alliance with Georg's banished friend. This explains, for example, why the father can declare himself to be the friend's "representative" at home (*Judgment*, 65; 86), and why he surrounds himself with memorials that remind him of the "dead mother" (*Judgment*, 58; 81).

When the father passes judgment on Georg, he does so not only in the name of the patriarch, but in the names of the mother and the friend, as well: he explicitly accuses Georg of having "disgraced [his] mother's memory, betrayed [his] friend, and stuck [his] father into bed so that he can't move" (*Judgment*, 64; 85). When he includes himself in the trinity of Georg's victims, the father implicitly identifies himself with mother and friend; and when a short time later he repeats this indictment, he again groups himself with these two representatives of the utopian potentials repressed in bourgeois patriarchal society. "What a long time it's taken you to mature/ripen [*reif werden*]," he remarks to Georg. "Your mother had to die, she couldn't live to experience the happy day; your friend is going to pieces in Russia, already three years ago he was yellow enough to be thrown away; and as for me, why you can see what kind of condition I'm in" (*Judgment*, 67; 87). The German phrase *reif werden*, with which the father describes Georg's maturation, designates not only the growth of the child to maturity, but the ripening of fruits, as well. When applied to Georg, whom the father has previously called his "little fruit" ("Früchtchen") (*Judgment*, 63; 84), it alludes to the fact that Georg, as a clone of the authoritarian patriarch, has brought to ultimate "fruition" the "devilish" aspects of the patriarchal model. When he drops from the bridge, Georg emblematically enacts the final stage of this ripening, the falling of the mature fruit from the tree: the "happy day" of Georg's maturation, if we follow this metaphorical allusion, is necessarily identical with the moment of his death.

Father, mother, and friend are fused in an alliance of solidarity from which Georg as their oppressor is excluded, and it is only by drawing on the strength of the dead mother and the banished friend that the father can assert his dominance over Georg. "I am still the much stronger one. Left alone I might have had to accede, but your mother has transferred her power to me, I have established a fine alliance with your friend" (*Judgment*, 65–66; 86).

With this incorporation—literally—of the utopian reserve identified with the mother and the friend, the father becomes an absolutely equivocal figure: in him, the paradigmatic representative of patriarchal authority and the images of resistance to this authoritarian behavior are fused. With this turn, which establishes the father as the resurrected model of the divided bourgeois subject, Kafka's text arrives at an irresolvable aporia: the judgment the equivocal father passes on Georg represents both the self-condemnation of patriarchal authority and the damning of this authoritarian behavior by the utopian alternative it viciously represses. Now, one might be able to avoid this dilemma by arguing, for instance, that the father's appropriation of the authority preserved in the mother and the friend merely represents the most deadly tactic in his cunning strategy to outmaneuver his son and adversary. Viewed from this perspective, his alliance with the mother and the friend would be but the final act of dissemblance in that overriding "comedy" of dissimulation in the service of mastery that the father admits to playing (*Judgment*, 65; 86), a comedy in which Georg also assumes a leading part. This line of argumentation would bring us back to the conclusion I drew from the double collapse of father and son, namely, that their fight to the finish emblematizes the self-undoing of the bourgeois patriarchal subject, its (self-) subjugation to the same abstract structures of bourgeois commerce over which it falsely presumes itself to be master. However, if we accept the father's assertion that the alliance he enters into with the mother and the friend is genuine—and the text gives us no reason to doubt this—then we must interpret his condemnation of Georg as the damning judgment passed by the utopian impulse of the bourgeois subject on its repressive alter ego, on the mimetically assimilated and reified agent of infinite commerce. This is the final line of interpretation I want to pursue, but to do so it is first necessary to elaborate on the twofold character of the father as authoritarian patriarch and utopian resistance.

As the figure that mediates between Georg as merchant and the friend as Georg's repressed opposition to bourgeois commercial practice, the father occupies the structural matrix of *The Judgment*. His function in the text is that of a perspectival shifter, a character whose qualities change according to the perspective from which it is viewed. The image that comes to mind to render this oscillation between two distinct articulations of the same figure is the hologram that reveals one or the other of two superimposed images depending on the angle at which it is viewed. For Georg—as well as the readers of *The Judgment*, who are tied to his perspective—the father appears as just such a hologram. At the moment he stands up and Georg recognizes that his father "is still a giant of a man" (*Judgment*, 59; 81), the father's oscillation between two images begins; and when he rises up in bed to denounce his son as a "devilish human being," he combines the authority of the family patriarch with the oppositional critique of the mother and the friend. Thus he takes sides not with the son who most closely replicates his own characteristics as merchant-patriarch, but rather with the ostracized friend, whom he now identifies as a "son after my own heart" (*Judgment*, 63; 85).

This equivocal function of the father is strikingly reminiscent of the ambivalence of the doppelgänger as conceived by Freud in the essay "The Uncanny." As I demonstrated in the previous chapter, Freud suggests that the double marks a waffling of allegiances in the self-understanding of the divided subject: it signals both the self-critique of the superego, which sides with external authority against the individual's unrealized potentials, and the censure of sociopolitical factors that force the individual to repress these utopian designs. The father in *The Judgment* represents Georg's double in this deeper sense, and as such he combines the agent of infinite commerce (Georg) and the socially estranged rebel (the friend) in a single figure. It is this oscillation in the character of the father that produces the mysterious, uncanny quality of Kafka's text. This principal equivocation, moreover, constitutes the structural center of *The Judgment* as psychic text insofar as it marks what Julia Kristeva calls the "matrix of enunciation" of narrative as a signifying practice. In narrative, she argues, the I of the author as the matrix of enunciation is a projection of the paternal role in the family, and she identifies this staging-ground of narrative as a point of perspectival mobility: "Although axial, this position is mobile; it takes on all the possible roles in intra- and inter-familial relations, and it is as changeable as a mask."[43] The chameleonlike quality of the father in *The Judgment*, his ability to identify alternatively with the perspectives of the mother, the son, and the utopian alter ego, defines him as the matrix of enunciation in this narrative. This implies that the literary-aesthetic breakthrough Kafka achieved in the story finds concrete expression in the oscillating nature of the father as doppelgänger, the figure that ties together the text's fictional events and its structural network. In a letter to Felice, Kafka noted the centrality in *The Judgment* of perspectival changes in the relations between father and son. "The 'Judgment' cannot be explained," he maintains, and he accounts for this inexplicability with the assertion: "The story may be a journey around father and son, and the friend's changing shape may be a change in perspective in the relationship between father and son. But I am not quite sure of this, either" (*Letters to Felice*, 396–97; 267). My interpretation confirms Kafka's insight that this story circles around perspectival changes in the relationship between father and son. However, contrary to Kafka's assessment, it is not the figure of the friend, but that of the father that incessantly changes shape.

Confronting in his father the friend's representative at home, Georg re-

sponds by conjuring up in his imagination the alter ego whose repression is
the condition of possibility for his success in the world of bourgeois commerce: "His friend in St. Petersburg, whom his father suddenly knew so well,
touched [Georg's] imagination as never before" (*Judgment*, 64; 85). Picturing
the friend in his plundered shop, Georg begins to identify with his alienated
condition, and this fulfills the necessary precondition for Georg's self-critique of his merchant persona from the perspective of this utopian reserve.
Only on the basis of this reconfiguration of Georg's self-assessment, in which
he begins to identify with the "friend" and the "mother" against the devious merchant "Georg," does his acceptance of the father's death sentence
make any sense whatsoever. The father "uncovers" for Georg the treachery
he has committed as the mediative agent of an all-encompassing system of
infinite commerce; and it is the return of this repressed knowledge that
makes Georg feel "driven toward the water" in which he will find his death
(*Judgment*, 67; 88).

With this *unheimlich* reversal, the father ceases to represent for Georg
solely the objective correlative of his own authoritarian superego and takes
on those traits that link him with the rebellious potential of Georg's repressed utopian reserve. At this moment the father becomes a mediator between Georg and his own repressed alter ego, thereby opening up a chink
in the armor of Georg's self-repression. It is through this chink, namely
through the shifting role of the father, that the repressed utopian Other consequently finds its way back into Georg's consciousness and avenges itself
on him. The relationship between Georg and his father, in other words, radically shifts gears during the course of their encounter. Initially the symbol
of socioeconomic success and authority, the father represents for the son his
own aspirations to become a successful merchant. In this configuration,
Georg's struggle to displace the father is grounded in a desire to inherit the
authority of the patriarch. Georg therefore adopts the principles of commercial intercourse and mimics the authoritarian behavior of the father to
underwrite his claim to the scepter of patriarchal power. But the father suddenly and unpredictably ceases to identify himself as the symbol of patriarchal authority and allies himself instead with the "innocent child"—that is,
with those aspects of his self that Georg had to squelch to pursue the strategy of mimetic adaptation to bourgeois economic and discursive practice.
The father's condemnation of Georg hence signals both the (self-)destruc-
tion of the bourgeois subject as it devolves into a mere agent in the structural network of infinite commerce, and the critique of such passive agency
from the perspective of the marginalized "reserve sphere" of utopian desire.
The shifting relationship between father and son reflects changes in Georg's

psychic constitution as he identifies with the different faces of his own divided subjectivity. As the "devilish human being" who is the successful merchant, Georg introjects patriarchal authority as a tyrannical superego and marginalizes his utopian potential; as "innocent child" he sides with the remainder of this repressed utopian potential and condemns the "respectable businessman" (*Judgment*, 65; 86) Georg Bendemann to death by drowning. The rift that divides bourgeois subjectivity from within has become unmendable, the rupture absolute, the bourgeois subject ineluctably aporetic. What survives the death of the dialectical subject is infinite commerce, on the one hand, and the marginalized utopian reserve embodied in the friend, on the other. But this reserve sphere has become a "reservation" in the sense of a domain totally cut off from the socioeconomic mainstream of bourgeois socioeconomic practice. Condemned to an absolutely insular autonomy, any emancipatory potency once inherent in this utopian reserve has been effectively neutralized.

The paradox that Georg's intercourse in the world of infinite commerce is a symptom of deep-seated antisocial behavior corresponds to the inverse paradox that in the friend, engagement for a more humane communitarian alternative is depicted only as the total absence of all human interchange. This paradox expresses a bitter, overarching pessimism that accompanies Kafka's insight into the hegemony of bourgeois infinite *Verkehr*: given the desubjectified conditions of the administered world, bourgeois subjectivity automatically ceases to be a terrain from which emancipatory sociopolitical projects can be launched. The fates of Georg Bendemann and his double project the extinction of critical bourgeois subjectivity as the absolute division of the poles of the dialectical subject into an aporetic and fatal either/or: either reification through mimetic assimilation to the structures of the administered world, or solitary confinement in a nether-realm beyond all social praxis. Viewed in this way, the friend's flight does not represent a genuine revolutionary alternative to Georg's sellout to the principles of bourgeois commerce; indeed, it takes on the character of a parodistic cipher for the self-delusion of a bourgeois consciousness that mistakenly deems itself capable of self-emancipation. The bourgeois ideal of sociopolitical autonomy, which theoretically guarantees the subject's independence from the coercive power of external authority and thereby guarantees its (self-)emancipatory energy, is unmasked at this historical station of the divided subject as a debilitating isolationism that bespeaks its ultimate sociopolitical impotence.

The social paralysis that results from this insularity is addressed when Georg imagines the friend confronted with the revolutionary upheavals that are taking place in Russia: while the friend is associated with these events, he is portrayed neither as a standard-bearer of the revolution, nor even as an engaged participant in these acts of rebellion, but merely as its passive bourgeois victim. "[Georg's] friend in St. Petersburg . . . touched his imagination as never before. Lost in the vastness of Russia he saw him. At the door of an empty, plundered warehouse he saw him. Among the wreckage of his showcases, the slashed remnants of his wares, the falling gas brackets, he was just barely still standing. {A trampling tumultuous mob of people marched past in waves}" (*Judgment*, 64; 85). I have quoted this passage once again with the addition of the sentence Kafka deleted from the manuscript, because it is only in this unretouched—that is, unrepressed—form that its full significance comes to the fore. I have already argued that this deletion signals the drive to expunge the sociopolitical motives associated with the marginalized friend. Moreover, without the reference to the tumultuous masses, which connect this vision to the revolutionary events of Bloody Sunday, the friend appears simply to suffer under some inexplicable, pseudometaphysical victimization, concretized as the wanton destruction of his shop and merchandise. As Georg's fantasy about the friend as his own alter ego, this passage projects his vision of the fate he would have suffered had he opted to resist rather than mimetically adapt to and assimilate the reifying structures of bourgeois sociopolitical and economic practice. The destruction of the friend's showcases and commodities by the revolutionary masses concretizes a disruptive assault on the infrastructure that underpins the networks of bourgeois commerce. However, this rebellious attack is not unleashed by the bourgeois subject, but is instead directed against it: revolt now has its source somewhere outside the sphere of bourgeois subjectivity, which ceases to be the driving force behind social history. In *The Judgment* Kafka thus identifies the culmination of bourgeois hegemony with its historical demise at the hands of a new revolutionary class.

If with the death of Georg Bendemann the collapse of bourgeois subjectivity as Unhappy Consciousness is depicted as the submersion of the subject in the infinite flow of commercial exchange, the marginalization of the friend indicates that the price of escape from the ideological web of the bourgeois epistemic formation is a self-imposed sociopolitical impotence. The implication of this aporetic choice is that at this historical juncture the bourgeois subject is so reified by the structures of instrumental rationality and abstract exchange, so enmeshed in the subjectless structural network of infinite commerce, that it can no longer formulate a productive critical alternative. What Kafka presents in *The Judgment* is the demise of Unhappy Consciousness, the collapse of a dialectical subjectivity that has spent every ounce of its critical potential. As depicted in Kafka's story, revolution no longer represents the self-liberation of the bourgeois subject from its self-destructive reliance on calculative rationality, as was true to varying degrees of Lessing, Schiller, Heine, Büchner, and even Hofmannsthal; instead, revolution signifies an attack on bourgeois hegemony from below, an assault that leaves the bourgeois subject "just barely standing" in the wake of the proletarian mass movements beginning to appear on the European horizon in 1912, when Kafka composed this story.

The fourteen years separating the composition of Hofmannsthal's *Tale of the Cavalry* and Kafka's *The Judgment* mark a crucial historical turning point in the self-understanding of the bourgeois subject. Where Hofmannsthal could still look back with—albeit, repressed—longing on the revolutionary upheavals undertaken by the bourgeoisie in 1848, Kafka projects the bourgeois subject only as the object of rebellion, no longer as its subject. *The Judgment* envisions the historical culmination of the divided bourgeois subject as a dead end in which it is confronted with a choice of equally catastrophic options: succumbing to the coercion of abstract exchange, it ceases to exist as subjective consciousness; resisting this demand for mimetic conformity, it continues to exist only as a historical anachronism in the emerging proletarian world. According to the analysis Kafka gives in *The Judgment*, the ambivalence of bourgeois Unhappy Consciousness achieves its historical culmination in the choice between alternative modes for the bourgeois subject's (self-)obliteration: its place becomes a genuine u-topia, a no-place that is its final resting place. In *The Judgment* Kafka creates one of the last great literary memorials to the inexorably divided bourgeois subject, a memorial that (yet) exploits the dialectical structure of Unhappy Consciousness in its literary aesthetic structures, but only to diagnose its historical extinction.

The Sociogenesis of Bourgeois Subjectivity

From Unhappy Consciousness to Liberal Ironism

> What is it that the Romantics ultimately craved if not the irresponsibly reflecting genius bound by the golden chains of authority?   —Walter Benjamin

> The rebel is careful to maintain intact the abuses from which he suffers in order to rebel against them. . . . He wants neither to destroy, nor transcend, but only to stand up against the order of things. The more he attacks it, the more he secretly respects it: the rights that he openly contests, he preserves intact in the depths of his heart.   —Jean-Paul Sartre

ALL WORKS of art contain, as Theodor Adorno has argued, an "unconscious historiography,"[1] and the foregoing interpretations of six acknowledged literary "masterworks" of German bourgeois literature have sought to recover the unconscious historiography of bourgeois subjectivity inscribed within these texts. The history of German bourgeois literary aesthetics, I have argued, evolves out of the dialectic of legitimation and contestation that characterizes the attitude of the bourgeois subject toward the ideological preconditions of bourgeois thought and social practice. Constitutive of the textual dynamics of these literary works is a fundamental equivocation between ideologically motivated compliance with, and ideology-critical resistance to, the instrumental rationality that underwrites the economic, discursive, and intersubjective practices of the bourgeois world. By examining changes in the relative balance between the submissive and the critical moments of these texts, I have attempted to outline certain transformations in the dialectical patterns that structure bourgeois subjectivity as Unhappy Consciousness. The (hi)story inscribed in the unconscious historiography of these literary texts tells of the atomistic breakup of this dialectically organized subjectivity: increasingly capitulating to the ideological demand that

it assimilate the authority-oriented behavior of the bourgeois patriarchal order, the bourgeois subject gradually shrinks into the mere affirmative agent
of the sociopolitical, economic, and discursive structures underwritten by
bourgeois ideology.

Parallel to this (hi)story of the disappearance of the subject in the infinite
networks of bourgeois traffic-commerce-intercourse-discourse (*Verkehr*), this
unconscious historiography also tells the (hi)story of the gradual atrophy of
that ideology-critical moment essential to the historical constitution of bourgeois subjectivity. German bourgeois literature from Lessing to Kafka thus
furnishes a critical counternarrative to the tale of the subject's progressive
self-realization as envisioned in the philosophic-historical accounts of German bourgeois philosophy. Indeed, far from projecting the historical self-realization of Unhappy Consciousness as the harmonious sublation of its dialectical opposites, as Hegel did in *Phenomenology of Spirit*, this literary counternarrative recounts the historical phylogenesis of the bourgeois subject as
a process of violent ideological self-disciplining in which its (self-)critical
drive is unremittingly repressed. This moment of utopian resistance, rather
than being dialectically integrated into bourgeois consciousness, is banished
to a privatized political unconscious, where it survives as an impotent
rem(a)inder of this lost emancipatory potential. But the literary texts considered here do not simply relate the (hi)story of this sociopolitical self-repression, they show it as well—in the Wittgensteinian sense—both in their
literary-aesthetic structures and in their signifying practices. The aesthetic
innovations concretized in these works function primarily as mechanisms
for the repressive self-disciplining of utopian sociopolitical drives that are out
of line with the precepts of bourgeois ideology. From the late eighteenth to
the early twentieth century, the sociocritical impulse of German bourgeois
literature is forced progressively further underground into the esoteric
depths of the text and its political unconscious. The growing marginalization of the ideology-critical moment of the bourgeois subject is thus reflected in this aesthetic occultation of sociopolitically resistant impulses.

Drawn inductively from sociosemiotic interpretations of historically disparate canonical texts, these speculative historical conclusions about the sociological evolution of German bourgeois literary aesthetics depart from
those assessments of the sociocritical component of modern literary discourse most frequently voiced in current theoretical debates. According to
my analyses, literature's aesthetic dimension does not simply circumscribe
a realm in which nonalienated subjectivity and difference seek refuge from
the reifying principles of the administered world, as Adorno, Marcuse, and
other adherents of German Critical Theory would have it; but neither does

it embody that ideology-resistant counterdiscourse envisioned by Foucault, Kristeva, and other representatives of French sociocritical post-structuralism. On the contrary, the otherness of literary-aesthetic discourse emerges, on the one hand, as a reflex of the ideologically assimilative drive to muzzle precisely such critical impulses, and on the other hand, as a—less and less effective—attempt to restore and articulate this critical position. The increasingly cryptic quality of German bourgeois literature thus appears as a consequence of the repressive privatization—the making *heimlich*, secret and private—of all opposition to the bourgeois epistemic-discursive formation, and the ever more insistent if violent return of this repressed utopian perspective. The intricate aesthetic advances made by these texts are produced by the pressure to force this sociocritical moment underground, out of the manifest and overt into the latent and covert layer of literary discourse.

If the self-critique of bourgeois discursive-economic practices is focused throughout the texts I have explored as an attack on symbolic mediation, then their gravitation toward ever more complex forms of discursive mediation in the fabric of their own textuality marks the ideological retrenchment of this literature against its own critical insights. Viewed from this perspective, the literary-aesthetic intricacies of High Modernist, avant-garde literary texts such as Hofmannsthal's *A Tale of the Cavalry* and Kafka's *The Judgment* reflect the ideologically affirmative capitulation of the bourgeois authorial subject to the alienating mediacy of bourgeois symbolic practices, the subject's ultimate submersion in the infinite *Verkehr* of bourgeois discourse. The bourgeois literary text, in other words, ultimately exercises the same mimetic adaptation to the meaning-alienating structures of bourgeois semiosis that it critically depicts in such characters as Büchner's Woyzeck and Kafka's Georg Bendemann.

The centrality of hermeneutics in the German bourgeois cultural formation from the end of the eighteenth century onward corresponds to the increasingly divided, opaque, and recondite character of its characteristic discourse, all qualities that are reflected in the signifying practices of bourgeois literary texts. However, even hermeneutics, as a science of interpretation, does not develop monolithically, as one might first believe, as a simple critical-emancipatory antidote that, when practiced correctly, can liberate the secret (*heimlich*) sociopolitical rebellion repressed by the disciplinary measures of bourgeois literary-aesthetic discourse. On the contrary, if the signifying practices that govern the production of German bourgeois literature emerge as a dialectic of revelation and occultation, the same can be said for the genesis of bourgeois hermeneutics as a set of interpretive practices that guide the reception of literary texts. Thus Heine's attempt to program a politically redemptive and therapeutic hermeneutical response into the text of *The Book Le Grand* finds its dialectical antithesis in the politically reactionary hermeneutrick characteristic of High Modernist psychic narratives and methodologically concretized in the repression of sociopolitical significance endemic to Freud's interpretive practice. The privatization of sociopolitical and discursive resistance first outlined as a literary-aesthetic strategy by Schiller in *The Robbers*, although initially conceived as a tactic deployed for the rescue and covert transmission of ideology-critical impulses, reverts ultimately into a device employed for their concealment. Both the productive and receptive dimensions of the German bourgeois literary institution, then, tend toward the generation of a privatizing cryptography that aims at the silencing and/or marginalization of all spontaneous opposition to bourgeois instrumental rationality and the socioeconomic, semiotic, and discursive exchanges it legitimates.

One of the most persistent symbolic manifestations of this marginalization of utopian desire makes itself evident throughout the texts investigated here as the bourgeois male subject's often violent mastery over the feminine. This motif is inaugurated in Lessing's drama *Emilia Galotti*, which depicts bourgeois tragedy as the sacrificial slaughter of those idealized virtues invested in its female heroine. While less overt in later texts, this problematic is never wholly absent, recurring, for example, in *The Robbers* as the exchange of Amalia's life in payment for Karl Moor's debt to the robbers;[2] in *Woyzeck* as the murder of Marie, an act calculated to establish Woyzeck as a mastering subject; and in *The Judgment* as the death of the mother—and parallel banishment of the friend—as the condition of possibility of Georg Bendemann's socioeconomic ascendancy. In all of these works, oppression of the feminine stands in for the self-repression of utopian alternatives to the authoritarian socialization procedures of bourgeois patriarchy. In this context Heine's *Book Le Grand* performs the function of the exception that proves the general rule: it ironically inverts the relative positions in this power struggle to jockey the male protagonist into the position of a desperate suitor who must woo the feminine back into his camp. The self-emancipatory wooing of madame, around which the narrative discourse of this text is structured, thereby suggests that both the sociological and the psychological emancipation of the bourgeois male subject can only occur if it actively courts the alienated feminine as the representative of utopian alternatives. Heine's text thus outlines the project of bourgeois self-liberation as the (re)establishment of a communicative interaction—one not grounded simply in the drive to repressive (self-)mastery—between the bourgeois inclination toward authority-behavior and its rebellious, authority-critical

Other. According to the diagnosis of historically subsequent works, however, this project, which would return a dialectical balance to Unhappy Consciousness, ultimately fails—with the result that the dialectical both / and structure of bourgeois subjectivity devolves into an aporetic either / or.

The dis-integrative historical momentum of Unhappy Consciousness inscribed in the unconscious historiography of these literary texts can be thrown into relief by briefly juxtaposing two works that represent opposite ends of this historical spectrum. Schiller's *The Robbers* and Kafka's *The Judgment* are ideally suited for such a historical cross-examination because, despite the temporal gulf that separates their composition, they display certain striking structural and characterological similarities. These resemblances are consistent enough to permit the hypothetical postulation of a structural paradigm against whose background divergences between these two texts take on the quality of historically significant transformations. Even the most cursory comparison of the fictional economies of *The Robbers* and *The Judgment* brings to light an array of remarkable analogies. On the most general level, both texts focus specifically on the interactions among male subjects in the institutionalized framework of the patriarchal family. In each work, moreover, the fictional events turn on the relations between two sons with antithetical characters and motivations who compete with one another for the right to inherit the power of a frail and aging patriarch. The agonal structures of the patriarchal institution that bonds this male triumvirate have a double representational function: on the one hand, they embody in microcosm the acrimonious relationships characteristic of *inter*subjective exchanges in bourgeois society as a whole; on the other hand, they emblematize tensions among the *intra*subjective agencies that operate in the psychic economy of the divided bourgeois (male) subject.

Both Schiller's *Robbers* and Kafka's *Judgment* tell the stories of sons who opt for divergent courses of action in their attempts to establish themselves as independent subjects in the bourgeois life-world. Like Georg Bendemann's friend in St. Petersburg, whom father Bendemann identifies as a son after his "own heart" (*Judgment*, 63; 85), Old Moor's favorite son Karl voluntarily enters into self-banishment from the patriarchal home. Their alter egos, Georg and Franz, by contrast, remain at the institutional center of patriarchal power and commit similar acts of semiotic treachery in their attempts to inherit the economic, sociopolitical, and discursive might attached to the role of the father. In fact, there are so many inherent similarities between Schiller's Franz Moor and Kafka's Georg Bendemann that we are justified in viewing them as closely related literary ancestors.[3] Both Franz and Georg, first of all, are obsessed with their own ascent to the seat of bourgeois power, and neither shies away from violence against his father or from the willful alienation of his "brother" to accomplish this socioeconomic end. Furthermore, both exploit the duplicity of an arbitrary and mediative semiotic to underwrite and conceal their brazen will to power, and in both texts this dissimulative design is paradigmatically manifest in epistolary intrigues deployed to effect the marginalization of their alter egos.

But Franz Moor and Georg Bendemann also differ in some significant respects. Where Franz, for example, literally buries his father alive, Georg only buries his father in a figurative sense, and this shift from the literal to the figurative reflects the increased sophistication and cunning of Georg's historically more advanced strategies of self-empowerment. But more important yet is the relative character of these sons in relation to that of their fathers; for whereas Georg Bendemann is truly his father's son in that his treachery merely mimetically reproduces the duplicitous Eros patterned by the father as bourgeois patriarch, Franz's behavior has no precedent in the actions of his father. Old Moor is not a representative of the bourgeois age of calculative rationality, as is father Bendemann; rather, he is one of the final avatars of that naive immediacy characteristic of the prebourgeois good-faith economy. Within the fictional economy of Schiller's play, then, Franz Moor functions as the character who introduces into the intersubjective relations of the bourgeois world a dissimulative discourse that operates by means of the malicious manipulation of arbitrary signs; in this sense he is—allegorically speaking—the progenitor of bourgeois purposive rationality. Franz's successful marginalization of both the father and Karl reflects the overthrow of this prebourgeois epistemic formation by the modern principles of calculative rationality. But where Schiller's drama portrays the historical moment at which the inverted world is institutionalized, Kafka's narrative depicts the socialization processes by which it, once instituted, guarantees its own self-perpetuation.

Now, to be sure, Schiller indicts as villainy the dissimulations of Franz Moor, and he ultimately sentences him to death; but the justice that expounds this verdict is merely poetic in nature, since the semiotic mediacy that he represents does not perish with him. Indeed, the conclusion of *The Robbers* presents the triumph of calculative rationality in the capitulation of Karl, the avatar of iconicity and immediacy, to the abstract, symbolic mediations of bourgeois economic and discursive exchange. The same holds true for Kafka's *The Judgment*: while the death of Georg and his father may reflect their condemnation before the court of poetic justice, the principles that motivate them remain intact at the story's conclusion. To the extent that it suggests that the structures of the administered world exist above and be-

yond the actions of human subjects, *The Robbers* already prefigures the absolutization of the infinite structural networks of bourgeois commercial-discur-
sive traffic diagnosed by Kafka in *The Judgment*. Read in this historical interrelation with Schiller's dramatic novel, Kafka's story appears as a literary
reckoning which, drawing the fatal consequences that follow from the hegemony of bourgeois purposive rationality, fictively portrays the fulfillment of
the pessimistic prophesy voiced by its literary antecedent over a century earlier.

The overweening pessimism of Kafka's diagnosis stands in contrast to the
optimism—to be sure, resigned—that characterizes Schiller's project of an
aesthetic redemption of the naive. That no such redemptive hope shines on
the fictional world of Kafka's *The Judgment* is signaled by the exceedingly minor role of the Petersburg friend. As the embodiment of a sociopolitical alternative to the mimetic adaptation practiced by Georg, this figure plays a
role that is structurally analogous to that of Karl Moor in Schiller's play. But
while this earlier text revolves fundamentally around Karl's utopian opposition to the "ink-smearing century" (*Robbers* I, ii, 502; 35), in Kafka's narrative the representative of this utopian drive is displaced to the very margins
of the text. The withering away of this figure that represents resistance to
bourgeois practice reflects the waxing atrophy of the bourgeois subject's
(self-)critical potential to mount effective opposition to the self-destructive
principles of the calculative rationality to which it subscribes. If in Karl
Moor's evolution we witness the birth of the divided subject out of the repressive privatization of this visionary critical impulse, in the mute helplessness of Georg Bendemann's nameless friend we become painfully aware
of the historical consequences of this privatizing repression of sociopolitical
opposition. What began as an underground resistance movement ends up
as self-imposed solitary confinement: the private-secret (*heimlich*) liberational
desire of the bourgeois subject is ultimately locked away in an isolation
ward, where it concedes its absolute impotence with regard to revolutionary sociopolitical praxis. Karl Moor's dream of revolutionary return is shattered in that moment when the rift that traverses bourgeois subjectivity
proves only to be mendable at the price of a repressive displacement that
forces the drive to critical resistance out of bourgeois consciousness and into
its repressed unconscious. If bourgeois subjectivity as Unhappy Consciousness first evolves as a dialectical dynamic of absolute unrest, this dialectical
system eventually disintegrates into its component parts, ending up as a sta-
tic, mutually exclusive counterposition between the ideological legitimation practiced in public life and the secrets of the private self. Personal fulfillment is thereby wholly dissociated from any form of intersubjective sol-

idarity other than those alienated interpersonal relations sanctioned by, and requisite for, the conditions of infinite commerce.

In his book *Contingency, Irony, and Solidarity*, Richard Rorty associates the phrase "liberal ironism" with a postmetaphysical philosophical position that legitimates precisely this absolute dissociation of the public from the private, and he dubs those who, like himself, adhere to the tenets of such a philosophy "liberal ironists." Liberal ironists, according to Rorty's definition, are those who "drop the demand for a theory which unifies the public and the private, and are content to treat the demands of self-creation and of human solidarity as equally valid, yet forever incommensurable."[4] Now, as *liberal* ironism, Rorty clearly understands the philosophical position he represents to be the historical, postmodernist heir to the tradition of bourgeois liberalism; and insofar as his theory attempts philosophically to codify as irreconcilable the rift between the bourgeois subject's public and the private personae, it does indeed represent the paradoxical culmination of that liberal tradition whose devolutionary history is captured in the unconscious historiography of German bourgeois literature. What Rorty calls "irony" refers, in fact, to nothing other than that aporetic choice, sketched in Kafka's *The Judgment*, between blindly committed adaptation to the given sociopolitical and discursive practices of bourgeois society, or retreat into a privatized, sociopolitically impotent selfhood that is totally segregated from all forms of intersubjective practice. The only thing that distinguishes Kafka's position from that of Rorty is that the former is still able to muster the critical energy to denounce as desubjectivizing capitulation to the structures of infinite commerce what the latter theoretically valorizes and legitimates as liberal—but by no means liberating—ironism. Kafka, in other words, still speaks with the distinctly modernist nostalgia of Unhappy Consciousness for a redemptive dialectical resolution of the conflict that scars bourgeois subjectivity, whereas Rorty's voice rings with the festive postmodernist affirmation of self-division as the hallmark of the decentered subject.[5]

Insofar as Rorty's defense of ironism is grounded, as he admits, on "a firm distinction between the private and the public," it harks back not so much to what he calls "the line of ironist thinking which runs from Hegel through Foucault and Derrida,"[6] as it does to the public/private distinction on which bourgeois self-conceptions have been based since the eighteenth century. In this sense it is Kant's self-contradictory delineation of the public and the private domains of the enlightened bourgeois subject that forms the foundation of Rorty's position. He expresses, without any of the skeptical trepidations of modernist writers such as Schiller or Kafka, the ultimate insight of bourgeois liberal culture when he advocates that we accept without hesitation the incommensurable contrariety of our impulses toward "private perfection" and "human solidarity." "The closest we will come to joining these two quests," he asserts, "is to see the aim of a just and free society as letting its citizens be as privatistic, 'irrationalist,' and aestheticist as they please so long as they do it on their own time."[7] Who can help but hear in this admonition the echo of the words Kant would have his ideal enlightened ruler direct at his subjects: "Argue as much as you will, and about what you will, but obey!"[8] It is this heritage, more than anything else, that lends Rorty's theory the quality of a retrospective philosophical apologia for the depoliticizing privatization of all practical sociocritical commitment, a tendency that has characterized the past two hundred years of bourgeois "liberal" culture. His insistence on our inherent inability to synthesize social commitment and self-creation, to discover a vocabulary that fuses the "shared" and the "private,"[9] thus reads like a theoretical corroboration of the unconscious historiography inscribed in German bourgeois literature, which relates the waxing disintegration of the divided bourgeois subject into, on the one hand, the mechanical agent of the public sociopolitical will, and, on the other hand, the creatively autonomous but politically impotent private individual. The belief that justice and freedom can somehow be realized in a self-administered bourgeois public sphere composed of autonomous and privatized monads is predicated on an ideologically motivated self-delusion; it is against this delusion that German bourgeois literature from Lessing to Kafka, in its never quite successfully repressed critical moments, raises its voice in protest. The "postmetaphysical culture" championed by Rorty,[10] by contrast, represents the absolute squelching of even this meager critical potential.

The historical juncture at which the nightmare of Kafka's trenchant literary visions turns into the self-fulfillment dream of bourgeois liberal justice marks the point at which the accommodation of the bourgeois subject to the self-deceptions of its own ideology reaches its apex. The tragic fate of the divided bourgeois subject, according to the historical disposition inscribed in German bourgeois literature, is to learn to love its fate as divided subjectivity. At the moment when the bourgeois liberal subject affirms with joyous *amor fati* its aporetic cleavage into public agency and self-repressed private utopian reserve, it ceases to exist as Unhappy Consciousness and enters instead into the state of liberal ironism. With this act of ultimate sociopolitical acquiescence, the curtain falls on the bourgeois tragedy of the divided subject, a tragedy whose first act is presented over two hundred years earlier in Lessing's *Emilia Galotti*.

Reference Matter

Notes

Introduction

1. Schulte-Sasse, "Einleitung," p. 27.
2. de Man, "Literary History," p. 165.
3. On the centrality of this dialectic and the need to develop interpretive procedures adequate to it, see Brenkman, pp. 46–56.
4. Horkheimer, "Rise and Decline of the Individual," p. 128.
5. Adorno, *Ästhetische Theorie*, pp. 312; *299*.
6. *Ästhetische Theorie*, pp. 168; *161*.
7. *Theorie der Avantgarde*, pp. 32; *25*.
8. See Goldmann, "Structure: Human Reality and Methodological Concept," p. 101.
9. Lyotard, p. xxiv.
10. On Lyotard's proximity to the thought of the early Frankfurt School theoreticians, see Berman, *Modern Culture*, pp. 3–9.
11. See Adorno, "Der Artist als Statthalter," pp. 120; *103*.
12. Deleuze and Guattari, *Kafka*, p. 18.
13. Lentricchia, p. 4.
14. Horkheimer, "Traditionelle und kritische Theorie," pp. 41; *223–24*.
15. Cf. Derrida, "Structure, Sign, and Play," pp. 278–80.
16. Huyssen, *After the Great Divide*, p. 213.
17. The most notable attempt to reassert a traditionalist view of the self-identical subject is undoubtedly Taylor's *Sources of the Self*, which seeks to retheorize the self by grounding it in the moral concept of the good.
18. See Frank, *Was ist Neostrukturalismus?* especially pp. 541–72; *425–49*. See also his *Die Unhintergehbarkeit von Individualität*.
19. Derrida, "Edmond Jabès," p. 75.
20. See Althusser.
21. Smith, p. xxxiv.
22. Smith, p. xxxv.
23. Horkheimer, "Rise and Decline of the Individual," p. 131.
24. Horkheimer, "Rise and Decline of the Individual," p. 128.
25. Adorno, "Gesellschaft," pp. 13–14; *148–49*.

26. See Baudrillard, *Simulations*.

27. See especially Goux's "Introduction," in *Symbolic Economies*, pp. 1–8.

28. Horkheimer and Adorno, pp. 147; *164*.

29. Saussure, p. 110.

30. Cf. Saussure, pp. 111–22.

31. Morris, p. 132.

32. See Marx, pp. 562–67; *375–80*.

33. See Turgot, "Value and Money" (1769), in *The Economics of A. R. J. Turgot*, p. 133.

34. Foucault, *The Order of Things*, p. 29.

35. See Brenkman, p. vii.

Chapter 1

1. Hegel, *Phänomenologie*, pp. 163; *126*.

2. Cf. *Phänomenologie*, pp. 155–63; *119–26*.

3. *Phänomenologie*, pp. 163–64; *126*.

4. Cf. *Phänomenologie*, pp. 165; *128*.

5. *Phänomenologie*, pp. 161; *124*.

6. *Phänomenologie*, pp. 168; *130*.

7. *Phänomenologie*, pp. 163; *126*.

8. *Phänomenologie*, pp. 150–55; *115–19*.

9. *Phänomenologie*, pp. 150; *115*.

10. *Phänomenologie*, pp. 162; *125*.

11. On the superego as the internalization of external structures of authority, see Freud, *Das Unbehagen*, pp. 250–52; *125–27*.

12. *Phänomenologie*, pp. 152; *117*.

13. See Kristeva, *Revolution*, p. 22.

14. See, for example, Benveniste, pp. 223–30, and Lacan, *The Language of the Self and Ecrits*.

15. Kristeva, *Revolution*, pp. 118, 215.

16. *Revolution*, p. 24.

17. *Revolution*, pp. 16–17.

18. Cf. *Revolution*, p. 88; Kristeva's conception of the avant-garde needs to be corrected and supplemented by the historicizing perspective Peter Bürger brings to the examination of this aesthetic phenomenon in his *Theory of the Avant-Garde*.

19. Cf. Heidegger, pp. 126–30; *162–68*.

20. *Revolution*, p. 82.

21. Adorno, "Der Artist als Statthalter," pp. 126; *107*.

22. Pp. 256; *245*.

23. See *Revolution*, pp. 25–30.

24. Coward and Ellis, p. 115; cf. also pp. 8, 44, and 155.

25. Foucault, *The Order of Things*, p. 62; on the constitution of "Classical" reason, see pp. 46–77.

26. *Phänomenologie*, pp. 152; *117*.

27. Weber, especially pp. 115–90; *95–183*.

28. On the church as ideological bastion, see Althusser, p. 144.

29. See Mauss's historical etiology of the categories of "person" and "self," p. 88.

30. Kant, "Was ist Aufklärung?" pp. 55; *87*; emphasis added.

31. See Habermas, *Strukturwandel*, pp. 45–46; *30–31*. Habermas points out the paradox that the bourgeois public sphere circumscribes a "public" constituted as a loose confederation of private individuals.

32. "Was ist Aufklärung?" pp. 55; *87*.

33. "Was ist Aufklärung?" pp. 55; *87*.

34. "Was ist Aufklärung?" pp. 55, 61; *87, 92*.

35. Koselleck, *Kritik und Krise*, pp. 9; *11–12*.

36. See Habermas, "Der Universalitätsanspruch der Hermeneutik," especially pp. 276–93; *190–209*.

37. See Habermas, *Strukturwandel*, pp. 44–58; *30–42*.

38. "Was ist Aufklärung?" pp. 54; *86*; emphasis added.

39. The metaphor of the human gait is borrowed from Kant himself; cf. "Was ist Aufklärung?" pp. 54; *86*.

40. Habermas, *Erkenntnis und Interesse*, pp. 14; *5*.

41. See Foucault, *The Order of Things*, pp. 25–34; Derrida, "Structure, Sign, and Play," pp. 278–79.

42. *Revolution*, pp. 86–89.

43. *Ästhetische Theorie*, pp. 16; *8*.

44. The controversy over the political status of aesthetic autonomy has been especially heated in German critical debate. See, for example, Janz. On autonomy as a response to bourgeois economics and the principles of commodification, see Hinz, as well as the other essays in the volume *Autonomie der Kunst*; cf. also Olechnowitz, pp. 92 98; and Warncken. On the emergence of the aesthetics of autonomy as a reaction against the subjugation of literary aesthetics to the structures and constraints of the developing bourgeois marketplace, see Christa Bürger, "Literarischer Markt und Öffentlichkeit," pp. 172–78. See also, in the same volume, Schulte-Sasse, "Das Konzept bürgerlich-literarischer Öffentlichkeit," especially pp. 99–106. Peter Bürger discusses the role of autonomy in idealist aesthetics, *Zur Kritik der idealistischen Ästhetik*, pp. 53–56. Marcuse and Adorno, of course, are the most noteworthy contemporary theoreticians of an aesthetic autonomy that preserves socially redemptive elements otherwise eliminated in the bourgeois world.

45. Marcuse, "Über den affirmativen Charakter der Kultur," pp. 64; *95–96*.

46. "Über den affirmativen Charakter der Kultur," pp. 66–67; *98*.

47. Koselleck, *Kritik und Krise*, pp. 29–39, 55–56; *37–50, 66–67*.

48. *Die Permanenz der Kunst*, pp. 11; *1*.

49. *Die Permanenz der Kunst*, pp. 9; *xii*.

50. Pp. 97; *90*.

51. On the prevalence of this dialectic between discursivity and figuration—an

inheritance from German idealist aesthetics—in contemporary theoretical discourses, see Wilke.

52. *Ästhetische Theorie*, pp. 152; 145.

Chapter 2

1. "Traditionelle und kritische Theorie," pp. 30–31; 210–11.
2. *Ästhetische Theorie*, pp. 72; 65.
3. *Ästhetische Theorie*, pp. 15–16; 7.
4. Hegel, *Vorlesungen über die Ästhetik* 1: 74–75; 1: 49.
5. Dvoretzky has traced the multifaceted receptive history of *Emilia Galotti* and sought its source in what he calls the "enigma" of the text itself; see *The Enigma*. The best analyses of the contradictions that disrupt the coherence of this drama are provided in the essays by Frank Ryder.
6. "*Emilia Galotti*," p. 330.
7. "*Emilia Galotti*," p. 331.
8. *Ästhetische Theorie*, pp. 420; 396.
9. See Adorno, *Ästhetische Theorie*, pp. 182, 205; 176, 197.
10. On this conflict between pedagogical mission and commercial marketplace, see Christa Bürger, "Literarischer Markt und Öffentlichkeit."
11. See Barner et al., p. 50.
12. For an excellent introduction to this debate and the issues it addressed, see Schulte-Sasse, "Der Stellenwert des Briefwechsels [über das Trauerspiel]."
13. See Lessing's letter of December 1, 1771, to his editor Christian Friedrich Voss (*LW* 9: 461).
14. See Lessing's famous comments in *Hamburgische Dramaturgie* (*LW* 6: 509), in which he blames the impossibility of a German national theater on the Germans' inability to constitute themselves either politically or morally as a nation; see also *LW* 9: 747–49, for further remarks on the idea of a national theater.
15. See Christa Bürger, "Literarischer Markt und Öffentlichkeit," p. 178.
16. See especially Stahl, pp. 102–3, who argues that these scenes perform the sole function of motivating the dramatic action on the psychological plane. But Stahl flatly denies that they serve Lessing as a medium for the presentation of aesthetic issues relevant to the drama itself. Cf. also Wells, p. 375.
17. Schmitt-Sasse, pp. 157–60; Lützeler, "Die marxistische Lessing-Rezeption," p. 44.
18. Wells, p. 377.
19. Appelbaum-Graham, pp. 4–9.
20. Flax, p. 52.
21. Flax, p. 40.
22. See Ebanks, p. 92.
23. For eighteenth-century aesthetic theory the concept of illusion thus performs a function similar to the notion of sensuality in Hegel's aesthetics. Whereas for Hegel the cultivated sensuality of art serves to lift humanity beyond crass sensuality,

for the eighteenth century the mimetic illusion of art serves to lift humanity beyond dissimulative illusion.

24. The original painting of Emilia, to be sure, is in the hands of her father, as Conti admits (see *EG* I, iv, 245; 9), and this opens up the possibility, at least, that the Emilia painting was likewise commissioned. The text is ambiguous on this matter, however, and it could just as easily be the case that Conti requested permission to portray Emilia, promising the portrait to her father as a way of ensuring that he attain the privilege of having her sit for him. From Conti's perspective as artist, at any rate, the portrait of Emilia derives from purely aesthetic considerations, and there is no mention of any monetary transaction having transpired between Conti and Odoardo. For Conti, in other words, it is emphatically not a commodity. The fact that he ultimately receives from the Prince whatever sum of money he desires for Emilia's portrait (*EG* I, iv, 245; 9) is a significant irony whose implications will be discussed below.

25. *Vorlesungen über die Ästhetik* 1: 20; 1: 7.

26. Mendelssohn, pp. 434, 435.

27. See Adorno, *Ästhetische Theorie*, pp. 253–60; *243–49*. Adorno argues that the concepts of the artistic "genius" and "originality," which evolved in the final decades of the eighteenth century, mark the attempt to generate an ideology of the organic work of art and thereby conceal its obvious artificiality.

28. Cf. *Ästhetische Theorie*, pp. 90–96, 114–21; *83–89, 108–14*.

29. On the demand for semiotic transparency see, for example, Lessing's *Laokoön* (*LW* 5: 294–95) and Mendelssohn, p. 443. Cf. also Wellbery, p. 8.

30. See Todorov, p. 19.

31. The distinction between the "expressive" or "symptomatic," and the "mimetic" dimension of communication is drawn by Bühler, p. 28.

32. Cf. Herder, p. 486, where language is defined as the "signature of the soul on a thing."

33. On the symbolic employment of natural signs in painting see *Laokoön* (*LW* 5: 83, 91).

34. Adorno draws this connection between the constructive principle of aesthetics and the tactics of what he terms the administered world, *Ästhetische Theorie*, pp. 334; *319*.

35. Cf. also *LW* 7: 177, where Lessing employs the example of Emilia's portrait to differentiate between first-order and second-order representations, between copies of nature and copies of copies.

36. Cf. Haug, *Kritik der Warenästhetik*, pp. 16; *15–16*.

37. Benjamin, "Das Kunstwerk im Zeitalter seiner mechanischen Reproduzierbarkeit," pp. 152–53; *223*.

38. Haug, *Kritik der Warenästhetik*, pp. 17; *16–17*.

39. Poster, p. 1.

40. This has been pointed out by Rickels, p. 45.

41. Wellbery, p. 194.

42. See Schulte-Sasse, *Literarische Struktur*, pp. 18–20.

43. It should be noted that his sentimentalism, as well as his emotional instability, casts the Prince in the role of a significant forerunner to the emotionally explosive if irresolute protagonists commonly presented by the Sturm und Drang writers of the next generation.

44. *Ästhetische Theorie*, pp. 51; *43*.

45. Zinkernagel documents this transition, pp. 209–10.

46. The infrequency of Emilia's stage appearances prompts Hatfield, for example, to dub her an "absentee heroine," p. 292.

47. On Odoardo as protagonist see, for example, Cowen, p. 12; Heitner, p. 486. On the Prince as protagonist see Merkel, pp. 232–39; Schenkel, pp. 179, 185.

48. Baudrillard, "On Seduction," p. 149.

49. Goux offers a penetrating analysis of this "isomorphism," as he calls it, between the economic and the psychological registers, pp. 9–63.

50. While it has been argued that *Emilia Galotti* forms an exception among Lessing's plays insofar as the middle-class merchant is not represented among its characters (see Barner et al., p. 200), in fact the Prince himself—or at the very least his middleman Marinelli—aptly fills this role.

51. Kant, "Was ist Aufklärung?" pp. 53; *85*.

52. *The Order of Things*, pp. 62–63.

53. This question dominated the contemporary reception of *Emilia Galotti*; see especially the reactions of Matthias Claudius, Herder, and Goethe, collected by Dvoretzky, *Lessing*, pp. 71, 113–15, 165.

54. Kristeva, "The Bounded Text," p. 50.

Chapter 3

1. Pp. 17–76.

2. Pp. 43–44.

3. *Was ist Neostrukturalismus?* pp. 146–48; *110–13*.

4. The reference to *Emilia Galotti* in Goethe's *The Sorrows of Young Werther* is but the most obvious index of the sympathetic reception this play received among young German bourgeois intellectuals. Schiller also refers to it in his foreword to *The Robbers*.

5. The debate about the revolutionary character of the Sturm und Drang and the causes for its failure are among the most persistent themes in scholarship on this period. For critical overviews see the essays in the collections by Hinck and Wacker, as well as the essay by Schmiedt. Significant contributions to this debate were made by Mattenklott with his theory that melancholy forms the basis for the internal failure of the movement, *Melancholie in der Dramatik des Sturm und Drang*, and by Huyssen, *Drama des Sturm und Drang*, who argues that the revolt of this generation was doomed by external sociopolitical factors deriving from the regressive conditions in the German states. This is also the position of Scherpe, who maintains, on the basis of an interpretation of *The Robbers*, that political conditions in

Germany were unripe for political revolt, leading intellectuals to seek ersatz-rebellion in literature; see his "Folgen eines 'naturwidrigen Beischlafs der *Subordination* und des *Genius.'"

6. Ehrmann, "On Articulation," p. 13.

7. Heine comments in *The Baths of Lucca* that the rift rending the historical world also split his poet's heart in two; see *HW* 2: 405–6.

8. Schulte-Sasse has pointed to the semiotic undercurrent that marks the revolutionary literary projects of this period, "Das Konzept bürgerlich-literarischer Öffentlichkeit," pp. 90–91; Wellbery's investigation into Lessing's semiotics also provides much background into the general evolution of semiotic thinking at this time, especially pp. 1–98.

9. See, for example, Herder, p. 486; Leibniz, p. 520; Hamann, p. 97. See Shell's investigation into monetary form and literature, especially pp. 1–4, 156–77, and 179–87. See also Riegel's essay on the isomorphism between monetary and linguistic systems, as well as Goux, pp. 96–111.

10. Nietzsche, "Über Wahrheit und Lüge im außermoralischen Sinn," pp. 314; 180.

11. *The Economics of A. R. J. Turgot*, pp. 62–63.

12. Cf. Riegel, pp. 63–65.

13. Herder, p. 481.

14. Herder, p. 428; emphasis added.

15. I am applying once again Bühler's terminology; see p. 28.

16. *The Order of Things*, p. 44.

17. See Schulte-Sasse, "Das Konzept bürgerlich-literarischer Öffentlichkeit," pp. 90–91, and Wellbery, pp. 5–8.

18. Frow, p. 117.

19. *Simulations*, p. 112.

20. *The Order of Things*, p. 27.

21. *The Order of Things*, p. 30.

22. *The Order of Things*, p. 34.

23. *The Order of Things*, pp. 62–63.

24. This assertion has been made by Huyssen, *Drama des Sturm und Drang*, pp. 48 and 75. Wacker has objected to this contention, viewing it as a projection of Horkheimer and Adorno's insights back onto the generation of the Sturm und Drang; see his "Einleitung," in *Sturm und Drang*, p. 12.

25. Seidlin, p. 131.

26. Such disruptive intermediacy is the very definition of corruption, according to Pocock, who writes (p. 122): "Every theory of corruption, without exception, is a theory of how intermediaries substitute their own good and profit for that of their supposed principals."

27. Seidlin, p. 134. This criticism is valid mutatis mutandis for Kieffer's interpretation, as well, since he follows Seidlin in most essential points; see his chapter "The Tragedy of Ideal Language," pp. 111–38.

28. Seidlin, pp. 134–35.

29. See the section entitled "On Writing" in Rousseau's *Essay on the Origin of Language*, pp. 249–54. Derrida, of course, develops his theory of "grammatology" on the basis of an interpretation of Rousseau's denigration of writing; see *Of Grammatology*, especially pp. 164–268. See also Herder, pp. 407–10.

30. Kieffer is stumped by the paradox that Karl's complaint about the bookishness of the age derives from the reading of a book (p. 125). His inability to provide an answer to this paradox points up the limitations of the solution offered by him and Seidlin, whose interpretation he follows.

31. Rousseau, *The Confessions*, p. 20: "Plutarch . . . was my especial favourite, and the pleasure I took in reading and re-reading him did something to cure me of my passion for novels."

32. "Literarischer Markt und Öffentlichkeit," pp. 165–69; see also her "Einleitung," pp. 17–19.

33. Schlunk, p. 186, was the first to point out the error of this interpretive tendency. He maintains that trust is the central quality of Karl's character, and that his gullibility merely reflects the negative side of this otherwise positive trait.

34. Habermas, "Der Universalitätsanspruch der Hermeneutik," pp. 277; *191*.

35. This interpretive error is thrown into relief when Schweizer, upon reading the letter, immediately recognizes that it is authored by a "scoundrel" (*Robbers* I, ii, 509; *42*).

36. Seidlin, p. 134.

37. The gullibility and childishness of which Schiller himself accuses the father in his review of *The Robbers* (*SW* I: 633) is thus just as applicable to Karl and Amalia, at least where their interpretive shortcomings are concerned.

38. Schiller's own employment of biblical allusions and motifs, one might hypothesize, reflects the desire to underwrite the authenticity of his own text by associating it with the verity of Scripture.

39. *Simulations*, p. 83.

40. Kant, *Kritik der Urteilskraft*, pp. 276; *206*.

41. Aesthetic autonomy has thus often been too narrowly construed as a reaction against the pedagogical, moralizing impulse of the literature of the Enlightenment; see, for example, Janz, pp. 1–2. On autonomy as a response to bourgeois economics and the principles of commodification, see Hinz, pp. 188–91; Olechnowitz, pp. 92–98; and Warneken, pp. 79–115. Marcuse and Adorno present conceptions of an aesthetic autonomy that preserves the socially redemptive elements otherwise eliminated in the bourgeois world. However, neither deals specifically with the semiotic dimension of literary discourse's autonomous status.

42. Horkheimer and Adorno, pp. 57; *62*.

43. Marx, pp. 566; *378–79*.

44. Marx, pp. 571–72; *383–84*.

45. Hess, p. 336.

46. Hess, p. 346.

47. Hess, pp. 346–47.

48. Cited by Sebeok, p. 6.

49. See Goux, pp. 41–42, 96–106.

50. This feature distinguishes not only Franz's discourse, but that of Moritz Spiegelberg as well, the other representative of semiotic exchange in this play.

51. Bourdieu, *Outline*, p. 173.

52. *Simulations*, pp. 84–86.

53. Habermas first developed this notion in *Erkenntnis und Interesse*, pp. 71–84; *53–63*; he expanded it into a full-fledged theory some years later in his *Theorie des kommunikativen Handelns*.

54. Michelsen, pp. 86–89, views Karl's revolt as an attempt to reestablish paternal authority; this thesis seems questionable, given Karl's earlier rejection of the father and the implicit rejection of the father a second time in the scene with the "Pater." It seems much more likely that Karl is attempting to reconstruct the blood-bonds of obligation that he feels have been disrupted.

55. See, for example, Best, p. 301; Finsen, pp. 23 and 31; Schings, "Schillers *Räuber*," p. 21; Seidlin, pp. 134–35. In all these instances Karl's capitulation is interpreted as acceptance of the principles against which he has hitherto fought.

56. In the rendition of *The Robbers* Schiller conceived as a "tragic drama" ("Trauerspiel")—that is, the version he rewrote specifically for the Mannheim stage production—Karl advises the robbers in the concluding scenes, "Serve the King, who is fighting for human rights"; Kosinsky and Schweizer he admonishes to "become good citizens," and he even concludes that he himself has become "a good citizen" (*SW* 1: 934). Far from simply making explicit certain implications contained in the original version of the play, these revisions eradicate entirely the re-volutionary thrust of the original drama, and as such they mark Schiller's own repression of his originary rebellious design.

57. Koselleck, *Kritik und Krise*, pp. 60; *75*. In the English translation "das Geheimnis" is inadequately rendered as "mystery." Aside from mystery, *Geheimnis* means "secret" in the sense of "I have a secret"; but the stem *heim* is also related to *heimlich*, and it thus shares the ambivalences of this term, "secret" and "private," that Freud examines in his essay on the uncanny.

58. This textual aspect is played up most in the "suppressed foreword" that Schiller withdrew and replaced with a modified version before the first publication of the play (*SW* 1: 481–84), but it remains in evidence in the revised preface as well (*SW* 1: 484–88).

59. Marcuse, "Über den affirmativen Charakter der Kultur," pp. 100; *132*.

60. Marcuse, "Über den affirmativen Charakter der Kultur," pp. 76–77; *108–10*.

61. Benjamin, *Ursprung des deutschen Trauerspiels*, pp. 206; *185*. Schiller's drama corresponds to Benjamin's definition of the "tragic drama" in numerous other respects, as well; indeed, it presents in its two protagonists, Franz and Karl, and in their respective plots, both the "drama of the tyrant" ("Tyrannendrama") and the "martyr-drama" ("Märtyrerdrama") that Benjamin postulates as different versions of the tragic drama; see pp. 60; *69*.

Chapter 4

1. "Die Wunde Heine," pp. 95; *80*.

2. On the notion of "tornness," see also Heine's comments in *Die Nordsee: Dritte Abteilung* (*HW* 2: 215, 240).

3. On the revolutionary aesthetic practice of Heine's *Travelogues* see especially Grossklaus, pp. 195–96; Jauss, "Das Ende der Kunstperiode," p. 12; Preisendanz, p. 343.

4. Gadamer presents a theory of such a productive hermeneutical dialectic, especially pp. 344–60; *325–41*.

5. Habermas, "Der Universalitätsanspruch der Hermeneutik," pp. 276–93; *190–209*.

6. Hegel, *Vorlesungen über die Ästhetik* 1: 25; *1: 11*.

7. On the background and implications of Hegel's assertion of the end of art, see the essays by Henrich and Oelmüller.

8. Hegel, *Vorlesungen über die Ästhetik* 1: 25–26; *1: 11*.

9. *Vorlesungen über die Ästhetik* 1: 24; *1: 10*.

10. *Vorlesungen über die Ästhetik* 1: 24; *1: 10*.

11. See *Vorlesungen über die Ästhetik* 1: 27; *1: 12*.

12. Schiller, *Über die ästhetische Erziehung*, pp. 579; *34*.

13. Hegel, *Vorlesungen über die Ästhetik* 1: 22–23; *1: 9*.

14. *Vorlesungen über die Ästhetik* 1: 24–25; *1: 10*.

15. Weber, pp. 135; *118–19*.

16. Hegel, *Vorlesungen über die Ästhetik* 1: 20; *1: 7*.

17. On the church as the principal ideological state apparatus, see Althusser, p. 144.

18. A general portrayal of the influence of censorship on the literature of this period is provided by Ziegler.

19. Heine himself pointed to the beneficial market effect that resulted from book banning; see his comments in *Reise von München nach Genua* (*HW* 2: 329). See also Windfuhr, "Heinrich Heines deutsches Publikum," p. 271.

20. One critic even goes so far as to claim that the threat of censorship constituted the condition of possibility of Heine's literary discourse; see Manfred Schneider, p. 86.

21. The notion of "idea smuggling" was coined in this period by Karl Gutzkow; on this conception and its impact on the development of specific literary strategies for the writers of Junges Deutschland, see Hömberg.

22. For other passages in which Heine acknowledges the furor that this volume created upon publication, see *HB* 1: 313, 335.

23. Wülfing gives an account of this conflict between literary use-value and commercial exchange-value and its impact on the literature of this period in *Junges Deutschland*, p. 156.

24. As a rule, those scholars who understand chapter fourteen of *Ideas* as a description of Heine's literary-satirical program—for example, Hofrichter, pp. 50–51,

and Pabel, pp. 163–65—ignore his own insights into the practical deficiencies of this method given his literary-political aims.

25. I have restored in the English translation Heine's repetition of the adverb "involuntarily," which the translators inexplicably delete.

26. On the relativizing "play" between satire and humor, politics and Romanticism in Heine's *Travelogues*, see Kolb, pp. 28, 30–31, 37; and Ronald Schneider, " 'Themis und Pan,' " 1–16, 24, and "Die Musa 'Satyra,' " pp. 15–17.

27. See Freud, *Das Unbehagen in der Kultur*, 250–52; *125–27*.

28. Hegel, *Vorlesungen über die Geschichte der Philosophie*, p. 482.

29. *Vorlesungen über die Geschichte der Philosophie*, p. 483.

30. Hegel, "Über die Bekehrten," p. 74.

31. We should note the intellectual-historical connection between Heine's ironic assertion of the ascendancy of the "insane" and Schiller's insistence in *The Robbers* that instrumental reason is always superior to and outmaneuvers the naive attitude.

32. On the Aristophanic comedy as model for *The Book Le Grand* see Schillemeit, p. 330.

33. The helplessness of irony as oppositional intellectual strategy has been lent philosophical codification by Rorty; see especially pp. 83–87.

34. Heine's projection of his reader as a woman also plays on the identification of women as the readers of popularized literature, which is a pervasive motif from the eighteenth century onward.

35. Sammons, p. 126.

36. For a survey of Heine's reception as Romanticist see Clasen, pp. 147–214; see also Hohendahl, "Geschichte und Modernität."

37. See Benjamin's epilogue to "Das Kunstwerk im Zeitalter seiner technischen Reproduzierbarkeit," pp. 167–69; *243–44*.

38. In the "Waterloo-Fragment," suppressed from the text of his "Geständnisse," Heine explicitly praises *Ideas* for its rehabilitation of Napoleon; see *HW* 6/1: 511–13.

39. See Habermas, *Strukturwandel*, pp. 112–71; *89–140*.

40. *Theorie der Avantgarde*, pp. 63–73; *47–54*. See also his *Zur Kritik der idealistischen Ästhetik*.

41. See Peter Bürger, *Theorie der Avantgarde*, pp. 76–116; *55–82*.

Chapter 5

1. Grimm, *Love, Lust, and Rebellion*, pp. 58–59.

2. On the implicit critique of realism that is contained in the reflections on art in *Lenz*, see Holub.

3. See Habermas, *Strukturwandel*, pp. 112–71; *89–140*.

4. As Büchner's literary sponsor, Gutzkow arranged for the initial publication of *Danton's Death*, for example, and also published excerpts from *Leonce and Lena* shortly after Büchner's untimely death.

5. Gutzkow's letter is reprinted in *BW* 2: 476–77.

6. *Ästhetische Theorie*, pp. 87; *80–81*.

7. This observation holds, we should note, for Derrida's deconstructive philosophy as well, and it signals his indebtedness to the modernist critical paradigm.

8. Pp. 4; *xiv.*

9. Pp. 4; *xiv.*

10. See pp. 3; *xiii.*

11. Pp. 4; *xv.*

12. Habermas, *Der philosophische Diskurs der Moderne*, pp. 144–45; *119–20.*

13. See, for example, *BW* 2: 422, 432, 436–37, 441; *256, 266, 270, 273–74.*

14. On Büchner's position as natural scientist see Döhner, "Neuere Erkenntnisse zu Georg Büchner's Naturauffassung und Naturforschung," pp. 126–27. The general history of scientistic rationalism is treated by Vietta, *Neuzeitliche Rationalität;* on Büchner, see especially pp. 97–98.

15. Habermas, *Erkenntnis und Interesse*, pp. 88–91; *67–69.*

16. This view has been defended by Müller-Seidel, pp. 207–10; see also Vietta, *Neuzeitliche Rationalität,* p. 120.

17. *Vorlesungen über die Ästhetik* 1: 24; *1: 10.*

18. The only mention of signs and semiotic problems in Büchner's writings arises in the context of his study of Plato's philosophy, where he gives a resumé of Plato's meditations on signs; see *BW* 2: 350.

19. Pp. 147; *164.*

20. The affidavit written by Clarus is reprinted by Mayer, *Georg Büchner, "Woyzeck,"* pp. 75–137, and will be cited as "Clarus Affidavit" with page numbers from this edition.

21. "Clarus Affidavit," p. 77.

22. "Clarus Affidavit," p. 122; his emphasis!

23. The abbreviations h1, h2, h3, and H4 in references to *Woyzeck* indicate the four extant versions of the manuscript, h1 being the earliest draft, h2 and h3 intermediary versions, and H4 the revision Büchner was working on just before his death. Roman numerals refer to the scene number of the respective manuscript.

24. "Clarus Affidavit," pp. 107, 111, 113, 114.

25. "Clarus Affidavit," p. 113; his emphasis!

26. "Clarus Affidavit," p. 113.

27. "Clarus Affidavit," p. 113.

28. "Clarus Affidavit," p. 113; emphasis added.

29. "Clarus Affidavit," pp. 76, 84.

30. "Clarus Affidavit," p. 125.

31. "Clarus Affidavit," p. 78.

32. "Clarus Affidavit," p. 76.

33. This thesis is defended most vociferously by Schings, *Der mitleidigste Mensch,* pp. 68–84, especially p. 79. See also Mautner, p. 536; May, pp. 248–49; Mayer, *Georg Büchner und seine Zeit,* p. 338; and Mayer, *Georg Büchner, "Woyzeck,"* pp. 67–68.

34. In his last revision, Büchner left space in the manuscript for these scenes, indicating his intention to include them in the final version of the play, perhaps in somewhat modified form.

35. Kristeva, *Desire in Language*, p. 78.

36. See Bakhtin's "Introduction," in *Rabelais and His World*, pp. 1–58.

37. P. 10.

38. For an account of this debate on the revolutionary potential of carnival, see Stallybrass and White, pp. 13–15. They ultimately come to the defense of carnival's destabilizing effect.

39. Pp. 13; *10*.

40. Pp. 13; *10*.

41. Pp. 5; *xvi*.

42. Pp. 53; *57*.

43. Glück, for example, insists on Woyzeck's victimization and rejects out of hand the idea that Woyzeck takes over the strategies of, and thus identifies with, his oppressors; see his "Der 'ökonomische Tod,' " pp. 172–75.

44. See Stallybrass and White, p. 53.

45. Pp. 13; *10–11*.

46. *The Order of Things*, pp. 43–44.

47. *Simulations*, pp. 84–86.

48. Pp. 222; *249*.

49. Pp. 12; *9*.

Chapter 6

1 Kracauer, pp. 61–76, especially pp. 64–67.

2. Freud, "Das Unheimliche," pp. 244; *220*.

3. "Das Unheimliche," pp. 245; *222*.

4. "Das Unheimliche," pp. 247; *223*.

5. "Das Unheimliche," pp. 249; *225*.

6. "Das Unheimliche," pp. 248; *224*.

7. "Das Unheimliche," pp. 250; *226*.

8. "Das Unheimliche," pp. 263; *241*.

9. *Kritik und Krise*, pp. 49–76; *62–97*.

10. On the relationship between psychological projection and the strategies of literary Expressionism, see Sokel, *The Writer in Extremis*, pp. 41–42.

11. Cohn, p. 100.

12. Cohn, p. 115.

13. Jauss, "Literaturgeschichte als Provokation," pp. 203–6; *42–44*.

14. Jauss, "Literaturgeschichte als Provokation," pp. 205; *43*.

15. "Das Unheimliche," pp. 250–51; *227*.

16. Goldmann, *Towards a Sociology of the Novel*, pp. 6–7.

17. Habermas has examined what he calls the "scientistic" self-misunderstanding of Freudian theory as a positive science in *Erkenntnis und Interesse*, pp. 300–32; *246–73*; see especially pp. 306–7; *251–52*.

18. See Swan, and Stallybrass and White, pp. 149–70.

19. *Fin-de-siècle Vienna*, p. 183.

20. *Fin-de-siècle Vienna*, pp. 202–3.

21. For the text of this dream and Freud's analysis, see *Die Traumdeutung*, pp. 218–26; *208–18*.

22. *Die Traumdeutung*, pp. 218; *209*.

23. *Die Traumdeutung*, pp. 225; *216–17*.

24. On the features of the sociocultural context that Freud and Hofmannsthal shared, see the chapter "Politics and the Psyche: Schnitzler and Hofmannsthal," in Schorske, *Fin-de-siècle Vienna*, pp. 3–23.

25. "Das Unheimliche," pp. 244; *220*.

26. See "Das Unheimliche," pp. 271–74; *249–52*.

27. Schleiermacher, pp. 31; *41*.

28. "Das Unheimliche," pp. 254; *230*.

29. "Das Unheimliche," pp. 254; *230*.

30. "Das Unheimliche," pp. 254–55; *231*.

31. "Das Unheimliche," pp. 255; *231*.

32. *Die Traumdeutung*, pp. 224; *215*; emphasis added.

33. *Die Traumdeutung*, pp. 218, 226; *209, 217*.

34. "Das Unheimliche," pp. 259, 271; *236, 249*.

35. "Das Unheimliche," pp. 258; *235*.

36. "Das Unheimliche," pp. 259; *236*; emphasis added.

37. See Freud, *Das Unbehagen in der Kultur*, pp 250–52; *125–27*.

38. This has been maintained by Martin Stern, p. 43.

39. See Träbing, "Hofmannsthals 'Reitergeschichte,' " for an overview of the critical interpretations on *A Tale of the Cavalry*.

40. Alewyn, p. 79.

41. Donop, p. 134.

42. Hugo Schmidt, p. 75.

43. *Hofmannsthal-Andrian Briefwechsel*, p. 109.

44. *Die Traumdeutung*, pp. 221; *211*.

45. See Schorske, *Fin-de-siècle Vienna*, pp. 193–94.

46. "Das Unheimliche," pp. 250; *226*.

47. "Das Unheimliche," pp. 246; *222*.

48. In this sense *A Tale of the Cavalry* would accomplish a jettisoning of Hofmannsthal's adolescent-rebellious political persona comparable with, and parallel to, the overcoming of his youthful poetic personality accomplished in "Letter to Lord Chandos," the central document testifying to the crisis of poetic language Hofmannsthal faced in this same period of his life.

49. Sokel has argued for an understanding of Kafka's texts as Freud-like narratives of the psyche; see his essay "Freud and the Magic of Kafka's Writing."

Chapter 7

1. For an overview of criticism on this text, see Neumann's excellent collection of materials and commentary, which also supplies a thorough bibliography (pp.

231–39). A substantial cross section of interpretations to this story is represented in Angel Flores's collection *The Problem of "The Judgment."*

2. Binder is the major representative of this direction in Kafka studies; see, among his many contributions, especially *Kafka in neuer Sicht* and *Motiv und Gestaltung bei Franz Kafka.* Psycho-biographical interpretations of *The Judgment* were initiated by the seminal early essay by Kate Flores, *"The Judgment."*

3. Bakhtin, p. 438. For a more thorough critique of biographism in Kafka criticism, see Gray, "Biography as Criticism in Kafka Studies."

4. See, for example, Corngold, "The Hermeneutic of *The Judgment*," and Nägele.

5. See Freud, *Die Traumdeutung*, pp. 122–23; *101–3.*

6. See especially Binder, "Kafkas Schaffensprozeß."

7. On Kafka's omission of this sentence from the manuscript, see Binder, "Kafkas Schaffensprozeß," p. 139, and Neumann, pp. 138–39, who points to the political relevance of the deleted passage.

8. See Beharriell, p. 34, who comments on the enigmatic quality of this passage.

9. Politzer has pointed to the likelihood of this historical allusion, p. 55.

10. See Wagenbach, *Franz Kafka: Eine Biographie seiner Jugend 1893–1912*, pp. 62, 74, 162. See also Janouch, pp. 122–23, 128.

11. The groundwork for such a sociopsychological approach to *The Judgment* has been laid by Neumann and Sautermeister.

12. Althusser, p. 153.

13. On this ideological aspect of the family, see also Althusser, pp. 146–48.

14. Horkheimer, "Autorität und Familie," pp. 359; *70.*

15. "Autorität und Familie," pp. 392; *102–3.*

16. Habermas, *Strukturwandel*, pp. 61; *43.*

17. Habermas, *Strukturwandel*, pp. 63; *46.*

18. On this connection between Kafka's oppressive family life and the oppressive mechanisms of bourgeois society, see Beicken, *Franz Kafka*, pp. 202–7; Neumann, pp. 80–81.

19. See, for example, Sokel, *Franz Kafka*, pp. 63–64.

20. Heinrich Mann's novel *Professor Unrat* (1905), filmed as *The Blue Angel*, and Robert Musil's *Young Törless* (1906) are two of the most notable examples of this literature attacking German educational methods and institutions. As fictional work, *The Judgment* shares a certain family resemblance with these texts.

21. Althusser, pp. 127–28.

22. Cf. Sokel, *Frank Kafka*, p. 69; Politzer, p. 55.

23. Habermas, "Theodor W. Adorno," p. 169.

24. "Autorität und Familie," pp. 345; *56.*

25. *Zur Genealogie der Moral*, pp. 805; *66–67.*

26. "Autorität und Familie," pp. 412; *122.*

27. "Autorität und Familie," pp. 391; *101.*

28. See "Autorität und Familie," pp. 390; *100.*

29. Deleuze and Guattari, *Kafka*, p. 38.

30. See Horkheimer, "Autorität und Familie," pp. 392–93; *102–3.*

31. "Autorität und Familie," pp. 398–99; *109*.

32. "Autorität und Familie," pp. 401; *111*.

33. "Autorität und Familie," pp. 397; *107*.

34. Adorno, "Zum Verhältnis von Soziologie und Psychologie," p. 60.

35. The thesis that the friend represents Georg's alter ego has been a constant motif in interpretations of *The Judgment* since first being proposed by Kate Flores.

36. Quoted by Szondi, p. 60.

37. *The Order of Things*, p. 173. We should recall here once more Peirce's definition of the sign as a relation requiring the cooperation of three subjects (Chapter 3).

38. The double meaning of this question has been pointed out by Sokel, *Franz Kafka*, p. 56

39. Rolleston, p. 144, interprets Georg's final words as evidence that to the very end he is an actor, playing out the part of the "dutiful son."

40. "Autorität und Familie," pp. 404; *114*.

41. Horkheimer, "Autorität und Familie," pp. 408; *118*.

42. The absence of any genuine communitarian perspective in the fictional present of the story is signaled by the scar the father bears, inflicted during his earlier participation in a supraindividual struggle (see *Judgment*, 64; *85*). This scar is but a sign of this absent communitarianism, and as sign, it can only mark, but never represent, this former social solidarity.

43. Kristeva, *Revolution*, p. 91.

Concluding Historical Postscript

1. *Ästhetische Theorie*, pp. 272; *262*.

2. Amalia's name alone, of course, suggests that she is a direct descendant of Emilia's.

3. Sokel has remarked on the similarity between Franz Moor and Georg Bendemann, without, however, developing the parallels in detail; see his *Franz Kafka*, p. 61.

4. Rorty, p. xv.

5. Derrida has specifically associated the attribute of nostalgia with the attitude of modernist metaphysics and affirmation with the postmetaphysical condition; "Structure, Sign, and Play," p. 292.

6. Rorty, p. 83.

7. Rorty, p. xiv.

8. Kant, "Was ist Aufklärung?" pp. 55, 61; *87, 92*.

9. See Rorty, p. xiv.

10. Rorty, p. xvi.

Bibliography

Adlam, Diana, Julian Henriques, Nicolas Rose, Angie Salfield, Couze Venn, and Valerie Walkerdine. "Psychology, Ideology and the Human Subject." *Ideology and Consciousness* 1 (May 1977): 5–56.

Adorno, Theodor. *Aesthetic Theory*. Trans. C. Lenhardt. London: Routledge and Kegan Paul, 1984.

———. "Der Artist als Statthalter." In Rolf Tiedemann, ed., *Noten zur Literatur. Gesammelte Schriften*, vol. 11, pp. 114–26. Frankfurt: Suhrkamp, 1974.

———. "The Artist as Deputy." In Rolf Tiedemann, ed., *Notes to Literature*, vol. 1, pp. 98–108. Trans. Shierry Weber Nicholsen. New York: Columbia University Press, 1991.

———. *Ästhetische Theorie*. Ed. Gretel Adorno and Rolf Tiedemann. Frankfurt: Fischer, 1970.

———. "Aufzeichnungen zu Kafka." In Rolf Tiedemann, ed., *Prismen: Kulturkritik und Gesellschaft*, pp. 250–83. Frankfurt: Suhrkamp, 1976.

———. "Gesellschaft." In Rolf Tiedemann, ed., *Soziologische Schriften I*, pp. 9–19. Frankfurt: Suhrkamp, 1979.

———. "Heine the Wound." In Rolf Tiedemann, ed., *Notes to Literature*, vol. 1, pp. 80–85. Trans. Shierry Weber Nicholsen. New York: Columbia University Press, 1991.

———. "Kulturkritik und Gesellschaft." In Rolf Tiedemann, ed., *Prismen: Kulturkritik und Gesellschaft*, pp. 7–26. Frankfurt: Suhrkamp, 1976.

———. *Prismen: Kulturkritik und Gesellschaft*. Ed. Rolf Tiedemann. Frankfurt: Suhrkamp, 1976.

———. "Society." *Salmagundi* 10–11 (Fall 1969–Winter 1970): 144–53.

———. "Die Wunde Heine." In Rolf Tiedemann, ed., *Noten zur Literatur. Gesammelte Schriften*, vol. 11, pp. 95–100. Frankfurt: Suhrkamp, 1974.

———. "Zum Verhältnis von Soziologie und Psychologie." In *Aufsätze zur Gesellschaftstheorie und Methodologie*, pp. 42–92. Frankfurt: Suhrkamp, 1970.

Alewyn, Richard. *Über Hugo von Hofmannsthal*. 4th ed. Göttingen: Vandenhoeck & Ruprecht, 1967.

Altenhofer, Norbert. "Chiffre, Hieroglyphe, Palimpsest: Vorformen tiefhermeneutischer und intertextueller Interpretation im Werk Heines." In Ulrich Nassen, ed., *Texthermeneutik: Aktualität, Geschichte, Kritik*, pp. 149–93. Paderborn: Schöningh, 1979.

————, ed. *Dichter über ihre Dichtung: Heinrich Heine*. 3 vols. Munich: Heimeran, 1971.

Althusser, Louis. "Ideology and Ideological State Apparatuses." In *Lenin and Philosophy*, pp. 121–73. Trans. Ben Brewster. New York: Monthly Review Press, 1971.

Angress, Ruth K. "The Generations in *Emilia Galotti*." *Germanic Review* 43 (1968): 15–23.

Anz, Heinrich. "Umwege zum Tode: Zur Stellung der Psychoanalyse im Werk Franz Kafkas." In Klaus Bohnen, Sven-Aaage Jorgensen, and Friedrich Schmöe, eds., *Literatur und Psychoanalyse*, pp. 211–30. Munich: Fink, 1981.

Appelbaum-Graham, Ilse. "Minds Without Medium: Reflections on *Emilia Galotti* and Werthers Leiden." *Euphorion* 56 (1962): 3–24.

Arendt, Peter. "Parabolische Dichtung und politische Tendenz: Eine Episode aus den 'Bädern von Lucca.' " *Heine Jahrbuch* 9 (1970): 41–57.

Arvon, Henri. *Marxist Esthetics*. Trans. Helen R. Lane. Ithaca: Cornell University Press, 1973.

Autonomie der Kunst: Zur Genese und Kritik einer bürgerlichen Kategorie. Frankfurt: Suhrkamp, 1972.

Babcock, Barbara, ed. *The Reversible World: Symbolic Inversion in Art and Society*. Ithaca: Cornell University Press, 1978.

Bakhtin, Mikhail. *Rabelais and His World*. Trans. Hélène Iswolsky. Bloomington: Indiana University Press, 1984.

Barner, Wilfried, Gunter Grimm, Helmuth Kiesel, and Martin Kramer. *Lessing: Epoche, Werk, Wirkung*. 4th ed. Munich: C. H. Beck, 1981.

Barnett, Stuart. " 'Über die Grenzen': Semiotics and Subjectivity in Lessing's *Hamburgische Dramaturgie*." *German Quarterly* 60 (1987): 407–19.

Bartels, Martin. "Der Kampf um den Freund: Die psychoanalytische Sinneinheit in Kafkas Erzählung 'Das Urteil.' " *Deutsche Vierteljahrsschrift für Literaturwissenschaft und Geistesgeschichte* 56 (1982): 225–58.

Baudrillard, Jean. "On Seduction." In Mark Poster, ed., *Selected Writings*, pp. 149–65. Stanford: Stanford University Press, 1988.

————. *Selected Writings*. Ed. Mark Poster. Stanford: Stanford University Press, 1988.

————. *Simulations*. New York: Semiotext(e), 1983.

Bauer, Gerhardt. *G. E. Lessing: "Emilia Galotti."* UTB 1433. Munich: Fink, 1987.

Bauer, Gerhardt, and Sibylle Bauer, eds. *Gotthold Ephraim Lessing*. Wege der Forschung, Bd. 211. Darmstadt: Wissenschaftliche Buchgesellschaft, 1968.

Baumann, Gerhart. *Georg Büchner: Die dramatische Ausdruckswelt*. Göttingen: Vandenhoeck & Ruprecht, 1961.

Baumann, Günter. *Poesie und Revolution: Zum Verhältnis von Kunst und Politik im Werk Heinrich Heines*. Europäische Hochschulschriften, Reihe 1, Bd. 561. Frankfurt: Peter Lang, 1982.

Bayerdörfer, Hans-Peter. *Poetik als sprachtheoretisches Problem*. Studien zur deutschen Literatur, Bd. 8. Tübingen: Niemeyer, 1967.

Beaujour, Michel. "Flight out of Time: Poetic Language and the Revolution." *Yale French Studies* 39 (1967): 29–49.

Beck, Evelyn Torton. "First Impact of the Yiddish Theater: 'The Judgment.' " In *Kafka and the Yiddish Theater: Its Impact on His Work*, pp. 70–121. Madison: University of Wisconsin Press, 1971.

———. "Kafkas 'Durchbruch': Der Einfluß des jiddischen Theaters auf sein Schaffen." *Basis* 1 (1970): 204–23.

Beckmann, Martin. "Franz Kafkas Erzählung 'Das Urteil.' Versuch einer Deutung." *Literatur für Leser* (1990): 44–59.

Beharriell, Frederick J. "Kafka, Freud und 'Das Urteil.' " In Manfred Durzak, Eberhard Reichmann, and Ulrich Weisstein, eds., *Texte und Kontexte: Studien zur deutschen und vergleichenden Literaturwissenschaft: Festschrift für Norbert Fuerst*, pp. 27–47. Bern: Francke, 1973.

Beicken, Peter U. *Franz Kafka: Eine kritische Einführung in die Forschung*. Frankfurt: Athenäum, 1974.

———. "*The Judgment* in the Critics' Judgment." In Angel Flores, ed., *The Problem of "The Judgment": Eleven Approaches to Kafka's Story*, pp. 238–51. New York: Gordion Press, 1977.

Benjamin, Walter. "Das Kunstwerk im Zeitalter seiner technischen Reproduzierbarkeit." In *Illuminationen*, pp. 148–84. Frankfurt: Suhrkamp, 1961.

———. *The Origin of German Tragic Drama*. Trans. John Osborne. London: New Left Books, 1977.

———. *Ursprung des deutschen Trauerspiels*. Frankfurt: Suhrkamp, 1972.

———. "The Work of Art in the Age of Mechanical Reproduction." In *Illuminations*, pp. 219–53. Trans. Harry Zohn. New York: Harcourt Brace, 1968.

Benn, Maurice B. *The Drama of Revolt: A Critical Study of Georg Büchner*. Cambridge, Eng.: Cambridge University Press, 1976.

Bensmaïa, Réda. "Foreword: The Kafka Effect." Trans. Terry Cochran. In Gilles Deleuze and Felix Guattari, *Kafka: Toward a Minor Literature*, pp. ix–xxi. Trans. Dana Polan. Minneapolis: University of Minnesota Press, 1986.

Benveniste, Emile. "Subjectivity in Language." In *Problems in General Linguistics*, pp. 223–30. Coral Gables, Fla.: University of Miami Press, 1971.

Berman, Russell A. *Modern Culture and Critical Theory: Art, Politics, and the Legacy of the Frankfurt School*. Madison: University of Wisconsin Press, 1989.

———. "Producing the Reader: Kafka and the Modernist Organization of Reception." *Newsletter of the Kafka Society of America* 6, no. 1–2 (June and Dec. 1982): 14–18.

Bernheimer, Charles. "Letters to an Absent Friend: A Structural Reading." In Angel Flores, ed., *The Problem of "The Judgment": Eleven Approaches to Kafka's Story*, pp. 146–67. New York: Gordion Press, 1977.

Best, Otto F. "Gerechtigkeit für Spiegelberg." *Jahrbuch der deutschen Schillergesellschaft* 22 (1978): 277–302.

Betz, Albrecht. *Ästhetik und Politik: Heinrich Heines Prosa*. Munich: Hanser, 1971.

Bezzel, Chris. "Dichtung und Revolution." *Konkrete Poesie: Text und Kritik* 25 (Jan. 1970): 35–36.

Binder, Hartmut, ed. *Kafka Handbuch*. 2 vols. Stuttgart: Alfred Kröner Verlag, 1979.

———. *Kafka in neuer Sicht: Mimik, Gestik und Personengefüge als Darstellungsformen des Autobiographischen*. Stuttgart: Metzler, 1976.

———. "Kafkas Schaffensprozeß, mit besonderer Berücksichtigung des *Urteils*: Eine Analyse seiner Aussagen über das Schreiben mit Hilfe der Handschriften und auf Grund psychologischer Theoreme." *Euphorion* 70 (1976): 129–74.

———. *Motiv und Gestaltung bei Franz Kafka*. Bonn: Bouvier, 1966.

Blochmann, Elisabeth. "Das Motiv vom verlorenen Sohn in Schillers Räuberdrama." *Deutsche Vierteljahrsschrift für Literaturwissenschaft und Geistesgeschichte* 25 (1951): 474–84.

Bloom, Harold. "Introduction." In *Franz Kafka*, pp. 1–16. New York: Chelsea House, 1986.

Bockelkamp, Marianne. "Ein unbekannter Entwurf zu Heines 'Ideen: Das Buch Le Grand.'" *Heine Jahrbuch* 12 (1973): 34–40.

Bohm, Arnd. "Possessive Individualism in Schiller's *Die Räuber*." *Mosaic* 20 (1987): 31–42.

Bohnen, Klaus. *Geist und Buchstabe: Zum Prinzip des kritischen Verfahrens in Lessings literarästhetischen und theologischen Schriften*. Kölner Germanistische Studien, Bd. 10. Cologne: Böhlau, 1974.

Bollacher, Martin. "'Tradition und Selbstbestimmung.' Lessings *Emilia Galotti* in geistesgeschichtlicher Perspektive." In Jürgen Brummak, ed., *Literaturwissenschaft und Geistesgeschichte: Festschrift für Richard Brinkmann*, pp. 99–118. Tübingen: Niemeyer, 1981.

Borchardt, Rudolf. "Revolution und Tradition in der Literatur." In Marie Luise Borchardt, ed., *Reden. Gesammelte Werke in Einzelbänden*, pp. 210–29. Stuttgart: Klett, n.d.

Borchmeyer, Dieter. "Rhetorische und ästhetische Revolutionskritik: Edmund Burke und Schiller." In Karl Richter and Jörg Schönert, eds., *Klassik und Moderne: Die Weimarer Klassik als historisches Ereignis und Herausforderung im kulturgeschichtlichen Prozeß*, pp. 56–79. Stuttgart: Metzler, 1983.

———. *Tragödie und Öffentlichkeit: Schillers Dramaturgie im Zusammenhang seiner ästhetisch-politischen Theorie und die rhetorische Tradition*. Munich: Fink, 1973.

Born, Jürgen, ed. *Franz Kafka: Kritik und Rezeption zu seinen Lebzeiten 1912–24*. Frankfurt: Fischer, 1979.

Bornscheuer, Lothar, ed. *Erläuterungen und Dokumente: Georg Büchner: "Woyzeck."* Reclams Universal-Bibliothek, Nr. 8117. Stuttgart: Reclam, 1972.

Bostock, J. Knight. "The Death of Emilia Galotti." *Modern Language Review* 46 (1951): 69–71.

Bourdieu, Pierre. *Distinction: A Social Critique of the Judgement of Taste*. Trans. R. Nice. Cambridge, Mass.: Harvard University Press, 1984.

———. *Outline of a Theory of Practice*. Trans. R. Nice. Cambridge, Eng.: Cambridge University Press, 1977.

Braendlin, Hans P. "The Dilemma of Luxury and the Ironic Structures of Lessing's

Emilia Galotti and Lenz's *The Soldiers."* *Studies on Voltaire and the Eighteenth Century* 151 (1976): 353–62.

Braun, Volker. "Politik und Poesie." *Weimarer Beiträge* 18, no. 5 (1972): 92–103.

Bredekamp, Horst. "Autonomie und Askese." In *Autonomie der Kunst: Zur Genese und Kritik einer bürgerlichen Kategorie*, pp. 88–172. Frankfurt: Suhrkamp, 1972.

Brenkman, John. *Culture and Domination*. Ithaca: Cornell University Press, 1987.

Breton, André, and Diego Rivera. "Manifesto: Towards a Free Revolutionary Art." *Partisan Review* 6 (1938–39): 49–53.

Brown, Christiane. " 'Der widerwärtige Mißbrauch der Macht' oder 'Die Verwandlung der Leidenschaften in tugendhafte Fertigkeiten' in Lessings *Emilia Galotti."* *Lessing Yearbook* 17 (1985): 21–43.

Brüggemann, Fritz. "Lessings Bürgerdramen und der Subjektivismus als Problem: Psychogenetische Untersuchung." In Gerhardt Bauer and Sibylle Bauer, eds., *Gotthold Ephraim Lessing*, pp. 83–126. Wege der Forschung, Bd. 211. Darmstadt: Wissenschaftliche Buchgesellschaft, 1968.

Brustein, Robert. "The Theatre of Revolt." In *The Theatre of Revolt*, pp. 3–33. Boston: Little, Brown, 1962.

Bubner, Rüdiger. "Moderne Ersatzfunktionen des Ästhetischen." *Merkur* 40 (1986): 91–107.

Büchner, Georg. *Complete Works and Letters*. Trans. Henry J. Schmidt. New York: Continuum, 1986.

———. *Werke und Briefe*. Ed. Fritz Bergemann. 7th ed. DTV Gesamtausgabe, 70. Munich: Deutscher Taschenbuch Verlag, 1973.

———. *Woyzeck*. Ed. Egon Krause. Frankfurt: Insel, 1969.

———. *Woyzeck*. In *Complete Works and Letters*, pp. 199–241. Trans. Henry J. Schmidt. New York: Continuum, 1986.

Buchwald, Reinhard. "In Tyrannos." In *Das Vermächtnis der deutschen Klassiker*, pp. 130–56. Frankfurt: Insel, 1962.

Bühler, Karl. *Sprachtheorie: Die Darstellungsformen der Sprache*. Frankfurt: Ullstein, 1978 [1934].

Bürger, Christa. "Einleitung: Die Dichotomie von hoher und niederer Literatur. Eine Problemskizze." In Christa Bürger, Peter Bürger, and Jochen Schulte-Sasse, eds., *Zur Dichotomisierung von hoher und niederer Literatur*, pp. 9–31. Frankfurt: Suhrkamp, 1982.

———. "Literarischer Markt und Öffentlichkeit am Ausgang des 18. Jahrhunderts in Deutschland." In Christa Bürger, Peter Bürger, and Jochen Schulte-Sasse, eds., *Aufklärung und literarische Öffentlichkeit*, pp. 162–212. Frankfurt: Suhrkamp, 1980.

Bürger, Christa, Peter Bürger, and Jochen Schulte-Sasse, eds. *Aufklärung und literarische Öffentlichkeit*. Frankfurt: Suhrkamp, 1980.

Bürger, Peter. "Institution Kunst als literatursoziologische Kategorie." In Peter Bürger, ed., *Seminar: Literatur- und Kunstsoziologie*, pp. 260–79. Frankfurt: Suhrkamp, 1978.

———. "Institution Literatur und Modernisierungsprozeß." In Peter Bürger, ed., *Zum Funktionswandel der Literatur*, pp. 9–32. Frankfurt: Suhrkamp, 1983.

———. *Theorie der Avantgarde*. Frankfurt: Suhrkamp, 1974.

———. *Theory of the Avant-Garde*. Trans. Michael Shaw. Minneapolis: University of Minnesota Press, 1984.

———. *Zur Kritik der idealistischen Ästhetik*. Frankfurt: Suhrkamp, 1983.

———, ed. *Seminar: Literatur- und Kunstsoziologie*. Frankfurt: Suhrkamp, 1978.

———, ed. *Zum Funktionswandel der Literatur*. Frankfurt: Suhrkamp, 1983.

Cantor, Jay. *The Space Between: Literature and Politics*. Baltimore: Johns Hopkins University Press, 1981.

Clasen, Herbert. *Heinrich Heines Romantikkritik: Tradition—Produktion—Rezeption*. Hamburg: Hoffmann & Campe, 1979.

Cohn, Dorrit. *Transparent Minds: Narrative Modes for Presenting Consciousness in Fiction*. Princeton: Princeton University Press, 1978.

Corngold, Stanley. *The Fate of the Self: German Writers and French Theory*. New York: Columbia University Press, 1986.

———. "The Hermeneutic of *The Judgment*." In Angel Flores, ed., *The Problem of "The Judgment": Eleven Approaches to Kafka's Story*, pp. 39–62. New York: Gordion Press, 1977.

———. "Kafka's Other Metamorphosis." In Alan Udoff, ed., *Kafka and the Contemporary Critical Performance: Centenary Readings*, pp. 41–57. Bloomington: Indiana University Press, 1987.

———. "Kafka's 'The Judgment' and Modern Rhetorical Theory." *Newsletter of the Kafka Society of America* 7, no. 1 (June 1983): 15–21.

Coward, Rosalind, and John Ellis. *Language and Materialism: Developments in Semiology and the Theory of the Subject*. Boston: Routledge and Kegan Paul, 1977.

Cowen, Roy C. "On the Dictates of Logic in Lessing's *Emilia Galotti*." *German Quarterly* 42 (1969): 11–20.

Csúri, Károly. *Die frühen Erzählungen Hugo von Hofmannsthals: Eine generativ-poetische Untersuchung*. Kronberg, Taunus: Scriptor, 1978.

David, Claude, ed. *Franz Kafka: Themen und Probleme*. Kleine Vandenhoeck Reihe, 1451. Göttingen: Vandenhoeck & Ruprecht, 1980.

Deleuze, Gilles, and Felix Guattari. *Anti-Oedipus: Capitalism and Schizophrenia*. Trans. Robert Harley, Mark Seen, and Helen R. Lane. Minneapolis: University of Minnesota Press, 1983.

———. *Kafka: Toward a Minor Literature*. Trans. Dana Polan. Minneapolis: University of Minnesota Press, 1986.

de Man, Paul. *Allegories of Reading: Figural Language in Rousseau, Nietzsche, Rilke, and Proust*. New Haven: Yale University Press, 1979.

———. *Blindness and Insight: Essays in the Rhetoric of Contemporary Criticism*. 2nd, rev. ed. Minneapolis: University of Minnesota Press, 1983.

———. "Literary History and Literary Modernity." In *Blindness and Insight: Essays in the Rhetoric of Contemporary Criticism*, pp. 142–65. 2nd, rev. ed. Minneapolis: University of Minnesota Press, 1983.

———. *The Resistance to Theory.* Minneapolis: University of Minnesota Press, 1986.

Denkler, Horst. "Revolutionäre Dramaturgie und revolutionäres Drama im Vormärz und Märzrevolution." In Helmut Kreutzer, ed., *Gestaltungsgeschichte und Gesellschaftsgeschichte,* pp. 306–37. Stuttgart: Metzler, 1969.

Denneler, Iris. " 'Das einzige Wort!'—'Buchstabieren Sie es zusammen!' Ein Versuch, *Emilia Galotti* neu zu lesen." *Germanisch-Romanische Monatsschrift* 37 (1987): 36–51.

Denner, Jürgen. *Franz Kafka: Der Dichter der Selbstreflexion: Ein Neuansatz zum Verstehen der Dichtung Kafkas, dargestellt an der Erzählung "Das Urteil."* Munich: Fink, 1973.

Derrida, Jacques. "Edmond Jabès and the Question of the Book." In *Writing and Difference,* pp. 64–78. Trans. Alan Bass. Chicago: University of Chicago Press, 1978.

———. *Of Grammatology.* Trans. Gayatri Spivak. Baltimore: Johns Hopkins University Press, 1974.

———. "Structure, Sign, and Play in the Discourse of the Human Sciences." In *Writing and Difference,* pp. 278–93. Trans. Alan Bass. Chicago: University of Chicago Press, 1978.

Desch, Joachim. "Emilia Galotti: A Victim of Misconceived Morality." *Trivium* 9 (1974): 88–99.

Döhner, Otto. "Georg Büchners Naturauffassung." Diss., Marburg University, 1967.

———. "Neuere Erkenntnisse zu Georg Büchners Naturauffassung und Naturforschung." *Georg Büchner Jahrbuch* 2 (1982): 126–32.

Donop, William R. "Archetypal Vision in Hofmannsthal's *Reitergeschichte.*" *German Life and Letters* 22 (1968–69): 126–34.

Doppler, Alfred. "Entfremdung und Familienstruktur: Franz Kafkas Erzählungen 'Das Urteil' und 'Die Verwandlung.' " In *Wirklichkeit im Spiegel der Sprache: Aufsätze zur Literatur des 20. Jahrhunderts in Österreich,* pp. 79–99. Vienna: Europa Verlag, 1975.

Durr, Volker O. "Der Tod des Wachtmeisters Anton Lerch und die Revolution von 1848. Zu Hofmannsthals *Reitergeschichte.*" *German Quarterly* 45 (1972): 33–46.

Durzak, Manfred. "Das Gesellschaftsbild in Lessings *Emilia Galotti.*" *Lessing Yearbook* 1 (1969): 60–87.

———. "Gesellschaftsreflexion und Gesellschaftsdarstellung bei Lessing." *Zeitschrift für deutsche Philologie* 93 (1974): 546–60.

———. "Lessing und Büchner: Zur Kategorie des Politischen." In Edward P. Harris, ed., *Lessing in heutiger Sicht,* pp. 279–98. Bremen: Jacobi, 1977.

Dvoretzky, Edward. "Death and Tragedy in Lessing's *Miss Sara Sampson, Philotas,* and *Emilia Galotti.*" *Rice University Studies* 55, no. 3 (1969): 9–32.

———. *The Enigma of "Emilia Galotti."* The Hague: Nijhoff, 1963.

———, ed. *Lessing: Dokumente zur Wirkungsgeschichte 1755–1968.* Göppinger Arbeiten zur Germanistik, 38–39. Göppingen: Kümmerle, 1971–72.

Eagleton, Terry. *Criticism and Ideology.* London: New Left Books, 1976.

———. "Text, Ideology, Realism." In Edward Said, ed., *Literature and Society,* pp. 149–73. Baltimore: Johns Hopkins University Press, 1980.

Ebanks, Milena Dolic. "Laokoön in Art and Literature." Diss., New York University, 1975.

Ehrmann, Jacques. "Foreword." *Yale French Studies* 39 (1967): 5–8.

———. "On Articulation: The Language of History and the Terror of Language." *Yale French Studies* 39 (1967): 9–28.

Eibl, Karl. "*Ergo todtgeschlagen*: Erkenntnisgrenzen und Gewalt in Büchners *Dantons Tod* und *Woyzeck*." *Euphorion* 75 (1981): 411–29.

———. "Identitätskrise und Diskurs: Zur thematischen Kontinuität von Lessings Dramatik." *Jahrbuch der deutschen Schillergesellschaft* 21 (1977): 139–91.

Elema, Hans. "Evelina und die Seelenwanderung: Zu Heines 'Ideen: Das Buch Le Grand.' " *Heine Jahrbuch* 12 (1973): 20–33.

Elias, Norbert. *Über den Prozeß der Zivilisation: Soziogenetische und psychogenetische Untersuchungen.* 2nd ed. 2 vols. Frankfurt: Suhrkamp, 1976 [1969].

Ellis, John M. "The Bizarre Texture of *The Judgment*." In Angel Flores, ed., *The Problem of "The Judgment": Eleven Approaches to Kafka's Story*, pp. 73–96. New York: Gordion Press, 1977.

Engels, Friedrich. *Der Ursprung der Familie, des Privateigentums und des Staats.* In *Karl Marx–Friedrich Engels: Werke*, vol. 21, pp. 25–173. Berlin: Dietz, 1975.

Engelsing, Rolf. *Analphabetentum und Lektüre: Zur Sozialgeschichte des Lesers in Deutschland zwischen feudaler und industrieller Gesellschaft.* Stuttgart: Metzler, 1973.

———. *Der Bürger als Leser: Lesergeschichte in Deutschland 1500–1800.* Stuttgart: Metzler, 1974.

Exner, Richard. "Ordnung und Chaos in Hugo von Hofmannsthals *Reitergeschichte*: Strukturelle und semiotische Möglichkeiten der Interpretation." In Roland Jost and Hansgeorg Schmidt-Bergmann, eds., *Im Dialog mit der Moderne: Zur deutschsprachigen Literatur von der Gründerzeit bis zur Gegenwart: Jakob Stewer zum 60. Geburtstag*, pp. 46–59. Frankfurt: Athenäum, 1986.

Falke, Rita. "Biographisch-literarische Hintergründe von Kafkas 'Urteil.' " *Germanisch-Romanische Monatsschrift* 41 (1960): 164–80.

Feldt, Michael. *Ästhetik und Artistik am Ende der Kunstperiode.* Heidelberg: Winter, 1982.

Fiedler, Theodore. "Hofmannsthals 'Reitergeschichte' und ihre Leser: Zur Politik der Ironie." *Germanisch-Romanische Monatsschrift* 26 (1976): 140–63.

Finsen, H. C. "Bürgerliches Bewußtsein zwischen Heroismus und Legalität am Ende des 18. Jahrhunderts: Eine literatursoziologische Skizze." *Germanisch-Romanische Monatsschrift* 59 (1978): 21–35.

Flaherty, Gloria. "*Emilia Galotti* in Fact and Fiction." *Lessing Yearbook* 15 (1983): 111–23.

———. "Emilia Galotti's Italian Heritage." *MLN* 97 (1982): 497–514.

Flavell, M. Kay. "Family Conflict in Lessing: Living Through the Fictions." *Lessing Yearbook* 14 (1982): 71–97.

Flax, Neil. "From Portrait to *Tableau Vivant*: The Pictures of *Emilia Galotti*." *Eighteenth-Century Studies* 19 (1985): 39–55.

Flores, Angel, ed. *The Kafka Debate.* New York: Gordion Press, 1977.

———, ed. *The Problem of "The Judgment": Eleven Approaches to Kafka's Story.* New York: Gordion Press, 1977.

Flores, Kate. *"The Judgment."* In Angel Flores and Homer Swander, eds., *Franz Kafka Today*, pp. 5–24. Madison: University of Wisconsin Press, 1958.

Foucault, Michel. *Language/Countermemory/Practice.* Ed. Donald F. Bouchard and Sherry Simon. Trans. Donald Bouchard. Ithaca: Cornell University Press, 1977.

———. *The Order of Things: An Archaeology of the Human Sciences.* New York: Vintage Books, 1973.

Frank, Manfred. *Die Unhintergehbarkeit von Individualität.* Frankfurt: Suhrkamp, 1986.

———. *Was ist Neostrukturalismus?* Frankfurt: Suhrkamp, 1983.

———. *What Is Neostructuralism?* Trans. Sabine Wilke and Richard T. Gray. Minneapolis: University of Minnesota Press, 1989.

Freier, Hans. "Ästhetik und Autonomie: Ein Beitrag zur idealistischen Entfremdungskritik." In *Deutsches Bürgertum und literarische Intelligenz*, pp. 329–83. Literaturwissenschaften und Sozialwissenschaften, Bd. 3. Stuttgart: Metzler, 1974.

Freud, Sigmund. *Civilization and Its Discontents.* In *The Standard Edition of the Complete Psychological Works of Sigmund Freud*, vol. 21, pp. 57–146. Trans. and ed. James Strachey. London: Hogarth Press, 1961.

———. *The Interpretation of Dreams. The Standard Edition of the Complete Psychological Works of Sigmund Freud.* Vols. 4–5. Trans. and ed. James Strachey. London: Hogarth Press, 1958.

———. *Die Traumdeutung.* Vol. 2 of *Freud-Studienausgabe.* Ed. Alexander Mitscherlich, Angela Richards, and James Strachey. 11 vols. Frankfurt: Fischer, 1974.

———. *Das Unbehagen in der Kultur.* In Alexander Mitscherlich, Angela Richards, and James Strachey, eds., *Freud-Studienausgabe*, vol. 9, pp. 197–270. Frankfurt: Fischer, 1974.

———. "The Uncanny." In James Strachey, trans and ed., *The Standard Edition of the Complete Psychological Works of Sigmund Freud*, vol. 17, pp. 217–56. London: Hogarth Press, 1955.

———. "Das Unheimliche." In Alexander Mitscherlich, Angela Richards, and James Strachey, eds., *Freud-Studienausgabe*, vol. 4, pp. 241–74. Frankfurt: Fischer, 1974.

Frieß, Ursula. " 'Verführung ist die wahre Gewalt': Zur Politisierung eines dramatischen Motifs in Lessings bürgerlichen Trauerspielen." *Jahrbuch der Jean-Paul-Gesellschaft* 6 (1970): 102–30.

Frow, John. *Marxism and Literary History.* Cambridge, Mass.: Harvard University Press, 1986.

Gadamer, Hans-Georg. *Truth and Method.* New York: Seabury Press, 1975.

———. *Wahrheit und Methode.* 4th ed. Tübingen: Niemeyer, 1975.

Gilbert, Mary E. "Hugo von Hofmannsthals 'Reitergeschichte': Versuch einer Interpretation." *Der Deutschunterricht* 8 (1956): 101–12.

———. "The Image of the Horse in Hofmannsthal's Poetic Work." *Modern Austrian Literature* 7 (1974): 58–76.

———. "Some Observations on Hofmannsthal's Two 'Novellen' *Reitergeschichte* and *Das Erlebnis des Marschalls von Bassompierre.*" *German Life and Letters* 11 (1957–58): 102–11.

Glück, Alfons. "'Herrschende Ideen': Die Rolle der Ideologie, Indoktrination und Desorientierung in Georg Büchners *Woyzeck.*" *Georg Büchner Jahrbuch* 5 (1985): 52–138.

———. "Der Menschenversuch: Die Rolle der Wissenschaft in Georg Büchners *Woyzeck.*" *Georg Büchner Jahrbuch* 5 (1985): 139–82.

———. "Militär und Justiz in Georg Büchners *Woyzeck.*" *Georg Büchner Jahrbuch* 4 (1984): 227–47.

———. "Der 'ökonomische Tod': Armut und Arbeit in Georg Büchners *Woyzeck.*" *Georg Büchner Jahrbuch* 4 (1984): 167–226.

Goebel, Gerhard. "Literatur und Aufklärung." In Peter Bürger, ed., *Zum Funktionswandel der Literatur*, pp. 79–97. Frankfurt: Suhrkamp, 1983.

Goldmann, Lucien. "Structure: Human Reality and Methodological Concept." In Richard Macksey and Eugenio Donato, eds., *The Structuralist Controversy*, pp. 98–124. Baltimore: Johns Hopkins University Press, 1972.

———. *Towards a Sociology of the Novel*. Trans. Alan Sheridan. New York: Tavistock Publications, 1975.

Goldstein, Bluma. "Bachelors and Work: Social and Economic Conditions in 'The Judgment,' 'The Metamorphosis' and 'The Trial.'" In Angel Flores, ed., *The Kafka Debate*, pp. 147–75. New York: Gordion Press, 1977.

Goldstücker, Eduard. "Kafkas Eckermann? Zu Gustav Janouchs 'Gespräche mit Kafka.'" In Claude David, ed., *Franz Kafka: Themen und Probleme*, pp. 238–55. Göttingen: Vandenhoeck & Ruprecht, 1980.

Görtz, Franz Josef. "Georg Büchner: Revolutionär und Schriftsteller." In Walter Hinderer, ed., *Literarische Profile: Deutsche Dichter von Grimmelshausen bis Brecht*, pp. 159–71. Königstein: Athenäum, 1982.

Goux, Jean-Joseph. *Symbolic Economies: After Marx and Freud.* Trans. Jennifer Curtiss Gage. Ithaca: Cornell University Press, 1990.

Gray, Richard T. "Biography as Criticism in Kafka Studies." *Journal of the Kafka Society of America* 10, no. 1–2 (June/Dec. 1986): 46–55.

———. *Constructive Destruction: Kafka's Aphorisms, Literary Tradition and Literary Transformation.* Tübingen: Niemeyer, 1987.

Grimm, Reinhold. "Georg Büchner and the Modern Concept of Revolt." *Annali Sezione Germanica. Studi Tedeschi* 21, no. 2 (1978): 7–66.

———. *Love, Lust, and Rebellion: New Approaches to Georg Büchner.* Madison: University of Wisconsin Press, 1985.

Grossklaus, Götz. "Heinrich Heine: 'Ideen: Das Buch Le Grand': Eine textsemantische Beschreibung." In Siegfried J. Schmidt, ed., *Zur Grundlegung der Literaturwissenschaft*, pp. 169–96. Munich: Bayerischer Schulbuch-Verlag, 1972.

Grubacic, Slobodan. *Heines Erzählprosa: Versuch einer Analyse.* Studien zur Poetik und Geschichte der Literatur, Bd. 40. Stuttgart: Kohlhammer, 1975.

Guthke, Karl S. "Der Glücksspieler als Autor: Überlegungen zur 'Gestalt' Lessings im Sinne der inneren Biographie." *Euphorion* 71 (1977): 353–82.

———. "Räuber Moors Glück und Ende." *German Quarterly* 39 (1966): 1–11.

Habermas, Jürgen. *Erkenntnis und Interesse.* Frankfurt: Suhrkamp, 1973 [1968].

————. "The Hermeneutic Claim to Universality." In Josef Bleicher, ed., *Contemporary Hermeneutics*, pp. 181–211. London: Routledge, 1980.

————. *Knowledge and Human Interests*. Trans. Jeremy J. Shapiro. Boston: Beacon Press, 1971.

————. *The Philosophical Discourse of Modernity*. Trans. Frederick Lawrence. Cambridge, Mass.: MIT Press, 1987.

————. *Der philosophische Diskurs der Moderne*. Frankfurt: Suhrkamp, 1985.

————. *The Structural Transformation of the Public Sphere: An Inquiry into a Category of Bourgeois Society*. Trans. Thomas Burger. Cambridge, Mass.: MIT Press, 1989.

————. *Strukturwandel der Öffentlichkeit: Untersuchungen zu einer Kategorie der bürgerlichen Gesellschaft*. 13th ed. Darmstadt: Luchterhand, 1982 [1962].

————. "Theodor W. Adorno: Urgeschichte der Subjektivität und verwilderte Selbstbehauptung." In *Philosophisch-politische Profile*, pp. 167–79. 3rd, expanded ed. Frankfurt: Suhrkamp, 1981.

————. *Theorie des kommunikativen Handelns*. 2 vols. Frankfurt: Suhrkamp, 1981.

————. *The Theory of Communicative Action*. 2 vols. Trans. Thomas McCarthy. Boston: Beacon Press, 1984–87.

————. "Der Universalitätsanspruch der Hermeneutik." In *Kultur und Kritik: Verstreute Aufsätze*, pp. 264–301. Frankfurt: Suhrkamp, 1973.

Hahn, Peter. "Kunst als Ideologie und Utopie." In Peter Bürger, ed., *Seminar: Literatur- und Kunstsoziologie*, pp. 236–59. Frankfurt: Suhrkamp, 1978.

Hamann, Johann Georg. "Vermischte Anmerkungen über die Wortstellung in der französischen Sprache." In Josef Simon, ed., *Schriften zur Sprache*, pp. 95–104. Frankfurt: Suhrkamp, 1967.

Härtling, Peter. "Literatur als Revolution und Tradition." *Akzente* 14 (1967): 221–23.

Hatfield, Henry. "Emilia's Guilt Once More." *MLN* 71 (1956): 287–96.

Haug, Wolfgang Fritz. *Critique of Commodity Aesthetics: Appearance, Sexuality and Advertising in Capitalist Society*. Trans. Robert Bock. Cambridge: Polity Press, 1986.

————. *Kritik der Warenästhetik*. Frankfurt: Suhrkamp, 1971.

————. "Zur Kritik der Warenästhetik." In Peter Bürger, ed., *Seminar: Literatur- und Kunstsoziologie*, pp. 394–417. Frankfurt: Suhrkamp, 1978.

Hegel, Georg Wilhelm Friedrich. *Aesthetics: Lectures on Fine Art*. Trans. T. M. Knox. 2 vols. Oxford: Clarendon Press, 1975.

————. *Phänomenologie des Geistes*. Vol. 3 of *Theorie-Werkausgabe*, ed. Eva Moldenhauer and Karl Markus Michel. Frankfurt: Suhrkamp, 1970.

————. *Phenomenology of Spirit*. Trans. A. V. Miller. Oxford: Clarendon Press, 1977.

————. "Über die Bekehrten." In Eva Moldenhauer and Karl Markus Michel, eds., *Berliner Schriften 1818–1831*. *Theorie-Werkausgabe*, vol. 11, pp. 72–82. Frankfurt: Suhrkamp, 1970.

————. *Vorlesungen über die Ästhetik*. 3 vols. Vols. 13–15 of *Theorie-Werkausgabe*, ed. Eva Moldenhauer and Karl Markus Michel. Frankfurt: Suhrkamp, 1970.

————. *Vorlesungen über die Geschichte der Philosophie*. Vol. 18 of *Theorie-Werkausgabe*, ed. Eva Moldenhauer and Karl Markus Michel. Frankfurt: Suhrkamp, 1971.

Heidegger, Martin. *Being and Time*. Trans. John Macquarrie and Edward Robinson. New York: Harper and Row, 1962.

———. *Sein und Zeit*. 7th ed. Tübingen: Niemeyer, 1953.

Heinburger, Käte. "Zur Struktur der belletristischen Prosa Heines." In Vincent J. Günther, ed., *Untersuchungen zur Literatur als Geschichte: Festschrift für Benno von Wiese*, pp. 286–306. Berlin: Erich Schmidt, 1973.

Heine, Heinrich. *Briefe*. Ed. Friedrich Hirth. 6 vols. Mainz: Florian Kupferberg Verlag, 1965.

———. *Concerning the History of Religion and Philosophy in Germany*. In Jost Hermand and Robert C. Holub, eds., *The Romantic School and Other Essays*, pp. 128–244. Trans. Helen Mustard. New York: Continuum, 1985.

———. *Geschichte der Religion und Philosophie in Deutschland*. In Klaus Briegleb, ed., *Sämtliche Schriften*, vol. 3, pp. 503–641. Munich: Hanser, 1969–75.

———. *Ideas: Book Le Grand*. Trans. Charles Godfrey Leland, Robert C. Holub, and Martha Humphreys. In Jost Hermand and Robert C. Holub, eds., *Heinrich Heine: Poetry and Prose*, pp. 174–228. New York: Continuum, 1982.

———. *Ideen: Das Buch Le Grand*. In Klaus Briegleb, ed., *Sämtliche Schriften*, vol. 2, pp. 245–308. Munich: Hanser, 1969–75.

———. *The Romantic School*. In Jost Hermand and Robert C. Holub, eds., *The Romantic School and Other Essays*, pp. 1–127. Trans. Helen Mustard. New York: Continuum, 1985.

———. *Die romantische Schule*. In Klaus Briegleb, ed., *Sämtliche Schriften*, vol. 3, pp. 359–504. Munich: Hanser, 1969–75.

———. *Sämtliche Schriften*. Ed. Klaus Briegleb. 6 vols. Munich: Hanser, 1969–75.

Heinrich, Ulrich. "Hugo von Hofmannsthals 'Reitergeschichte': Eine Interpretation." *Wirkendes Wort* 21 (1971): 313–18.

Heise, Wolfgang. "Krise eines Weltanschauungssystems: Emilia Galotti." *Impulse* 10 (1987): 5–26.

Heitner, Robert R. "*Emilia Galotti*: An Indictment of Bourgeois Passivity." *Journal of English and Germanic Philology* 52 (1953): 480–90.

Henrich, Dieter. "Kunst und Kunstphilosophie der Gegenwart: Überlegungen mit Rücksicht auf Hegel." In Wolfgang Iser, ed., *Immanente Ästhetik. Ästhetische Reflexion*, pp. 11–32. Poetik und Hermeneutik, 2. Munich: Fink, 1966.

Herder, Johann Gottfried. *Abhandlung über den Ursprung der Sprache*. In Erich Loewenthal, ed., *Sturm und Drang: Kritische Schriften*, pp. 399–506. 3rd ed. Heidelberg: Lambert Schneider, 1972.

Hermand, Jost. *Der frühe Heine: Ein Kommentar zu den Reisebildern*. Munich: Winkler, 1976.

———. "Heines 'Briefe aus Berlin': Politische Tendenz und feuilletonistische Form." In Helmut Kreuzer, ed., *Gestaltungsgeschichte und Gesellschaftsgeschichte*, pp. 284–305. Stuttgart: Metzler, 1969.

Hess, Moses. "Über das Geldwesen." In Auguste Cornu and Wolfgang Mönke, eds., *Philosophische und sozialistische Schriften 1837–1850*, pp. 329–48. Berlin: Akademie Verlag, 1961.

Hessel, Karl. "Heines 'Buch Le Grand.' " *Vierteljahresschrift für Literaturgeschichte* 5 (1892): 546–72.

Heydermann, Evelyne. "Institution und Autonomie: Zur Diskussion des Aufsatzes von G. Goebel: 'Literatur und Aufklärung.' " In Peter Bürger, ed., *Zum Funktionswandel der Literatur*, pp. 98–106. Frankfurt: Suhrkamp, 1983.

Hinck, Walter, ed. *Sturm und Drang: Ein literaturwissenschaftliches Studienbuch*. Frankfurt: Athenäum, 1978.

Hinderer, Walter. "Freiheit und Gesellschaft beim jungen Schiller." In Walter Hinck, ed., *Sturm und Drang: Ein literaturwissenschaftliches Studienbuch*, pp. 230–56. Frankfurt: Athenäum, 1978.

Hinz, Berthold. "Zur Dialektik des bürgerlichen Autonomie-Begriffs." In *Autonomie der Kunst: Zur Genese und Kritik einer bürgerlichen Kategorie*, pp. 173–98. Frankfurt: Suhrkamp, 1972.

Hodge, Robert, and Gunther Kress. *Social Semiotics*. Ithaca: Cornell University Press, 1988.

Hofmannsthal, Hugo von. *Reitergeschichte*. In Heinz Otto Bürger, ed., *Sämtliche Werke*, vol. 28, pp. 39–48. Frankfurt: Fischer, 1975.

———. *A Tale of the Cavalry*. In *Hugo von Hofmannsthal: Selected Prose*, pp. 321–31. Trans. Mary Hottinger and Tania and James Stern. New York: Pantheon, 1952.

Hofmannsthal-Andrian Briefwechsel. Ed. Walter H. Perl. Frankfurt: Fischer, 1968.

Hofrichter, Laura. *Heinrich Heine*. Oxford: Cambridge University Press, 1963.

Hohendahl, Peter Uwe. "Geschichte und Modernität: Heines Kritik an der Romantik." *Jahrbuch der deutschen Schillergesellschaft* 17 (1973): 318–61.

———. "Literarische und politische Öffentlichkeit: Die neue Kritik des Jungen Deutschland." In *Literatur und Öffentlichkeit*, pp. 102–27. Munich: Piper, 1974.

———. "Von der politischen Kritik zur Legitimationswissenschaft: Zum institutionellen Status der Literaturgeschichte nach 1848." In Peter Bürger, ed., *Zum Funktionswandel der Literatur*, pp. 194–217. Frankfurt: Suhrkamp, 1983.

Holub, Robert C. "The Paradoxes of Realism: An Examination of the *Kunstgespräch* in Büchner's *Lenz*." *Deutsche Vierteljahrsschrift für Literaturwissenschaft und Geistesgeschichte* 59 (1985): 102–24.

Hömberg, Walter. *Zeitgeist und Ideenschmuggel: Die Kommunikationsstrategie des Jungen Deutschland*. Stuttgart: Metzler, 1975.

Hörisch, Jochen. "Die Tugend und der Weltlauf in Lessings bürgerlichen Trauerspielen." *Euphorion* 74 (1980): 186–97.

Horkheimer, Max. "Authority and the Family." In *Critical Theory: Selected Essays*, pp. 47–128. Trans. Matthew J. O'Connell. New York: Continuum, 1989.

———. "Autorität und Familie." In Alfred Schmidt, ed., *Gesammelte Schriften*, vol. 3, pp. 336–417. Frankfurt: Fischer, 1988.

———. "Rise and Decline of the Individual." In *Eclipse of Reason*, pp. 128–61. New York: Continuum, 1992 [1947].

———. "Traditional and Critical Theory." In *Critical Theory: Selected Essays*, pp. 188–243. Trans. Matthew J. O'Connell. New York: Continuum, 1989.

————. "Traditionelle und kritische Theorie." In *Traditionelle und kritische Theorie: Vier Aufsätze*, pp. 12–64. Frankfurt: Fischer, 1970.

————. "Vorwort" [zu den *Studien über Autorität und Familie*]. In Alfred Schmidt, ed., *Gesammelte Schriften*, vol. 3, pp. 329–35. Frankfurt: Fischer, 1988.

Horkheimer, Max, and Theodor Adorno. *Dialectic of Enlightenment*. Trans. John Cumming. New York: Continuum, 1988.

————. *Dialektik der Aufklärung*. Frankfurt: Fischer, 1969 [1947].

Horn, Peter. " 'Ich meine für menschliche Dinge müsse man auch menschliche Ausdrücke finden': Die Sprache der Philosophie und die Sprache der Dichtung bei Georg Büchner." *Georg Büchner Jahrbuch* 2 (1982): 209–26.

Huyssen, Andreas. *After the Great Divide: Modernism, Mass Culture, Postmodernism*. Bloomington: Indiana University Press, 1986.

————. *Drama des Sturm und Drang: Kommentar zu einer Epoche*. Munich: Winkler, 1980.

Jacobs, Carol. "The Critical Performance of Lessing's *Laokoön*." *MLN* 102 (1987): 483–521.

Jacobs, Jürgen. "Nach dem Ende der 'Kunstperiode': Heines Aporien und ihre Aktualität." In Wolfgang Kuttenkeuler, ed., *Heinrich Heine: Artistik und Engagement*, pp. 242–55. Stuttgart: Metzler, 1977.

————. "Zu Heines 'Ideen: Das Buch Le Grand.' " *Heine Jahrbuch* 7 (1968): 3–11.

Jameson, Fredric. "Introduction." In Henri Arvon, *Marxist Esthetics*, pp. vii–xxiv. Trans. Helen R. Lane. Ithaca: Cornell University Press, 1973.

————. *The Political Unconscious: Narrative as a Socially Symbolic Act*. Ithaca: Cornell University Press, 1981.

————. "Reflections in Conclusion." In *Aesthetics and Politics*, pp. 196–213. London: New Left Books, 1977.

Janouch, Gustav. *Gespräche mit Kafka: Aufzeichnungen und Erinnerungen*. Expanded ed. Frankfurt: Fischer, 1968.

Jansen, Deborah. "The Emancipation Which Enslaved." *New German Review* 1 (1985): 15–27.

Janz, Rolf-Peter. *Autonomie und soziale Funktion der Kunst: Studien zur Ästhetik von Schiller und Novalis*. Stuttgart: Metzler, 1973.

Jauss, Hans Robert. "Das Ende der Kunstperiode: Aspekte der literarischen Revolution bei Heine, Hugo und Stendahl." In *Literaturgeschichte als Provokation*, pp. 107–43. Frankfurt: Suhrkamp, 1970.

————. "Literaturgeschichte als Provokation der Literaturwissenschaft." In *Literaturgeschichte als Provokation*, pp. 144–207. Frankfurt: Suhrkamp, 1970.

————. *Toward an Aesthetic of Reception*. Trans. Timothy Bahti. Minneapolis: University of Minnesota Press, 1982.

Johnson, Pauline. *Marxist Aesthetics: The Foundations within Everyday Life for an Enlightened Consciousness*. Boston: Routledge and Kegan Paul, 1984.

Jürgens, Martin. "Bemerkungen zur 'Ästhetisierung der Politik.' " In *Ästhetik und Gewalt*, pp. 8–37. Gütersloh: Bertelsmann Kunstverlag, 1970.

Kafka, Franz. *Beschreibung eines Kampfes: Novellen, Skizzen, Aphorismen aus dem Nachlaß*. Ed. Max Brod. New York: Schocken Books, 1946.

———. "Brief an den Vater." In *Hochzeitsvorbereitungen auf dem Lande und andere Prosa aus dem Nachlaß,* pp. 162–223. Frankfurt: Fischer, 1953.

———. *Briefe 1902–1924.* Ed. Max Brod. Frankfurt: Fischer, 1958.

———. *Briefe an Felice.* Ed. Erich Heller and Jürgen Born. Frankfurt: Fischer, 1967.

———. *Briefe an Milena.* Ed. Jürgen Born. Expanded ed. Frankfurt: Fischer, 1983.

———. *Briefe an Ottla und die Familie.* Ed. Hartmut Binder and Klaus Wagenbach. Frankfurt: Fischer, 1974.

———. *The Complete Stories.* Ed. Nahum N. Glatzer. Trans. Willa and Edwin Muir. New York: Schocken Books, 1971.

———. *Dearest Father: Stories and Other Writings.* Trans. Ernst Kaiser and Eithne Wilkins. New York: Schocken Books, 1954.

———. *The Diaries 1910–1923.* Trans. Joseph Kresh and Martin Greenberg. New York: Schocken Books, 1976.

———. *Erzählungen.* Ed. Max Brod. Frankfurt: Fischer, 1952.

———. *Hochzeitsvorbereitungen auf dem Lande und andere Prosa aus dem Nachlaß.* Ed. Max Brod. Frankfurt: Fischer, 1953.

———. *The Judgment.* In Nahum N. Glatzer, ed., *The Complete Stories,* pp. 77–88. Trans. Willa and Edwin Muir. New York: Schocken Books, 1971.

———. *Letters to Felice.* Trans. James Stern and Elisabeth Duckworth. New York: Schocken Books, 1973.

———. *Letters to Friends, Family, and Editors.* Trans. Richard and Clara Winston. New York: Schocken Books, 1977.

———. *Letter to His Father.* Trans. Ernst Kaiser and Eithne Wilkins. New York: Schocken Books, 1966.

———. *Tagebücher 1910–1923.* Ed. Max Brod. Frankfurt: Fischer, 1949.

———. *Das Urteil.* In *Erzählungen,* pp. 53–68. Frankfurt: Fischer, 1952.

Kaiser, Gerhard. "Krise der Familie: Eine Perspektive auf Lessings *Emilia Galotti* und Schillers *Kabale und Liebe.*" *Recherches germaniques* 14 (1984): 7–22.

Kant, Immanuel. "Beantwortung der Frage: Was ist Aufklärung?" In Wilhelm Weischedel, ed., *Werke in sechs Bänden,* vol. 6, pp. 53–61. Frankfurt: Insel, 1964.

———. *Critique of Judgment.* Trans. Werner S. Pluhar. Indianapolis: Hacket, 1987.

———. *Kritik der Urteilskraft.* Vol. 10 of *Kant Werkausgabe,* ed. Wilhelm Weischedel. Frankfurt: Suhrkamp, 1974.

———. "What Is Enlightenment?" In *"Foundations of the Metaphysics of Morals" and "What Is Enlightenment?"* pp. 85–92. Trans. Lewis White Beck. Indianapolis: Bobbs-Merrill, 1959.

Kellner, Douglas. *Critical Theory, Marxism, and Modernity.* Baltimore: Johns Hopkins University Press, 1989.

Kemper, Hans-Georg. "Gestörte Kommunikation: Franz Kafka, 'Das Urteil.' " In Silvio Vietta and Hans-Georg Kemper, eds., *Expressionismus,* pp. 286–305. UTB 362. Munich: Fink, 1975.

Kieffer, Bruce. *The Storm and Stress of Language: Linguistic Catastrophe in the Early Works of Goethe, Lenz, Klinger, and Schiller.* University Park: University of Pennsylvania Press, 1986.

Kittler, Friedrich A. " 'Erziehung ist Offenbarung': Zur Struktur der Familie in Lessings Dramen." *Jahrbuch der deutschen Schillergesellschaft* 21 (1977): 111–37.

Klotz, Volker. *Geschlossene und offene Form im Drama.* Munich: Hanser, 1969.

Knapp, Gerhard P. *Georg Büchner.* Sammlung Metzler, M 159. Stuttgart: Metzler, 1977.

Kobel, Erwin. *Georg Büchner: Das dichterische Werk.* Berlin: de Gruyter, 1974.

Kobligk, Helmut. " ' . . . ohne daß er etwas Böses getan hätte . . . ': Zum Verständnis der Schuld in Kafkas Erzählungen 'Die Verwandlung' und 'Das Urteil.' " *Wirkendes Wort* 32 (1982): 391–405.

Koc, Richard. "Fathers and Sons: Ambivalence Doubled in Schiller's *Räuber.*" *Germanic Review* 61 (1986): 91–104.

Kolb, Jocelyn. "The Sublime, the Ridiculous, and the Apple Tarts in Heine's *Ideen: Das Buch Le Grand.*" *German Quarterly* 56 (1983): 28–38.

Koopmann, Helmut. "Joseph und sein Vater: Zu den biblischen Anspielungen in Schillers *Räuber.*" In Gerald Gillespie and Edgar Lohner, eds., *Herkommen und Erneuerung: Essays für Oskar Seidlin,* pp. 150–67. Tübingen: Niemeyer, 1976.

Koselleck, Reinhart. *Critique and Crisis: Enlightenment and the Pathogenesis of Modern Society.* Oxford: Berg, 1988.

———. *Kritik und Krise: Eine Studie zur Pathogenese der bürgerlichen Welt.* Frankfurt: Suhrkamp: 1973 [1959].

———. "Der Zufall als Motivationsrest in der Geschichtsschreibung." In *Vergangene Zukunft: Zur Semantik geschichtlicher Zeiten,* pp. 158–75. Frankfurt: Suhrkamp, 1979.

Köster, Udo. *Literarischer Radikalismus: Zeitbewußtsein und Geschichtsphilosophie in der Entwicklung vom Jungen Deutschland zur Hegelschen Linken.* Frankfurt: Athenäum, 1972.

———. *Literatur und Gesellschaft in Deutschland 1830–1848: Die Dichtung am Ende der Kunstperiode.* Sprache und Literatur, 120. Stuttgart: Kohlhammer, 1984.

Kracauer, Siegfried. *From Caligari to Hitler: A Psychological History of the German Film.* Princeton: Princeton University Press, 1947.

Krapp, Helmut. *Der Dialog bei Georg Büchner.* Munich: Hanser, 1958.

Krauss, Hennig. "Die Zurücknahme des Autonomiestatus der Literatur im Frankreich der vierziger Jahre." In R. Kloepfer, ed., *Bildung und Ausbildung in der Romania,* vol. 1, pp. 267–78. Munich: Fink, 1979.

Kristeva, Julia. "The Bounded Text." In Leon S. Roudiez, ed., *Desire in Language,* pp. 36–63. Trans. Thomas Gora, Alice Jardine, and Leon S. Roudiez. New York: Columbia University Press, 1980.

———. *Desire in Language.* Ed. Leon S. Roudiez. Trans. Thomas Gora, Alice Jardine, and Leon S. Roudiez. New York: Columbia University Press, 1980.

———. *Revolution in Poetic Language.* Trans. Margaret Waller. New York: Columbia University Press, 1984.

Krusche, Dietrich. *Kafka und Kafka-Deutung: Die problematisierte Interaktion.* Kritische Information, 5. Munich: Fink, 1974.

Kurz, Paul Konrad. *Künstler—Tribun—Apostel: Heinrich Heines Auffassung vom Beruf des Dichters.* Munich: Fink, 1967.

Labroisse, Gerd. "Emilia Galottis Wollen und Sollen." *Neophilologus* 56 (1972): 311–23.

Lacan, Jacques. *Ecrits: A Selection.* Trans. Alan Sheridan. London: Tavistock, 1977.

————. *The Language of the Self: The Function of Language in Psychoanalysis.* Trans. Anthony Wilden. Baltimore: Johns Hopkins University Press, 1968.

Laing, R. D. *The Divided Self: An Existential Study in Sanity and Madness.* 2nd ed. Harmondsworth, Eng.: Penguin, 1965.

Lakin, Michael. "Hofmannsthals *Reitergeschichte* und Kafkas *Ein Landarzt.*" *Modern Austrian Literature* 3 (1970): 39–50.

Lamport, J. F. " 'Eine bürgerliche Virginia.' " *German Life and Letters* 17 (1963–64): 304–12.

Larsen, Svend Erik. "The Symbol of the Knife in Büchner's *Woyzeck.*" *Orbis Litterarum* 40 (1985): 258–81.

LeFebvre, Joël. "Zur Autonomie der Literatur in der frühen Neuzeit." In Peter Bürger, ed., *Zum Funktionswandel der Literatur,* pp. 61–78. Frankfurt: Suhrkamp, 1983.

Lehmann, Ursula. *Popularisierung und Ironie im Werk Heinrich Heines: Die Bedeutung der textimmanenten Kontrastierung für den Rezeptionsprozeß.* Europäische Hochschulschriften, Reihe 1, Bd. 164. Frankfurt: Peter Lang, 1976.

Lehmann, Werner R. *"Geht einmal euren Phrasen nach": Revolutionsideologie und Ideologiekritik bei Georg Büchner.* Darmstadt: Eduard Roether Verlag, 1969.

Leibniz, Gottfried Wilhelm. *Unvorgreifliche Gedanken, betreffend die Ausübung und Verbesserung der teutschen Sprache.* In Ernst Cassirer, ed., *Hauptschriften zur Grundlegung der Philosophie,* vol. 2, pp. 519–55. Hamburg: Meiner, 1966.

Leithäuser, Gerhard. "Kunstwerk und Warenform." In Peter Bürger, ed., *Seminar: Literatur- und Kunstsoziologie,* pp. 21–36. Frankfurt: Suhrkamp, 1983.

Lentricchia, Frank. *Criticism and Social Change.* Chicago: University of Chicago Press, 1983.

Lessing, Gotthold Ephraim. *Emilia Galotti.* In Paul Rilla, ed., *Gesammelte Werke,* vol. 2, pp. 237–318. East Berlin: Aufbau, 1954.

————. *Emilia Galotti: A Tragedy in Five Acts.* Trans. Edward Dvoretzky. New York: Ungar, 1962.

————. *Gesammelte Werke.* Ed. Paul Rilla. 10 vols. East Berlin: Aufbau, 1954–58.

————. *Nathan der Weise.* In Paul Rilla, ed., *Gesammelte Werke,* vol. 2, pp. 319–481. East Berlin: Aufbau, 1954.

————. *Nathan the Wise.* Trans. Bayard Quincy Morgan. New York: Ungar, 1955.

Leventhal, Robert S. "The Parable as Performance: Interpretation, Cultural Transmission and Political Strategy in Lessing's *Nathan der Weise.*" *German Quarterly* 61 (1988): 502–27.

Levin, Harry. "The Rhetoric of Revolution." In Stanley A. Corngold, Michael Curshmann, and Theodore Ziolkowski, eds., *Aspekte der Goethezeit,* pp. 183–203. Göttingen: Vandenhoeck & Ruprecht, 1977.

Lindenberger, Herbert. *Georg Büchner.* Carbondale: Southern Illinois University Press, 1964.

Loewenthal, Erich. *Studien zu Heines "Reisebildern."* Berlin: Mayer & Müller, 1922.

Löwenthal, Leo. *Literature and the Image of Man.* Boston: Beacon Press, 1957.

362 Bibliography

Lukács, Georg. "Der faschistisch verfälschte und der wirkliche Georg Büchner." In Wolfgang Martens, ed., *Georg Büchner*, pp. 197–224. Wege der Forschung, Bd. 53. Darmstadt: Wissenschaftliche Buchgesellschaft, 1965.

Lützeler, Paul Michael. "Lessings *Emilia Galotti* und *Minna von Barnhelm*: Der Adel zwischen Aufklärung und Absolutismus." In Peter Uwe Hohendahl and Paul Michael Lützeler, eds., *Legitimation des deutschen Adels 1200–1900*, pp. 101–18. Literaturwissenschaften und Sozialwissenschaften, Bd. 11. Stuttgart: Metzler, 1979.

———. "Die marxistische Lessing-Rezeption: Darstellung und Kritik am Beispiel der *Emilia Galotti*-Interpretation in der DDR." *Lessing Yearbook* 8 (1976): 42–60.

Lyotard, Jean-François. *The Postmodern Condition: A Report on Knowledge*. Trans. Geoff Bennington and Brian Massumi. Minneapolis: University of Minnesota Press, 1984.

McCarthy, John A. "Some Aspects of Imagery in Büchner's *Woyzeck*." *MLN* 91 (1976): 543–51.

McInnes, Edward O. " 'Eine bürgerliche Virginia'?: Lessing's *Emilia Galotti* and the Development of the Bürgerliches Trauerspiel." *Orbis Litterarum* 39 (1984): 308–23.

Marcuse, Herbert. *The Aesthetic Dimension: Toward a Critique of Marxist Aesthetics*. Boston: Beacon Press, 1978.

———. "The Affirmative Character of Culture." In *Negations: Essays in Critical Theory*, pp. 88–133. Trans. Jeremy J. Shapiro. Boston: Beacon Press, 1968.

———. *Die Permanenz der Kunst: Wider eine bestimmte marxistische Ästhetik*. Reihe Hanser, 206. Munich: Hanser, 1977.

———. "Über den affirmativen Charakter der Kultur." In *Kultur und Gesellschaft I*, pp. 56–101. Frankfurt: Suhrkamp, 1965.

Marson, Erich L. "Franz Kafkas 'Das Urteil.' " *AUMLA* 16 (1961): 167–78.

Martens, Wolfgang, ed. *Georg Büchner*. Wege der Forschung, Bd. 53. Darmstadt: Wissenschaftliche Buchgesellschaft, 1965.

Marx, Karl. *Economic and Philosophical Manuscripts*. In *Karl Marx: Early Writings*, pp. 279–400. Trans. Rodney Livingstone and Gregor Benton. New York: Random House (Vintage), 1975.

———. *Ökonomisch-philosophische Manuskripte aus dem Jahre 1844*. In *Karl Marx–Friedrich Engels: Werke*, Ergänzungsband, Teil I, pp. 465–588. Berlin: Dietz, 1968.

Mattenklott, Gert. *Melancholie in der Dramatik des Sturm und Drang*. 2nd ed. Königstein, Taunus: Athenäum, 1985.

———. "Was bedeutet die Sprache der Bilder für eine realistische Ästhetik: Überlegungen zu Lessings *Laokoön*." *Zeitschrift für Germanistik* 1 (1980): 215–19.

Mattenklott, Gert, and Klaus R. Scherpe. *Demokratisch-revolutionäre Literatur in Deutschland: Vormärz*. Literatur im historischen Prozeß, Bd. 3/2. Kronberg, Taunus: Scriptor, 1974.

Mauser, Wolfram. "Fatalität der Identitätsstörung: *Reitergeschichte*." In *Hugo von Hofmannsthal: Konfliktbewältigung und Werkstruktur: Eine psychosoziologische Interpretation*, pp. 101–17. Munich: Fink, 1977.

Mauss, Marcel. "A Category of the Human Mind: The Notion of Person, the Notion of 'Self.' " In *Sociology and Psychology: Essays by Marcel Mauss*, pp. 57–94. Trans. Ben Brewster. London: Routledge and Kegan Paul, 1979.

Mautner, Franz H. "Wortgewebe, Sinngefüge und 'Idee' in Büchners 'Woyzeck.' " In Wolfgang Martens, ed., *Georg Büchner*, pp. 507–54. Wege der Forschung, Bd. 53. Darmstadt: Wissenschaftliche Buchgesellschaft, 1965.

May, Kurt. "Büchners 'Woyzeck.' " In Wolfgang Martens, ed., *Georg Büchner*, pp. 241–51. Wege der Forschung, Bd. 53. Darmstadt: Wissenschaftliche Buchgesellschaft, 1965.

Mayer, Dieter. "Vater und Tochter: Anmerkungen zu einem Motiv im deutschen Drama der Vorklassik." *Literatur für Leser* (1980): 135–47.

Mayer, Hans. *Georg Büchner und seine Zeit*. Wiesbaden: Limes, 1959.

———. *Georg Büchner, "Woyzeck": Wirklichkeit und Dichtung*. Frankfurt: Ullstein, 1963.

———. "Schillers *Räuber*." *Theater Heute* 9, no. 10 (Oct. 1968): 1–6.

———. "Schillers Vorreden zu den *Räubern*." In *Von Lessing bis Thomas Mann: Wandlungen der bürgerlichen Literatur in Deutschland*, pp. 134–54. Pfullingen: Neske, 1959.

Meier, Albert. "Georg Büchners Ästhetik." *Georg Büchner Jahrbuch* 2 (1982): 196–208.

———. *Georg Büchners Ästhetik*. Munich: Fink, 1983.

———. *Georg Büchner: "Woyzeck."* UTB 975. Munich: Fink, 1980.

Meier, Ulrich. "Soziologische Bemerkungen zur Institution Kunst." In Peter Bürger, ed., *Zum Funktionswandel der Literatur*, pp. 33–58. Frankfurt: Suhrkamp, 1983.

Meltzer, Francoise. "Reiter- (writer- reader-) Geschichte." *Monatshefte* 77 (1985): 38–46.

Mendelssohn, Moses. *Über die Hauptgrundsätze der schönen Künste und Wissenschaften*. In *Gesammelte Schriften*, vol. 1, pp. 423–52. Stuttgart: Frommann Verlag, 1971.

Merkel, Frank-Volker. "Der Prinz: ein Wollüstling? ein Tyrann? Zu Lessings *Emilia Galotti*." *Neuphilologische Mitteilungen* 79 (1978): 232–39.

Merkel, Johannes, and Rüdiger Steinlein. "Schillers *Die Räuber*: Modelversuch bürgerlich-revolutionärer Umgestaltung des feudalistischen Deutschland." In Walter Raitz and Erhard Schütz, eds., *Der alte Kanon neu: Zur Revision des literarischen Kanons in Wissenschaft und Unterricht*, pp. 109–35. Opladen: Westdeutscher Verlag, 1976.

Metzger, Michael M. "Soziale und dramatische Struktur in Lessings *Emilia Galotti*." In Leonard Forster and Hans-Gert Roloff, eds., *Akten des V. Internationalen Germanisten-Kongresses, Cambridge 1975*, vol. 3, pp. 210–16. Frankfurt: Peter Lang, 1976.

Michelsen, Peter. *Der Bruch mit der Vater-Welt: Studien zu Schiller's "Räuber."* Euphorion Beihefte, 16. Heidelberg: Winter, 1979.

Mitchell, W. S. T. *The Politics of Interpretation*. Chicago: University of Chicago Press, 1983.

Mollenhauer, Peter. "Wahrnehmung und Wirklichkeitsbewußtsein in Hofmannsthals *Reitergeschichte*." *German Quarterly* 50 (1977): 283–97.

Morris, Charles W. "Esthetics and the Theory of Signs." *Journal of Unified Science* 8 (1939–40): 131–50.

Mueller, Peter. "Glanz und Elend des deutschen 'bürgerlichen Trauerspiels': Zur

Stellung der *Emilia Galotti* in der zeitgenössischen deutschen Dramatik." In Helmut Brandt and Manfred Beyer, eds., *Ansichten der deutschen Klassik*, pp. 9–44. East Berlin: Aufbau, 1981.

Müller, Klaus-Detlef. "Das Virginia-Motif in Lessings *Emilia Galotti*: Anmerkungen zum Strukturwandel der Öffentlichkeit." *Orbis Litterarum* 42 (1987): 305–16.

Müller-Seidel, Walter. "Natur und Naturwissenschaft im Werk Georg Büchners." In Eckehard Catholy and Winfried Hellmann, eds., *Festschrift für Klaus Ziegler*, pp. 205–32. Tübingen: Niemeyer, 1968.

Murrill, V., and W. S. Marks III. "Kafka's 'The Judgment' and 'The Interpretation of Dreams.' " *Germanic Review* 48 (1973): 212–28.

Nägele, Rainer. "Kafka and the Interpretive Desire." In Alan Udoff, ed., *Kafka and the Contemporary Critical Performance: Centenary Readings*, pp. 16–29. Bloomington: Indiana University Press, 1987.

Nehring, Wolfgang. "Dramatische Funktionalität und epische Breite in Schillers *Räuber*." *Aquila* 1 (1968): 110–20.

Neumann, Gerhard. *Franz Kafkas "Das Urteil": Text, Materialien, Kommentar.* Hanser Literaturkommentare, 16. Munich: Hanser, 1981.

Nietzsche, Friedrich. *On the Genealogy of Morals.* Vol. 13 of *The Complete Works of Friedrich Nietzsche*, ed. Oscar Levy. Trans. Horace B. Samuel. New York: Macmillan, 1924.

———. "On Truth and Falsity in Their Ultramoral Sense." In Oscar Levy, ed., *The Complete Works of Friedrich Nietzsche*, vol. 2, pp. 172–92. Trans. Maximilian Mügge. London: Allen and Unwin, 1911.

———. "Über Wahrheit und Lüge im außermoralischen Sinn." In Karl Schlechta, ed., *Werke in drei Bänden*, vol. 3, pp. 309–22. Munich: Hanser, 1966.

———. *Zur Genealogie der Moral.* In Karl Schlechta, ed., *Werke in drei Bänden*, vol. 2, pp. 761–900. Munich: Hanser, 1966.

Nölle, Volker. *Subjektivität und Wirklichkeit in Lessings dramatischem und theologischem Werk.* Berlin: Erich Schmidt, 1977.

Northey, Anthony D. "The American Cousins and the *Prager Asbestwerke*." In Angel Flores, ed., *The Kafka Debate*, pp. 133–46. New York: Gordion Press, 1977.

———. *Kafkas Mischpoche.* Kleine kulturwissenschaftliche Bibliothek, 6. Berlin: Wagenbach, 1988.

Oelmüller, Willy. "Hegels Satz vom Ende der Kunst und das Problem der Philosophie der Kunst nach Hegel." *Philosophisches Jahrbuch* 73 (1965): 75–94.

Olechnowitz, Harry. "Autonomie der Kunst: Studien zur Begriffs- und Funktionsbestimmung einer ästhetischen Kategorie." Diss., Free University of Berlin, 1981.

Pabel, Klaus. *Heines "Reisebilder": Ästhetisches Bedürfnis und politisches Interesse am Ende der Kunstperiode.* Munich: Fink, 1977.

Pascal, Roy. *Kafka's Narrators: A Study of his Stories and Sketches.* Cambridge, Eng.: Cambridge University Press, 1982.

Peacock, James L. "Symbolic Reversal and Social History: Transvestites and Clowns of Java." In Barbara Babcock, *The Reversible World: Symbolic Inversion in Art and Society*, pp. 209–24. Ithaca: Cornell University Press, 1978.

Peter, Klaus. *Stadien der Aufklärung: Moral und Politik bei Lessing, Novalis und Friedrich Schlegel*. Wiesbaden: Akademische Verlagsgesellschaft Athenaion, 1980.

Piel, Edgar. "Die Schwäche, der Eifer und die Ich-Sucht: Kafkas Erzählung 'Das Urteil' als 'Gesellschaftsroman.' " *Sprache im technischen Zeitalter* 75 (1977): 167–79.

Pocock, J. G. A. "The Mobility of Property and the Rise of Eighteenth-Century Sociology." In *Virtue, Commerce, and History: Essays on Political Thought and History, Chiefly in the Eighteenth Century*, pp. 103–23. Cambridge, Eng.: Cambridge University Press, 1985, pp. 103–23.

Politzer, Heinz. *Franz Kafka: Parable and Paradox*. 2nd ed. Ithaca: Cornell University Press, 1966.

Pondrum, Cyrena Norman. "Coherence in Kafka's 'The Judgment': Georg's Perceptions of the World." *Studies in Short Fiction* 9 (1972): 59–79.

Poschmann, Henri. *Georg Büchner: Dichtung der Revolution und Revolution in der Dichtung*. East Berlin: Aufbau, 1983.

———. "Heine und Büchner: Zwei Strategien revolutionär-demokratischer Literatur um 1835." In Akademie der Wissenschaften der DDR, ed., *Heinrich Heine und seine Zeitgenossen: Geschichtliche und literarische Befunde*, pp. 203–28, 320–22. East Berlin: Aufbau, 1979.

Poster, Mark. "Introduction." In Jean Baudrillard, *Selected Writings*, pp. 1–9. Stanford: Stanford University Press, 1988.

Preisendanz, Wolfgang. "Der Funktionsübergang von Dichtung und Publizistik bei Heine." In Hans Robert Jauss, ed., *Die nicht mehr schönen Künste: Grenzphänomene des Ästhetischen*, pp. 343–74. Poetik und Hermeneutik, 3. Munich: Fink, 1968.

Quabius, Richard. *Generationsverhältnisse im Sturm und Drang*. Cologne: Böhlau, 1976.

Ransmeier, John C. "Heines 'Reisebilder' und Laurence Sterne." *Archiv für das Studium der neueren Sprache und Literatur* 118 (1907): 289–317.

———. *Das Räuberbuch: Die Rolle der Literaturwissenschaft in der Ideologie des deutschen Bürgertums am Beispiel von Schillers "Die Räuber."* Frankfurt: Verlag Roter Stern, 1974.

Reeves, Nigel. *Heinrich Heine: Poetry and Politics*. Oxford: Oxford University Press, 1974.

Reh, Albert M. "*Emilia Galotti*: 'Großes Exempel der dramatischen Algebra' oder 'Algebra der Ambivalenz'?" *Lessing Yearbook* 17 (1985): 45–64.

Richards, David G. *Georg Büchner and the Birth of the Modern Drama*. Albany: State University of New York Press, 1977.

Rickels, Laurence A. "Deception, Exchange, and Revenge: Metaphors of Language in *Emilia Galotti*." *Lessing Yearbook* 16 (1984): 37–54.

Rieder, Heinz. "Hugo von Hofmannsthals 'Reitergeschichte.' " In Alois Eder, ed., *Marginalien zur poetischen Welt: Festschrift für Robert Mühlher zum 60. Geburtstag*, pp. 311–23. Berlin: Dunckert & Humblot, 1971.

Riegel, Klaus F. "Comparison Between Monetary and Linguistic Systems." In *Foundations of Dialectical Psychology*, pp. 60–70. New York: Academic Press, 1979.

Robertson, Ritchie. "The Dual Structure of Hofmannsthal's *Reitergeschichte*." *Forum of Modern Language Studies* 14 (1978): 316–31.

Rolleston, James. "Strategy and Language: Georg Bendemann's Theater of the Self." In Angel Flores, ed., *The Problem of "The Judgment": Eleven Approaches to Kafka's Story*, pp. 133–45. New York: Gordion Press, 1977.

Rorty, Richard. *Contingency, Irony, and Solidarity*. Cambridge, Eng.: Cambridge University Press, 1989.

Rosenberg, Harold. "Literary Form and Social Hallucination." *Partisan Review* 27 (1960): 638–51.

Rosenberg, Rainer. "Die Wiederentdeckung des Lesers." In Akademie der Wissenschaften der DDR, ed., *Heine und seine Zeitgenossen*, pp. 178–202. East Berlin: Aufbau, 1979.

Rousseau, Jean-Jacques. *The Confessions*. Trans. J. M. Cohen. Harmondsworth, Eng.: Penguin, 1954.

———. *Essay on the Origin of Language*. In Victor Gourevitch, trans. and ed., *The First and Second Discourses and the Essay on the Origin of Language*, pp. 239–95. New York: Harper and Row, 1986.

Ruhleder, Karl H. "Franz Kafka's 'Das Urteil': An Interpretation." *Monatshefte* 55 (1963): 13–22.

Ryan, Judith. "Die 'allomatische Lösung': Gespaltene Persönlichkeit und Konfiguration bei Hugo von Hofmannsthal." *Deutsche Vierteljahrsschrift für Literaturwissenschaft und Geistesgeschichte* 44 (1970): 189–207.

Ryan, Lawrence. " 'Zum letzten Mal Psychologie!' Zur psychologischen Deutbarkeit der Werke Kafkas." In Wolfgang Paulsen, ed., *Psychologie in der Literaturwissenschaft: Viertes Amherster Colloquium zur modernen deutschen Literatur*, pp. 157–73. Heidelberg: Lothar Stiehm, 1971.

Ryder, Frank G. "Emilia Galotti." *German Quarterly* 45 (1972): 329–47.

———. "Emilia Galotti and the Algebra of Ambivalence." In Luanne T. Frank and Emery E. George, eds., *Husbanding the Golden Grain: Studies in Honor of Henry W. Nordmeyer*, pp. 279–94. Ann Arbor: University of Michigan, Department of Germanic Languages and Literatures, 1973.

Said, Edward. "Opponents, Audiences, Constituencies, and Community." In W. S. T. Mitchell, *The Politics of Interpretation*, pp. 7–32. Chicago: University of Chicago Press, 1983.

———, ed. *Literature and Society*. Baltimore: Johns Hopkins University Press, 1980.

Sammons, Jeffrey L. *Heinrich Heine: The Elusive Poet*. New Haven: Yale University Press, 1969.

Sanders, Hans. *Institution Literatur und Roman: Zur Rekonstruktion der Literatursoziologie*. Frankfurt: Suhrkamp, 1981.

Saussure, Ferdinand de. *Course in General Linguistics*. Ed. Charles Bally and Albert Sechehaye. Trans. Wade Baskin. New York: McGraw-Hill, 1966.

Sautermeister, Gert. "Sozialpsychologische Textanalyse: Franz Kafkas Erzählung 'Das Urteil.' " In Dieter Kimpel and Berte Pinkerneil, eds., *Methodische Praxis der Literaturwissenschaft*, pp. 179–222. Kronberg, Taunus: Scriptor, 1975.

Schenkel, Martin. " 'Wer über gewisse Dinge den Verstand nicht verlieret, der hat keinen zu verlieren': Zur Dialektik der bürgerlichen Aufklärung in Lessings *Emilia Galotti*." *Zeitschrift für deutsche Philologie* 105 (1986): 161–86.

Scherpe, Klaus R. "Folgen eines 'naturwidrigen Beischlafs der *Subordination* und des *Genius*': Friedrich Schillers *Die Räuber*." In *Poesie der Demokratie: Literarische Widersprüche zur deutschen Wirklichkeit vom 18. zum 20. Jahrhundert*, pp. 43–78. Cologne: Pahl-Rogenstein Verlag, 1980.

———. "Historische Wahrheit auf Lessings Theater, besonders im Trauerspiel *Emilia Galotti*." In Edward P. Harris, ed., *Lessing in heutiger Sicht*, pp. 259–77. Bremen: Jacobi, 1977.

———. "Schillers *Räuber*—theatralisch." *Der Deutschunterricht* 35, no. 1 (1983): 61–77.

Schieder, Theodor. "Das Problem der Revolution im 19. Jahrhundert." *Historische Zeitschrift* 170 (1950): 233–71.

Schillemeit, Jost. "Das Grauenhafte im lachenden Spiegel des Witzes: Zum historischen Kontext einer ästhetischen 'Idee' in Heines 'Buch Le Grand.' " *Jahrbuch des freien deutschen Hochstifts* (1975): 324–45.

Schiller, Friedrich. *On the Aesthetic Education of Man in a Series of Letters*. Trans. Reginald Snell. London: Routledge and Kegan Paul, 1954.

———. *On the Naive and Sentimental in Literature*. Trans. Helen Watanabe-O'Kelly. Manchester, Eng.: Carcanet New Press, 1981.

———. *Die Räuber*. In Gerhard Fricke and Herbert G. Göpfert, eds., *Sämtliche Werke*, vol. 1, pp. 491–618. Munich: Hanser, 1960.

———. *The Robbers*. Trans. F. J. Lamport. Harmondsworth, Eng.: Penguin, 1979.

———. *Sämtliche Werke*. Ed. Gerhard Fricke and Herbert G. Göpfert. 2nd ed. 5 vols. Munich: Hanser, 1960.

———. *Über die ästhetische Erziehung des Menschen in einer Reihe von Briefen*. In Gerhard Fricke and Herbert G. Göpfert, eds., *Sämtliche Werke*, vol. 5, pp. 570–669. Munich: Hanser, 1960.

———. *Über naive und sentimentalische Dichtung*. In Gerhard Fricke and Herbert G. Göpfert, eds., *Sämtliche Werke*, vol. 5, pp. 694–780. Munich: Hanser, 1960.

Schillers Briefe. Ed. Fritz Jonas. 7 vols. Stuttgart: Deutsche Verlags-Anstalt, 1893–96.

Schings, Hans-Jürgen. *Der mitleidigste Mensch ist der beste Mensch: Poetik des Mitleids von Lessing bis Büchner*. Munich: C. H. Beck, 1980.

———. "Philosophie der Liebe und Tragödie des Universalhasses: *Die Räuber* im Kontext von Schillers Jugendphilosophie." *Jahrbuch des Wiener Goethe-Vereins* 84–85 (1980–81): 71–95.

———. "Schillers *Räuber*: Ein Experiment des Universalhasses." In Wolfgang Wittkowski, ed., *Friedrich Schiller: Kunst, Humanität und Politik in der späten Aufklärung*, pp. 1–21. Tübingen: Niemeyer, 1982.

Schleiermacher, Friedrich. *Hermeneutics: The Handwritten Manuscripts by F. D. Schleiermacher*. Trans. James Duke and Jack Forstmann. Missoula, Mont.: Scholars Press, 1977.

———. *Hermeneutik*. Ed. Heinz Kimmerle. Heidelberg: Carl Winter Verlag, 1959.

Schlunk, Juergen E. "Vertrauen als Ursache und Überwindung tragischer Verstrickung in Schillers *Räuber*: Zum Verständnis Karl Moors." *Jahrbuch der deutschen Schillergesellschaft* 27 (1983): 185–201.

Schmidt, Henry J. "A New Source for Georg Büchner's *Woyzeck?*" *German Quarterly* 58 (1985): 423–24.

———. *Satire, Caricature and Perspectivism in the Works of Georg Büchner*. Stanford Studies in Germanics and Slavics, vol. 8. The Hague: Mouton, 1970.

Schmidt, Hugo. "Zum Symbolgehalt der *Reitergeschichte* Hofmannsthals." In Karl S. Weimar, ed., *Views and Reviews of Modern German Literature: Festschrift für Adolf D. Klarmann*, pp. 70–83. Munich: Delp, 1974.

Schmiedt, Helmut. "Wie revolutionär ist das Drama des Sturm und Drang?" *Jahrbuch der deutschen Schillergesellschaft* 29 (1985): 48–61.

Schmitt-Sasse, Joachim. *Das Opfer der Tugend: Zu Lessings "Emilia Galotti" und einer Literaturgeschichte der "Vorstellungskomplexe" im 18. Jahrhundert*. Wuppertaler Schriftenreihe Literatur, Bd. 22. Bonn: Bouvier, 1983.

Schneider, Heinrich. "Emilia Galotti's Tragic Guilt." *MLN* 71 (1956): 353–55.

Schneider, Manfred. *Die kranke schöne Seele der Revolution: Heine, Börne, das "Junge Deutschland," Marx und Engels*. Frankfurt: Syndikat, 1980.

Schneider, Ronald. "Die Muse 'Satyra': Das Wechselspiel von politischem Engagement und poetischer Reflexion in Heines 'Reisebildern.' " *Heine Jahrbuch* 16 (1977): 9–19.

———. " 'Themis und Pan': Zu literarischer Struktur und politischem Gehalt der 'Reisebilder' Heinrich Heines." *Annali Sezione Germanica. Studi Tedeschi* 18, no. 3 (1975): 7–42.

Schorske, Carl E. *Fin-de-siècle Vienna: Culture and Politics*. New York: Knopf, 1980.

———. "Generational Tension and Cultural Change: Reflections on the Case of Vienna." *Daedalus* 107, no. 4 (Fall 1978): 111–22.

Schulte-Sasse, Jochen. "Einleitung: Kritisch-rationale und literarische Öffentlichkeit." In Christa Bürger, Peter Bürger, and Jochen Schulte-Sasse, eds., *Aufklärung und literarische Öffentlichkeit*, pp. 12–38. Frankfurt: Suhrkamp, 1980.

———. "Das Konzept bürgerlich-literarischer Öffentlichkeit und die historischen Gründe seines Zerfalls." In Christa Bürger, Peter Bürger, and Jochen Schulte-Sasse, eds., *Aufklärung und literarische Öffentlichkeit*, pp. 83–115. Frankfurt: Suhrkamp, 1980.

———. *Literarische Struktur und historisch-sozialer Kontext: Zum Beispiel Lessings "Emilia Galotti."* Paderborn: Schöningh, 1975.

———. "Der Stellenwert des Briefwechsels [über das Trauerspiel] in der Geschichte der deutschen Ästhetik." In Jochen Schulte-Sasse, ed., *Lessing, Mendelssohn, Nicolai: Briefwechsel über das Trauerspiel*, pp. 168–237. Munich: Winckler, 1972.

Schunicht, Manfred. "Die frühen Erzählungen Hugo von Hofmannsthals." *Germanisch-Romanische Monatsschrift* 15 (1965): 275–92.

Schwerte, Hans. "Schillers *Räuber*." In Jost Schillemeit, ed., *Deutsche Dramen von Gryphius bis Brecht: Interpretationen*, pp. 147–71. Frankfurt: Fischer, 1965.

Sebeok, Thomas A. *Contributions to a Doctrine of Signs*. Studies in Semiotics, vol. 5. Bloomington: Indiana University Press, 1976.

Seidler, Ingo. "Das Urteil: 'Freud natürlich'? Zum Problem der Multivalenz bei Kafka." In Wolfgang Paulsen, ed., *Psychologie in der Literaturwissenschaft: Viertes Amherster Colloquium zur modernen deutschen Literatur*, pp. 174–90. Heidelberg: Lothar Stiehm, 1971.

Seidlin, Oskar. "Schiller's 'Treacherous Signs': The Function of the Letters in His Early Plays." In John R. Frey, ed., *Schiller 1759/1959: Commemorative American Studies*, pp. 129–46. Urbana: University of Illinois Press, 1959.

Shell, Marc. *Money, Language and Thought: Literary and Philosophical Economies from the Medieval to the Modern Era*. Berkeley: University of California Press, 1982.

Silverman, Katja. *The Subject of Semiotics*. New York: Oxford University Press, 1983.

Smith, Paul. *Discerning the Subject*. Minneapolis: University of Minnesota Press, 1988.

Sokel, Walter H. *Franz Kafka: Tragik und Ironie*. Frankfurt: Fischer, 1976.

———. "Freud and the Magic of Kafka's Writing." In J. P. Stern, ed., *The World of Franz Kafka*, pp. 145–58. New York: Holt, Rinehart & Winston, 1980.

———. "From Marx to Myth: The Structure and Function of Self-Alienation in Kafka's *Metamorphosis*." *Literary Review* 26 (1983): 485–95.

———. "Frozen Sea and River of Narration: The Poetics Behind Kafka's 'Breakthrough.'" *Newsletter of the Kafka Society of America* 7, no. 1 (June 1983): 71–79.

———. "Kafka's Poetics of the Inner Self." *Modern Austrian Literature* 11, no. 3/4 (1978): 37–58.

———. "Language and Truth in the Two Worlds of Franz Kafka." *German Quarterly* 52 (1979): 364–84.

———. "Perspectives and Truth in *The Judgment*." In Angel Flores, ed., *The Problem of "The Judgment": Eleven Approaches to Kafka's Story*, pp. 193–237. New York: Gordion Press, 1977.

———. *The Writer in Extremis: Expressionism in Twentieth-Century German Literature*. Stanford: Stanford University Press, 1959.

Speirs, Ronald. "Movement, Time, Language: Forms of Instability in Kafka's 'Das Urteil.'" *Forum for Modern Language Studies* 23 (1987): 253–64.

Stahl, Ernst. "Lessing: *Emilia Galotti*." In Benno von Wiese, ed., *Das deutsche Drama*, vol. 1, pp. 101–12. Düsseldorf: August Basel, 1958.

Stallybrass, Peter, and Allon White. *The Politics and Poetics of Transgression*. Ithaca: Cornell University Press, 1986.

Steffen, Hans. "Kafkas 'Urteil': Drei Lebensmodelle und ihre Verurteilung." In Luc Lambrechts and Jack de Vos, eds., *Jenseits der Gleichnisse: Kafka und sein Werk*. Bern: Peter Lang, 1986.

Steinbach, Dietrich. "Das Interesse an Franz Moor, oder: Leseprozesse als Erkenntnisprozesse: Anmerkungen zur literarischen Hermeneutik." *Der Deutschunterricht* 33, no. 2 (1981): 91–103.

Steinberg, Erwin R. "The Judgment in Kafka's 'The Judgment.'" *Modern Fiction Studies* 8 (1962): 23–30.

Steinmetz, Horst. "Verstehen, Mißverstehen, Nichtverstehen: Zum Problem der Interpretation, vornehmlich am Beispiel von Lessings *Emilia Galotti*." *Germanisch-Romanische Monatsschrift* 37 (1987): 387–98.

Stern, J. P. "Franz Kafka's *Das Urteil*: An Interpretation." *German Quarterly* 45 (1972): 114–29.

———. "Guilt and the Feeling of Guilt." In Angel Flores, ed., *The Problem of "The Judgment": Eleven Approaches to Kafka's Story*, pp. 97–113. New York: Gordion Press, 1977.

Stern, Martin. "Die verschwiegene Hälfte von Hofmannsthals *Reitergeschichte*." In Roland Jost and Hansgeorg Schmidt-Bergmann, eds., *Im Dialog mit der Moderne: Zur deutschsprachigen Literatur von der Gründerzeit bis zur Gegenwart: Jakob Stewer zum 60. Geburtstag*, pp. 41–45. Frankfurt: Athenäum, 1986.

Sussman, Henry. *Franz Kafka: Geometrician of Metaphor*. Madison: Coda Press, 1979.

Swan, J. "Mater and Nannie: Freud's Two Mothers and the Discovery of the Oedipus Complex." *American Imago* 31, no. 1 (1974): 1–64

Szondi, Peter. *Die Theorie des bürgerlichen Trauerspiels im 18. Jahrhundert*. Frankfurt: Suhrkamp, 1973.

Tarot, Rolf. "*Reitergeschichte*." In *Hugo von Hofmannsthal: Daseinsformen und dichterische Struktur*, pp. 332–53. Tübingen: Niemeyer, 1970.

Taylor, Charles. *Sources of the Self: The Making of Modern Identity*. Cambridge, Mass.: Harvard University Press, 1989.

Thorn-Prikker, Jan. *Revolutionär ohne Revolution: Interpretationen der Werke Georg Büchners*. Literaturwissenschaft-Gesellschaftswissenschaft, 33. Stuttgart: Klett-Cotta, 1978.

Todorov, Tzvetan. "Ästhetik und Semiotik im 18. Jahrhundert: G. E. Lessing, *Laokoön*." In Gunter Gebauer, ed., *Das Laokoön Projekt: Pläne einer semiotischen Ästhetik*, pp. 9–22. Stuttgart: Metzler, 1983.

Träbing, Gerhard. "Hofmannsthals 'Reitergeschichte': Interpretationen und Observationen 1949–1979." *Sprache im technischen Zeitalter* 79 (1981): 221–36.

———. "Hugo von Hofmannsthals 'Reitergeschichte': Beitrag zu einer Phänomenologie der deutschen Augenblicksgeschichte." *Deutsche Vierteljahrsschrift für Literaturwissenschaft und Geistesgeschichte* 43 (1969): 707–25.

Träger, Christine. "Lessing und das bürgerliche Trauerspiel." *Impulse* 4 (1982): 26–43.

Turgot, Anne Robert Jacques. *The Economics of A. R. J. Turgot*. Ed. and trans. P. D. Groenewegen. The Hague: Nijhoff, 1977.

Udoff, Alan, ed. *Kafka and the Contemporary Critical Performance: Centenary Readings*. Bloomington: Indiana University Press, 1987.

Ueding, Cornelie. *Denken, Sprechen, Handeln: Aufklärung und Aufklärungskritik im Werk Georg Büchners*. Tübinger Studien zur deutschen Literatur, Bd. 2. Frankfurt: Peter Lang, 1976.

Ullman, Bo. "Die sozialkritische Thematik im Werk Georg Büchners und ihre Entfaltung in 'Woyzeck.' " Diss., Stockholm University, 1970.

Vacano, Stefan. *Heine und Sterne: Zur vergleichenden Literaturgeschichte*. Berlin: F. Fontane, 1907.

Vásquez, Adolpho Sánchez. *Art and Society: Essays in Marxist Aesthetics*. Trans. Maro Riofrancos. New York: Monthly Review Press, 1973.

Veit, Philipp E. "The Strange Case of Moritz Spiegelberg." *Germanic Review* 44 (1969): 171–85.

Vierhaus, Rudolf. "Deutschland im 18. Jahrhundert: soziales Gefüge, politische Verfassung, geistige Bewegung." In Jungius-Gesellschaft, ed., *Lessing und die Zeit der Aufklärung*, pp. 12–29. Göttingen: Vandenhoeck & Ruprecht, 1968.

Vietta, Silvio. *Neuzeitliche Rationalität und moderne literarische Sprachkritik: Descartes, Georg Büchner, A. Holz, Karl Kraus*. Munich: Fink, 1981.

———. "Sprachkritik bei Büchner." *Georg Büchner Jahrbuch* 2 (1982): 144–56.

Vormärz 1830–1848. Erläuterungen zur deutschen Literatur. Kollektiv für Literaturgeschichte. 10th ed. Leipzig: Verlag Volk und Wissen, 1977.

Wacker, Manfred, ed. *Sturm und Drang*. Darmstadt: Wissenschaftliche Buchgesellschaft, 1985.

Wagenbach, Klaus. *Franz Kafka: Eine Biographie seiner Jugend 1893–1912*. Bern: Francke, 1958.

———. *Franz Kafka in Selbstzeugnissen und Bilddokumenten*. Rowohlts Monographien, 91. Reinbek: Rowohlt, 1964.

Warneken, Bernd Jürgen. "Autonomie und Indienstnahme: Zu ihrer Beziehung in der Literatur der bürgerlichen Gesellschaft." In *Rhetorik, Ästhetik, Ideologie: Aspekte einer kritischen Kulturwissenschaft*, pp. 79–115. Stuttgart: Metzler, 1973.

Weber, Max. *The Protestant Ethic and the Spirit of Capitalism*. Trans. Talcott Parsons. Gloucester, Mass.: Peter Smith, 1988.

———. *Die protestantische Ethik und der Geist des Kapitalismus*. In Johannes Winkelmann, ed., *Die protestantische Ethik I*, pp. 27–277. Gütersloh: Verlagshaus Mohn, 1984.

Weigand, Hermann J. "The Double Love Tragedy in Heine's *Buch Le Grand*: A Literary Myth." *Germanic Review* 13 (1938): 121–26.

———. "Heine's *Buch Le Grand*." *Journal of English and Germanic Philology* 18 (1919): 102–36.

———. "Warum stirbt Emilia Galotti?" *Journal of English and Germanic Philology* 28 (1929): 467–81.

Weimar, Klaus. "Vom Leben in Texten: zu Schillers *Räubern*." *Merkur* 42 (1988): 461–71.

Wellbery, David. *Lessing's "Laokoön": Semiotics and Aesthetics in the Age of Reason*. Cambridge, Eng.: Cambridge University Press, 1984.

Wellmer, Albrecht. "Adorno, Anwalt des Nicht-Identischen: Eine Einführung." In *Zur Dialektik von Moderne und Postmoderne: Vernunftkritik nach Adorno*, pp. 135–64. Frankfurt: Suhrkamp, 1985.

Wells, George A. "Conti's Functions in *Emilia Galotti*." *Lessing Yearbook* 16 (1984): 375–78.

Werner, Hans-Georg. "Büchners *Woyzeck*: Dichtungssprache als Analyseobjekt." In Willi Steinberg, ed., *Funktion der Sprachgestaltung im literarischen Text*, pp. 14–48. Halle: Martin-Luther-Universität Halle-Wittenberg, 1981.

Werner, Hans-Georg, and Gotthard Lerchner. "Lessings *Emilia Galotti*: Prolegomena zu einer Interpretation." *Zeitschrift für Germanistik* 3 (1982): 39–67.

Werner, Michael. *Genius und Geldsack: Zum Problem des Schriftstellerberufs bei Heinrich Heine*. Hamburg: Hoffmann & Campe, 1978.

Wertheim, Ursula. "Lessings Trauerspiel *Emilia Galotti* und das 'Heinzi'-Fragment:

Zum Problem des bürgerlichen Helden." *Wissenschaftliche Zeitschrift der Friedrich-Schiller-Universität Jena* 30 (1981): 65–78.

Wessel, Leonard P., Jr. "The Function of Odoardo in Lessing's *Emilia Galotti.*" *Germanic Review* 47 (1972): 243–58.

Wetzel, Heinz. "Die Entwicklung Woyzecks in Büchners Entwürfen." *Euphorion* 74 (1980): 375–96.

Wexler, P. "Structure, Text and Subject." In Michael Apple, ed., *Cultural and Economic Reproduction in Education*, pp. 275–303. London: Routledge and Kegan Paul, 1982.

Weyland, Peter. "Determinierte Autonomie: Kritische Überlegungen zur Kategorie 'Institution Kunst.'" In K. Kloepfer, ed., *Bildung und Ausbildung in der Romania*, vol. 1, pp. 254–66. Munich: Fink, 1979.

White, John J. "Franz Kafka's 'Das Urteil': An Interpretation." *Deutsche Vierteljahrsschrift für Literaturwissenschaft und Geistesgeschichte* 38 (1964): 208–29.

———. "Georg Bendemann's Friend in Russia: Symbolic Correspondences." In Angel Flores, ed., *The Problem of "The Judgment": Eleven Approaches to Kafka's Story*, pp. 97–113. New York: Gordion Press, 1977.

Wierlacher, Alois. "Das Haus der Freude oder Warum stirbt Emilia Galotti?" *Lessing Yearbook* 5 (1973): 147–62.

Wiese, Benno von. "Reitergeschichte." In *Die deutsche Novelle von Goethe bis Kafka*, vol. 1, 284–303. Düsseldorf: August Basel, 1964.

Wilke, Sabine. *Zur Dialektik von Exposition und Darstellung: Ansätze zu einer Kritik der Arbeiten Martin Heideggers, Theodor W. Adornos und Jacques Derridas*. New York: Peter Lang, 1988.

Williams, Anthony. "The Ambivalences in the Plays of the Young Schiller about Contemporary Germany." In *Deutsches Bürgertum und literarische Intelligenz 1750–1800*, pp. 1–112. Literaturwissenschaften und Sozialwissenschaften, Bd. 3. Stuttgart: Metzler, 1974.

Windfuhr, Manfred. "Heine und der Petrarkismus: Zur Konzeption seiner Liebeslyrik." *Jahrbuch der deutschen Schillergesellschaft* 10 (1966): 266–85.

———. "Heinrich Heines deutsches Publikum (1820–60): Vom Lieblingsautor des Adels zum Anreger der bürgerlichen Intelligenz." In Alberto Martino, ed., *Literatur in der sozialen Bewegung: Aufsätze und Forschungsberichte zum 19. Jahrhundert*, pp. 260–83. Tübingen: Niemeyer, 1977.

———. "Das Junge Deutschland als literarische Opposition: Gruppenmerkmale und Neuansätze." *Heine Jahrbuch* 22 (1983): 47–69.

Witte, Bernd, ed. *Vormärz: Biedermeier, Junges Deutschland, Demokraten*. Vol. 6 of *Deutsche Literatur: Eine Sozialgeschichte*, Horst-Albert Glaser, gen. ed. Reinbek: Rowohlt, 1980.

Wittkowski, Wolfgang. "Bürgerfreiheit oder -feigheit? Die Metapher des 'langen Weges' als Schlüssel zum Koordinatensystem in Lessings politischem Trauerspiel *Emilia Galotti.*" *Lessing Yearbook* 17 (1985): 65–87.

———. *Georg Büchner: Persönlichkeit—Weltbild—Werk*. Reihe Siegen, Beiträge zur Literatur- und Sprachwissenschaft, Bd. 10. Heidelberg: Winter, 1978.

———. "Stufenstruktur und Transzendenz in Büchners *Woyzeck* und Grillparzers Novelle *Der arme Spielmann.*" *Georg Büchner Jahrbuch* 3 (1983): 147–65.

Wülfing, Wulf. *Junges Deutschland: Texte-Kontexte, Abbildung, Kommentar.* Reihe Hanser, 244. Munich: Hanser, 1978.

————. *Schlagworte des Jungen Deutschland.* Philologische Studien und Quellen, Heft 106. Berlin: Erich Schmidt, 1982.

Wunberg, Gotthart. " 'Erblicken des Doppelgängers': *Reitergeschichte."* In *Der frühe Hofmannsthal: Schizophrenie als dichterische Struktur,* pp. 57–67. Stuttgart: Kohlhammer, 1965.

Zeller, Rosmarie. "Kafkas 'Urteil' im Widerstreit der Interpretationen." In Albrecht Schöne, ed., *Akten des 7. Internationalen Germanisten-Kongresses. Göttingen 1985,* Bd. 11, pp. 174–82. Tübingen: Niemeyer, 1986.

Ziegler, Edda. *Literarische Zensur in Deutschland 1819–1848: Materialien, Kommentare.* Hanser Literaturkommentare, 18. Munich: Hanser, 1983.

Zimmermann, Werner. "Hugo von Hofmannsthal: Reitergeschichte." In *Deutsche Prosadichtungen der Gegenwart,* Teil I, pp. 130–44. Düsseldorf: Pädagogischer Verlag Schwann, 1962.

Zinkernagel, Franz. "Die Katastrophe in Lessings *Emilia Galotti."* *Germanisch-Romanische Monatsschrift* 6 (1914): 206–12.

Zons, Raimar St. *Georg Büchner: Dialektik der Grenze.* Abhandlungen zur Kunst-, Musik- und Literaturwissenschaft, Bd. 208. Bonn: Bouvier, 1976.

Index

In this index an "f" after a number indicates a separate reference on the next page, and an "ff" indicates separate references on the next two pages. A continuous discussion over two or more pages is indicated by a span of page numbers, e.g., "57–59." *Passim* is used for a cluster of references in close but not consecutive sequence.

Library of Congress Cataloging-in-Publication Data

Gray, Richard T.
  Stations of the divided subject : contestation and
  ideological legitimation in German bourgeois literature,
  1770–1914 / Richard T. Gray.
      p.   cm.
  Includes bibliographical references and index.
  ISBN 0-8047-2402-4
  1. German literature—History and criticism.   2. Literature
  and society—Germany.   3. German literature—Social
  aspects.   4. Middle class in literature.   5. Middle class—
  Germany—History.   I. Title.
  PT111.G7   1995
  830.9´355—dc20   94-33723
                                                          CIP

∞ This book is printed on acid-free, recycled paper.